'Captain Bligh' is a cliché of our times for the extravagant and violent misuse of power. In fact, William Bligh was one of the least physically violent disciplinarians in the British navy. That paradox inspires this book to ask why, then, did he have a mutiny? Its answer is to display the theatricality of naval institutions and the mythologising power of history. The theatre of the *Bounty* lay not just in its rites of power on the quarterdeck and in the fo'c'sle but also on the beaches at Tahiti and in the murderous settlement at Pitcairn, on the stage in London, on altar stones and temples of sacrifice, on catheads from which men were hanged.

MR BLIGH'S BAD LANGUAGE

Mr Bligh's
Bad Language

*Passion, Power and Theatre
on the Bounty*

GREG DENING

CAMBRIDGE
UNIVERSITY PRESS

Published by the Press Syndicate of the University of Cambridge
The Pitt Building, Trumpington Street, Cambridge CB2 1RP
40 West 20th Street, New York, NY 10011-4211, USA
10 Stamford Road, Oakleigh, Victoria 3166, Australia

First published 1992

Printed in the United States of America

Library of Congress Cataloging-in-Publication Data
Dening, Greg.
Mr Bligh's bad language : passion, power and theatre on the
Bounty / Greg Dening.
p.   cm.
Includes bibliographical references.
ISBN 0-521-38370-6
1. Bounty Mutiny, 1789.   2. Bligh, William, 1754–1817.
3. Pitcairn Island – History.   I. Title.
DU800.D43   1992
996.1'8–dc20   91-34318
                                                          CIP
A catalog record for this book is available from the British Library.

ISBN 0-521-38370-6 hardback

For the memory
of my father,
Alec Seymour Dening
(1898–1953).
He was a sailor
and told me many yarns of the sea.
I wish he had heard mine.

Contents

Illustrations

Acknowledgements

I feel sad now, as I count my debts, that my long voyage with the *Bounty* is nearing its end. The *Bounty* has been bountiful to me. I cannot say who gave her the name or whether there was any discussion of its aptness to the ambitions that sent her into the Pacific to deliver a source of mass subsistence, the breadfruit, to West Indies slave plantations. But the hours of enjoyment, the years of learning have been a bounty for me. The *Bounty* is my first acknowledgement.

My second is my students. For twenty years they have represented the *Bounty* to me in narratives, reflections, poetry, plays and even paintings. They will find in this book how much I owe them.

An older generation of scholars has made research into all things concerned with the *Bounty* much easier than they themselves experienced. Markedly these were Owen Rutter, George Mackaness and John C. Beaglehole. I have two mentors, Harry E. Maude and Douglas Oliver, whose contributions will be just as lasting.

There are some modest cliometrics in this study. Pat Grimshaw helped me in the collation of data on which the statistics are based. Wayne Wescott helped in the counting. Mark Gallagher, of the University of Hawaii, managed an experimental computer programme for me.

The University of Melbourne, in the research leave given me; the Faculty of Arts, through various research grants; the Department of History, in the prolonged assistance of its administrative staff, led by Lynn Wrout, and the support of academic colleagues, made the creation of this book possible for me. The Institute for Advanced Studies, Princeton, New Jersey, housed and fed me in the final year, 1988–9, of research and writing. More importantly, the permanent fellows – notably Clifford Geertz, Joan Scott and John Eliot – and the cohort of scholars who shared my good fortune nourished my mind and spirits. A Senior Fulbright Fellowship got me to this academic nirvana.

Donna, my wife, has read everything I have written and has saved me from myself innumerable times. My true bounty in the *Bounty* has been the freedom her care has allowed me.

Vivienne Burrows puzzled with me over how best the land- and seascapes of the voyagings in this book could be represented. Her maps are my delight.

The list of institutions and persons to which and to whom I am beholden for giving me permission to publish material in their care and possession is long. Their courtesy is acknowledged in the appropriate places in this book. The institutions are these: The Museum of Art and the Baillieu Library of The University of Melbourne; the National Maritime Museum, Greenwich; the Mitchell Library, Sydney, State Library of N.S.W.; the National Library of Australia, Canberra; the Museum of Garden History, Lambeth; the Manx Museum, Isle of Man; the National Portrait Gallery, London; the Newberry Library, Chicago; the British Museum, London; the Bishop Museum, Honolulu; the New Yorker Magazine, Inc. I also thank these authors for allowing me to use their material: John McKay, Gavin Kennedy, Douglas Oliver, Harry Maude, Niel Gunson, J. B. Handelsman.

'Nothing is written until it has been read' has been a tenet of my teaching for many years. Among the readers who have helped make me a writer are Frank Smith, Executive Editor of Cambridge University Press, New York. His wisdom and enthusiasm have supported me greatly. Shelley Abelson, Copy Editor, and Judi Steinig, Production Editor, have eased my pain in discovering how error prone I am with kind encouragement and a sure eye. Dr Elizabeth Wood Ellem, a Pacific scholar in her own right, contributed the index. Although I count her as my student, she has been my teacher too. I thank all these readers for their crafting skills.

Prologue

The voyage of this book, like Bligh's voyage in the *Bounty*, has ended in theatre. By long tradition, theatre needs a prologue. The prologue is more than just a beginning. The prologue fills that marginal space between the conventionalities of everyday living and the conventionalities of being in the theatre. The prologue mediates one and the other, educates the audience to its own role, blinkers the audience to its different way of seeing, prepares it for reflexivity and criticism, and, most dangerously, liberates the audience's interpretive skills. By tradition, too, the deliverer of the prologue enters by a 'stage door' that is not part of the scenery but marks a special entry place of someone who for the moment is neither actor nor audience, but in between, distant by being a didact, dangerous by being an ironist, disturbing by being a relativist. On him or her there traditionally focused a deep antitheatrical prejudice. The imagination he or she sparked was dialogic and by that the audience was enticed into the conspiracy of its own engagement in making realism. For those convinced by religion or politics or philosophy that realism was not of their own making, this representative of representing was a very dangerous clown.

Let me begin my prologue by saying I love prefaces and overtures. Prefaces have the courage of ignorance before the event and the clarity of hindsight after it. Overtures anticipate the whole. My notes are full of prefaces of books I have never written. For *Mr Bligh's Bad Language*, there are no less than three prefaces, each written at a bicentenary moment – December 23, 1987, the anniversary of the *Bounty*'s sailing; April 28, 1989, the *Bounty*'s mutiny; March 14, 1990, Bligh's return to England. They are critical entries in the log of my voyage and a prologue for yours.

December 23, 1987. On December 23, 1787, the *Bounty* sailed from Portsmouth. As she did, William Bligh cursed the Admiralty for losing him three weeks of fair winds by delaying the delivery of his orders. By that, the *Bounty* was thrown into an Atlantic storm with seas so high that the crew and Bligh had to risk their lives to repair the damages and rescue ruined supplies. The three weeks' delay lost them a passage round the Horn, put out the fine timetabling of their circumnavigation, made them stay five long, disturbing months at Tahiti. Who knows? Had it been December 2, not 23, when she left Portsmouth, I would have no bicentenary to celebrate, not of all that the *Bounty* has come to mean, at any rate.

I am on vacation. It is my summer task to complete this ethnographic history of the *Bounty*. This summer is full of celebrations, although the aboriginal Australians are rightly protesting that they have nothing to celebrate; 1988 is the bicentenary of white settlement in Australia. The fleet carrying convicts for the first settlement at Botany Bay had left England six months before Bligh and would arrive at Botany Bay on January 26, 1788. The *Bounty* and the convict settlement were the first exploitation by the British of their Pacific discoveries. The *Bounty* joined east and west hemispheres by bringing breadfruit from what was seen to be a Tree of Life in the islands of Paradise to feed slaves, the living dead of the Caribbean. The First Fleet joined north and south hemispheres with an expedient solution of a social problem that gave an imperial presence in an empty sea as well. Now there is a 'First Fleet' re-enacting the voyage from Portsmouth to Botany Bay. There are Tall Ships, as well, rendezvousing for a spectacular entry into Sydney Harbour. My desk, as I write, looks out over Bass Strait. Bass Strait is the seaway that separates the island of Tasmania from mainland Australia. Perhaps I shall see some of the Tall Ships and the 'First Fleet' as they sail past my window. A 'Bounty' is part of this born-again 'First Fleet'. This 'Bounty' has an auxiliary engine and a steel hull. No use being fussy about detail in this sort of symbol making. No use asking what the 'Bounty' is doing in a 'First Fleet'. No use saying that the last time we saw this same 'Bounty' was on television as Cook's 'Endeavour', and then as his 'Resolution'. This 'Bounty' is a sort of Platonic idea, a Kantian noumenon of 'sailingness'. It is a theatrical prop, plastic enough for comedy, tragedy, irony – any mode of history that one would like to make of it.

I am not much for re-enactments. Re-enactments tend to hallucinate a past as merely the present in funny dress. They give modernity and fashion a fillip by making the past look quaint. They patronise the human condition in hindsighted superiority. They remove the responsibility of remedying the present by distracted, unreflective search for details of a past whose remedying will make no difference. I have an ambition in this history of the *Bounty* to be ethnographic. I hope this ethnographic history is not considered a re-enactment.

If I were asked what ethnographic history may ultimately be, I would answer that it is an attempt to represent the past as it was actually experienced in such a way that we understand both its ordered and its disordered natures. We live in a world already made for us but also of our own making. We live in a world that has its clarities and its ambivalences. We live in a world that is at the same time full of meanings that are simple and of meanings that are multiple. These qualities of the world of the present, we must assume, were qualities of the world of the past. If I ambition to tell what actually happened, I must ambition as well to describe the painful mix of force and freedom that life tends to be. I will begin with the trial and execution of the *Bounty* mutineers. Their court martial and death can be a parable about all I want to say – about history, about power, about symbol making, about force and freedom, about theatre.

For all my queasiness at grand historical re-enactment, I have my own re-enactments, of course. What historian does not? I re-text the already texted past. I have no experience of the past that I re-present other than that past transformed into words, symbolised. The past I experience is shaped by the genres of its expression and the ways of its preservation. That past for me now, on December 23, 1987, is a facsimile reproduction of Bligh's log, the transcriptions of the mutineers' trial, my files of notes taken after hours of chasing old newspapers, reminiscences and letters. For that matter, that past is the images I have made of Bligh and Christian and the *Bounty* in the lectures I have given and the articles I have written. It is the images made for me by Charles Laughton and Marlon Brando.

That past will even be the wooden model of the *Bounty* I have set myself the summer relaxation of completing. But will this model be the *Bounty* of the Deptford Naval Yard plans or the adaptations made of them? When was the *Bounty* the *Bounty*? Will I set the mainmast a little lower following Bligh's plan to lower the power of her sails, or shall I raise it following his second thoughts at the Cape of Good Hope? Even the *Bounty* was process. At what moment shall my model freeze it and falsify it for what it was at every other moment? What model will ever catch process? What text? An ethnographic history that claims to re-present symbolic realism must surely catch process – not just change, but the changing too.

That past I re-present is my microfilm-reader glaring at me now with the *Bounty's* muster roll on its screen. The muster's column headed 'D., D.D. or R.' stands out. D. (Discharged), D.D. (Discharged Dead), R. (Ran). There are many 'Rs' on the *Bounty* muster. The mutineers all 'Ran'. But others 'Ran' before the voyage began – John Charlton, John Cooper, George Armstrong, John Swan, Samuel Sutton, James Kainey, Charles Page, William Bell, Robert Barclay, William Ray, Luke Dods, Alexander Tyre, John McTaggett, Alexander Johnston. They presumably got wind of where the *Bounty* was going and made their choice. I cannot chase these fourteen, now that I am about to begin. They 'Ran' out of my history too. But I would have liked to know how they counted their fortune in having run from the *Bounty* – good or bad? And I would have liked to have heard them narrate the ironies of that experience in their sailors' yarns. With such a trope for such a past they must have made fine ethnographic history. Maybe I should begin again.

April 28, 1989. The Mutiny is over. Bligh has been thrust into his launch. It rocks unsteadily in the smooth sea as the eighteen men with him settle over the piles of clothes and provisions that have been thrown into her. These are galling, frightening moments. The launch is still attached to the *Bounty* by its painter. The men do not know how far the jeers and curses and threats being poured over them will go. They do not know whether they are being played with as the *Bounty* drifts ahead and pulls them along.

Bligh is hoarse from his own angry shouting. He is conscious, too, of pain, now that his hands have been untied. He has made the awful decision to cut the painter. It was an acknowledgement of the finality of what had been done. Possibly the decision was made easier by the sight of a column of steam rising over the horizon from the volcano on Tofua. Bligh and all the *Bounty* crew had watched the volcano's reflections in the clouds the night before, never dreaming that some of them would count on it for a beacon. Now they have nine or ten hours of rowing and sailing to make a landfall. They take a north-east tack. The *Bounty* continues on her west-north-west course. How often the men in the launch looked back at her, or if they did, we do not know. But we know that they saw young Tom

Figure 1.
Robert Dodd, *Lieutenant Bligh Leaving the Bounty,* Aquatint, July 1790. (Russell Grim-
wade Collection, The Museum of Art, The University of Melbourne.) Robert Dodd's
aquatint of the mutineers turning Bligh adrift in the launch was published just three
months after Bligh's return to England. Fletcher Christian is depicted standing on the
railing behind the *Bounty*'s flag box. The painter of the launch is still attached to the
Bounty. The four swords, allowed the launch people only at the last moment, are being
thrown to them. Details are so correct that a viewer might wonder whether the faces of
the crew are recognisable.

Ellison scamper to the shrouds and loosen the sails. Their memory of the
sprightly way he performed an act that seemed so wanton of their lives
would one day be his death sentence.

Bligh thought the *Bounty's* west-north-west course was a blind. She
would turn for Tahiti. Tahiti, Bligh thought, was the cause of his mutiny. In his mind he had already begun to write his *Narrative of the Mutiny.* Suspicious even of his companions in the launch, he began days of
questioning them about the conspiracies against him. He called up the
names of every man still on board, one by one. We have the records still:
the water-stained and blotted pages of this description of the mutineers,
the notebook he began to keep of this new voyage of discovery in his
launch, and the journal into which he transcribed his thoughts.

Of his mutiny he wrote: 'Just before Sunrise Mr Christian and the Master at Arms came into my cabbin while I was fast asleep, and seizing me tyed my hands with a cord and threatened instant death if I made the least noise. I however called sufficiently loud to alarm the officers, who found themselves equally secured by centinels at their door. There were now three men at my Cabbin door and four inside (a) (Fletcher Christian, Alexander Smith, John Sumner, Mathew Quintal) Mr Christian had a Cutlass and the others were armed with Musquets and Bayonets – I was now carried on deck in my Shirt in torture with a severe bandage around my wrists behind my back, when I found no man to rescue me. I ask'd the reason for such a violent act but I was threatned to be put to death if I said a word.'

Of the causes of his mutiny, he speculated: 'It is certainly true that no effect could take place without a Cause, but here it is equally certain that no cause could justify such an effect – It however may very naturally be asked what could be the reason for such a revolt, in answer to which I can only conjecture that they have Idealy assured themselves of a more happy life among the Otaheitians than they could possibly have in England, which joined to some Female connections has most likely been the leading cause of the whole business.

'The Women are handsome – mild in their Manners and conversation – possessed of great sensibility, and have sufficient delicacy to make them admired and beloved – The Chiefs have taken such a liking to our People that they have rather encouraged their stay among them than otherwise, and even made promises of large possessions. Under these and many other attendant circumstances equally desirable it is therefore now not to be Wondered at, 'tho not possible to be foreseen, that a Set of Sailors led by Officers and void of connections, or if they have any, not possessed of Natural feelings sufficient to wish themselves never to be seperated from them, should be governed by such powerfull inducements but equal to this, what a temptation it is to such wretches when they find it in their power however illegally it can be got at, to fix themselves in the most of plenty in the finest Island in the World where they need not labour, and where the alurements of disipation are more than equal to anything that can be conceived.'

That debate on why there was a mutiny on the *Bounty* has been long. Who can – who would want to – end it? Not I. I am a coward for causes but a professor of parables. Bligh, some of his contemporaries would have said, was no gentleman. Power without a gentleman's authority created contradictions. Bligh, his later defenders have countered, has been slandered, and with him, the British navy. An age of indiscipline, like our own, the argument goes, will slander men and institutions of power. Now, late in the twentieth century, when the battlefields of life seem not to be about power and authority or about discipline but about gender relations and sexuality, there are those who know the true cause of the mutiny on the *Bounty* to be in the secret recesses of Bligh's and Christian's psyches. And I? How can I not be product of my times? Look to Mr Bligh's bad language, I say, and all that that may mean. Our lives are a double helix of past and present. We are the language of our representations. We are caught in our webs of significance.

March 14, 1990. Bligh landed at Portsmouth ten months and fifteen days after his mutiny. The Dutch ship on which he had travelled from the Cape of Good Hope dropped him there on the very day that London discovered from France by way of a faster vessel that there had been a mutiny on the *Bounty*. Bligh had only his secretary and his servant with him. The others of the launch he had left in the East Indies. Four of the men had not been strong enough after their ordeal to withstand the fevers of Batavia and were already dead and buried. Hatred and fear among the rest had broken out into drunken fury, mutiny, legal threats and affidavits. Bligh was filled with a blazing energy to defend himself and had spent the leisure time of his homeward voyage writing drafts of his narrative, composing letters of explanation to officials, and calculating his personal losses down to the last stolen nightcap.

Bligh was home before all his letters describing his disasters. His wife, Elizabeth, his patron, Sir Joseph Banks, his superiors in the Admiralty heard from his lips what he had carefully rehearsed on paper. He wrote notes to an anxious group of relatives of the men of the *Bounty*. To Mrs Tosh, mother of Thomas McIntosh, he wrote tenderly, explaining that he had asked her son to stay on board the *Bounty* after the mutiny. To Mrs Heywood, mother of Peter Heywood, midshipman, he wrote savagely that her boy was undeserving of any care. Bligh had grown to hate Peter Heywood, a boy of sixteen, as much as he had grown to hate Christian.

Bligh's energies in vindicating himself held him high. His health did not break, nor did reaction to the traumas of his escape set in until he was on his way back into the Pacific on his second breadfruit voyage to Tahiti.

Within six months of his return to England, the admirals sent him back to Tahiti on the *Providence* to do what he had failed to do on the *Bounty*. A few weeks into this second voyage, he thought he was near to death. Those around him thought he had gone insane.

In the first days back in England, there was nothing but praise for Bligh's extraordinary achievements and nothing but condemnation for all that had been done to him. But he must have been given pause by a report in the London *Times*, March 26, 1790. It pointed to three circumstances 'unparralleled in the annals of mutiny': 'one, [that] out of forty-seven men, eighteen should suffer themselves to be pinioned and put on board a boat at the almost certainty of death without the least resistance; two, [that] the secret of the conspiracy should be so well kept by twenty-seven men (most of them very young) as not to give the least suspicion to the rest of the crew; three, [that] after having carried through this successful mutiny, the question might be asked – cui bono? as in those seas there was no possibility of plunder or committing the smallest act of piracy.'

The *St James Chronicle or British Evening Post*, March 20–23, also gave pause to those who might have been tempted to condemn the mutiny too loudly. 'The perpetrator of the outrages on the Bounty', it reported of Fletcher Christian, 'is of respectable connections. His mother is a most worthy woman. He has two brothers resident in London, both respectable characters of legal professions.'

Fletcher Christian's family was indeed respectable. A long line of Deemsters of the Isle of Man stretched behind him, and his own generation had married well. He numbered, among his first cousins, two bishops and three Members of Parliament. He had an uncle who was High Sheriff of Cumberland. Another uncle was Bishop of Carlisle. His own immediate family had fallen on hard times, but not before his mother had educated his elder brothers, John and Edward, at Peterhouse and St John's College, Cambridge University. Not sizars they, or poor scholars – at least not John – but fellow commoners, a somewhat giddier brand of gentleman scholar. Edward Christian was a professor of law at Cambridge—'a sixpenny Professor', Bligh called him. He served as professor of law at the East India College in Hertfordshire as well. He was to become a rather eccentric Chief Justice of Ely, operating, one of his relatives would nastily note, 'in the full vigour of his incapacity'.

For a short time, Bligh could bask in the fame of his courage, but he would quickly begin to know who had been touched by his mutiny and resented the shame of it. Edward Law, later Chief Justice of England, first cousin of Fletcher Christian, was one. Law was the defender of Warren Hastings, whose epic trial stretched all through these years. John Christian Curwen was another. He had just taken the name of his wife, the heiress Isabella Curwen. (There are those who still believe that Fletcher Christian returned to England after the mutiny and that he hid out on Isabella's Belle Isle in the middle of Lake Windermere. Christian named his Tahitian wife 'Isabella'. There is a suspicion that Christian went to sea disappointed that his uncle, John, had married his ward Isabella. Isabella was much nearer Fletcher Christian in years.) Indeed, it seems that the County of Cumberland felt itself shamed by the mutiny. Cockermouth, the birthplace of Fletcher Christian, probably stirred as few imaginations as to its historical importance then as it does now. But between 1790 and 1795 a sort of Cockermouth connection proudly found its roots through Fletcher Christian and the *Bounty* – through Fletcher Christian because the community knew him in his family as something other than a mutineer, through the *Bounty* because the mutiny scored the basic paradox: the *Bounty* was transporting the breadfruit tree, the very symbol of a free and unencumbered life, from the island of freedom, Tahiti, to the islands of bondage, the West Indies and their slave plantations. The Cockermouth connection included William Wordsworth, who at one time attended the same school as Fletcher Christian and at another time studied under the headmastership of his brother Edward. In these years Wordsworth was beginning to discover his disenchantment both with St John's College, Cambridge, and also with his brief but heady radicalism towards the French Revolution. He was, with his sister Dorothy, also indebted to Edward Christian's legal skills in winning them their rightful inheritance. Through Wordsworth the Cockermouth network finds its way to his uncle, Canon Cookson, of Windsor, Preceptor of the king's sons; to Dr Fisher, also Canon of Windsor and intimate friend of Edward Law; to his cousin Captain John Wordsworth of the East India Company; to his friend James Losh, a sympathiser with the Revolution and saved by Marat in Paris in 1792; to tutors and associates at St John's – Dr Freire, a friend of Wilberforce, and the Reverend M. Antrobus, chaplain of the Bishop of London. It was a formidable connection in family and politics. In an age of antislavery and in the first triumphs of the French Revolution, they were on the edge of radical politics.

Bligh had his connections, too. They made an apt opposition to the connections of the Christians. Sir Joseph Banks, his patron, had been a scandalous example of the decadence Tahiti could create. In the instance of the *Bounty,* he was an agent and lobbyist at court for West Indian slaveowners. As soon as Bligh was acquitted by court martial of the loss of the *Bounty,* he was presented to King George III at a levee. It had been the King's encouragement of conservative politics and mercantile interests that had closed the West Indies to the importation of cheap food for slaves from the newly liberated American colonies. Breadfruit from the Pacific was a possibility. Banks helped foster an ecological imperialism by which the ends of the earth were joined in productivity.

Bligh's connections were familial too. He was a customs officer's son married to a customs officer's daughter. Elizabeth Bligh was the daughter of Richard Betham, born in Glasgow but moved to the Isle of Man. David Hume and Adam Smith had been friends of the family in Glasgow. Elizabeth took pleasure in what we now call the Scottish Enlightenment. After Bligh's death, Sotheby's would auction her brilliant collection of sea-shells and her thousands of prints of virtually every school of European art. Duncan Campbell was her uncle. Campbell was a merchant trading with the West Indies and an entrepreneur managing the convict hulks on the Thames – the *Dictionary of the Vulgar Tongue* called the hulks 'Campbell's Academies'. It was Campbell who hired Bligh to captain his merchant vessels, *Lynx, Bethia* and *Britannia* to the West Indies at five hundred pounds per annum. It was Campbell who suggested to Sir Joseph Banks that Bligh would be a good man to command the breadfruit voyage for which the West Indies plantation owners were lobbying. Even though this meant a reduction in income from five hundred pounds p.a. to fifty pounds Bligh saw it as the main chance of his life. There would be prizes from the plantation owners. There would surely be the most important prize – and insurance – of all, a post-captaincy. There would be patronage of the great. It was really Duncan Campbell who stamped Jamaica, Tahiti and Botany Bay on Bligh's soul. In the end, when he had to face the Cockermouth connection, Bligh would not find much sympathy from those who thought they had Righteousness, Freedom and Reform stamped on theirs.

'Connections' is a softer word than 'systems'. I could have written: cheap subsistence made slave labour cheap enough to make the sugar trade profitable, and that made sweetness (and tea) an affordable luxury by which the working-class poor of the Industrial Revolution became dependent on systems of world trade. I would have joined *Mr Bligh's Bad Language* with Sydney Mintz's *Sweetness and Power* in showing world systems at work in the most trivial artefacts and actions. I could have written: the delirious discovery that there was a Tree of Life in Paradise that gave food without work was transformed into a discovery that the environments of distant places could be exploited for the sake of genteel living at home. By that, I would have joined myself to Eric Wolf in his *Europe and the Peoples without History* to show what hegemony of a world encompassed might actually mean. But it is the prerogative of listeners to prologues in the theatre to interpret for themselves what the play really means. If you see the systems at work in my narrative, I am happier for that than telling you that they are there.

On March 14, 1790, Bligh returned to his home in Lambeth, across the river from the Houses of Parliament in London. He lived there in two different houses till his death in 1817. He was away from there for the two years of his *Providence* voyage, for about nine years of distinguished wartime service in a number of vessels, for about five years as governor of New South Wales. But he has been in Lambeth many more years than that. He is buried there at St Mary's Church. St Mary's Church itself is now a Garden Museum and the small cemetery a Tradescant Garden. Bligh must rest happily there. The only good memories he would have had of the *Bounty* would have been of the hours in his shirt sleeves potting plants under a tarpaulin on the quarterdeck minding all the species he was bringing home for Sir Joseph Banks and the Kew Gardens. The memory of him carved on his grave mentions his Fellowship of the Royal Society. Years before, when he had just married Elizabeth and set up house on the Isle of Man, he had remarked that there were plenty of books. 'I can improve myself', he wrote. He did improve himself. He was proud of his Fellowship of the Royal Society, although he was constantly jealous of how others might improve themselves. 'Vice Admiral of the Blue', the gravestone also reads. There were bitter memories in that, recollections of the days after his return on the *Resolution* following Cook's death in Hawaii. Cook had chosen Bligh as Master of the *Resolution* at the age of twenty-two. Yet Bligh was denied promotion, even recognition of how much he had contributed. Being made post-captain came late, only after his return from the *Bounty*. It was a slow ride up the seniority ladder as death tipped off those above him. In the end, however, he was Vice-Admiral of the Blue. He would have been proud of that.

Figure 2.

The tomb of William Bligh in the graveyard of the Church of St Mary, Lambeth, now The Museum of Garden History administered by the Tradescant Trust. Bligh's grave was restored in 1888 by the Society of Arts. (Courtesy of the Museum of Garden History, Lambeth.)

'Celebrated Navigator', 'first transplanted the bread fruit tree from Otaheite to the West Indies', 'bravely fought the battles of his country' – these are the other epitaphs of the things Bligh did. He himself had a tendency to make history of the things done to him. He is better served on his tombstone.

Elizabeth is buried with him. On the side of the grave is also carved a memorial to his twin sons, William and Henry. They had only one day of life, March 21, 1795. Young William and Henry would have been conceived in the days following his return on the *Providence,* in Bligh's darkest days, in which he was to discover how strong the force of public opinion against him had become. To read the inscription for these dead boys is to realise how dark those dark days must have been. Anne, the last of his daughters born before these boys, was born epileptic and mentally handicapped. She was the object of Bligh's tenderness his whole life long. What do I really know of him? Be warned, Prologue-Reader, how much else there is to learn than what you will know from this drama.

ACT ONE.
The Ship

THE *BOUNTY* was a beautiful ship. Her masts and sails stood improbably high and delicate: her hull lay low in the water and was clean-lined. We can know her well – to the last rope and pulley. The officers of the Deptford Naval Yard surveyed every inch of her in August 1787 as she lay at Wapping Stairs under the name *Bethia*. Then the Naval Yard drew plans for her alteration, as Sir Joseph Banks began to fuss with her. He wanted to ensure the safe delivery of breadfruit trees to the English West Indian plantations. He wanted botanical specimens for the new gardens at Kew as well. So he made a plant nursery of the *Bounty*'s great cabin. Two skylights were set in the deck above, with scuttles for air in the side and a stove for heat. The floor was of lead and carried the surplus water into storage on the deck below.

Space and the language to describe it make a ship. Space was inseparable from the authority it displayed and the relationships it enclosed. The 'quarterdeck' in naval parlance was a place – the upper deck abaft of the mainmast. It was also a social group – those who had the privilege of walking the quarterdeck and using the space associated with it, usually the great cabin and the wardroom. From the earliest times the quarterdeck had been a sacred place for shrines of the gods of the sea and seamen. By the eighteenth century, the quarterdeck was sacred to the presence of sovereign power in displays of etiquette and privilege. It was the captain's territory – his to walk on alone, his to speak from but not to be spoken to unless he wished it. But the captain himself also owed the quarterdeck a deference. He too saluted this shrine as a sign that he was subordinate to the power that others saluted in him. The quarterdeck embodied his commission from the King. It was the space of his sovereign's power, and all its trivial gestures and etiquette were its geography. The quarterdeck, for officers of a fighting ship, was also a space for very deep plays. It was there that an officer was expected to stand exposed, shielded only by his honour, when others on the ship might fight with more protection. That dread possibility but also the hope that any officer might have of treading where captains trod touched even the most trivial gesture with solemnity.

From the start, the main social space of the *Bounty* was subordinated to its botanical function. Sir Joseph Banks' plant nursery pushed the crew's living space forward and down. Bligh, the captain, and Fryer, the master, were squeezed into tiny cabins opposite one another in a lobby around the stairs of the rear hatchway. The arms chest stood between them. As a result, Bligh, instead of enjoying the small grandeur of a great cabin where he could work at his drawings, write his journals, be the 'experimental gentleman', and make a table for his quarterdeck, as Cook had done, spent his days in an airless, dark, temporary 'dining room', divided from the open space of the lower deck only by a bulk-head, perhaps only by a canvas wall. Thirty-three men slept, cooked, ate and spent their leisure time in a space twenty-two-by-thirty-six feet on the other side of that divide. No wonder Bligh was mystified by the conspiracy of mutiny against him. In the stew of humanity that was daily living, there could not have been a sound or smell or sight that all would not have shared.

Distance in naval command is something acted out, sometimes in so small a thing as a term of address, an invitation to dinner. Distance could be blurred by countervailing signs of relationships other than military. Ominously, there were many signs of spaces and relationships other than military on the *Bounty*.

The politics of captaincy for those with ambitions was to be chosen young and be bespoken for by a captain, be in some way stamped by him and moved by him along an upward path. 'Followers' was how an arch-conservative of the Old Navy's ways, Admiral W. H. Smyth, de-scribed them in his *Sailor's Word Book* (1867). 'The young gentlemen [were] introduced into the Service by the captain and reared with a fa-ther's care, moving with him from ship to ship; a practice which pro-duced most of our best officers formerly, but innovation has broken through it, to the great detriment of the Service and Country.' For Bligh, Cook should have played this role. His death had been a disaster for Bligh's ambitions. Bligh had missed out on inevitable promotion when those who took Cook's place had no interest in taking him along with them. When he began to man the *Bounty* for its voyage, the gran-deur of his ambitions conflicted with the modesty of the field from which, in turn, he could choose. After his voyage with Cook he had fulfilled his navy service in marginal ways and in fringe places, pursuing smugglers from the Isle of Man. Then he had joined the merchant service. He was something of an outsider to navy politics and considerably more subject to influences from the circle of those to whom he owed some social debt. So when he began to make his quarterdeck on the *Bounty,* he had no wide and open choice of 'young 'uns'. He had to listen to his own family and his own patrons urging their concerns for young men affected by poverty and death who must find a place in life with his help. So he listened to the Heywoods whose house he had rented in the Isle of Man, to the Stewarts whose hospitality he had enjoyed in the Orkneys, to the Christians in hard times, to the Halletts and the Haywards who had the ear of his wife, to Sir George Young whom he knew from the West Indies. Peter Heywood, George Stewart, Fletcher Christian, John Hallett, Thomas Hayward, Edward Young would be his 'young gentlemen'. They would be that cluster of ratings – midshipmen, able seamen with quarterdeck potential, master's mates – whose careers he would manage by promotions and on whom he would be dependent to fulfil his own ambitions. One day he would come to curse their incompetence, to berate their lack of commitment, to despair at their irresponsibility. He always had the sour sense that they had somehow been put upon him. And they, to judge from their extravagant ineptitude, had a sense that they were owed, more than that they were owing. His and their military relationship was skewed by this intervention of the personal. It did not make for an easy theatre of command.

There were other relationships that blurred the social space by their ambivalences. These ambivalences were institutional among navy ships but were, by the chance of personalities, made more acutely painful on the *Bounty* than most. There was, in the first place, some contradiction between the authority that came from 'commission' and that which came from 'warrant'. The Commission, direct from the Crown, in some way displaced the person commissioned, leaving much more room for a sense of public altruism and its rhetoric. The Warrant, a certificate of some personal capital in knowledge and skill outside the gift of the Crown, was much more privatising and entrepreneurial. In an institution as dependent as the navy on both the effectiveness of military command and the mastery of a complex artisanry of the sea, there had long been a contradiction between the authority of those who in some way were born to power by being a gentlemen with commissions and the authority of

those who had to make themselves powerful in their particular domain
by years of experience and learning and who served under warrant.

Bligh was the only commissioned officer on the *Bounty*. Self-serving
though he was and always ready to grasp the main chance, he could sub-
limate his *Bounty* voyage to the very highest ideals of king and country.
He had much to win by doing so, and he could not understand why
others did not find such righteousness rewarding. His Warrant Officers
were John Fryer, master, Thomas Huggan, surgeon, William Peckover,
gunner, William Purcell, carpenter, and William Cole, boatswain.
Bligh would be at odds with all of them before the voyage was done, but
most seriously Fryer, Huggan and Purcell. He could not raise their ambitions to his expectations. Nor could he cope with the obligation on
him as their commander to show loyalty to their authority and to restrain his contempt for their abilities. He saw Fryer, Huggan and Purcell as destroying the brilliance of his voyage by their preoccupation
with the boundaries of their own positions. He was forced to his first
flogging because Fryer insisted upon reporting Matthew Quintal for mutinous behaviour. To that moment he thought he had a perfect voyage,
but that was now spoiled by his dependence on what he considered another's poor judgement. The drunken, obese surgeon, Thomas Huggan,
was everything unclean and disgusting that Bligh had wanted the ship
not to be. When Huggan diagnosed scurvy as the cause of the first death
on the *Bounty*, Bligh's rage that this would have to be a matter of public
record convulsed the whole ship. Purcell, the carpenter, was always measuring of his obligations and of the small capital of his skills and tools.
When the need was public – to ingratiate the Tahitians by sharpening
their tools, to work for the ship beyond his carpentering duties – Purcell
held back. Captaining for Bligh was managing the contradictions of
these spaces of power, and he did it not very well.

Bligh was his own purser. He was thus commissioned and warranted
at the same time. This was a contradiction that ran through his own
person. In accepting command of the *Bounty* he had taken an extraordinarily large drop in yearly income, from five hundred pounds to fifty
pounds. The anxiety this created for him was real. It can be seen at all
moments of the voyage. He took every opportunity to make money, and
above all he put great energy into avoiding being loaded with debt. It
was not unheard of in the navy for a captain to be his own purser. Cook

had been purser. But it was recognised as a dangerous combination. Pursers were objects of almost universal suspicion because they distributed provisions, accounted for every ounce of food and every farthing of expense. Pursers were the brokers of every transaction on a ship and had to find a profit in these transactions if they were to win back the surety they had laid down. They were responsible to the Naval Victualling Board. The Board, out of long experience, had learnt every trick there was to squeeze a farthing. It made all its own rules, none to its disadvantage. It took any amount of time between six months and fifty-seven years, as N. A. M. Rodger has written in *The Wooden World* (1986), to settle its own debts. Shipwreck, mutiny or accident was never a reason to compensate a purser for his losses. Any man who became purser had to have some genius for knowing what would adversely affect him and had to labour instantly to record whatever he counted and measured. A mean spirit and calculating shrewdness were his chief defences. The altruism expected of a captain glimmered lowly behind the parsimony anticipated from a purser. It was to be expected that the *Bounty* crew would be suspicious of cheeses that disappeared and pumpkins that served as substitutes for bread. They would be worried whether they would really get their 'pinchgut money' for going on two-thirds allowance. They would all count their coconuts and yams very carefully. When it came to captains who were also pursers, sailors' stomachs were also spaces of power.

The arboretum in the Great Cabin cramped the social space forward and below. The warrant officers and supernumeraries – the boatswain, carpenter, gunner, surgeon, botanist and the captain's clerk and steward – clung to their privilege of a private space, even though it was the darker for being a deck lower and perched on a mezzanine platform fore and aft of this merchant ship's hold. Thomas Huggan, the surgeon, cocooned himself in foetid solitude in one of these holes till he died at Tahiti. Bligh, sitting in his dining room above the surgeon's cabin, debated the whole twelve months of their voyage together just how private he could allow the surgeon's private space to be. Huggan was an institutional scandal, the stuff that Random Smollett could write a novel about. While the officer responsible for their health was so comfortable in his dirt, how could Bligh persuade the 'people' to accept the pain of being healthy by constantly cleaning their clothes, washing the ship

down in warm vinegar and pumping the bilges till they were as clean as
the seawater Bligh had them pour into the ship's bottom? It was not till
the last days of Huggan's life that Bligh dared invade his private space
and clear out his cabin. It was a dilemma of his command, this measuring of the niceties of a subordinate's authority. His patience with Huggan – not counting the cost of his rage at others because of it – was the
exception of a lifetime. In the *Bounty* or later, Bligh was never really to
know where his quarterdeck ended and others' private space began.

Meanwhile, the Admiralty was counting every penny spent on scuttles
and hatches, lead trays, pot stoves, shelving, mezzanine platforms and
everything else that was transforming the *Bethia.* In the end, the cost of
the *Bounty* and her preparations was more than £6,406, three times as
much as the Admiralty had intended to pay. The politics of empire were
expensive. Lobbyists among the West Indian plantation owners could
persuade the Admiralty to fund the supply of breadfruit as a cheap subsistence food for their slaves. Gentlemen scientists, such as Sir Joseph
Banks, could manoeuvre government to service pet ideas. Once the
needs of politics were met, overruns in cost really did not matter. And
costs of making symbols of power mattered even less. So in 1790, the
admirals would send a frigate, the *Pandora,* to retrieve a *Bounty* lost on a
voyage they did not really care about. Then they could mount an even
more expensive breadfruit expedition in the *Providence* and *Assistant.* The
West Indian slaves never would change their eating habits for the im-
ported breadfruit. But, by then, the *Bounty* had been transformed from
being a sign of entrepreneurial adventures into being a parable of trans-
gressed sovereignty. To win in such display of unambivalent power, material costs were unimportant.

A naval vessel assumed an inexorable logic in her spaces of power simply by being rated. The *Bounty* was rated as 'H. M. Armed Vessel'. That
rating gave her the number of her crew (forty-five), the number of servants (one), the number of marines (nil), and the unchangeable presumption that she could only have a commander, not a post-captain. In
Bligh's estimation, but not in Admiralty logic, she was something more
than an 'Armed Vessel'. She was a ship of discovery, a great experiment.
She was encompassing the world in a voyage of major significance. In
this there was always a contradiction between what he was doing and
what the ship would be allowed to do by the structures imposed upon her.

The forty-six men aboard the *Bounty* (add the botanist, David Nelson, to her allowed complement) can be described with as much precision as the *Bounty* herself. The muster roll was both an institutional profile and a purser's portrait of them. Indeed, it was a mark of what Bligh valued most highly on the *Bounty* that his clerk managed to secure the muster roll during the mutiny and protected it from sea and sun in the launch all the way home to England. Of course, the muster's profile was a peculiar one — of 'slops' supplied, 'venereals' treated, beds bought, tobacco used and wages advanced: it was a sailor seen through a purser's eyes. But there is history in that. Poor Thomas Huggan is there in the *Bounty*'s muster, in the column of 'Dead Men's Clothes'. The crew had auctioned his effects on the afternoon he was buried at Point Venus on Tahiti. Twenty-four crew found something to buy for a total of £87/7/2 debit. In the way of the navy, the auction would not have been a sad affair. In his log, Bligh wrote that he stopped the sale of thirty-three shirts because they were being offered at less than half their real value. One wonders what George Simpson bought for 6d; or Fletcher Christian for £2/16/6, James Morrison for £3/13/6, or the 'boy', Robert Tinkler, Fryer's stepson, for £8/10/0. They would not have been icons to cherish a memory, one would have thought.

Twenty-four of the complement of forty-five men were rated 'A.B.', able seaman, a man able to 'hand' (furl the square sails to the yards), 'reef' (shorten sail in strong winds) and 'steer' (direct the ship by the steering wheel). In practice on the *Bounty*, 'A.B.' described men performing a wide range of roles. The midshipmen — George Stewart, Thomas Hayward, Peter Heywood, Edward Young, John Hallett — were rated 'A.B.' but were nonetheless always privileged to the quarterdeck. Robert Tinkler, who messed with the midshipmen and was rated 'A.B.', was always referred to by Bligh as 'boy', no doubt to remind Fryer of his debt to Bligh's patronage and to anger him with his contempt. The cook's assistant (William Muspratt), Bligh's servant (John Smith), the half-blind Irish fiddler (Michael Byrne), the surgeon's assistant (Thomas Ledward), young Thomas Ellison, whom Bligh had brought with him from the *Britannia* with John Norton, Lawrence Lebogue and Fletcher Christian — all were rated 'A.B.' Yet there would not have been more than twelve to fourteen true 'A.B.'s to hand, reef and steer. With three watches, that would have been about four able seamen to a watch. The men seemed to make homely and familiar groups, a far cry from 'divisions', the instrument of discipline and order that the navy was discover-

ing at the time. In 'divisions' each man was numbered and assigned to a
group that was set against other groups in competitive efficiency and
obedience. There was no sign of 'divisions' on the *Bounty*. Indeed, what
glimpses we have of her watches at work show them winking at one another's breaches of rule – such as sleeping on watch (a death penalty in
the Articles of War), being late for watch – or they are lessening the
distance between themselves and their officers in easy familiarity and informal exchange. All but three of these true 'A.B.'s were engaged ac-
tively in the mutiny. It has been suggested that on them had fallen a
disproportionate share of the physical rigours of the voyage. But when
she was a merchant ship, the *Bethia* would have had only a total complement of fifteen, officers included. Perhaps it was not so much the rigour
of their lives as the blurring of their spaces of power that disturbed
them. The navy was discovering that discipline was best sustained when
men identified themselves by a sense of pleasure in work well done. It is
difficult to find any sense of pleasure in the *Bounty*.

By the chance that the physical characteristics of the wanted mutineers were described, we know how tall the men of the *Bounty* were.
They averaged five feet seven inches, the shortest being Thomas Ellison
at five foot three, the tallest being Isaac Martin at five foot eleven.
Fletcher Christian at five foot nine would have stooped a little over his
bowlegs as he walked about the cramped quarters of the *Bounty*. Most of
the men would have stooped. Headroom was only five feet seven inches.

The muster roll tells us the crew's age. They averaged twenty-six
years. The three youngest were fifteen years, the oldest was thirty-nine.
Bligh was thirty-three years old. Of the crew, 15.21 percent were older
than Bligh and more than thirty-six years old. Older men among seamen
were repositories of knowledge, lore and experiential authority. The
Bounty was skewed by this age factor more than any other naval ship to
enter the Pacific at this time. Bligh had considerable competition as to
who could be considered the true 'father' of the ship.

Place of origin was registered on the musters. Mostly, the 'Bountys'
came from the west, north-west and south-east of England. There were
also eight Scots and one Irishman. There was a significant cluster of men
from islands – one from Guernsey, one from the Orkneys, one from the
Shetlands, one from the Isle of Wight, two from the Isle of Man. There
were also a West Indian, two Americans and a German. All, excepting
three or four men, smoked or chewed tobacco. By the time of the mu-

tiny, most had spent more than three of their sixteen months' wages on this comfort. Thirty-nine percent were found to be with 'venereals' and were docked fifteen shillings for the surgeon's costs at least once. Only one other ship in the Pacific at this time had more 'venereals' – 59 percent of the crew on the *Chatham* on Vancouver's expedition were treated for the condition. On the *Bounty,* Bligh was never niggardly with liquor. A gallon of beer a day, while it lasted (preservatives for beer were as yet undiscovered), and a daily half-pint of 'grog' after that, must have taken some of the pain of their hard lives away. However, the spirits they learned to distil after the mutiny would cause them more pain.

Knowing how tall the masts or crew of the *Bounty* were hardly discovers the sense of the ship to those who sailed her. There was probably no single sense of the *Bounty,* anyway. None of those who were called on as witness in trial testimony, affidavit or informal recollection could be guided to an agreed-upon image. Individual sureness of perception fell away when a man was asked to describe unambivalently the trivialities with which structure and power were clothed. The Ship is much more an outsider's image, part of other conversations. The Ship, for the insider – in all its spaces, in all its relationships, in all its theatre – was always being re-made, was always in process. Its story had not ended. The partial history men made of it was always creating something new.

The Ship of the *Bounty,* in my outsider's image of it, had many signs of ambivalence. She was navy and, by that, should have been most unambivalent. The distances of status, the spaces of authority, the rules of role, the functions of officers should have been measured precisely and staged with clearly specific rubric and ceremony. 'Ceremony', it has been written of the navy, 'is to a marked degree the cement of discipline and upon that discipline the service rests. Worth of ceremony rests mainly upon the fact that it binds to the past while, at the same time, it lends an air of dignity and respect in all official relations. . . .' Ceremony binds to the past. Ceremony focuses on the ways in which things have always been done. Ceremony emplots relationships in unambivalent spaces.

In contrast, the *Bounty* was an unceremonious ship in a ceremonious institution. She had an entrepreneurial rather than a navy air. She was in the service of West Indian 'nabobs'. She was the toy of a social dilettante. Her commander's loyalties were more civilian than military. As he pursued his main chance, patronage flowed to Bligh and made him in

turn patron more than captain. At the same time his men were institutional men. Such institutional men are alienated by their sense of powerlessness over the structures they know they create by their own deferences. But their alienation can be their defence. The institution does not
touch them in their souls. They have some independence in this dialectics of dominance and deference. Blurred genres of behaviour – being
somewhere between personal and institutional, between entrepreneurial
and naval – can make the trivial momentous, can breach their private
space. The ship of the *Bounty,* with Bligh as her captain, was full of such
dangerous ambivalences.

Figure 3. Spaces of the *Bounty.* (Figures 3a–d courtesy of John McKay, *Anatomy
of the Ship, The Armed Transport Bounty.* 1989. London: Conway Maritime Press.)

John McKay's reconstructions of the *Bounty* best set our images. The great cabin
(Figure 3b), empty on the voyage out to Tahiti, allowed overhead space to sling
hammocks, which Bligh permitted when the decks leaked too badly. Bligh's
sleeping cabin (starboard) and Fryer's cabin (port) were cramped, approximately
7′ × 8′. Beyond the captain's pantry and dining/day room and behind the bulk-
head was space for master's mates and midshipmen. Christian, Hayward, Hallett,
Stewart, Heywood, Elphinstone, Young and Tinkler would have slept and messed
there. Behind a canvas bulkhead, thirty-three seamen filled the rest of the space,
approximately 22′ × 36′. Note the Brodie stove and galley in the fore starboard
section. And note the open space opposite the galley. The bosun's cabin of the
Bethia was removed from here, and the bosun, William Cole, berthed in a cabin
immediately below in the hold. This meant that one of the petty officers most
concerned with discipline and ordinarily on hand with the people was isolated
and out of the way.

   Mezzanine floors had been constructed aft and fore of the hold (Figure 3c). The
breadroom, damaged in the very first storm in the Atlantic, was immediately
below the great cabin. Then, on the port side, was a storeroom, surgeon Huggan's cabin, the clerk Samuel's and the botanist Nelson's cabins. Gunner Peckover's was the last cabin on the starboard side, then the captain's storeroom. The
mizzenmast, the run-off barrels from the nursery and the elm-tree pumps denied
them space outside these cabins. A scuttle gave them air indirectly, but not much
light. On the port side in the fore mezzanine, there was first a storeroom, then
bosun Cole's cabin, the sail room, the bosun's and gunner's storerooms, the pitch
room. Carpenter Purcell's cabin had been moved from the lower deck to make

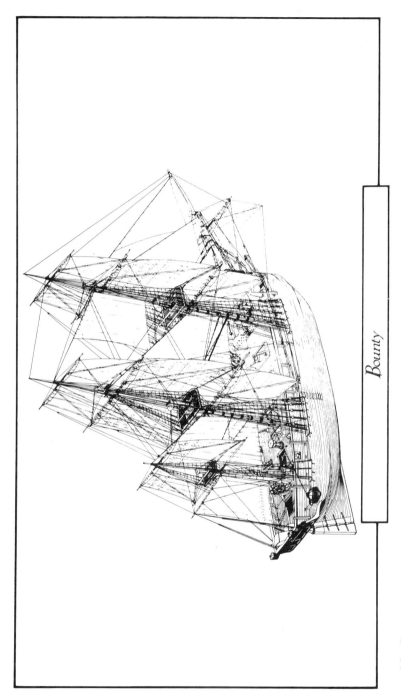

Bounty

3a. The *Bounty*.

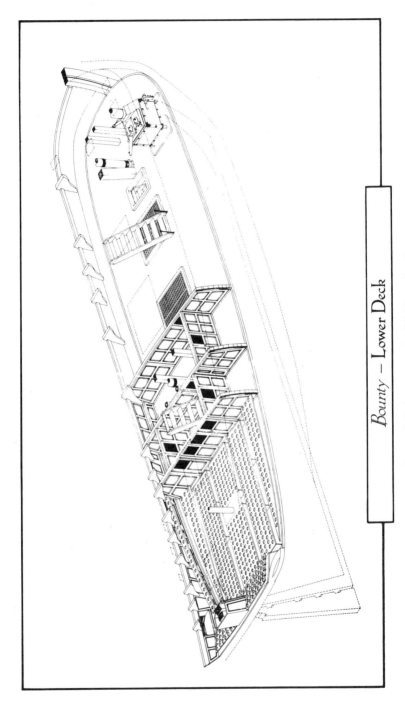

Bounty – Lower Deck

3b. The lower deck: great cabin, Bligh's cabin and dining space, the fo'c'sle and galley.

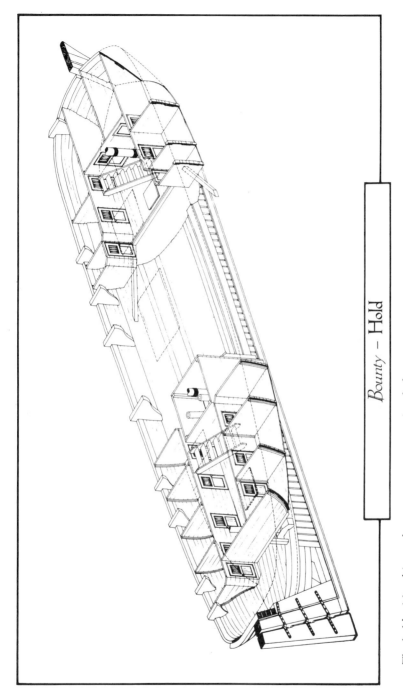

Bounty – Hold

3c. The hold with cabins and storerooms on mezzanine deck.

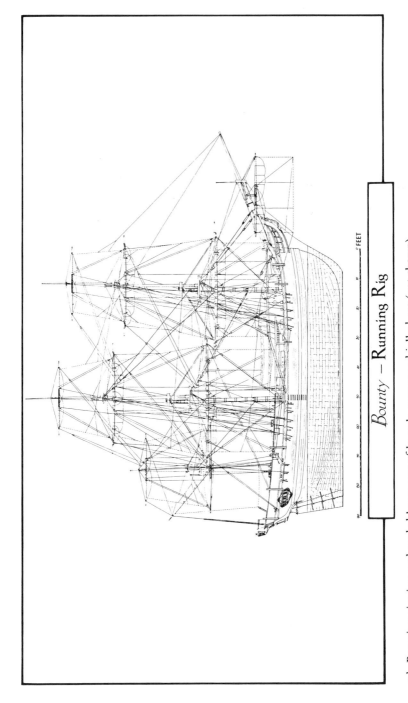

Bounty – Running Rig

3d. Running rigging and probable storage of launch, cutter and jolly-boat (not shown).

32

room for the galley. So he, too, was down in the dark, which may account for his perpetual bad temper. He had his storeroom beside his cabin.

Thus eight of the 'Bountys' had an opportunity for some privacy in their cabins. The rest spent their working and leisure hours and performed every bodily function in public.

Exactly how the three boats − the 23-foot launch, the 20-foot cutter and the 16-foot jolly-boat − were stored between main and foremast on the upper deck is a matter of conjecture and debate (Figure 3d). Bligh's insistence on largish, stout boats with which to provision the *Bounty* in the Pacific saved his life, but these boats crowded out the only public social space on board. So much so that it is difficult to imagine how and in what numbers they did their dancing. The morning of the mutiny must have been so much the more confused by the jostling and elbowing for space. However, as they put the three boats into the water trying to decide which would and which would not be Bligh's death warrant in its unseaworthiness, they made a stage on the deck for Christian's theatre.

So universally admired is Bligh's feat of navigation in the launch, that inevitably there have been reconstructions of the launch itself and re-enactments of the voyage (see Shackleton 1989). Just as inevitably history has no answers for all the questions replicating demands. Was the launch carvel or clinker or both? Was it built by Thomas White at Gosport or John Burr a naval contractor? Was the planking of larch? If so, was the larch from Yorkshire where it was better for its slower growing? Bligh was so proud of her that he included her builder's lines in his *Narrative of the Mutiny*. But they do not nearly answer all the questions. Above all, they do not answer what to those who have reconstructed her and sailed the reconstruction is the most important question of all − how could Bligh have managed eighteen men in a boat that feels so crowded with six?

❧   ❧   ❧

Scene i. *Narrative*

FATAL HISTORIES

Tattoo (*tatau*) is a Polynesian word. A tattoo was the badge of a voyage to Polynesia in the eighteenth century. The crew of the *Bounty* were much tattooed. Fletcher Christian had a star on his breast and some other undescribed mark on his buttock, perhaps the broad black band that all Tahitian men wore. Other seamen enjoyed the irony of a tattooed star, the insignia of the Order of the Garter. James Morrison, the bosun's mate, took the irony farther. He had a garter tattooed around his thigh with the motto *Honi soit qui mal y pense*. John Millward had a Tahitian feather gorget (*taumi*) on his chest.

Peter Heywood was described by Bligh in 1789 as 'very much tattowed and on the Right leg is tattowed the Three Legs of Man as that coin is. At this time he [Heywood] had not done growing – He speaks with Strong Manks or Isle of Man Accent'. Bligh added later: 'I have now reason to curse the day I ever knew a Christian, a Heywood or any Manxman'. The three legs of the crest of the Isle of Man with its Latin motto, *Stabit, Jeceris, Quocunque* (Whichever way you throw him, he will stand) must have cartwheeled in Bligh's mind. He probably knew the ballad:

> However through the world they're tost
> However disappointed crost
> Reverses, losses, fortunes frown
> No chance nor change keep Manxmen down
> Upset them anyway you will
> Upon their legs you'll find them still
> Forever active, brisk and spunky.
> Stabit, Jeceris, Quocunque.

Whichever way the Christians and Heywoods were tossed, Bligh no doubt felt, they were still left standing.

Heywood, trying to soften the shock to his mother of his many tattoos, explained them in a letter from Batavia after his capture: 'I was tattooed, not to gratify my own desire, but theirs [the Tahitians], for it was my constant endeavour to acquiesce in any little custom which I thought wou'd be agreeable to them, tho' painful in the process, provided I gained by it their friendship and esteem.'

The youngest of the *Bounty* crew, a boy of fifteen years, Thomas Ellison, simply had a date on his right arm, '25 October, 1788'. It was the date that the 'Bountys' first saw Tahiti. They all must have remembered that date well. Few of them, however, celebrated many anniversaries of it. Thomas Ellison celebrated only four. He was hanged from the yard of HMS *Brunswick* on the morning of 29 October 1792.

John Millward, with his tattooed gorget, and Thomas Burkitt, scarred by smallpox as well as tattoos, hanged with Thomas Ellison. On these three men fell the whole pain of retribution for the mutiny of the *Bounty*. The forty-three other seamen on the *Bounty* had also paid their price. Four had drowned in irons in the wreck of the *Pandora,* trapped in a 'Pandora's Box' that was their prison. Two were murdered at Tahiti. Christian himself was within a few months of his murder along with three others on his hideaway at Pitcairn. Five of Bligh's party were dead too, one killed by the islanders of Tofua, four taken by fever in Batavia and Timor. Two others had died before the mutiny. All told, seventeen of the forty-six who sailed on this Voyage to the South Seas on 23 December 1787 were dead by 29 October 1792, or were soon to die.

Only Ellison, Millward and Burkitt were hanged, however. As they shuffled out along the catheads of the *Brunswick,* barefoot, hands tied, ropes around their necks, they could have wondered why it was on them alone that the King's Majesty fell with such awful show.

They were a humble remnant on which to wreak vengeance. Young Tom Ellison had been doing his 'trick' at the helm on the morning of the mutiny, April 28, 1789. He was barely observant of the trivial tasks of the dawn watch, the chopping of the wood for the galley fire that caused a yell of annoyance from someone wakened down below, the coiling of the ropes in preparation for washing the deck, the preoccupation of midshipman Hayward with a shark along the ship's side.

The mutiny was over before Ellison knew what was happening. There was Christian, musket, bayonet and cartouche box in one hand, pistol and cutlass in the other. 'He looked like a Madman, is long hair was luse, is shirt Collair open', Ellison wrote in his own defence. (Ellison had been learning to write on the *Bounty*. Bligh and his secretary had been teaching him.) 'I must have been very Ingreatful if I had in any respect assisted in this Unhappy Affair against my Commander and Benefactor, so I hope, honorable Gentlemen, yo'll be so Kind as to take my Case into Consideration as I was No more than between Sixteen and Seventeen years of Age when this was done, Honorable Gentlemen, I leave myself at the Clemency and Mercy of this Honourable Court.'

There, suddenly, was Bligh, bare-arsed, his nightshirt caught in the ropes that bound his wrists behind. And Bligh, even in this absurd situation, seeing the ship standing to land, snapped an order to the distracted Ellison to attend the helm, which he promptly obeyed.

In the half-light, in the space filled with Bligh's botanical gifts to Sir Joseph Banks and piled with yams and coconuts collected by the crew, with the boat, cutter and launch crowding the deck and with forty or so anxious and nearly hysterical men, Ellison could not know that where he stood, what he held, whether he smiled or wept, what he said would become parables of something else. He could not know that out of all the sights and sounds that engulfed him in confusion and fear someone would make history and hang him for it.

That history-making hanged John Millward too. He was asleep when all this was happening. Practised at not hearing the clatter of other watches and only just into his hammock at 4:00 A.M., he had to be wakened to be told that Christian had taken the ship. He knew he was doomed the moment he heard. Not that he knew anything of a plot. Nobody did. There had been no plot, only extravagant decisions instantly made. He knew the hatred, however. He had been involved in a 'foolish business' at Tahiti. He had deserted with Charles Churchill and William Muspratt. They had stolen eight stands of arms and ammunition. Bligh had dragged them back, flogged Millward and Muspratt with two dozen lashes, given Churchill a dozen, and put them all in irons for a month in Tahiti's February heat. He then repeated the dose of floggings. Bligh had also extracted a letter from them declaring their gratitude that he had not court-martialled them. Millward knew that Churchill, at Christian's side now in the mutiny, would never let him escape the hatred that the ingratiating letter disguised. He, of them all, knew the killer in Churchill. He also knew that no matter how convincingly he revealed his ambivalences to others, or how strenuously he might show his good intentions to help take back the ship by use of the arms with which the mutineers entrusted him, he was doomed by everybody's presumptive history of who he was. In any case, every man was preoccupied with his own signals. None had time to read the nuances of Millward's.

Thomas Burkitt, the third to be hanged, looked the ugly mutineer. But Burkitt was no leader, no man of independent action. He was always on the edge of things. He, like Ellison, was on Christian's morning watch on April 28. He was plucking a fowl for midshipman John Hallett. It was Hallett's week to supply the 'young 'uns' mess. Burkitt was protesting his inability to pluck fowls when the mutiny swept him by and caught him along. Christian was suddenly shouting that arms be taken out of the arms chest to shoot the shark that Mr Hayward had seen or to perform the exercises that Mr Bligh had been supposed to have ordered. He did not know which. Then they were in Bligh's cabin. Bligh, with the scene seemingly etched in his mind, later said that Burkitt was among them. John Fryer, the master, testified that Burkitt emerged from Bligh's cabin armed. Burkitt said no, he had never left the deck. Christian, he said, 'with fury in his eyes', came up the fore hatchway that led to the arms chest, and forced a musket on him with a threat as he passed him. William McCoy backed Christian by cocking his piece and saying, 'Why don't you lay hold of it and go aft as Mr Christian desires you?' It was only in this way, Burkitt claimed, that he might have been seen standing armed at the aft hatchway. When Bligh came up, it was he who loosed the nightshirt from the ropes and got Bligh's clerk to bring clothes. 'The officers being now all up, I look'd for some attempt to be made, but, to my utter surprise and astonishment, saw None.' Now that it was begun, how could it be ended by those who had no authority to lead and no example from those who did?

At their trial Ellison, Millward and Burkitt had had to make history to save their lives. Each had to tell a story of all the uncertainties *in* the event against the certain knowledge of what happened *after* the event. After the event there had been mutiny and piracy. That is what all those confused actions and undirected words had meant. But that hindsighted certainty never described what actually happened while the mutiny unfolded, never revealed the intentions of actions, never showed their secret fears or how they distanced themselves from the principal actors. Ellison, Millward and Burkitt were only masters of their own experience, not of how others experienced their signs. In the court they had to tell stories that had no context other than what they had done in the two and a half hours between 5:30 A.M. and 8:00 A.M., April 28, 1789. They had to make a history of an event that had no past, not in Bligh's pettiness, not in Christian's turmoil, not in Churchill's hatred. Such history without time and without circumstance — it was called 'evidence' — requires a peculiar poetic to be made and to be read. There needs to be a certain discipline to see the past so artfully. Courts that hang a man put great discipline into constructing such a blinkered view. Ellison, Millward and Burkitt were hanged by a very artful history indeed. In fact their hanging made the court's history come true.

The trick of making such artful history seem real rather than contrived is to surround its reading with signs of cultural propriety. Ellison, Millward and Burkitt were hanged with high propriety. It was October 1792. In France, the King was already in prison and the London newspapers were full of the politics of revolution. The Terror was still to come but the disorder was full of foreboding. In the *Gentleman's Magazine,* where Englishmen were apt to reflect contentedly on how different they were to foreigners, there had been comment on how civilised the English process of legal execution was.

In England the punishment of crimes is tempered with mildness and humanity. The most atrocious villain when he has been tried and found guilty by an equitable judge and an impartial jury is put to death with all the lenity that can possibly attend capital punishment. But in France criminals are frequently executed with circumstances of the most shocking barbarity. The offender is condemned to the most horrible of tortures; he is racked in the brodeguin, he is broiled, he is burnt alive, he is torn to pieces, or broken on the wheel. In the meantime an innumerable multitude of both sexes are viewing the dreadful spectacle with the usual levity, and, for the most part, with an unfeeling and inhuman exultation.

As it happened, there was a crowd of many thousands to see the mutineers hang. They were in a festive mood, 'as if instead of a solemn scene of sorrow, it had been a spectacle of joy', wrote one witness. From nine o'clock when the warning gun had been fired and the yellow flag raised, men, women and children had gathered on the harbour shore and ringed the *Brunswick* around in hired wherries.

This audience, no more nor less tumultuous than a Tyburn hanging crowd, was kept at a distance. Cutters from every naval vessel in port made an inner ring around the *Brunswick.* Its decks were lined with officers of those same ships. In the waist were three columns of seamen, yard-

arm ropes stretched over each man's hands. Ellison, Millward and Burkitt
would be run to the yard in a practised way. The crowd at a distance was
a rabble who would see the meanings of the ritual as they might. Within
the theatre of the execution, men fussed with the rubrics of where they
should stand, how they should look, what they should say. Distracted by
their duties of holding a cutter in line, of firing a gun, raising a flag,
processing the prisoners, with no time at all to reflect on the larger meanings of the moment, the inner audience was nonetheless disciplined to be
entertained by the signs. 'Hanging wonderfully concentrates the mind',
said Dr Samuel Johnson. But so does preoccupation with the trivia of
symbolising power.

For this final reading of the history of the *Bounty* mutiny, it was important that all the signs be seen in high hyperbole, all the gestures be
strongly accentuated, all the charades be precisely formal. The better to
make theatre of these signs, the *Brunswick* was sealed off for only those
who would see what was to be seen. It did not matter, sailors used to say,
whether he who would piss when he could not whistle slipped or was
hauled from the cathead. He was hanged all the same. But to make the
rituals work there needed to be solemn deferences to all the signs. Nothing should be accidental. Nor should the mutineers disturb the right
order of things. Later, Richard Parker, the leader of the Great Mutiny at
Nore, disturbed things greatly by jumping from the cathead and thus
taking his own life, not having it taken. Ellison, Millward and Burkitt
must be proper sacrificial victims. Their hanging made the court's history
true.

To the crowd outside the ritual space there were uncertainties in the
history and the signs. The crowd buzzed with rumours. 'Many respectable
inhabitants purposely left town till the melancholy scene closed', reported
the *London Chronicle*. There was unease at the executions. The unease sprang
from the suspicion that 'money bought the lives of some and others fell
sacrifice to their poverty'. Ellison, Millward and Burkitt had not been the
only ones sentenced to death for the mutiny. Peter Heywood, midshipman, nephew of a soon-to-be admiral, and a gentleman, had also been
sentenced, but had won the King's Mercy. There were 'great murmurs
and vulgar notions' that he was the heir to a fortune of thirty thousand
pounds. Untrue murmurs. James Morrison, the bosun's mate, and William Muspratt, the assistant cook, had been sentenced to death. Morrison
won a King's Pardon at the recommendation of the court. Muspratt was

freed on a legal technicality. It was common knowledge that Morrison had letters and journals of the *Bounty* voyage. The rumours of what was in them had persuaded many that Bligh had been the cause of his own mutiny. Heywood's family had used these papers to persuade some that a history of the events of the *Bounty* confined to the legalism of a court martial might not be a just history. Indeed, the Reverend William Howells, who acted as protector of Morrison, agreed not to publish the papers on condition that the Admiralty would treat Morrison well after his pardon. Muspratt, like Heywood, had a lawyer to defend him. The lawyer exploited the conservative pursuit of court-martial precedence by the court's president, Lord Hood, to show that in a matter of life and death there was a serious discrepancy between civil and military law. While the others were executed, Muspratt was freed with an admonition about his future conduct.

The hint of corruption was wrong. What was sensed, however, was correct. Under the binding hegemony proclaimed by the rhetoric of the King's majesty and law was an arbitrariness that invented criminality rather than discovered it. The artifices of making distinctions between those who would hang did not hide the fact that in the end it was class or relations or patronage that made the difference. What assuaged a little the conscience of all who witnessed the theatre of execution was that those who were hanged finally took upon themselves the responsibility for their hanging. Millward, who was spokesman for the other two on the cathead, was reported to have made a speech that was 'nervous, strong and eloquent, and delivered in an open and deliberate manner'.

You see before you three lusty young fellows about to suffer a shameful death for the dreadful crime of mutiny and desertion. Take warning by our example never to desert your officers and, should they behave ill to you, remember it is not their cause, it is the cause of your country that you are bound to support.

That was his speech or that was what was heard. He had no family or fortune to protect in purging his guilt. He had no ulterior motive in pleading his guilt. It was the pure libation of a victim. His born-again innocence made the sacrifice seem right. His sacrificers were well satisfied. Those who heard his speech gave an accolade to the British tars they ruled.

The tension between the formal definition of who they were and whom they experienced themselves to be had tortured all the mutineers in the twenty months since their capture by Captain Edwards in the *Pandora*.

Edwards had had his own mutiny a few years before or, more accurately
had forestalled it from ever happening. He had had seven of his crew
hanged for that non-event. When Edwards sailed for Tahiti he was under
orders to bring the mutineers back for trial. It was of little matter that
Bligh had publicly declared that four of the men were innocent and had
been kept against their will. Edwards forced each of the fourteen survivors
into 'Pandora's Box', an eleven by eighteen foot prison he had built on
the *Pandora's* deck. For five months, manacled hand and foot, with the
scuppers running with vermin and sweat, food lowered through the tiny
scuttle in the roof that was their only light and ventilation, the men
endured one another's innocence and guilt. In their misery, they fought
and wrangled. When the *Pandora* was wrecked on the Australian coast,
they scrabbled for the key of their manacles. A guard, against Edwards'
orders, had thrown it into their box in the *Pandora's* last minutes. Four
of them lost in that mad fight for an escape and were drowned. Then
those still living lay in irons on the bottom of open boats for a thousand-
mile voyage to Timor. They were not taken out of irons until they were
delivered to the *Vengeance* at Sheerness. There, for the first time in seventeen months, they may have felt some comfort. The commander of Sheerness was Captain Thomas Pasley, Peter Heywood's uncle.

The brutality towards them had only become more genteel. They were
still indiscriminately prisoners and pirates. That charade was maintained.
The four named by Bligh as innocent, including a half-blind Irish fiddler,
Michael Byrne, whom Bligh had brought on the *Bounty* to make his sailors exercise by dancing of an evening, still had to endure the terror of not
knowing what chance piece of evidence would take their lives. When the
trial was under way, every day there were scenes of piteous self-degrada-
tion as Byrne, whom everybody despised, played the lawyer and argued
for his life which no court in the land would take from him for his being
blind, but which, for the form of the theatre, no one would say they
would not take.

The prisoners all found that God, if not the Law, had come a little
closer. They were visited by evangelical ministers of the newly forming
Mission Society, London. The Society was about to send missionaries to
Tahiti whence the mutineers had come. Soon those missionaries, innocent
of any other knowledge or strategy, were to go to Tahiti armed with a
vocabulary and grammar compiled for them by Peter Heywood and ethnographic notes about Tahitian culture out of Morrison's journal. It was

not a bad bargain. The evangelical ministers quickly spread abroad edi-
fying tales of the prisoners' piety. Rumours about Mr Bligh grew apace.

The court martial began on Wednesday, September 12, 1792. The
court heard the prosecutor's evidence for four days, defence for one and
passed sentences on Tuesday, September 18. Lord Hood, Vice-Admiral of
the Blue and Commander-in-Chief of His Majesty's Ships and Vessels at
Portsmouth and Spithead, was president of their trial. Twelve captains of
the fleet in port sat beside him left and right in order of their seniority.
One was a baronet, two were knights. Their names rang with quality –
Albemarle Bertie, Andrew Snape Hammond, Andrew Snape Douglas, John
Nicholson Inglefield. . . . The Great Cabin of the *Duke* was packed with
spectators as well – judges, admirals, naval officers of high rank, lawyers,
lords. The mutineers' trial being 'a very interesting discussion of some
part of our military arrangements', as one naval officer wrote, some made
it a principle to attend all sessions. It was a theatre for the hegemony of a
special sort of common sense. Institutional structures lay bare in the extravagant care for playing roles. The prisoners were tried under the Articles of War in 22 Geo. II, cap. 33 (1749).

The critical point in the trial was, as Captain Pasley wrote to Peter
Heywood's mother, 'The man who stands neutral is equally guilty with
him who lifts his arm against his Captain'. The great divide between those
for and against Bligh had become the launch. Those who went with him
in the launch were loyal; those who stayed on the *Bounty* were mutineers
and pirates. But who went in the launch had been something of a lottery.
There were a number in the launch who would have stayed on the *Bounty*
if they could, notably midshipman Hallett. His tears and protests at going,
then his shame at the memory of them, made him a cruel witness and the
death of others. There were other men, who, by the chance of having
skills that the core of the mutineers needed, by the luck of the launch
being too full, by the accident of being out of sight on the deck of the
Bounty, were compelled to be 'neuter' by the same fears that kept those
with Bligh from making even the slightest gesture in support of him.
Being on the ship and not the launch did not necessarily make one group
guilty and the other not.

The witnesses of the court were those who survived that famous launch
voyage from Tonga to Timor. The exception, of course, was Bligh, who
was off on his second breadfruit voyage in the *Providence* – a remarkable
decision on his part and a sign of his tenacious ambition, an outrageous

decision on the Admirality's part when they had already commissioned the *Pandora* to pursue their 'pirates'. The witnesses had not much doubt as to the real cause of their sufferings. Brilliant as the launch voyage was, they had experienced all over again Bligh's tantrums, his self-centred preoccupations, his hatreds. In the launch itself, there were three mutinous occasions when they bowed to Bligh's power but challenged his authority. At the trial, however, the prescriptions of the court about their evidence — what they could say on oath about their actual observation — reduced the complexity of their experiences to a thin veneer. They were blinkered by the court's rules of evidence. None of them could record what really happened. Their own futures depended on their making uncomplicated histories.

Edward Christian, Fletcher's brother, was a professor of law at Cambridge University and later a judge. He appreciated the make-believes of courts. Indeed, he reflected in later life on the effectiveness of the court's theatre. When the *Bounty* trials were over and the executions carried out, he wrote a pamphlet showing how different a history of what actually happened could be to that of a court's. 'The court', he wrote, 'confined the witnesses as much as possible to the question who were actually engaged in the mutiny? For that being the crime which will admit of no legal justification, the relation of previous circumstances could not be material or legal evidence'. The Crown itself, he recognised, was threatened by a mutiny. The King's commission in the captain was scorned. Any mutinous action was a parable for the overthrow of the ultimate power of the state over life and death. As for the *Bounty*'s crew, any action done under the gaze of their trussed-up captain at the command of Christian was mutinous, unless Christian's command was violently enforced upon them. But there was not a single action of such high clarity that a man's life would depend on it the whole mutiny long. Even the half-instinctive act of helping Bligh safe into the launch was somehow cooperating with Christian. Even arming oneself on the chance of taking the ship away from the mutineers was a sign of willingness to use armed power outside the jurisdiction of the captain. Even obedience to Bligh's explicit request that some men not board the launch and the terrified pleas of his companions not to overcrowd it was a sign of willingness to stay under unlawful command. Even to have surreptitiously accepted a dram of pure rum when Christian ordered it for his men could hang a man. Watered down rum was the only licit drink. There was not a man among them who did not hear and find hope in Bligh's shout from the launch: 'Men, I will do you justice when I get back to England'. They heard him say that he had seen their confusion and would protect them. When the prisoners faced the witnesses and sought to find out of the confusion of those wild two hours some concordance of a word or a look or a gesture, they knew that their personal memory, clear and vivid, would be seen as self-seeking, and the witnesses' forgetfulness arising out of their other preoccupations would be seen as objective truth.

Only two of the prisoners, Peter Heywood and William Muspratt, had lawyers. The other eight managed by their own wits. Some did very well. 'The ship seems to have abounded with men above the common herd of illiterates', wrote one spectator. 'The boatswain's mate [Morrison] stood his own counsel, questioned all the evidences, and in a manner so arranged and pertinent, that the spectators waited with impatience for his turn to call on them, and listened with delight during the discussion.' Morrison – he with the tattooed Order of the Garter – played the theatre for his life, and won. Heywood had it played for him in another way. His uncle, Captain Pasley, directed him very closely. Pasley was a close friend of several of the captains on the court martial. When it was all over and Peter Heywood stood pardoned, they – including the President of the Court, Lord Hood – competed to offer him patronage. Heywood won his lieutenant's commission in two years and his captaincy in six, in spite of having been condemned to death for mutiny. Before the trial, Pasley had contacted all the witnesses to measure the effectiveness of their evidence. He also employed a lawyer, Francis Const, but relied more on the experience of a friend, Aaron Graham, who had acted as Deputy Judge Advocate in courts martial for twelve years, and John Delafons, who was to write a treatise on naval courts martial. Knowing the aversion of navy men to lawyers, they directed Heywood's counsel to play a discreet and guiding role. Their strategy was to let the midshipman be seen by the court only in clichéd deference. All Heywood's statements to the court were written and read by a friend. 'Owing to the long and severe Confinement he had suffered he was afraid he was not capable of delivering it with that force of Expression which it was required.' Even when he received the King's Mercy, as was remarked at the time in Knapp and Baldwin's *Newgate Calendar* (1820) of executions, 1792, he 'anticipated his inability to speak' and read a prepared statement. Perhaps there was more to his clichés than legal strategy, however. His correspondence with his mother and his sister Nessie is extant, as are Nessie's poetry and intimate diary. There could not be a world more full of bathetic intensity than theirs.

Why William Muspratt, assistant cook on the *Bounty,* born at Maidenhead, had the good sense and fortune to have a lawyer, Stephen Barney, we do not know. Barney delivered the masterstroke of the trial when Lord Hood called upon his prerogative to try the prisoners collectively rather than individually. Barney called on two prisoners, Norman and Byrne, who were certain to be acquitted, as witnesses in Muspratt's defence. By precedent the naval court did not allow one accused to defend another. By that they ran counter to civil practice, especially in cases of capital punishment. Muspratt, found guilty, was pardoned on that legalism, and naval attorneys, lawyers and counsels glowed with a sense of justice in the triumph of it. Along with Edward Christian's pamphlet, Barney published his own transcription of the proceedings of the court. To an audience wider than the spectators who reinforced the theatricality of the court by their presence, the transcriptions were a disturbing revelation of the trivialities on which life and death had hung.

On the morning of Tuesday, September 18, 1792, the court passed sentence that 'the Charges had been proved against the said Peter Heywood, James Morrison, Thomas Ellison, Thomas Burkitt, John Millward and William Muspratt, and did adjudge them and each of them to suffer Death by being hanged by the Neck, on board such of His Majesty's Ship or Ships of War, at such time or times and at such Place or Places, as the Commissioners for executing the Office of Lord High Admiral of Great Britain and Ireland, etc., or any three of them, for the time being, should in Writing, under their Hands direct'. Heywood and Morrison were recommended for the King's Mercy. Norman, McIntosh, Coleman and Byrne were acquitted. Muspratt's legal petition was accepted. Within half an hour Aaron Graham was writing assuring letters to Peter Heywood's relatives that his life was safe. It was, he wrote, 'as safe as if he was not condemned', and he had that from the King's Attorney General (Sir Archibald Macdonald) and Judge Sir William Henry Ashurst who were spectators in the court. Everyone was quite pleased at the set of charades. Awful majesty was displayed and manipulated at one and the same time.

Ellison, Millward and Burkitt were brought to the *Brunswick* the evening before their execution. 'W. L.', the naval officer who had followed their trial, was a lieutenant aboard the *Brunswick*. 'I expected to have seen

them emaciated, wan and half-expiring with the keenness of their afflic-
tion, but to my astonishment, they tripped up and down the ladders with
the most wonderful alacrity, and their countenances, instead of being (as
I expected) the index of woeful depression of mind, were perfectly calm,
serene and cheerful' ('W. L.' 1792)

The gunroom where they spent the night was screened and closed to
light. They were surrounded with appropriate funereal gloom. Around
their cubicle in the corner gathered a 'melancholy group of mournful spectators' who watched them talk and read and sleep the night through.
Millward read Dodd's sermons to the other two. They were practised in
religion. Four chaplains would lead them to the cathead on the morrow.
The Reverend Williams Howells, not to be outdone in this didactic moment, would preach to them their last sermon out of Hebrews 13:17,
'Obey them that have authority over you'. Morrison, pardoned of the guilt
that was taking their lives, would fill the last half-hour of their lives with
devotions. The signs were that they would die well. They would be pliant
victims. Their dying would be sacramental of all the proprieties their
execution displayed.

Except in one ugly respect. The provost marshal, their gaoler on the
Brunswick, had seen it all before and was not going to go unrewarded for
so famous an occasion. He stole their three nightcaps as souvenirs, and,
over the murmur of the prisoners' devout talk, declared that the 'young
one's a hardened dog'. Ellison, who had been called a 'running dog' by
Bligh and a 'little monkey' by Christian, was probably less disturbed by
it than 'W. L.'. He ordered the provost out of the gunroom. The provost
'went to the berth of the serjeant of marines, where the infernal brute sat
down to drinking with the most cheerful countenance you can possibly
imagine. Oh! how I wished for the pen of a Sterne.'

Ah, indeed! 'The pen of a Sterne.' Power thrives on a cliché. It was
important to them all that the proper emotions be displayed with hyperbole. It was important to them all that the 'three lusty young fellows'
transform themselves in clichéd ways. Ellison, Millward and Burkitt must
balance for their last act on the catheads, the solid stumpy projections on
each side of the ship to which the anchors were hauled. Sailors joked about
the cathead with the bravado that the dominated show for the instruments
of their domination. But it was bad luck, nonetheless, to climb a yard
from which a man had been hanged, and seamen would not go there if
they could avoid it. The executioners were always the victim's own mates.

Those who shared the burden of giving deference to authority carried the duty of doing the killing.

Ellison, Millward and Burkitt were very proper victims. In their last speeches, they said the right things about law and order. Those who think themselves civilised have often agreed that they are civilised because they have resigned the power to do violence to an institution outside themselves, to something they reify as the state or Crown. Obeisance to sovereignty is the acknowledgement of both the limit on self and the openness of self to the invasion of power. Yet this thing outside of self needs many plays to make it present and real. Not least among the plays is the victim's demeanour, his or her acceptance and resignation. There is horror at executions when the victims see the shams and will not be killed quietly. Their transformations are their ultimate socialisation. And those that witness these transformations are shriven of the responsibility of their power.

'At 11.00 o'clock the gun was fired and their souls took flight in a cloud, amid the observations of thousands. They behaved with manly firmness that would have dignified a superior state, merited a better fate, and was the admiration of all.' Ellison, Millward and Burkitt were sacrificial victims, not raised to gods, but lifted a class or two.

There was, by naval rubric, no work in the fleet while their bodies hung from the yard for an hour or so. Captain Hammond of the *Brunswick* reported to the Admiralty that 'the example seems to have made a great impression upon the minds of all the ships' companies present'. Perhaps it did, perhaps it did not. Five years later, most of these ships' companies mutinied against most of these ships' captains in the mutiny at Great Nore. After Nore thirty-six men were hanged.

Figure 4.   The Faces of the *Bounty*

Portraits, like autobiographies, are puzzling sources of history. They freeze the subjects to a moment of the artist's perception of them. For Bligh we have a succession of these stilled moments. Make of them what we will. Bligh had a penchant for portraits, not just out of his sense of history and his role in it, but also because he had connections with painters, engravers and publishers. The earliest portrait we have of Bligh is attributed to John Webber (Figure 4a). If it was John Webber — and the likelihood of it being so is supported by Webber's

a. William Bligh (1755–6). John Webber. (From a Private Collection.)

b. William Bligh (1790). Engraving by J. Conde after a watercolour by J. Russell. (Frontispiece, William Bligh, *A Voyage to the South Seas*. 1792. London: G. Nicol. Baillieu Library, The University of Melbourne.)

c. William Bligh (1803). Pencil watercolour by J. Smart. (National Portrait Gallery, London.)

d. Elizabeth Bligh (1782). John Webber. (From a Private Collection.)

e. Fletcher Christian (1790). Detail from an aquatint by Robert Dodd. (See Figure 1.)

f. Thursday October Christian (1817). Engraving from J. Shillibeer, *A Narrative of the* Briton's *Voyage to Pitcairn Island.* Taunton: Lawrence and Whittaker. (Baillieu Library, The University of Melbourne.)

g. John Fryer (1787–1817). Oil portrait by Gurtano Calleja. (Mitchell Library, State Library of N.S.W. Sydney. Ref: ZHL 413.)

h. Peter Heywood. Oil. Artist unknown. (Manx Museum, Douglas, Isle of Man.)

i. Peter Heywood. Oil. Artist unknown. (National Maritime Museum, Greenwich. Ref: A1072.)

j (i–ix). Nine of the twelve members of the court martial of the *Bounty* mutineers. j. (i) Viscount Samuel Hood. By L. F. Abbatt. (National Portrait Gallery, London.)

j. (ii) Sir Andrew Snape Hammond. By T. Lawrence. (National Maritime Museum.. Ref: D3981.)

j. (iii) Captain John Thomas Duckworth. By W. Beechey. (National Maritime Museum. Ref: 6379.)

j. (iv) Captain John Knight. By J. Smart. (National Maritime Museum. Ref: A9259.)

j. (v) Sir Richard Godwin Keats. By J. Jackson. (National Maritime Museum. Ref: D3982.)

j. (vi) Sir John Colpoys. By P. Pellegrini. (National Maritime Museum. Ref: B91.)

j. (vii) Captain John Nicholson Inglefield. By Engelhart. (National Maritime Museum. Ref: A1031.)

j. (viii) Sir Albemarle Bertie. Artist unknown. (National Maritime Museum. Ref: A7508.)

j. (ix) Sir Roger Curtis. By W. Hamilton. (Trustees of the British Museum)

k. Commodore Thomas Pasley. Thomas Rowlandson. (National Maritime Museum. Ref: 2726.

l. 'The Pusser'. Thomas Rowlandson. (National Maritime Museum. Ref: 1461.)

signed and dated (1782) portrait of Elizabeth Bligh (Figure 4d) – then it was done on the eve (1775–6) of Webber's and Bligh's voyage with Cook. Bligh was about twenty-one years old. Webber was just back in London after years of training and experience in Berne. Perhaps these two unknowns celebrated their mu-- tual good fortune in this portrait. There is a pensive gentleness in the painting that is still discernible in the public's first view of Bligh in the engraving by J. Conde of the drawing by J. Russell that appeared as the frontispiece to Bligh's *Voyage to the South Seas* (Figure 4b). Bligh sat for the portrait in his captain's uniform which he earned on December 15, 1790. He was famous then after his mutiny and his voyage in the launch. Russell emphasised the 'ivory or marble whiteness' of Bligh's pallor that contemporaries noted. It can be seen again in the pencil and water colour drawing by John Smart (Figure 4c), engraved for the Camperdown action commemorative plate. There are several other portraits and miniatures by George Dance, Henry Aston Barker and unknown artists that catch the sardonic toughness of a veteran commander and something of the wry, human quality that men noticed in him. Then in later years there is strain and sadness in his face.

John Webber painted Elizabeth Bligh in 1782 (Figure 4d). She had married Bligh in February, 1781, and had been living in Douglas, the Isle of Man, while Bligh was in service on the *Cambridge,* relieving Gibraltar. It was likely that Elizabeth was pregnant with their first child, Harriet Maria. It is likely, too, that these were the days in which her affectionate relationship with her uncle, Duncan Campbell, was leading to an offer to Bligh of a command on a West Indian trader. The prospect of establishing a family on the half-pay of a naval lieutenant could not have been encouraging.

The face of Fletcher Christian is missing from our collection. The face created by R. R. Dodd in July 1790 in his famous painting of the moments after the mutiny will have to do (Figure 4e). The painting is accurate enough in many details for us to suspect that Dodd worked from eyewitness descriptions. So maybe Christian wore a hat in the mutiny! How fanciful is it to see something of his face in his son's, Thursday October Christian (Figure 4f)?

John Fryer, forever in his master's uniform, is caught in an oil painting by Gurtano Calleja (Figure 4g). Peter Heywood is caught twice by unknown artists. In the one he is tough, almost barnacled, as befitted his twenty-seven years at sea (Figure 4h). In the other he is strong and pensive, as befitted the poet and the pain in him (Figure 4i).

There is a gallery of portraits of those whose lives touched or were touched by the *Bounty*. Most of those who presided at the mutineers' court martial found themselves preserved on canvas. Gavin Kennedy in his illustrated edition of Sir John Barrow's *Mutiny of the Bounty* (1980) has hung (figuratively!) most of the court martial panel for us. Nine of the twelve are then represented (Fig 4j, i–ix). Admiral Sir John Colpoys seems to have been the most brutal among them. He lost his command in accession to mutineers' demands at Nore. Captain John Knight was held in high esteem by the mutineers and acted as a defence witness for Richard Parker. But others, including Sir Roger Curtis, Captain John Duckworth, Sir Richard Keats, Captain John Bazely (not figured in the portraits) were subjects of protest from the mutineers. Captain Albemarle Bertie, related by marriage to Peter Heywood's family, was one of the most important contacts for Thomas Pasley (Heywood's uncle) and Aaron Graham (Heywood's legal adviser).

Such galleries of faces catch their subjects well prepared to represent who and what they were. We have only one not quite so prepared, Commodore Thomas Pasley (Figure 4k). Probably Commodore Thomas Pasley. There has to be some doubt at least in date of attribution of the drawing. Thomas Rowlandson pursued his 'tough old commodore' type through many cartoons. Pasley, however, was reported to have had a face – 'out of drawing' or symmetry – and a body – round fore and aft, square port and starboard – that cried out for satire. He lost his leg in battle on the Glorious First of June 1794. That means he did not quite look like the cartoon at the court martial in 1792. He probably looked enough like it, however, to make the scenery in the great cabin of the *Duke* grotesque enough to allow all the theatrical 'behind the scenes' interplay that made their judgement seem so commonsensical.

Let Rowlandson have the last image – of 'The Pusser'. It might have been the face of Bligh as his men really saw it (Figure 4l).

ॐ   ॐ   ॐ

MR BLIGH'S BAD LANGUAGE

When criticisms of Bligh first began to be raised in public, it was his language that was seen to be his most offensive trait, not his violence. It seems odd that there should have been such complaints. Sailors are not ordinarily hypersensitive about language. In the community at large, and for several centuries, there has been a tolerance for the extravagant expressions that a harsh existence at sea can produce. Indeed, the land has had a propensity to borrow from the sea and forget the origin of its phrases. 'Shake a leg', we say, forgetting that it meant showing discreetly whether the lump in a sailor's hammock was male or female. 'Learning the ropes' gives us a more comfortable sense of induction than the rough initiation into so particularly a named environment as a ship, which, in the words of one eighteenth-century sailor, was the 'first Rhudiment of that University [of the ship]'. 'Taken aback' we will say, and we will 'cut and run' or be at 'loggerheads' 'to the bitter end', forgetting that it is the wind that takes a ship aback, that urgency sometimes demanded that ropes be axed to let furled sails run free, that the anchor's cable was held by a bitt and the bitter's end was that part of the cable that stayed on board, that loggerheads were balls of iron on handles; heated loggerheads were used to melt tar; hot or cold they could crack other sorts of heads.

To borrow a nautical phrase is not to become nautical. This osmosis of language was as much a sign of distance as of closeness. Seamen were men apart. They were 'to be numbered neither with the living nor the dead', wrote one eighteenth-century cleric. The precise, terse, unequivocal language by which seamen controlled their 'wooden world' was thought to be incongruous and laughable on land. Otherness, like the grotesque − like natives, as we shall see − is often controlled by a joke. Georgian England invented the jolly, simple, incongruous tar. The more the country became dependent on the exploitation of seamen's brilliant skills, the more sure it became that seamen were 'children' − improvident, intemperate, profligate. They were 'lazy children' who could have no politics or independence. Seamen 'must be watched like children', Bligh used to maintain. He was only voicing a common prejudice and a common metaphor.

So if, at a later date, the loyal sailors of HMS *Pinafore* gave three hearty cheers and one cheer more for a captain who never, well, hardly ever, used a big, big D——, they were only acting out of a social satire that helped to control sailors through the late eighteenth and nineteenth centuries. 'Captain Brilliant' of John Davis' (1813) *Post Captain* was only one seaman about whom it was appropriate to laugh. His amorous world was a joke set in nautical *double entendre*. 'Can any face', he said of his Cassandra, 'be more angelic? Such toplights! Or can any form be more ravishing? Such a pair of cat-heads! And, Oh! what hair! By——, one might take a sheepsshank in it!' Sailors were managed in their distinctiveness by a satirical tolerance of their language.

The otherness of the 'wooden world' is difficult to describe. It is humbling now to live so vicariously out of dictionaries and 'Sailors' Companions'. Such book learning will discover words, but not really a language.

Joseph Conrad called seamen's language 'a flawless thing for its purpose'. A century later, the historian of the sea, J. H. Parry (1948), knowing that the force of seamen's language lay in its capacity to relate actions to a precisely named environment, invited his readers to enjoy the crispness in the sequence of orders given to haul a boat on board: 'Hook On – Haul Taut Singly – Marry the Falls – Hoist Away – High Enough – Ease to the Life Lines – Light to!' Precision, economy, definitional correspondence to coordinated actions were the mark of a seaman's language. The language itself was sacramental to his sailor's skills and his control over his dangerous environment.

When the ship's machinery was being energised by their own bodies, seamen's language created a remarkable sense of rhythm and tempo. It transformed itself easily into song and chantey. That the ship's most skilled seamen would also be the ship's best dancers was not unexpected. Speed, reflexivity, coordination married aesthetics with practicality. There was much choreography in sailing a ship.

Silence and chorus were both signs of discipline. With a well-coordinated crew, a long train of mandatory words such as 'Let go the bowlines! In topgallants! Up courses! Down jibs and staysails!' might be reduced to 'Shorten sail!' 'No hailing from aloft is needed, and none should be tolerated' was one principle of discipline. But just as important was a sense of presence of others. Sailors in the shrouds were like birds on a branch. They filled their territory with chatter. To a sailor, the text of his life was in knowing every degree of the relationship of his wooden world to the wind and sea and land outside it and the relationship of every place, role and action within it to himself. The pleasure of that text was as erotic for him as a composition could have been to Mozart, and just as self-identifying, and just as disturbing to others.

It is not easy to discover what triggered Bligh's rage at how distant the wooden world of the *Bounty* was from what he ambitioned it to be. His rage was directed not so much at his men as at his officers, and often in what seemed to be the simplest manoeuvres of his ship – keeping watch, maintaining equipment, warping and towing the *Bounty* in Matavai Bay, controlling relations with the Tahitians. All of these occasions were concerned not so much with the *Bounty* at sea as with the *Bounty* at Tahiti. There, in such an ambivalent space, even the language of the crew began to change. What stuck in the memory of those who tried to describe Christian on the morning of the mutiny was the sort of Tahitian-English pidgin he was using. 'Mammoo' (*mamu*), 'Silence', they remember him shouting. While it is difficult to point to anything stronger than hints in James Morrison's and Peter Heywood's accounts of the mutiny, there is a suggestion that the crew of the *Bounty* had been marked by something more than tattoos at Tahiti. They had begun to intersperse Tahitian words in their speech with one another. By the time Edwards had collected them in the *Pandora,* this pidgin had made them bilingual. It was a highly threatening strangeness to Edwards, and he promised extreme punishment, even gagging, if a word of Tahitian was spoken. On the *Bounty,* their pidgin would not have been to exclude others' understanding what they were saying, but to underscore a relationship changed by their Tahitian experience. It bred familiarity. It lessened distinction between them and increased distance between their present and their former selves. It blurred the genres of their sailors' talk. Bligh might rage at their seamanship, but it was more than their incompetence that angered him. They were touched and changed by something outside their wooden walls. They showed it on their skin and in their speech.

No one suggested, of course, that Bligh's language was obscene. It was thought to be abusive and intemperate. Edward Christian, Fletcher's brother, collected a few examples. Bligh used to call his officers 'scoundrels, damned rascals, hounds, hell-hounds, beasts and infamous wretches'. What stuck in memory was a terrible scene the day before the mutiny on the deck of the *Bounty.* Bligh had assembled the whole crew to berate them for having stolen some of his coconuts. Clearly the men, marshalled in their ranks and suffering this tirade in silence, gave signals of contempt for his pettiness. His rage grew uncontrolled. He taunted them with what he thought to be their fear of Endeavour Straits still to come. He thrust his fist in their faces, perhaps even put a pistol to McCoy's head, and said that he would make them jump overboard before the voyage was done and would make them eat grass like cows.

Bligh's supporters among the crew accepted that he 'damn[ed] the people, like many other captains' and that 'any seafaring gentleman must be convinced that situations occur in a ship when the most mild officers will be driven, by the circumstances of the moment, to utter expressions which the strict standards of politeness will not warrant'. But they felt that those were all passing storms. 'He did not dislike any man', said one defender, suggesting that Bligh's language was not the measure of the man and that his anger blew away with the breath of his words.

Young George Tobin, who was with Bligh on the *Providence* in 1790, heard of his death in 1817 and wrote of him to a colleague: 'Those violent tornados of temper when he lost himself' produced dissatisfaction. 'Once or twice, indeed, I felt the unbridled licence of his power of speech, yet never without soon receiving something like a plaister to heal the wound. . . . When all, in his opinion, was right, who could be a man more placid and interesting.'

As it happened, Bligh was court-martialled for bad language in March 1805, long after the *Bounty*. The charges against him were 'tyranny, un-officerlike conduct and ungentlemanly behaviour'. By 1805 he had experienced both battle and mutiny and was about to be appointed governor of the new penal colony at Botany Bay. He was now a Fellow of the Royal Society, of which Sir Joseph Banks was president. In his defence against the court martial charges, Bligh told the twelve captains who were his peers: 'I candidly and without reserve avow that I am not a tame and indifferent observer of the manner in which officers placed under my orders conduct themselves in the performance of their several duties. A signal or any communication from a commanding officer has ever been to me an indication for exertion and alacrity to carry into effect the purport thereof and peradventure I may occasionally have appeared to some of these officers as unnecessarily anxious for its execution by exhibiting an action or gesture peculiar to myself to such.' And he added: 'if the circumstances which elapsed in the course of twelve months were to be scraped together, who is there so virtuous? who is there so wise? who is there so perfect as to be able to say I am not he against whom a charge can be passed?' The charge had been brought by a litigious officer, himself under court martial, and Bligh was acquitted; but the court admonished Bligh to be more careful in his language. In the quiet after the trial, Bligh wrote to Banks asking him to use his influence to make life uncomfortable for those who had charged him and witnessed against him. He admitted that his 'high sense of professional duty' made him 'sometimes too particular in the execution of it'. But he cited 'instances of doing good and rendering service since my youth' and bemoaned the 'sort of low men accept into the service'. 'To govern a ship is not an easy matter, altho' a captain's responsibility is as great or greater than ever.'

The transcript of the court martial gave samples of Bligh's bad language. It was directed principally at his commissioned, warrant and petty officers. To a lieutenant: 'What, Sir, you damn'd scoundrel, never was a man troubled with such a lot of blackguards as I am. Take care, Sir, I am looking out for you.' To the bosun, 'Shaking fist at head': 'if he had him in a dark corner he would do for him.' To the master: 'vile man', 'shameful man', 'disgrace to the service', 'damn you you lubber', 'jesuit, old rogue, let me have none of your rigadoon steps here', 'old thief', 'liar'. To the gunner: 'damn'd long pelt of a bitch'. To the carpenter: 'dastardly, cowardly old man'. Vivid language, one would think, and not likely to endear. But all things are relative, and there was also testimony that 'ungentlemanlike' language was never heard, that Bligh used a 'great deal of action with his hands, as if he was going to knock any person down, without particular meaning to it'. There was doubt expressed that insult was intended. Even the man most hardly done by, the 'old jesuit' of a master, said that there were good times and bad, and that while he had sometimes contemplated getting 'public reckoning' from Bligh, he had also been much instructed by Bligh in nautical matters. He may even have enjoyed Bligh's inventiveness of language. The complicated steps of a rigadoon made a suitable dance for a 'jesuit'. Bligh had other admirers of his choice of phrase. One seasoned curser in New South Wales blushed at his inadequacies in the presence of Bligh. Indeed, Bligh had a picturesque phrase to describe himself. He suffered, he said, 'ebullition of the mind' when confronted by dereliction of duty. 'Ebullition' is the agitation of boiling water, fire, lava or humours. Bligh's 'ebullition of the mind' convulsed his body as well as his tongue.

The court martial's deconstruction of Bligh's language was unlikely to uncover the actual meaning of these exchanges. It had no context for their meaning. Or rather, it could only accept Bligh's contexting, in the revelation of his good intentions and the assurance of the witnesses that the language did not define relationships but only clothed them with the idiosyncrasy of Bligh's character. But the issues of the court martial were the same issues as those raised in the case of the *Bounty*. The occasions of his 'bad language' were the same. He was his most abusive when he chose to see the actions of others as somehow impinging on his role as commander. The officer who brought the charges in 1805 and to whom Bligh was most abusive gave an order while Bligh was on the quarterdeck. Bligh told him on his peril that if he ever set the sails or gave an order while he was on deck he would confine him and make him rue it. To Bligh every gesture of his subordinates was an instant performance that defined relationships. Every order was a sign of their relationship to him, challenging his authority and changing the landscape of power on his quarterdeck. But his own words and gestures, in his eye, were always circumstanced by the occasion of their expression. Or he was extravagantly vituperative when someone – such as the ship's carpenter back in 1805 and on the *Bounty* – measured his engagement in work by the rules of his role rather than by the purer motives of 'professional duty'. Bligh found it difficult to grasp the metaphors of being a captain, how it could mean something different to those being captained. He could not understand that those less powerful could think that power had its own rewards, that they could be more measuring in the service of the institutions that ruled them. Bligh tended not to hear the good intentions or catch the circumstances and context in the language of others but demanded that others hear them in his. If others did not share his sublimations, he damned them for their dereliction.

Language is notoriously difficult to recapture in history or in a courtroom. An inflection, a look in the eye, a turn of the lip could make even words like 'scoundrels, damned rascals, hell-hounds' terms of endearment and familiarity, not insult. Or the words could cascade over hearers so constantly that they would not be heard at all. The question is whether and in what way Bligh's bad language penetrated, wounded and festered. I make the thesis that Bligh's bad language was the ambiguous language of his command. It was bad, not so much because it was intemperate or abusive, but because it was ambiguous, because men could not read in it a right relationship to his authority.

It is the common myth of the twentieth century that Bligh's command was violent. Being a 'Captain Bligh' is a cliché of our times. Popular films and novels have fantasised all the violent punishments of the British navy – keelhauling, running the gauntlet, flogging around the fleet, indiscriminate flogging, masting, press-ganging – and laid it at the feet of Bligh the tyrant or 'Bligh the Bounty Bastard', as the mutineers at Great Nore called him. Yes, Bligh had a mutiny at Great Nore, too. Yes, he had his mutiny as governor of New South Wales. Mythmakers that we are – by way of our films, for example – we cope more easily with a tyranny that is distanced from our everyday lives by being extravagantly violent. Such violence makes larger heroes of those rebelling against it, and at the same time, the rebellion itself reinforces the hegemony of the authority that should have been good. Out of the same mythmaking, we are uncomfortable with mutinies or revolutions or even social changes that

come by ambivalences. We do not want our institutions to be so fragile
or nurturing of evil so banal.

Bligh was not a physically violent man. His pale, composed face peering from portraits should alert us to that. His delicate appearance, of
course, does not lessen the possibility of aggressive violence, but his looks
surprise. They are not at all those of a blustering, swearing, brutal sea-
captain. He was, we know, continually wracked by nervous headaches,
which might account for his excessive paleness, and his becalmed stillness
is also consistent with the sort of bad language I am going to attribute to
him. But, by any measures we have of him, as against other captains of
his day, he was not a physically violent man. On his two voyages to the
Pacific in the *Bounty* and the *Providence* he flogged fewer of his crew, actually and proportionately, than any other captain who came into the
Pacific in the eighteenth century. He was much milder than Cook, and
milder by far than Vancouver, the most violent of all the British naval
captains in the Pacific.

Seamen had a high tolerance of violence done to them by their superiors, especially in the Pacific. Any crew sailing south down the Atlantic
to the Pacific passed the bleak, low island of Port St Julian on the Pata-
gonian coast. There Magellan had hanged his mutineers, and Drake, in
the shadow of the same gibbet, beheaded Thomas Dougherty for plotting.
The gibbet was an ominous portal to the Pacific, a symbol of how high
the stakes were. The number of lives lost in the Pacific in the two decades
before the *Bounty* – from careless seamanship, from unforeseen dangers,
from native attacks – was large enough to ensure that lower-deck seamen
were fairly accepting of the navy's ordinary measures of discipline. If Bligh
had gone beyond those measures, he would not have survived his mutiny.
Every other mutiny in the Pacific and in the British navy that had a
captain's violence as the cause, ended in carnage. The hegemony of mutual trust founded on the skills and high performance of seamen's duties
was difficult to dislodge. The bad language had to be very bad indeed.

I have the right to say that Bligh was milder in displaying physical
violence than most British captains who came into the Pacific in the eighteenth century because I have counted all the lashes British sailors received
and the occasions of their receiving them. The eminent French historian
Emmanuel le Roy Ladurie has said: 'History that is not quantifiable cannot claim to be scientific'. This is my cliometric moment. From 1765,
when John Byron made his dash across the Pacific in the *Dolphin*, until

1793, when George Vancouver tried to ease Spain off the northwest coast of North America, fifteen British naval vessels came into the central Pacific for purposes of discovery and appropriation, or, like the *Bounty* and *Providence*, for purposes of exploitation. Fifteen hundred and fifty-six British sailors were aboard those fifteen vessels. Of them, 21.5 percent were flogged. Cook flogged 20 percent, 26 percent and 37 percent, respectively, on his three voyages. Vancouver flogged 45 percent of his men. Bligh, on the *Bounty*, flogged 19 percent and, on the *Providence*, 8 percent. It was among the least number of men punished on any ship that came into the Pacific. One could expect a mean of five lashes would be given for every crew member who sailed into the Pacific. Vancouver's mean was 21. The *Bounty*'s mean was 1.5. In addition, there were variables at work other than the captain's sense of authority. Marines were objects of scorn to seamen. They lacked the skills that gave others a sense of purpose and were always in trouble. Of all marines, 47 percent were flogged. Irishmen and Welshmen, although proportionately few in these naval vessels, were twice as likely to be flogged as Englishmen and Scots. Being found with the 'venereals' was not an offence for which a sailor might be flogged. For 'venereals', there was a fine of fifteen shillings (more than half a month's pay) to be paid to the ship's surgeon. But as the surgeons had no cure either for gonorrhea or syphilis, sufferers paid the fine repeatedly. It was, one might say, a sore point with sailors; 36 percent of those recorded as having 'venereals' were flogged, more than twice the proportion of those free of the disease. And then there was age. A twenty-three-year-old Irish marine on Vancouver's voyage would have been the 'ideal type' to be flogged and could expect to have a very painful voyage. Bligh, on the *Bounty*, was lucky. He had no marines, had only one Irishman, the half-blind fiddler, and a crew with the average age of twenty-six years. But then 40 percent of his crew had the 'venereals', which may explain why he always blamed Tahiti for his troubles.

Flogging occurred in two ways on naval vessels. One was by what the Americans called the 'colt' and the other by what they and the British called the 'cat'. The 'colt' was a single rope, and with it the bosun or the bosun's mate would beat or 'start' anyone slow to move or careless in his actions. Often a man would be beaten, at the instigation of a lieutenant, just as he stood. Witnesses reported at such times that other sailors would simply stop their work and stand around or go on without curiosity as the offender received his flogging. In many ways, a flogging with a colt was

not a ceremonious play about discipline and authority, but it especially
degraded a grown man who had to stand freely and without response or
objection while violence was done to him. It was a dangerously undisci-
plined form of control, practised although forbidden. In the case of the
Bounty, it is difficult to think of the bosun, William Cole, or the bosun's
mate, James Morrison, 'starting' the crew. The crew's complement was
small and their physical proximity too confined to allow the social distancing that the colt required. More than once, one can sense frustrations
so deep in Bligh that he himself was on the edge of personally striking
somebody. The only two occasions reported, however, were those when
he slapped the midshipman, John Hallett, for being fussily reluctant to
enter the water from a boat and later when he gave Robert Lamb, of his
launch party, a beating for greedily eating raw the birds he had caught
and not putting them in the common pot.

Flogging with the cat was altogether more formal. It was usually performed on a Sunday after divine service and the reading of the Articles of
War. The recipient was bare-back and spread-eagled against an upright
grating set against the quarterdeck or mast. His hands and ankles were
bound. The crew were mustered on one side of the mainmast, the officers
on the other. Marines bearing arms faced the crew. The offender was in
between. The captain was judge and jury. He was limited by the Articles
of War to ordering twelve lashes for a single offence, without sending the
offender to a court martial. It was an article easily bypassed, however, by
multiplying the offences or by separating the floggings. The offender had
no rights or redress. The usual procedures of civil trials were entirely
overthrown. The precise procedures of evidence, delay and judgement by
peers − so carefully observed for officers − were never observed for the
crew. The surgeon was always present. The cat rarely broke the skin in a
dozen lashes. But it raised severe dark bruises. Reactions to floggings were
seldom recorded in the sources. Such as there are stress how differently
men responded. Bravado and silent, sullen acceptance, were two ways of
reacting, but others broke into miserable howling, careless of self-respect.
Most witnesses spoke of the change in a man made by his first flogging.
Charles Nordhoff, searching for a word to catch what he saw in the faces
of the flogged, wrote of them as being 'down'. The binding of the hands
and ankles in public was always talked of as an awful symbol of the individual's subjection to the power of others.

Four months into the _Bounty_'s voyage, Bligh recorded that 'untill this afternoon I had hoped I could have performed the voyage without punishment to anyone'. It was a note made on the afternoon when he gave Matthew Quintal two dozen lashes for 'insolence and contempt'. The cliometrics of flogging, as we shall see, suggest that physical punishment came in cycles on a voyage. After an initial period in which the crew got used to a command or discovered means of manipulating it, the frustrations of the quarterdeck exhibited themselves in intense displays of violence, which then subsided till another peak was reached some months later. Bligh, whatever his ambitions of a voyage without punishment, had been threatening to flog anyone who would not eat the pumpkin that he as purser had purchased at Tenerife for use instead of bread. Yet his disappointment in Quintal's case was directed more at his officers than the crew. John Fryer, as master, had reported Quintal for 'mutinous behaviour', which Bligh had changed to 'insolence and contempt' in his log. He was, no doubt, inclined to believe that Fryer had not handled his authority properly but was forced nonetheless to support him. His perfect voyage was thus spoiled by the incompetence of those on whom he depended. It had been the Admiralty at the start. Now it was Fryer. Soon it would be his surgeon, his carpenter, his acting lieutenant and his midshipmen.

The intensity with which Bligh wanted his perfect voyage needs to be understood. Bligh had been master of the *Resolution* on Cook's third and fatal voyage. Being master under Cook was difficult, with a man so intrusive on matters of navigation as Cook and a man so sensitive of the boundaries of his office as Bligh. Bligh was bitterly resentful that his work of mapping and surveying had been given so little credit in the publications on the *Resolution*'s voyage. There was also some hint that actions of his contributed to Cook's death. His hatred is written into the margins of a copy of James Cook's *A Voyage to the Pacific Ocean . . .*(1784) in the Admiralty Library. So it was with a highly inflated sense of its importance that he grasped at the chance of taking the *Bounty* to Tahiti and the West Indies. The Admiralty did not share his ambitions. They were responding to the lobbying of West Indian plantation owners by providing the minimum: the cheapest ship and the smallest number of men. They were also delighted that it was something for Sir Joseph Banks to fuss about. So, although it was the most flattering moment of William Bligh's life to be made a confidant of Banks on things botanical, on the health of seamen and on matters of discovery, he simply could not understand how, on a voyage of scientific discovery just as important as Cook's, the navy could not give him a captain's commission and send him to Tahiti, not as Mr Bligh, Lieutenant Commander of H.M. Armed Vessel _Bounty_ but as Captain Bligh. But if he did not go as captain, he meant to come back to be one, after a perfect voyage.

The intensity of Bligh's passion for an unblemished voyage found expression in the intensity of his busyness in the short six weeks of preparations before sailing. He had old ideas about beating scurvy – 'a disgrace to a ship', he wrote: plenty of sauerkraut and 'inspissated juice of wort' (malt extract). He had new ideas that were around: ground wheat and sugar for hot breakfasts, barley in lieu of oatmeal, and five hundredweight of 'portable soup' for broths. And he had his own ideas: the health of seamen was dependent on their 'chearfulness' and cleanliness. So he hired the fiddler, Michael Byrne, to give the men exercise by providing music for dancing in the dogwatch, between 4:00 P.M. and 6:00 P.M. He planned his routines for hygiene – daily, even hourly, pumping of the bilges, washing of all quarters with vinegar, two men of every watch to dry clothes, two sets of hammocks for every man, three watches instead of two for the uninterrupted rest they allowed. Banks and his gardeners, David Nelson and William Brown, had already renovated the great cabin of the West Indian trader _Bethia_, become _Bounty_, as a breadfruit nursery. Meanwhile, Bligh supervised the manufacture of 234 dozen 'toeys' (or adzes) and other ironware implements to meet Tahitian requirements. He planned that these and six dozen shirts, fourteen dozen threepenny and sixpenny looking glasses, eighty pounds of white, blue, and red glass beads, and twenty-two dozen stained-glass earring drops would be his currency in exchange for the breadfruit. He negotiated with admirals and generals, who were looking for his patronage for their unemployed relatives. He entered the scientific world of Banks and his salon, eager to learn what it was that these 'experimental gentlemen' would want to learn from him. With no commissioned officers to support him and with no inclination in his character to delegate responsibility even if he had had officers, he came to see the _Bounty_'s voyage more intensively as his own. Just a few days before he flogged Matthew Quintal, he had written to Banks relating that all that they had planned and prepared had succeeded marvellously. 'I am happy and satisfied with my little ship and we are now fit to go around half a score of worlds. Both men and officers are tractable and well disposed and cheerfulness and content in the countenance of everyone. I am sure nothing is more conducive to health. I have no cause to inflict punishment for I have no offenders and everything turns out to my most sanguine expectations.' At that moment, he was riding a dangerous high.

The first strains were about to come. The Admiralty had been slow in delivering his orders to sail. Because of his frenetic efforts, the *Bounty* was ready to sail but was delayed because Bligh had no papers. By that, they missed the opportune time to pass Cape Horn. By that, in fact, they would miss the fair winds that would take them through Endeavour Straits on their return journey from Tahiti by the Moluccas, where they were to collect more trees for the West Indies. Bligh's ambitions were already threatened by the incompetence of others. The Horn, when he reached it, was impassable. Its storms, he wrote, 'exceeded anything that I had met with and seas higher than I had ever seen before'. He himself was magnificent in his care for his men at this time, especially those who came down frozen from the snow-heavy yards. They could not speak with the cold and their exhaustion. He allowed them to set their hammocks in the great cabin over the empty breadfruit pots. He had himself lashed to the mast on deck to make his observations. He had the 'waisters' – those who did not have to go to the yards – endure the smoke of fires that served to dry clothes and warm food. When he decided to turn and run to the Cape of Good Hope and make for Tahiti along the southern westerlies, the whole company cheered. He was disappointed and exhilarated at the same time. 'I have suffered much fatigue but I always thrive best when I have the most to do and I never was better in my life.' There was, however, something that had begun to worry him. His company of forty-six men was badly balanced. There were only ten able seamen on whom the hard daily tasks of sailing the vessel fell. They were rested, three or so in a watch, but effectively, in times of hard going, these ten were on watch all the time. Any navy man would know how this would bind such a group together. These ten would be, as it turned out, the hard core of the mutineers.

There has always been a tarnish to Bligh's brilliance at Cape Horn. There was the story that he had 'masted' the young midshipman, Peter Heywood, in the middle of these storms. He was said to have ordered the boy up the mast in punishment for some misdemeanour and told him to stay there beyond the point of all endurance. Film and fiction have made much of this grotesquely inhumane behaviour. And the wardrooms of the navy debated for years after Bligh's death whether or not it had happened, whether or not Peter Heywood had told this or that friend that it was true.

An indefatigable searcher for material sources that throw light on the *Bounty*, Glynn Christian, discovered in the *Cumberland Paquet* of November 26, 1788, a 'letter from a midshipman (aged sixteen) on board His Majesty's ship Bounty' written from Simon's Bay in False Bay, Cape of Good Hope, June 17, 1788. The *Cumberland Paquet* served the Isle of Man and the northern districts where all the Heywood and Christian connexions would have had an interest. It is clearly a letter of Peter Heywood to his family. His family, no doubt with some sense of pride and excitement and knowing it would interest many in the Isle of Man and the Cumberland district, published the letter – in some slight contravention of agreements as to who had the right to publish accounts of the *Bounty*'s voyage. The letter, as Glynn Christian (1982) puts it, is a fresh and exuberant description of the voyage of the *Bounty* to that point. It is too long and not to our purpose to be quoted in full. It exudes the dreamy pleasure of sailing the Atlantic in 'the most pleasant weather imaginable', catching fish and birds, drawing them and describing them, shooting whales to drive them away from the ship as they spouted water all over her, being delighted at the vast number of seals and porpoises and birds of all kinds as they reached the southern latitudes. Then Cape Horn: 'During twenty-nine days we were beating off the Cape, we had to encounter the most violent storms that I suppose were ever experienced; and I can safely say, the wind was not twelve hours easterly during that time, and we never had more canvas spread than close reefed top sails; but most chiefly, when not lying to, reefed courses. . . . After beating about three weeks, to no purpose, and the ship at last beginning to be leaky, so as to oblige us to pump every hour; and many people being ill by the severity of the weather, and want of rest (there being seldom a night but all hands were called three or four times), the captain . . . thinking it dangerous and very improper to lose so much time, bore down on the Cape of Good Hope, to the great joy of every one on board. . . . I suppose there never were seas, in any part of the known world, to compare with those we met off Cape Horn, for height, and length of swell; the oldest seamen on board never saw anything to equal that, yet Mr Peckover (our gunner) was all the three voyages with Captain Cook.'

The run from Cape Horn to the Cape of Good Hope was as easy as its preliminaries had been difficult. 'I dare say, as great a run in the time, as ever performed; and I have the happiness of telling you that the Bounty is as fine a sea boat as ever swam. She does not sail very fast; her greatest rate is 8 or 9 knots; but once she went ten, quarterly, which is quite sufficient.'

No mention of 'masting' in this account, nor even a suggestion of anything except coordinated action of a united crew against the elements. Much evidence, though, of all we have said of the life of a ship – of pleasure and pride in skills exhibited, of the binding character of shared hardship, of the role of experience – Peckover's for example – and of yarning in shaping a crew, of deference to authority wisely exercised.

By the time the *Bounty* reached Adventure Bay in Van Diemen's Land, August 21, 1788, Bligh's exhilaration had disappeared. John Adams, the lone survivor of the mutiny, said many years later that something had come between Bligh and Christian at the Cape of Good Hope. Adams thought it had to do with money. It was a shrewd, independent and dispassionate comment. Bligh had entered the *Bounty* in an entrepreneurial spirit. Making money was a matter of necessity for him. He had to make up in some way the income he had lost as one of Duncan Campbell's merchant captains. He had learned as a merchant captain to trade in bills of credit by buying at discounts of up to 50 percent and then redeeming the bills at their full face value or selling them at a smaller discount. In fact, he paid a discounted bill of the *Bounty* to a Cape Town merchant out of his own pocket on credit to the Victualling Board and asked Duncan Campbell to redeem it in full, and so 'make a little cash'. He asked a suspicious William Muspratt and a more knowing Thomas Hayward to countersign his credit as if they were respectable merchants. It was a perfectly proper exchange in the system as it was practised, and if William Muspratt – and with him all who came back in the 'Pandora's Box' – viewed the transaction as a 'pusser's' shady ways, they were wrong. It may also have been perfectly proper to lend Fletcher Christian money and send the bill of credit straightway to Duncan Campbell with the demand that Edward Christian redeem it as some percentage of profit. But it was not wise. Christian, borrowing on his as yet unearned wages, was thus in debt to two people. Bligh never learned what these sorts of dealings did to his command. When he reached Batavia after the mutiny with the penniless, wasted survivors of the launch, he would give them no credit – make them no loans to buy passage home – unless they gave what they saw as unwarranted security. Thomas Ledward, the assistant surgeon, wrote from Batavia to his uncle in the United States, warning him of what must be expected if he did not survive. 'The captain denied me, as well as the rest of the gentlemen who had no agent, any money unless I would give him my power of attorney and also my will, in which I was to bequeath him all my property, this he called by way of security'. Again this was not improper or unrespectable, given Bligh's uncertainty of his own future and its effect on his family. But it was sour and small to those who had to endure the humiliation of it.

The sourness of being lent money in these sorts of conditions stayed with Christian. Bligh began to remind Christian of some obligation whenever differences arose between them. Other men always thought that the relationship between Christian and Bligh was strange. Christian had sailed with Bligh twice before, on West Indian trading runs. Mates on those voyages also remarked on Bligh's infatuation with the active, charming young man who had begged – for the experience of it – to join his crew even at no pay, so long as Bligh permitted him 'to mess with the gentlemen'. 'We midshipmen are gentlemen', Christian had written to Bligh, 'we never pull at a rope; I should be glad to go one voyage in that situation, for there may be occasions when officers may be called upon to do the duties of a common man'. There is something uncomfortable in the language of that letter, and in the expectancies of how it would be read. Bligh took Christian on board the *Bounty* under much the same conditions, mustering him as 'A.B.' but raising him, by captain's orders, three months into the voyage, to Acting Lieutenant. That act introduced a first ambivalence into the status structures of this naval vessel. A lieutenant who was not a lieutenant, who was dependent on status by personal favour and subject to being reminded continually of this and other obligations had the high potential to be 'in hell'. 'I am in hell, Mr Bligh, I am in Hell' were Christian's words to Bligh on the decks of the *Bounty* when Bligh asked him why he could not go back a step from mutiny. Then in the launch, with water lapping the gunwale, with his secretary in great difficulty penning his words with quill and ink, Bligh gave this description of Fletcher Christian: 'Age 24. Masters mate. 5ft 9in high. Blackish or very dark brown Complexion. Dark Brown Hair. Strong Made. A star tatowed on his left Breast, and tatowed on the backside. His knees stand a little out and he may be called a little Bowlegged. He is subject to

Violent perspiration, particularly in his hands, so that he Soils anything he handles.' What language is that? we may ask, what message?

If Bligh's exhilaration was dissipated by Adventure Bay, there too his ambition was deflated beyond measure. Jo Valentine, able seaman, had died, and the surgeon, Thomas Huggan, reported that he died of scurvy. Bligh simply could not believe it. His rage poured out at the 'drunken sot' of a surgeon. Huggan's obesity, the squalor of his cabin, his personal uncleanliness, his drunken lethargy, all were the antipathetic image of Bligh's notion of cheerfulness, cleanliness and well-exercised contentment. Convinced that Valentine had died of Huggan's incompetence – at this distance, we may suspect a blood infection from a careless bleeding of the patient – and thinking that Huggan might have diagnosed scurvy out of spite and to have a victory in the official records of the voyage, Bligh countered by going into a frenzied application of all his medicinal and dietary remedies. He had already complained that 'seamen were like children' and had stood them in a line while watching them swallow every last drop of his antiscorbutic concoctions. Now he had them vigorously pumping the bilges, drinking half a pint of elixir vitriol and eating barley and essence of malt. Above all, he would have them 'chearful', so they must dance. When two of the crew refused to dance, he cut their grog and promised something worse.

Bligh's language was getting very bad. Many a naval captain had used the reversed ritual of 'skylarking' in the dogwatch to relieve the institutional tensions of a ship. 'On deck and skylark' was a quaint and seemingly contradictory order to participate in exuberant physical play, to transfer the conflicts of messes and watches and the tensions created by the skilled work that stratified them to giddy games. The spontaneity of skylarking was fragile and needed to be managed by those who knew what the games really were about. Skylarking did not need careful management by the very power whose authority was being metaphorically tested. Bligh's estranging carefulness had also been shown in that other reverse ceremony of a ship, the 'Crossing of the Line'. He had forbidden the ducking over the ship's side of those who had not sailed south of the equator, calling it cruel and dangerous. But a man's capacity to endure a ducking two times, four times or ten times before agreeing to pay Neptune's fine was a matter of personal achievement and boasting. In a group undifferentiated in the deference it owed to the single authority of the ship, there needed to be other intervening authorities at work to negotiate the pains of such def-

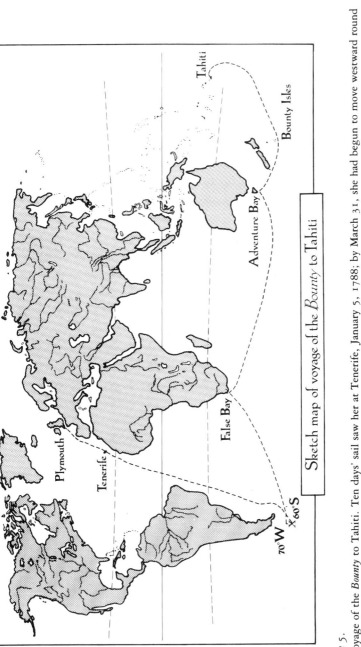

Figure 5.

Sketch map of voyage of the *Bounty* to Tahiti

The voyage of the *Bounty* to Tahiti. Ten days' sail saw her at Tenerife, January 5, 1788; by March 31, she had begun to move westward round Cape Horn at latitude 60° S. A week's working saw them at longitude 76° 58' W, the farthest west they reached. Then for two weeks they were battered eastward till Bligh turned and ran for the Cape of Good Hope. May 24 saw them anchored at False Bay where they recuperated for thirty-eight days. Six weeks' easy sail along the route to the Central Pacific pioneered by Cook, in weather that Bligh called 'boisterous', took them to Adventure Bay, Van Diemen's Land, August 20. There two weeks' rest was no rest at all because of growing tensions aboard. A discovery of rocky islets, which they named The Bounty Isles, marked their voyage to Tahiti south of New Zealand. Bligh rated the fifty-two days' sailing from Van Diemen's Land to Tahiti as 'moderate'. 'It may not be unworthy of remark' wrote Bligh in his log, 'that the whole distance which the ship had run by the log, in direct and contrary courses, from leaving England to our anchoring at Otaheite, was twenty-seven thousand and eighty-six miles, which, on an average, is at the rate of an hundred and eight miles each twenty-four hours.'

erence. Bligh spoke badly to them in not allowing them to find their own levels of authority independent of his.

Ducking, yarning and dancing need a moment's reflection. The ways human beings exercise power over one another in an institution such as a ship, whether exaggerating it or fending it off, are subtle and complex. Hegemony is made of trivia. If a description of these trivia deflates an expectancy that high drama is caused only by momentous action, so be it. One defence against the power of exaggerated rage is to watch its boiling theatre with mockery. Bligh did not win his duel with his crew over dancing, because, as Michael Byrne fiddled, they mocked their captain in the ditties they sang and the steps they danced. They enjoyed their connivance at this, with all the knowing looks and stifled laughs of their behind-the-scenes cunning. Bligh was always teased by the inconsistencies in his people's responses. On his launch voyage, there was a terrible scene on Sunday Island off the Australian coast. Eighteen men had survived thirty days of terrible danger in the open. Hunger, fear and now relief at their escape made them selfish and careless of discipline. That sunny beach was the place of one of Bligh's most terrible rages. He was 'calling Everybody the Names he could think of', 'telling them that if it had not been for him they would not have been there'. His skills had saved them. He called Purcell, the carpenter, 'a damned scoundrel'. 'Yes', said Purcell, 'we would not be here if not for you'. The implication of such ambivalent agreement was too much for Bligh. He took up his cutlass and would have fought with Purcell, had not John Fryer intervened and Purcell backed away. Such teases once begun were never ending. Bligh's mutiny, had he reflected on it, may have begun in a ditty.

Those who observed them closely have said that sailors defended themselves in harsh conditions by various rituals of sociability. Yarning was high among them. Herman Melville told of the solace topmen took in yarning to one another high up in the yards and in secluded niches in the sails. Yarning exchanged the politics of experience. It enlarged the boundaries of interpretation by giving a measure of what was exceptional and what was usual. Yarning was a very political thing. It educated participants in the language and signs of institutions. Sailors, in the public view, may have been reckless, profligate, intemperate and profane, but even those most scandalised at their character ascribed them minds that seemed to act much more rapidly than those of other orders of men. Sailors raised grumbling to an art form. 'They were peculiarly sensitive and selfish as to what they required as their rights', one chaplain said of them. Each was 'led to look well at his own rights and to quarrel with jealous care against the encroachment of others'. In verbalising their way of life, let us say, they were peculiarly susceptible to language that got it wrong.

Yarns are lost on the breath of the voice. A historian can never experience yarning. So the *Bounty*'s yarning is a matter of surmise. We have, however, the admiring judgement of one officer who witnessed the court martial of the mutineers and who testified that 'this ship seems to have abounded with men above the common herd of uninformed illiterates'. Whether the *Bounty* was exceptional, or whether the 'common herd' simply did not have the *Bounty*'s stage on which to exhibit their practised skills, does not matter. As they fought for their lives, the *Bounty* men exhibited in their advocacy how much narratives emplotted the institution.

There is one quite brilliant text of their yarning. It is James Morrison's *Journal* (1935). Written in part as he waited for his trial, then in full as he rested on the Isle of Wight after receiving the King's Mercy, the *Journal* is a narrative selected and sculpted in hindsight. Some historians have berated Morrison for that. Yet the earlier months of living naked and shackled in a verminous 'Pandora's Box' were not conducive to authorship on paper. Nor was it, for that matter, conducive to yarning as a ritual of sociability. But it was suitable for a mental dramatisation of the past expressed in a language in which the institution of the *Bounty* was literally yarned about. Without doubt, yarning emplotted the *Bounty* in Morrison's *Journal*. Read it not for whether it is true or not, not for whether Bligh was morally indictable or not, but for its semiotics, and you have a study in Bligh's bad language.

Many of these incidents of bad language are famous now after 200 years of debate. There is the yarn about the missing cheeses. A number of cheeses, on a count of 'Pusser' Bligh, were missing. He threatened the whole crew with punishment. John Williams declared he was ordered to take the cheeses to 'Pusser' Bligh's own home. 'Nipcheese' was the nautical nickname for 'pussers'. Williams' yarn did not have to be true to be believed. The crew, playing politics with the purser, refused to eat butter on Banyan (non-meat) days without cheese, lest they compromise their stand of innocence.

Pumpkins were the subject of a second story. The men disputed the one-pound replacement of pumpkin for two pounds of bread. Then, 'they would eat grass', Bligh responded. Instead they ate the potatoes they themselves had bought at Tenerife. They could hear through the bulkhead the complaints of the 'young gentlemen' as they were forced to eat the pumpkin, the 'young gentlemen' being a little nearer to Bligh. There was also grumbling on the light weight of their peas rationed out and suspicion that the best meat was going to the cabin. They wanted to know what four gallons of Mrs Dubois' portable soup with peas and sauerkraut that Bligh provided was equivalent to? And were oil and sugar a fair replacement for butter and cheese? Who would eat a dead sheep that Bligh served in place of pork? Bligh's pride, his hot breakfast of wheat and barley in place of burgoo, was so small a dish (for all its dietary richness) that four men in a mess would draw lots for it. The galley, with its Brodie stove, in the forward starboard corner of the lower deck, was on the edge of their messes and hammocks. It became a place of fights as the messes tried to divide a gallon of wheat and two pounds of barley among forty-six men. The pint of hot sweetwort that Bligh had wanted them to drink each day had to be heated with the hatches shut. They drank their medicine with smoke in their eyes.

Then, when the dam of Bligh's rage burst over them at Adventure Bay, there was nothing they could do that would satisfy him. They fell into disputes among themselves as they actually undid each other's work so that his rage would fall on someone else. They were quite convinced, and no doubt pleased with the conviction, that none of his medicines for scurvy had worked. They had pains in their limbs. Bligh called it 'rheumaticks', but they thought it was scurvy.

At Tahiti, Bligh commandeered nine-tenths of every provision the crew brought aboard. It was 'pusser's' profits in their eyes. Then there were thefts by natives – of buoys, of the cutter's rudder, of hooks and thimbles in the rigging. There was the running aground in Matavai Bay. There was the desertion of Churchill, Millward and Muspratt, and the discovery of a list of names of others (Christian's among them) on a piece of paper left by Churchill in his boxes. The cable was cut, a cask stolen. The spare sails were found rotting in their locker. There were Bligh's punishments of those sleeping on watch. Morrison is telling us all their talk.

Morrison's memory of the crew's leaving Tahiti was this: 'Everybody seem'd in high spirits and began already to talk of home, affixing the length of the passage and count[ing] up the wages and one would readily

have imagined that we had just left Jamaica instead of Taheiti so far
onward did their flattering fancies waft them'. Once on their way to the
west and Endeavour Straits, he wrote, their minds again became obsessed
with food. Were six plantains a day equal to the bread allowance that
should have been theirs? What was equivalent to a pound of fresh pork
and, when that was gone, to what was a pound of yam or taro a day
equivalent? The voyage home suddenly began to look longer. In anticipation of its privations just a few hours before the mutiny, they went into
a frenzy of trading with the natives. They purchased 'mats, spears, curiosities, yams, coconuts and everything the natives would dispose of'. 'There
were yams and clubs in all quarters of the ship with scarcely room to stir.'

How they must have talked – and principally about what Samuel Pepys
called the sailors' 'tenderest point' – their bellies. How large all that
touched upon this 'tenderest point' must have loomed! How small it now
seems to be through history's turned-around telescope! Through it all,
Bligh was writing to himself, yarning to himself, in his logs and letters.
'Happy and satisfied is my little ship and we are now fit to go around a
score of worlds. Both men and officers tractable and well disposed and
cheerfulness and content on the countenances of everyone.' 'I never saw a
more healthy set of men and so decent looking in my life.' 'As to the
officers I have no resources or do I ever feel myself safe in the few instances
I trust them.' 'Seamen will seldom attend to themselves in any particular
and simply to give directions that they are to keep themselves decent and
dry as circumstances allow is of little avail. They must be watched like
children.'

And ducking – we were reflecting on dancing and ducking. For centuries, ducking had been a way of trial and punishment in Europe. Sailors
had a different name for it. They called it 'baptism', in token of its being
something of a rebirth into some other condition. Knowledge, as we have
seen, was the sailor's most important capital. But knowledge could come
only by experience, not by birth, not by gift, not vicariously. The most
important knowledge was that of a seaman who had gone where others
had not been, beyond that point, beyond that cape, beyond that sea. Such
has a power on which all the others were in some way dependent. From
the eighteenth century and beyond, 'baptism' was the sailor's certificate
of having that kind of knowledge.

Going south was no unimportant thing for a European whose world
was north. Once the world was encompassed, once Europe, in J. H.

Parry's (1974) wonderful phrase, 'discovered the sea', discovered that the whole inhabited earth was set in one ocean that could be sailed by those who had the knowledge and technology to do so, then the known world had only one edge. It was that Line that divided it into hemispheres, the equator. That Line marked entry into a topsy-turvy world – into an antipodes, a place of mirror opposites, where seasons were reversed, where even the unchanging heavens were different. As it happened, the threshold of the Line was the Doldrums, where a ship might be broiled and becalmed, and where captains would have to discover some bustle to keep the devil out of sailors' heads. So the Line came to be just beyond the Horse Latitudes. The sailors would have had charades, would have thrown overboard the 'dead horse' of working off their advanced wages. For several months captains would have 'flogged the dead horse' of their dispirited working for nothing. Beyond the Horse Latitudes crews began their anticipations again and entered into the small but engulfing conspiracies of being sailors.

'Crossing the Line' in the eighteenth century was no affair of starched whites and excited squeals as later P and O cruises made it. Henning Henningsen (1954, 1961), who knows the ceremony more than any other scholar, found observers using these words to describe it: ridiculous, childish, foolish, stupid, silly, ludicrous, bizarre, grotesque, crazy, repulsive, burlesque, profane, superstitious, shameless, outrageous, revolting, tiresome, dangerous, barbarous, brutal, cruel, coarse, rapacious, vindictive, riotous, licentious, mad. Bligh added his own adjectives: 'of all customs it is the most brutal and inhuman'. We have to sense that Crossing the Line was play of a serious and disturbing sort.

Across time and between nationalities, the ceremonies differed, but their expressions had a common character. Firstly, they played out a reversed world in which for a time the true authority of the ship belonged to those who had already Crossed the Line, and not to any by right of their commissions or warrants or appointments. So, for example, John Gore, who had been twice around the world with Byron and Wallis, made a novice out of Captain Cook in his first voyage of the *Endeavour*. Cook was made to know that as yet his world was small. A second common quality was that the theatre of the ceremony was always a grotesque satire on institutions and roles of power. The satire could be about the sacraments of the state – the accolade of a knight – or the sacraments of the church – baptism by the priest. On English ships in the late eigh-

teenth century the satire was of kingship and the power over life and
death.

We have no real way of knowing how Bligh read the ceremony on his
ship, but, believing it 'most brutal and inhuman', he forbade its key
element, the ducking from the yardarm. Here is what he wrote in his log
on February 9, 1788: 'This afternoon those who had never crossed the line
before underwent the usual ceremony except ducking, which I never would
allow for of all the customs it is the most brutal and inhuman. Twenty
seven men and officers therefore tarred and shaved with a piece of iron
hoop. And the officers to pay two bottles of rum and the men one, which
I promised to answer for, and gave everyone a half pint of wine as soon as
the business was over, and dancing began.'

Here we can see him removing the sting of the satire, by intruding
with commander's grace the allowance of an institutional binge on half a
pint of wine. For twenty-seven officers and men he negated the cost of
their inexperience by standing in for their forfeit with perhaps some thirty-
five bottles of rum. The ceremonies were transformed from reverse world
rituals into quaint customs. Now the signified meaning of the ceremony
was not the measured deference that sailors gave to power, but the grace
with which they were commanded. The sailors would not sense their independence and vigour, but their dependent gratitude. The uncomfortable
feeling that Bligh experienced in the ambivalent language of his men, he
seemed also to have felt in reading the ambivalent gestures of ritual. It is
not the violence that disturbs him so much as the grotesque theatre.

The 'usual ceremony' of Crossing the Line began with those who had
already been baptised making preparations with highly officious secrecy,
usually behind a screen set up on the quarterdeck. There, no doubt ex-
uding all the pretentious signs of being by right on this otherwise exclusive spot, crew who had already crossed the Line put together Neptune's
gear – his dolphin skin, his crown, his trident, his wig (a deck swab), his
beard of roping, the nightgown of his consort (Amphritite) and her outrageous jewellery and cosmetics, a tub of tar, galley fat, sowse, droppings
from the henhouse, resin, the costumes of Neptune's secretary and the
Barber. On ships larger than the *Bounty* and given more elaborate charades, there would have been the Devil or Davey Jones, mermaids, fakirs,
clowns, tailors, wandering Jews and farmers. Dangling from the yardarm
was the ducking stool. On the *Providence* it was described as a 'most alarm-
ing machine', made up of iron cross and collar with a handspike for a seat,

all suspended through a block on the foreyard arm. Meanwhile lists would be made certifying the credentials of those who had crossed the line. Each would take an oath over some map. There were nineteen men on the *Bounty* who had crossed the line. We know the names of six or seven, including Fletcher Christian. The dozen others had probably been to India or the East Indies. The ducking stool dangled from the same yard from which a man might hang. The preparations included all the plays on the unknown for the novices − setting them to watch for the Line, tricking them into seeing it in tampered-with telescopes, offering exaggerated hints about the fearsome rubrics of the day.

Neptune usually made a preliminary visit the day before the ceremonies to collect his lists and negotiate his command. He eked out the occasion of his equality with a drink at the captain's table. Then on the day itself he came over the stern and quarterdeck in procession with his court. He would perform some farcical charade of the officers' navigational tasks and declare that the ship had infringed on his domain. A mock trial of those guilty of the infringement would then begin. The trial was full of insults, humiliations, injustices, erotic oaths, and compromising choices. A novice, for example, would have to choose between shouting 'God Save the King!' and getting 'shaving cream' shoved down his throat when he opened his mouth. In the end, and after being shaved, each would be condemned to hang in the ducking stool but would be also expected to buy off all or some of this punishment in some way. Officers would ransom themselves immediately without a ducking. The test for the rest was how many times they would be ducked before forfeiting some part of their grog allowance. They were run to the yard by their own mates, as also happened in a hanging. From there they would be dropped into the sea as many times as they could bear. How many times would be a matter of their later boasting. Two or three times was usual, ten and eleven times a matter for recording. Most would not have been able to swim. So most would not forget this terrifying experience of being overboard, of being in the power of others in a joking relationship that was always nearly serious. They would be bound by the memory of it, and like all initiates, be the surer to see it happen to others as well. Ducking belonged to the oldest Articles of War of which we have a record. Richard Coeur de Lion, going to the Crusades, declared that if one man struck another, he must be ducked three times. Ducking was the first moments of keelhauling. Ducking was a play on hanging. Ducking was play on the edge of not being play at all.

The whole of Crossing the Line was play on the edge of not being play. Certainly its brutality and inhumanity were a satire on the brutality and inhumanity of sailors' lives. But the bravado with which the brutality was endured could be a social quality of the crew as well as a sign of an individual's strength. A man like Bligh who was uncomfortable with that social strength of the crew behind their deferences wanted some other sacrament of power than that of a reversed world. He wanted such ceremonies reduced to folklore.

There were other problems at Adventure Bay. On the long haul from the Cape of Good Hope, Fryer and Bligh had grown totally intolerable to one another. They dined separately. Their tiny cabins across the lobby of the rear hatchway were like nation–states on the edge of war. They communicated with punctiliously polite hatred. At Adventure Bay, Fryer refused to sign the account books without some commendation from Bligh that he, Fryer, had done nothing amiss. Bligh immediately mustered the whole crew, read the Articles of War at Fryer and forced him, in public humiliation, to sign the books before everybody.

We have already noted the structural contradiction on a naval ship between those with power by the King's commission and those with the authority of their skills as seamen. On a fighting ship, especially one of early modern times, that division lay between those commissioned to take their soldiers aboard and fight – the captain and his lieutenants – and those warranted or certified in their navigating and sailing skills – the master and his warrant officers, the bosun, carpenter, sailmaker and their mates. The commissioned officers were gentlemen by birth, while the warrant officers were not, although they were, in varying degrees, given gentlemen's privileges. Naval historians have insisted that the division was strong and consequential in the French and Spanish navies at this time but was not so marked in the British navy of the eighteenth century. Be that as it may. Bligh's fighting and sailing roles may have become blurred in his captaincy by the evolution of naval custom. But he blurred power and authority more dangerously.

In one sense, power of the captain was public, impersonal, dependent on rituals of reification and signs of distance. Authority was private, personal, dependent on interpretive wisdom and signs of adaptability. A man could have power without authority. A man could have authority without power. Bligh could have the power to force a humiliation on Fryer by invoking the authority of his commission. But just as surely he lost the true authority that came from using power wisely. Fryer was a weak man. The only authority he had on the *Bounty* came from the sympathy his humiliation roused in the rest. Christian was different. Christian had authority – by being better than any at the seamen's skills that seamen admired, by being recognisably the gentleman. That is how it came to be between Bligh and Christian. To captain with both power and authority, a man needed to blend the public and the private within himself. But Bligh blurred the public and private in his relations with others, and was in peril in this.

The *Bounty* was a small ship, ninety-one feet long and twenty-three feet wide. It had been made smaller by Sir Joseph Banks' making room for 750 pots of breadfruit in the great cabin. Bligh had made it smaller again by converting the aft half into a botanical garden. 'I looked at [the plants] with delight every day of my life', wrote Bligh. There was little or no private space in such confinement and less on the *Bounty* than on most ships. A merchant seaman or a whaling man might have a bunk. The nearest things a navy man could call private space were the number on the hooks for his hammock and the fourteen inches his hammock spanned when he slept in it. Creating some sort of private space was an art, a privilege for some and a right for all. Topmen might do it in the shrouds, yarning there in elite companionship. Or in the quiet stretches of the night watches, private spots on the deck or along the gunwales could be found, spaces to nap, to sew, to fish, to watch the sea. Privacy was not a matter of walls. It was a matter of behaviour, closing the windows of one's soul. Except for this, the essence of a sailor's existence was to be utterly without space he could call his own, to have all his possessions calculated narrowly, to be a totally public man to his peers and to be totally public to superiors who could muster him twice daily at his quarters.

There were boundaries nonetheless. The boundaries were not just between quarterdeck and lower deck, not just between watched and idler. They were between messes, watches, divisions, between foremast, mainmast and mizzenmast men, between waisters and topmen, between afterguard and fo'c'sle, to say nothing of all the distinct functionaries between captain and boy and all their mates. Daily life was full of plays and gestures that marked status and privilege, that established group and subgroup existence, that drew and redrew boundaries according to the needs of maintaining the ship. Life was full of conflicts that boundary drawing engendered and full of rituals that resolved the conflicts. Life was also a matter of numbers, of the number of a man's hammock, of his mess, of his gun, and a matter of knowing a man's group, his watch, his quarter watch, his station at any prescribed moment of the day or in emergency. On a ship, as on a battlefield, every event needed to be predictable and every response instinctual. So every place, every occasion, every action had its definition and its rules. However, unlike a battlefield where the experience of the unforeseen is usually a small part of a soldier's life, on a ship, every day and night, men experienced the value of efficient, instinctual behaviour in the face of the unpredicted.

Rules and definitions, in measuring things so minutely, were double-edged. They controlled subordinates but they also protected subordinates' privilege against authority. They marked what an institutional man could and could not do, but they also measured the limits that institutions could reach. Rules gave instinctual predictability, but they also gave protective privacy. So, arithmetic on a ship was everywhere. It was present in meals that gave seamen two ounces of butter on Mondays, a half a gill of peas on Fridays, and a pound of this or a pint of that on every other day. In the same way the hours of a seaman's watch, the inches of his hammock, the pennies of his expenses and fines, his half-pint of grog or gallon of beer a day, the lashes of his floggings were not only known and counted constantly but were ceremonially measured that all might be secure in the different boundaries around their lives. The navy did its arithmetic to captains, court-martialling them if they lost their ship or any significant part of it. The navy counted the men in every purser's muster. The captains calculated with cooks and pursers, counting every piece of salted beef as it came from a barrel. The men made arithmetic with one another as they divided their food in their messes. Deviance from the measurement that ensured order was the principal crime; encroachment on calculated rights the principal tyranny; playing tricks that manipulated order and measurements was the chief sport. James Cook cursed the conservatism of his sailors for preferring the rotten salt beef that they had by right to the sauerkraut he gave them out of generosity. It was only when he declared sauerkraut a privilege for officers that the crew demanded to have some as their right.

Such a public and measured life was hard. It was not necessarily oppressive. The social contract of a total institution is to be public. The personal in such a contract is disturbing. The personal creates ambivalences and blurs the boundaries between control and protection. Such public presence, however, requires ceremony. Order, the good things, values are supported by ceremony. Ceremony is an act of commonsense. If the goal of an institution is efficiency — moving a large number of men with the least idiosyncrasy on their part and without the distraction of conflict with one another — then it can seem natural, commonsensical, to focus men's whole attention on the totally trivial, but ordered, realities of ceremony and custom. Prompt response to orders, salutes, straight lines at muster, reverence shown to the sacred spaces of the quarterdeck, a language of address that confirms a depersonalisation of role, deferential rituals; regulations covering all of time and space — these are effective signs. They establish as socially real what they signify. An efficient ship is its straight lines and smart appearance. Smart appearance is a sacrament of order.

It is wrong to think this is inhuman or unrewarding. For officers and men there is considerable satisfaction in smartness: one has only to look at the competitiveness between groups on a ship and between ships to see that satisfaction. And human beings get large satisfaction not simply from contribution to the order of the systems of which they are a part but also from observing their own efforts to beat those systems, from finding a rough equilibrium between defiance and conformity.

When Bligh reflected on the cause of his mutiny, his first thought was that his men had been unsettled by their lust for Tahitian promiscuity and licence. His second thought was that he had no marines on the *Bounty*. Perhaps he judged that he would have been safer behind a marine guard continuously at his cabin door. But marines could sleep on duty as well as midshipmen. More plausibly, marines would have given him some ceremonial distance in his role as captain. Distance was what he lacked. He had no real wardroom, only a makeshift dining room behind canvas bulwarks. The surgeon took meals out of a bottle. The master, John Fryer, was cantankerous and easily wounded. Bligh was always picking at some scab in their relationship. So they did not eat together. Bligh made his wardroom a matter of privilege among the 'young 'uns', the midshipmen. Whether they, including Christian, ate with him was a measure of his changing favours.

But the dangerous lack of distance was also in himself and how he blurred the boundaries between public and private in other ways. He was his own purser, and he had to care about money. James Cook had been his own purser, too, but the *Endeavour* and *Resolution* were large enough to delegate his purser's role to a secretary. Pursers were known entrepreneurs. They had an investment to save and make good. Profit and surplus were their perks. So whenever Bligh, for motives of health, put his men on half or two-thirds of an allowance that was theirs by immemorial right and replaced it with something he had acquired cheaply, say pumpkin, he was seen as infringing on a space not his and doing so for private gain, not the common good. For the whole five months of the *Bounty*'s stay at Tahiti, he set up an account book at the ship's gangway. All foodstuffs brought on board were counted and weighed and entered in the book. Ninety percent of it went to the ship's store. For men who counted every pea they had as right from a measuring navy, paying for their own living in this way was an outrage, and they knew that Bligh profited by it.

The most troublesome man on the *Bounty* for Bligh was William Purcell, the carpenter. A carpenter, like a purser, was also entrepreneurial, in that his tools were his private capital and he belonged to an artisan guild as well as the navy. When Purcell drew a boundary around what was his – by questioning whether he had to blunt his chisels in order to allow Bligh to make some gift to the Tahitian 'king', or whether it was his task to load provisions – it enraged Bligh to think that Purcell would not subordinate his self-interests to the greater plan of the perfect voyage. He would not allow Purcell the distinction of public and private he insisted on for himself as purser.

Bligh blurred the boundary of public and private in his punishments as well. Not all of them. The floggings he gave to John Williams (six lashes), to Alexander Smith [alias John Adams] (twelve), to William Muspratt (twelve), and to John Sumner (twelve) – all for 'neglect of duty' – fell under an acceptable rubric in one way or another. They were finished with in the giving of them: they were for lapses a self-respecting sailor would accept as lapses. They created no guilt or obligation. But with other men, Bligh used the Articles of War as a measure of personal loyalty. When Fryer at Adventure Bay refused to sign the account books, Bligh's reading of the Articles of War at him was overkill. When Churchill, Muspratt and Millward deserted at Tahiti, he publicly berated the midshipman, Hayward, who had been asleep on watch, and put him in irons for nineteen days. He flogged the three deserters with a hundred and twenty lashes all told, then to protect himself from having gone beyond his powers – by navy rule he should not have given more than thirty-six lashes – he extracted a written acknowledgement from them that they were thankful for his leniency.

Bligh was by then so out of countenance with all of the men that when a Tahitian stole a compass and some bedding, he had him seized. The man's chiefs were not averse to having him shot. Bligh gave him 100 lashes. One can sense his puzzlement that the native was not broken by this terrible punishment. He thought that this insensitivity was a sign of his uncivilised nature. 'He bore it surprisingly and only asked me twice to forgive him although he expected to die.' When the Tahitian later escaped the irons that he had been put in to await a further lashing, it was another midshipman, George Stewart, who was given the blame. 'Such neglectfull and worthless Petty officers I believe never was in a ship as we are in this. No order for hours together were obeyed by them and their conduct in general is so bad that no confidence or trust can be reposed in them, in short, they drove me to everything but corporal punishment and that must follow if they do not improve.' Bligh was reducing the oppositions of the *Bounty* to their raw simplicity – him against all the rest.

The *Bounty* was anchored in Matavai Bay, Tahiti, for five months. This was one cause of Bligh's rising tensions. A ship in port is an ambivalent space in itself. A graph of eighteenth-century naval floggings in the Pacific and elsewhere would show peaks at every port of call, 'civilised' or 'uncivilised'. Cook would never have stayed five months in one place. He would have been off 'discovering'. On the *Bounty* routine disappeared at Matavai Bay. With Bligh preoccupied with the diplomacy and the botany of his breadfruit, no one had an eye for maintenance or for busyness, the busyness that good order required. The women could not be kept off the ship; the sailors could not be kept off the land. Bligh, suffering his headaches in the heat and distracted by his plants and all his moves to keep face with the 'king' of Tahiti, had no energy except for rage. The liminal space that should have been made for signifying his authority became instead a liminal space for signifying licence against the institution of the ship.

That is not to say that the 'people' of the *Bounty* were unwilling to give up paradise. Very few of them – John Adams later named only Matthew Quintal, while John Fryer named only Stewart and Morrison – had established lasting relationships at Tahiti. When April 4, 1789, came and they weighed anchor, there was more talk of what was to come than regret for what had been left behind. 'Everybody was in high spirits', we have heard Morrison say. 'Fluttering fancies' had wafted them out of Tahiti to Jamaica and home. The 'people' had become entrepreneurial too. They would never make their fortunes out of wages, but they would still do well out of the 'artificial curiosities' they had collected. The *Bounty*, already overcrowded, was now full of clubs and spears, Tahitian cloth, fans and feathers. There were other ambitions as well. Months earlier, when they had first discovered their destination and the purpose of the voyage, some had laid plans to break into the publishing market and make their fortunes there.

It was Bligh who dispelled their high spirits and their nostalgia for home. His breadfruit cuttings had taken root and were growing well. Though he looked the gentleman gardener puttering under the tarpaulin on the quarterdeck, he was now the navigator again. He had 100 ducats in his cabin to buy 'Mangosteens, Duriens, Jacks, Nancas, Lansas, and in short all the fine fruits. . . , as well as the Rice Plant which grows upon dry land' in Java. But he had to sail the dangerous waters between New Guinea and mainland Australia, and he was late for the winds that would make it easier. There were island discoveries still to be made on his route. He must do it all himself, for he now knew there were none to help him. He flogged the crew bitterly with his tongue.

Three weeks along, they were off Nomuka in the Tongan Islands. Bligh had visited it earlier with Cook. Now he landed for water, wood, food and the replacement of some breadfruit cuttings. He was unsuccessful in his trading, but, left behind on the *Bounty*, the men were making spectacular bargains exchanging their Tahitian curiosities for food. Clearly, the crew were laying in supplies against the hard times that would be coming, and they were doing it with some sense of triumph at beating Bligh's system of accountancy. Bligh returned to the ship with a miserable load of coconuts, only to find their private piles of yams and fruits abounding. No doubt they winked and smirked at having beaten his system. And he found that there had been native thefts from the other watering party under Christian's command. Almost as if he were testing Christian, Bligh had sent him unarmed and unable because of that to prevent the thefts that Bligh now raged about. In the night, some of Bligh's coconuts were missing. To placate Bligh, Fryer suggested that the piles

might merely have been trodden down. Christian said he had taken a
coconut to slake his thirst. Bligh called him a thief. Then, on the same
day, there were other native thefts, and Bligh held three chiefs on board
as hostages. The day became a storm of charges and more charges. He
turned the crew's triumph sour with threats of cutting their allowances
and of what he would do to them when the sailing became hard. Then,
in the whirlwind, he turned quiet, freed the chiefs, played the beneficiary
with rich gifts, invited Mr Christian to dinner and, when Mr Christian
declined, invited Mr Hayward instead, and finally retired to his cabin.

That night, many of the crew stayed late on the deck watching the
volcanic displays off Tofua. They congratulated themselves that a new
moon off Tofua would mean a full moon off the Australian coast and a
better sight of its dangerous reefs. The whirlwind, quiet at the centre,
was still wild at its edges. Christian, distraught and in tears, had wan-
dered the ship asking what he would do. He got little comfort from those
who thought he was just a little worse off than they. In the night, he
made a raft out of spare yards, tore up all his papers, and collected a few
stores as part of some mad plan to drift ashore. Someone, in that night,
persuaded him that he should take the ship instead. Perhaps it was George
Stewart; more probably it was Matthew Quintal. Christian, of them all,
seemed to know how final either solution would be. His greatest fear
seemed to be that his family, with its professors of law and its friends
among the Wordsworths and Coleridges, with its members already victims of stress, would be pulled into his more private hell. When he came
on deck, armed for mutiny and no doubt sweating profusely and soiling
everything he touched, he looked the madman Bligh had made him.

There was not much that Bligh had to say on the morning of his mutiny. He told the mutineers that it was not too late to turn back. He
reminded Christian that he had dandled Bligh's children on his knees. He
negotiated for what would give him and the men in the launch a chance
at survival. When, in the end, he looked up from the launch to the crowded
rails of the *Bounty*, he saw faces of hate, faces of despair, faces of incom-
prehension; he heard jeers and threats and insults and pleas for understanding and messages for people back home. He told that undifferentiated crowd, 'Never fear, my lads, I will do you justice if ever I reach
England'. Each one heard him as each wanted. His language was ambivalent to the end.

MR CHRISTIAN'S LOT

So the *Bounty* was now Christian's problem. If Bligh had a problem with blending his power and authority, how would Christian manage? Later the surprise – and the fear – arising out of the Great Nore Mutiny, was that ordinary seamen, supposedly anarchic towards established authority, could govern themselves so well. By their self-government, the Nore mutiny became a revolution with its own parliament, its own decision-making processes, its own system of justice. The *Bounty*'s mutiny had certainly been unpremeditated, but now the mutineers must have a plan not just for tomorrow but forever. Everyone knew, now that it was over, that whether Bligh survived or perished, they had conspired in their own self-destruction. The navy would never let them go. Once discovered, they would be rescued by neither truth nor lie. Among the twenty-five men left on board, there were those, perhaps nine, who believed they had a chance of explaining their actions away. The rest, perhaps sixteen, must have been fatalistic: they would have a few years' freedom or they must hide away for life. The division made for factions of Christian's government.

Christian never doubted that he must find a hideaway for life. He would never be dragged back to disgrace his family. It was not he who cried, 'Huzzah for Otaheiti' – unless 'Otaheiti' was a general metaphor for a freer life. Tahiti was the last place they could go, because it was the first place to which the navy would come. Christian scoured Bligh's books and charts and chose Tubuai, an island Cook had seen on his third voyage.

It should be no surprise that the first act of the mutineers was to throw overboard the breadfruit plants. Their second set of actions may surprise, however. They made themselves uniform jackets by cutting up the royals and then the main topsail and the mizzenmast top staysail. Then they divided all the wearing apparel and Tahitian curiosities of those gone in the launch. It was an intense preoccupation of theirs, this perfectly equal distribution of whatever wealth they had out of a common store. And they had a mechanism of drawing lots that satisfied them. But why the uniform jackets? They did not say. Officers had jackets and hats, but ordinary seamen at this time had only the uniformity of 'slops' on which they were dependent on long voyages. Tahitians, they knew, had a discerning eye for symbols of status. On whatever island they landed, they proposed that none should have an advantage over another. They would all wear jackets.

The men had no hesitation in acknowledging a hierarchy of status according to their seamen's skills. They knew the dangers of ships and seas and islands. They had had no time for incompetence and would not suffer it when their lives were at risk. They would bow to power that had the authority of expertise. Christian had dazzled them the whole voyage long with his feats of physical ability, and, in retrospect, they thought him as good a navigator, or better, than Bligh. He predicted to within a half-hour when they would see Tubuai, one man later said appreciatively. And George Stewart was the second most skilled and experienced officer, better than Peter Heywood, though less popular. Christian became their commander and Stewart his lieutenant. And if they were communistic in the distribution of their common wealth, they nonetheless knew that power needed its spaces. They therefore gave those officers the cabins and comforts of command. In fact, they re-established the great cabin now that the breadfruit had gone, and the *Bounty* was a proper ship again.

Tubuai was not Tahiti. It had the double-island appearance of Tahiti, but its twin peaks were less. It had a drier, barer look than Tahiti. The men would not have been tempted, one suspects, to tattoo themselves with the date of their arrival at Tubuai. They discovered the only passage through the reef and warped their way along to virtually the only safe anchorage.

Tubuai was not the Tahiti of their *Bounty* experience in another sense. Their Tahiti was twenty years into its European experience. Those years had blunted the violence of early contact. Cook had seen and mapped Tubuai but not landed because it 'appeared of little consequence'. He had spoken to some of the islanders in their canoes through Omai, the Tahitian whom he was returning to Tahiti after his visit to George III. Cook learned the name of the island was 'Toobouai'. One of the islanders, Cook wrote, blew a 'conch most part of the time they were near us, what this might mean I cannot say, but I never found it the messinger of Peace'. The *Bounty* men heard a conch, too, and came to agree that it was not the messenger of peace. Being the first European strangers to land at Tubuai, they began a re-play of first contacts throughout the Pacific – of misread signs, of mythical presumptions, of killings. As they warped inside the reef, Tubuaians harassed the boat guiding them. Burkitt was speared, so they fired on the canoes. 'Bloody Bay' they were to call it, after their muskets took effect. Then the women appeared in a double canoe and, as they had done in first contact at Tahiti and Hawaii, they tried to mesmerise these strangers, these 'gods from beyond the skies', with their dances.

The men's comfort and dreams ended there, however. Tubuai was not Tahiti. There were no more women and there was no meat. There _were_ politics, as always. The place of their landfall had depended on their finding safety for their ship. That chance discovery, however, disturbed the politics of the chiefs, three men who ruled the island's different parts. Food and women became the currency of power in the jealousies that the _Bounty_'s presence created. The _Bounty_, its crew soon realised, needed an independent supply of food and women if they were to be free of Tubuai's politics.

Within ten days, they sailed back to Tahiti to collect meat and women. They were more successful with meat than women. They packed the _Bounty_ with either four hundred and sixty or three hundred and twelve hogs – they were still doing the arithmetic that Bligh had demanded of them, but not very well – fifty goats (or thirty-eight), eight dozen fowl, dogs, cats (needed to attack the rats that infested Tubuai), a bull and a cow. But only nine women returned with the twenty-five men. (Why only nine women were brought back is something of a puzzle. It is a sign, I think, that the hard-core mutineers – nine would eventually go to Pitcairn – had already formed.) Meanwhile they had told the Tahitians some story that Bligh had met up with Captain Cook at Aitutaki (Bligh had concealed Cook's death from them) and was now sending Titreano (Christian) to gather supplies for a settlement. They took on board eight Tahitian men and seven boys as well as the nine women. Also taken was Hitihiti. He had mediated Cook's and Bligh's exchanges with Tahiti and would do the same for Vancouver and then Bligh again. Hitihiti became their greatest asset. He made sense of the strangers to the Tubuaians and strengthened their connections with Tahiti.

Christian came back to Tubuai to build a fort – 'Fort George', no less. With a Union Jack flying on a staff, Fort George was a hundred yards square, with a surrounding ditch eighteen feet wide, earthen walls twenty feet high and twelve feet wide at their narrowest, a drawbridge, the _Bounty_'s four pounders in the corners and swivel guns on the walls. It was Robinson Crusoe stuff. Maybe it was Freudian stuff too, for Christian was born in or within sight of Moorland Close, his mother's border fortification become farmhouse. Its high walls looked like ramparts. Were they also a hundred yards around? The watchtower guarding the easily defended entryway must have been a place of play for Christian. Maybe 'Fort George' was too. The remains of 'Fort George' are still to be seen, 200 years on. There is a monument to their hard labour still in the middle of it – a breadfruit tree.

Not all the men were prepared to humour Christian. Once they were back at Tubuai – it was early July, only eight weeks after the mutiny – it became clear that there were more factions than two on board the *Bounty*. Sumner and Quintal immediately broke ranks and went on shore, without leave, as it were. 'The ship is moor'd and we are now our own Master', they said. A ship in port is, I have said, a liminal space. Christian's response was to shout: 'I'll let you know who is Master', and put a pistol to their heads. They were put in irons until they begged his pardon. They were punished not just on Christian's word but on a majority vote, and that majority then decided to allow two of their number on shore each night.

The men's lust for women off the ship was more easily controlled than their lust for liquor on the ship. Drunken fights and threats to one another's lives became common. 'Those abaft' – Christian and Stewart – began wearing pistols. They knew that those who were murderous – McCoy, Thompson, Churchill, Quintal – would become murderers. They knew who it was they had had to restrain from killing Bligh – from 'blowing the bugger's brains out' – on the day of the mutiny. Christian had no solution to his problem of discipline, save by siphoning off the liquor until there was none, and putting the men to work.

So Christian farmed out tasks. Brown, Sir Joseph Banks' gardener, and the Tahitians, with their local knowledge, were set to clearing ground for growing yams. McCoy and Coleman, the armourer who had been forced to stay by the mutineers because of his blacksmith's skills, were to man the forge and construct spades, hoes and mattocks. Henry Hilbrant, a Hanoverian with a strong accent, was not asked to use his cooper's skills, but was expected to cook. Michael Byrne and Ellison would mind the boats, along with the Tahitian boys. The rest would labour on the fort, their arms under sentinel.

They worked strenuously for about six weeks, raising the earthen walls to at least six or seven feet, digging a hundreds yards of the ditch, staking the walls, posting the gates and drawbridge. But hard work did not distract them from their lusts – it probably only increased them – and building a fort on native land did not give them possession of an island.

Whatever they were in native eyes when they first arrived at Tubuai – gods, mythic strangers from the skies – the men were now an invading force. The Tubuaians might have mediated the force of their arrival through women in the first days, but now they refused them women altogether, and stole whatever they could. Neither would the Tubuaians trade for food. Christian's authority now desperately depended on his finding women. The men would not give him his fort until he did.

Armed parties went plundering for wives, burning houses, shooting and bayoneting those who resisted. To force negotiations, Christian ravaged a *marae,* a sacred place, and seized all the statues of gods and sacred paraphernalia, together with the arsenal of clubs and spears that were kept there. Then, when Tinarou, the chief, offered peace ceremonies around the drinking of *kava* but refused to guarantee wives, Christian flew into a passion. He had sat, like Cook and Bligh before him at Hawaii and Tahiti, surrounded by cloth and gifts in a place of sacrifice, but he stomped off in a rage. A week later, another armed party from the *Bounty* marched behind a Tahitian holding a Union Jack aloft. This time, they were looking for their wandering stock of hogs, goats and cattle, as well as women. They were ambushed by 700 Tubuaians and had to fall back. Ambushed a second time, they stood and fired and claimed later to have killed 120 men and women.

Within the camp and on the ship, there was also trouble. There were thefts from the common store, especially of red feathers, the currency that was most likely to buy a woman. Churchill had begun to challenge Christian's position. Some men were conspiring to disable the *Bounty* and escape in the cutter. To cope with a disintegration of order, the men contrived a covenant. It comprised 'Articles' in which Churchill and Christian specified mutual forgiveness of all past grievances and that every man was obliged to swear to and sign. Matthew Thompson alone refused to comply.

Preoccupied with their own divisions, the mutineers did not know how close they were to being discovered. A Swedish trader, the *Mercury* under Captain Cox, had arrived at Tahiti after they had returned there. The captain was bemused by stories of Titreano. By chance, the *Mercury* sailed south to Tubuai on leaving Tahiti. Coming on the island in the evening,

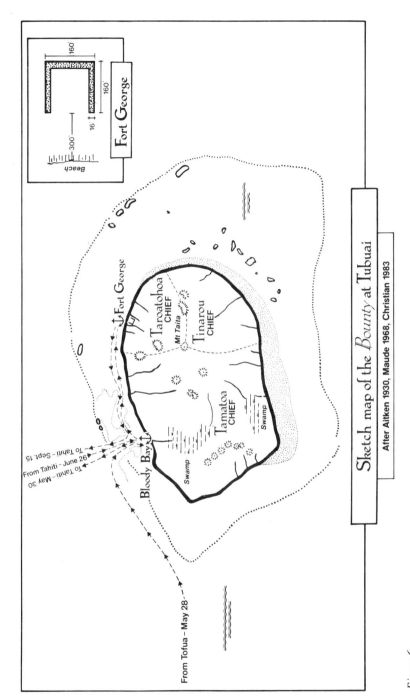

Figure 6.
Tubuai and 'Fort George'.

the crew sailed off 'Bloody Bay' in the dark. They saw the light of fires on shore. They fired a cannon as possible signal for anyone who could read it. It was August 9. Perhaps the *Bounty* men were weary from their ditch-digging or perhaps the surf hid the sound. In any case, they did not respond.

By the first week of September, Christian's authority had all but wasted away. Those not of his faction, and those who had no wives, now refused to work at the fort. They proposed to enslave the Tahitian men to do their work, and were about to cast lots for them. Others proposed a mad scheme to kill off all the Tubuaian men and take their women.

They then began three days of debate about their future. No one was for staying on Tubuai. The question was whether they would return to Tahiti. Christian was weary of it all and made only one stipulation: that if they returned to Tahiti, he would be given the *Bounty*. He would sail her, alone if necessary, anywhere she would take him. It was a moment of truth for them all. They could not escape the consequences of their decision, and they had to enter into some social contract of mutual support. When the debate was ended, they voted. Sixteen men voted to return to Tahiti. Eight voted to go with Christian on the *Bounty*. They agreed to make an equal distribution of all the arms and movable goods. They sailed from Tubuai on September 15. George Stewart and Peter Heywood, who had been keeping their logs like good midshipmen, du-tifully recorded that they lost three fathoms of very rubbed cable in the sailing.

They were back in Matavai Bay in four days. Each man had his 'lotts', a musket, pistol, cutlass, bayonet, cartridge box, seventeen pounds of lead and three gallons of wine. Except Michael Byrne. No one liked Byrne. He was of a 'troublesome disposition'. They did not trust him with a musket. For those staying at Tahiti, there were some common stores – an anvil, a grindstone, a kettle and musketoons. Christian got his 'lott', the *Bounty*, and his chance to start again.

At Matavai, the men unloaded expeditiously in a few hours. The *Bounty* sailed off in the same night, no one knew where or in what direction. No one was really sure how many Tahitian men and women went with Chris-tian. In fact, twelve Tahitian women and one female infant, as well as five Tahitian men and one Tubuaian man sailed with him and his crew of eight. Wantonly they had put overboard some women and men they did not want. Bligh, on that September 21, was just a few days off leaving Timor for home.

The eight men who sailed with Christian must have believed that they had no choice. Not one of all those who stayed on the *Bounty* after the mutiny is recorded as blaming Christian in his moment of madness for their lot. None of them seemed to say to Christian what was said to Bligh, we are here because of *you*. Now this final remnant was freed of those who had challenged him on Tubuai. It is doubtful that he had already decided on Pitcairn. That most knowledgeable of Pacific historians, H. E. Maude (1968), has shown that the *Bounty*'s last voyage was a long one – to the west by Rarotonga as far as Ono-i-lau in Fiji, then back east in a long southerly loop through the Tongan Islands to Pitcairn. In the end, Pitcairn was as near the ideal hideaway as Christian could have hoped for. It must have been the only uninhabited high island in the whole Pacific. Polynesians had settled it but had either gone away or died. It had no reef or anchorage. It was off the known wind routes that sailing ships would follow. It was a place to hide and start again. But Christian never seemed to slough off his deep depression at what he had done. That, with the *Bounty*, was his unequal lot.

The sixteen men who elected to stay at Tahiti are difficult to define. They included the four who, by any definition except a legalistic one, were innocent of mutiny and were there against their will: Norman, McIntosh, Coleman and Byrne. They included four who must have known they were doomed, if they were discovered: Churchill, Thompson, Sumner and Burkitt; three were there who were convinced in their own minds of their innocence and believed they had some chance of convincing others – Heywood, Stewart, Morrison. Five must have felt a Tahitian interlude was worth the gamble either of the navy's discovery of them or of casting their lot with Christian – Millward, Muspratt, Ellison, Hilbrant, Skinner.

Thompson was psychotically violent and was a danger to them all. But soon he was murdered by Tahitian friends of Churchill – whom he had previously murdered. Churchill, the only man who seemed to have ambitions to be captain over both Bligh and Christian, had had his ambitions fulfilled by being made chief of a Tahitian group. Indeed, he had reached a higher status even than that of being made equal to a god: when he was killed, his skull, together with Thompson's, was archived in a place of sacrifice.

What the sixteen men made of their beach – and what the eight men with Christian made of their island – belongs to our coming narrative. It is their world-turned-upside-down on the ship that now needs a reflection. With Bligh's ambivalences gone, they had their own ambivalences with which to cope. In many ways they coped well. True authority went immediately to those who had demonstrated their mastery over a dangerous environment. They solved their problems by use of systems that had protected them against intrusion of unwarranted power – simple systems, such as distribution by equal lot and by lottery. They invested those with authority with symbols and perquisites of their position. They bowed to a hegemonic commonsense of how a ship should be run. They were well aware that there was a violence among them that could easily erupt. They had no qualm at its violent suppression. Though some of them had jeered at those going in the launch, taunting them that now they would truly feel the cost of short allowances, all the old and serviceable arithmetic of food and space seemed to remain. They remained clustered too, if not in messes, then in twos and threes of mateship.

But it is the mark of such institutions as a ship to be temporary. A voyage begun is a voyage to be ended. Its temporariness is its hegemony. The harshness of its order lasts only for a time, and men can subordinate themselves to its violence. But when a ship is only the doorstep to a residence, as the *Bounty* was to the beach at Tubuai, then subordinations were not so easy. The mutineers had entered another set of time. In this other time, they had to be inventive of the sorts of deferences they would owe one another. 'Fort George' was a madness. What metaphor of freedom was in it? They may as well have 'Huzza'd' for a prison. The only good it did was to dampen their divisiveness by focusing their toil and roles to one end. They must have known, even Christian, that they would never draw its drawbridge. Their inventions did not work, more than anything, because they feared the untrammelling of the violence among themselves. Their encampments around Christian on the *Bounty* and around the moderate faction at Tahiti were first steps toward distancing themselves from this violence. They still had to discover the irony that their violence was within them. It was the hegemony of their ship that had tamed it for a time.

SAD PASSION AND DAMNED OECONOMY

On the day of his mutiny, Christian was all threats of death to Bligh, but his actions belied his bluster. In his 'madness' he seemed to have had no plan for either Bligh's survival or his destruction. His followers kept protesting that he was giving Bligh too many chances for escape. By letting the carpenter take his tools, he enabled those with Bligh to build a bigger boat in a month, they said. He denied the men in the launch charts but secretly gave them his own best sextant. He allowed them only five days' provisions but he must have presumed they would make a landfall. Landing without arms, however, was dangerous – they had just spent two days trying without success to impose discipline in their relations with the natives of Nomuka – so he gave the men with Bligh four cutlasses. Perhaps he thought they would make for Botany Bay or that they would play the lottery of waiting for some ship to come and collect them. If he knew Bligh at all – and perhaps with all his preoccupations with himself he did not – he would know that Bligh's resolve was unfathomable.

In fact, on that same day and 'scarcely a furlong' from the *Bounty* in the launch, Bligh was remarking to himself how strong his spirits were. 'I began to reflect on the vicissitudes of human affairs, but in the midst of all I felt a universal happiness which prevented any depression of my spirits, conscious of my own integrity and anxious solicitude for the good of the service I was on, I find my mind wonderfully supported and began to conceive hopes notwithstanding so heavy a calamity to be able to re-count to my King and Country my misfortune.' Buoyed by the certainty that he would one day tell his story, and supplied with the means to record it in a near-empty signals notebook belonging to Thomas Hayward, and in his own precious log, he closed down the world around him to the space of the launch. For a short time, perhaps a day or so, he even began to love this closed-down world of fellow sufferers. He admired their silent courage and resolve. He praised their submission to his plans. He almost thought they were comfortable in their distress.

Bligh had sailed past Tofua twelve years before, when he was master of the *Resolution*. Now, as he saw it, he was unsure how much he could remember of it. Tofua was a platform of rock, rising sheer out of the sea, its volcano not greatly pronounced. The *Resolution* had passed it on its south and southwest sides, where the slopes of coconut tree and vegetation made it look idyllic. From the islanders of Nomuka, Cook had learned of a crater lake and that the island was visited by islanders from the east for its black stone. He was told that the island's volcano was a god called Lofia.

The *Resolution* did not see the northern and western sides of Tofua, which were barren and bare and without beaches. The only vegetation there was scattered in deep ravines. It was to the western side that Bligh brought the launch, seeking shelter from the southeast wind. In the dusk there was no safe landing place to be seen. The men spent an uncomfortable and nervous night at sea. The half-pint of grog and quarter-pint of wine each that Bligh allowed them may have taken the edge off their nerves.

The next day brought no relief. A party was able to land and scramble up the cliffs by clinging to vines, but found little food or water. There was no making for sea because the winds had freshened. Bligh's plan now, in any case, was to increase their provisons so that when they ran for one of the larger islands – Tongatabu or Nomuka – they would have some security if they were blown into the deep ocean.

On the second day they found a cove, not safe enough for them to beach the launch but where they could land through the surf. It had a cave where a few of them slept tormented by mosquitoes, and where Bligh retired to write up his log. A search party found some coconuts and a little water and contacted some islanders who came down to the cove to trade. Then a canoe arrived and slowly the stony beach began to fill with islanders from Nomuka till there were about 200 of them. Among those from Nomuka were chiefs and a young man who remembered Bligh from his visit in the *Resolution*. They asked about Captain Cook and Captain Clerke, who was with Cook and in command of the *Discovery*. They asked about the *Bounty*. They looked greedily at the launch held by a grapnel over the bow and a line to the shore thrown over the stern. They were trying to cope with this new experience of European strangers come amongst them without their usual trappings of power. Bligh began to threaten with his cutlass any islander who tried to pull the launch ashore and began moving his men and the few provisions they had collected quietly to the launch. As dusk began to fall, it was clear they would not survive the night if they stayed in the cave. When Bligh told the chiefs that he would sleep in the launch, he thought he heard them say 'then we will kill you'. In the gloom, the natives began to clack their stones. Bligh had heard that clacking before, in Hawaii, after the death of Cook, as Bligh had waited to be attacked. He ordered everyone to the launch. 'We walked down the beach', he wrote, 'everyone in a silent kind of horror'. John Norton, the largest man on the *Bounty*, stayed to loose the line. Purcell, on Bligh's orders, stood with Bligh as the others moved through the surf. Not one man in twenty would have done what Purcell did, John Fryer reported, giving some justice to a man much maligned. As the stones began to fly, Bligh was last into the launch, pulling himself out of the water as stones as heavy as eight pounds battered them. There was no saving John Norton. He was dead and stripped before they cut the line.

The survivors pulled themselves along the grapnel line out of the cove, only to find that the grapnel had fouled. It held them until its fluke broke. Canoes were all around them filled with natives stoning them. Ineffectually, they could only fling back those stones that landed in the launch. In the end they escaped by an old trick. They flung clothes overboard and, while the islanders were distracted and fighting over this booty, they sailed and rowed out into the dark.

Everyone was bruised. For all they had suffered to gain them, their supplies were not much greater than what remained from the *Bounty*. In the dark, in disorder, far out at sea, they must now decide what they must do. Fryer reports that he asked Bligh at the time whether he had had trouble when he was at Nomuka in the *Resolution*. If there had been trouble, it would have been dangerous to make for that island. Bligh answered, yes, there had been thieving. We do not know what troubles . Bligh personally had had at Nomuka. His logs aboard the *Resolution* have never been found, perhaps disappearing in the *Bounty* with his maps and other papers. We know – and Peckover in the launch would have known – that Cook, more irritable with natives on his last voyage than he had ever been, had acted out some extravagant charades that embarrassed his more liberal colleagues, his surgeon William Anderson among them. Cook had flogged a chief with a dozen lashes for stealing part of a small winch and then had had the chief's hands bound behind his back while he was held ransom for a pig. 'That he should be confined in painfull posture for some hours after a ransom demanded after proper punishment for the crime had been inflicted I believe will scarcely be found consummate with principles of justice or humanity upon the strictest scrutiny', Anderson reflected. Whatever the natives remembered of it, it was a memory the launch people could not trust. They looked for somewhere else to go. Peckover had been to Timor with Cook on the *Endeavor*. On board the launch were Hamilton Moore's *The Practical Navigator and Seaman's New Daily Assistant* as well as the *Tables Requisite* to be used with the *Nautical Ephemerides for finding the Latitude and Longitude at Sea*. Transcribed from these – by Thomas Hayward, evidently making what little effort he ever made to be a proper midshipman (they are on the first page of his signals notebook) – are half a dozen positions in the New Hebrides, and for

Timor: 100° 23′S − 123° 59′W. By these positions they were on a nearly direct westward course to Timor, within the equatorial plane. With a Ramsden ten-inch sextant, a quadrant, an Adams compass, navigational tables, and luck in clear noon sightings, they could do their latitudinal navigation with no great difficulty. To estimate their longitude, they would have to make a logline and train themselves in counting out the seconds and calculating their speed. Bligh had them practice all these skills in case something happened to him. By the time they made their landfall on the Australian Great Barrier Reef, after thirty-one days of sailing, they were in error of only two minutes of latitude and nineteen and a half minutes of longitude − a mere eighteen miles.

The morning after their decision to sail directly to Timor, the wind was blowing a 'severe gale' but then abated to a 'mere storm'. The seas were so high that the launch's sails were becalmed in the troughs but were dangerously stretched on the peaks. The men were bailing all the time. The seas were curling into the boat. This was only a taste of what was to come.

Once on the way to Timor, once having 'returned God thanks for our miraculous preservation', once again confident that it was on his skills that all were dependent, Bligh's spirits, slightly subdued, became more buoyant. 'I had a mind more at ease than I had before felt.'

'Sad passion' was John Fryer's favourite description of Bligh's rages. 'Oeconomy' was Bligh's own approving word for managing resources. 'His damned oeconomy' was the phrase that a weak and dying David Nelson used to describe the cause of their sufferings. Much of the ease of mind that Bligh felt at the beginning of this terrible voyage came from the 'oeconomy' he planned for it and engaged his men to follow. His 'sad passions' came mostly from the breaches and suspicions he detected in the working of his 'oeconomy'.

Bligh first made space in the boat. The three watches of five to six men he created needed room and seating to work the boat. Those not on watch lay as best they could on the bottom, moving delicately every four hours, but suffering terrible cramps from their inactivity.

Each was allowed two sets of clothing. The rest of the clothing was thrown overboard. For all their fears of dying of mad thirst in these tropic waters, their greatest pain came ironically from wet cold. It rained almost the whole of their passage to the Great Barrier Reef. In the end Bligh ordered them to soak their spare clothes in sea water, which was warmer than the rain, and change into these soggy garments every few hours. The food, already wet and rotting, he put into the carpenter's chest. Purcell, the owner of the chest, gave them some comfort by raising the aft quarters of the launch nine inches, using the stern seating. Bligh calculated the probable days for sailing to Timor and divided their food accordingly, making scales of coconut shells weighted with a musket ball (1/24 lb). He offered them an 'oeconomy' of 1/24 pound of bread twice a day, an occasional ounce of salted pork, an occasional teaspoon of rum, and a quarter of a pint of water a day. He secured their engagement to this oeconomy as 'a sacred promise forever to their memory'. As it happened they were fated never to catch a fish, save one, in this abounding sea. But they did catch one noddy and seven booby birds, each of which they divided into eighteen parts down to their beaks and feet. They ate what they were given by seaman's lottery from whatever was in Bligh's hands behind his back. Bligh told stories at dinner parties in his later years about the nauseating bits he was forced to eat. He recorded the 'prodigious' sickness he suffered following the catching of that one fish and his revulsion at 'the oily nature of part of the stomach of the fish which it had fallen to my lot at dinner'. From his careful record of every item consumed, we can say with fair accuracy that the total food each man had in forty-eight days was this: seven pounds bread, one pound salt pork, one pint rum, five ounces wine, two and one-quarter coconuts, one banana, one pint coconut milk, one and one quarter raw seabirds, four ounces fish. On reaching the Australian coast, each man also consumed four pints of oysters and clams and some uncalculated amount of cabbage palm, berries and wild peas. A sailor's ordinary food allowance has been calculated at about 4,450 calories a day. On the figures I have given her, a nutritionist estimates that the launch people were reduced to 345 calories a day. This would mean a possible daily energy deficit of 4,105 calories and a total weight loss of some 56 pounds.

Added to cramps and the rheumatic pains deep in their bones that probably came from vitamin C deficiency, the men suffered cruel pain in their bowels. Bligh called it tenesmus, which is a medical term for a continual straining to evacuate the bowels. Their lack of fibre intake would have created constipation from costiveness or a hardening of the faeces. Late in the passage, when they were feeling their worst, Bligh made this reflection: 'For my part, wonderful is it for me to relate, I feel no extreme hunger or thirst. My allowance satisfies me, knowing I can have no more. This perhaps does not admit me to be a proper judge on a story of miserable people like us at last driven to the necessity of destroying one another for food, but if I may be allowed, I deny the fact in its greatest extent. I say I do not believe that among us such a thing could happen, but death through famine from any violent diseases. Served 6 oysters and 1/24 lb bread for dinner'. Hunched in the rear of his launch, sheltering his notebook and journal from spray and rain, gazing at men blankly staring at him, Bligh made this little academic aside on cannibalism at sea. He also filled the notebook with rough surveys and horizon profiles of the islands they passed. He is apologetic in his journal that circumstances do not allow the excellence of survey and description that his ordinary standards would have demanded. The fierce intensity of his will to report to 'King and Country' this voyage of discovery, interrupted now only by the mutiny, is patient. It is exclusive, too. He would not allow John Fryer a piece of paper or a pencil to make his record of what was happening. Bligh had always a sense of the power of archives.

That does not detract from his achievement. It only points to its preemptive character. We who are readers of his experience, not sufferers of it, can remind ourselves to be humble by extracting a few sentences from his journal: 'May 10. We spent a very distressing night without sleep but such as could be got in the midst of the rain. We had no relief with the day but its light. The sea was constantly breaking over us and kept two persons bailing, and we had no choice how to steer for we were obliged to keep before the waves to avoid filling the boat.' 'May 23. The miseries of this day have exceeded the preceeding. The night was dreadful. The sea flew over us with great force and kept us bailing with horror and anxiety. At dawn of day I found everyone in a most distressed situation and I now began to fear another such night would produce the end of several who were no longer able to bear it.'

On May 28, the launch came on the Great Barrier Reef in the night and had to lie along the breakers till light and then find a passage. Once through a passage into smooth waters, the men saw salvation in view. Small islands lay around and the Australian coast was on the horizon. They nonetheless waited until noon so that they could get an accurate reading of their position. Bligh thought their passage was somewhere near Providence Channel, which was the break in the reef that had saved Cook, too.

It was a sense of restrained relief that the launch people experienced on landing on Restoration Island, named by Bligh for the Restoration of Charles II, on May 29, and for the restoration of hope it gave them. As they reeled like drunken men onto the spit of white sand that was their beach, they had no strength for exuberance and little spirit for it: they still had far to go. So they divided almost immediately between those who thought they should stay to recuperate and those who thought they should go on while they still had strength. Inevitably Bligh heard these natural debates among men concerned for their lives as mutterings about whatever decision he would make in command.

Bligh was worried for their safety on the island. They found native implements of the sort they had seen in Van Diemen's Land (Tasmania). There were as well tracks of what they presumed to be a kangaroo. The skeleton of a snake was hanging on a tree. They could not be sure that they would not be visited by aborigines. Since Tofua they had fled every sight of natives whether in canoes or on land. Bligh warned them against making large fires. The first of his 'sad passions' came when a spark caused a brushfire that could be subdued only by pulling out the grass before it.

Bligh had no oeconomy for the beach. Who would gather oysters for whom? Would there be a common pot? What berries could they safely eat? How much food would be dangerous to consume in their wasted state? Again, every suggestion offered to answer these questions was seen by him as some usurpation of his authority, every difference of opinion a muttering. Every look was high hyperbole of something else.

On their first night, half of the men slept in the boat, half on shore. During the night, the gudgeon – the metal plate carrying the eye for the pin of the rudder – fell off and was lost. Had it happened in the open sea, they would have skewed in the waves and overturned. It was a startling and seemingly divine providence and it shook Bligh deeply. The next day he took himself away from everybody and sat writing in his journal. Thomas Hayward brought him a share of the food they scavenged. The men thought he was doing his maps and surveys. But he was composing a prayer, giving thanks to the Almighty and petitioning His help. Bligh inscribed it in his notebook, so that he could have it handy every morning and evening. The prayer rolls in the grand phrase of the Book of Common Prayer. All is 'we' and 'us' in mercies granted and distresses relieved. It stumbles only once into the singular – 'strengthen my mind and guide our steps'. But that is how he saw it still. His men were children, out-

siders to the oeconomy in his mind. He might have trembled, too —
except that he was not a man to see ironies — that here he was about to
enter Endeavour Straits and it was he who was eating the grass. The day
before his mutiny, that had been his terrible threat to his men of the
Bounty. They left Restoration Island within two days, seeing aborigines
on the mainland beach, shouting and hallooing at their intrusion.

Bligh was brooding again, counting those who were for him and those
who were against him. It was at the next landfall, Sunday Island, that the
ugly incident with Purcell occurred, with Bligh drawing his cutlass. No
matter what the rights and wrongs were, listen to him musing in his
journal at the logic of it all: 'The carpenter began to be insolent to a high
degree. He told me with a mutinous aspect he was as good a man as I
was. I did not see where this was to end, I therefore determined to strike
a final blow at it, and either to preserve my command or die in the attempt, and taking hold of a cutlass I ordered the rascal to take hold of
another and defend himself, when he called out that I was going to kill
him and began to make concessions. I was now only assisted by Mr.
Nelson, and the Master very deliberately called out to the Boatswain to
put me under arrest and was stirring up a greater disturbance, when I
declared if he interfered when I was in the execution of my duty to preserve order and regularity and that in consequence any tumult arose I
could certainly put him to death the first person. This had a proper effect
on this man and he now assured me that on the contrary I might rely on
him to support my orders and directions for the future. This is the outlines of a tumult which lasted about a quarter of an hour. I saw there was
no carrying command with any certainty and order but by power, for
some had totally forgot every degree of obedience. I saw no one openly
scouting the offenders altho they were known, and I was told that the
master and the carpenter at the last place were endeavouring to produce
altercation and were the principal cause of the murmuring there. Such is
generally the case under such disastrous circumstances as mine. I now
took a cutlass determined never to have it from under my seat or out of
my reach, as providence had seemed pleased to give me sufficient strength
to make use of it. I did not suffer this to interfere with the harmony of
the well disposed.'

Bligh did not publish much of this account in his *Narrative of the Mutiny* (1790). Properly so, as there was much bad language in it. He listed
in his journal the names of the nine whom he thought well disposed.

David Nelson's name headed the list. Nelson indeed was loyal, and Bligh loyal to him. When Nelson died in Timor six weeks later, Bligh wrote of Nelson's honesty, integrity, and courage, and of how he had accomplished, through great care and diligence, all the tasks he had been set by Sir Joseph Banks to do. But amid all this sad passion over oysters and cutlasses, it was Nelson who was heard to say what a damned oeconomy Bligh's was.

The last leg of the launch's voyage from Restoration Island to Timor up the coast of Australia inside the reef gave some respite. But when they turned westward through Torres Straits into open seas all the horrors of their situation returned. The sea washed over them constantly. They were never free of bailing the boat. They were still in doubt how long they would be at sea, so Bligh above their protests imposed an even more stringent oeconomy in rationing their food. Continued exposure began to ravage their wasted bodies. Bligh looked at them and wrote: 'An extreme weakness, swell'd legs, hollow and gastly countenances, great propensity to sleep and an apparent debility of understanding, give me melancholy proofs of an approaching dissolution of some of my people.' They were past caring that their divisions showed. There were thefts of food. The coordination that came from deferring to the knowledge and skill of another mate was gone. Every piece of advice, every suggestion and command was now a point of argument. The lethargy of their bodies only intensified their spite.

The wind and an ignorance of the place where the Dutch administrative centre of Kupang lay on Timor drove them down the east coast of the island. Then they beat up the west coast to its northern tip. For three days they lay in tantalising touch with their salvation, seeing the fruitfulness of the shore, arguing whether they should risk a landing. When they did land, on the last afternoon of their voyage, some 'malays' showed them that they had little distance to travel to Kupang. It was a long way, nonetheless. The wind died and they were forced to row till 1000 in the evening when they 'came to a grapnel', and, as Bligh wrote, 'for the first time I issued a double allowance of bread and a little wine to each person'. Then after three hours of 'the most happy and sweetest sleep the men ever had', they began rowing again, often making no headway, until, just before dawn, they stood off the beach at Kupang. It was a moment for which Bligh was well prepared. Somehow in the chaos of the launch he had made sketches of the flag of the Royal Navy and then managed to sew some signal flags into a Great Union flag of England and Scotland. Off the beach at Kupang, he hoisted this small jack in the main shrouds as a signal of distress. He also had his papers. On the morning of his mutiny, Samuel, his clerk, had secured his commission, his journal and the *Bounty*'s papers. 'Without these I had nothing to certify what I had due, and my honor and character would have been in the power of calumny without a proper document to have defended it.' With proper flags and papers, proprieties were established for his meeting with the Dutch governor.

The men of the launch were objects of pity and considerable charity in this isolated settlement, and they were not to be the last refugees from the *Bounty* to receive Dutch kindness. The survivors of the *Pandora*'s wreck would follow them, and find the first convicts escaped from Botany Bay. But they must have been objects of curiosity as much as pity for the Dutch, who must have wondered why their shared suffering did not make them more patient with one another. Their divisions were irreparable. They squabbled over every right and duty and propriety. Bound together now not by the sides of the launch but by the walls of the houses lent them by the Dutch, they evaluated every piece of furniture and every morsel of hospitality for what it said of what was or what was not owed to their differing statuses. Overarching all was Bligh's frenzied sensitivity about what was being said to whom about his mutiny.

To move on, these navy men without a ship must make a ship all over again and endure each other as sailor and captain once more. Bligh bought a small schooner and made of it HMS *Resource.* He left for Surabaja, giving some thought to taking John Fryer home as a prisoner, but in the end stifled his revenge. He towed the launch behind. He had some hopes, not to be fulfilled, of taking it to England. It was a precious relic of his grandest achievement.

Surabaja was even worse than Kupang. Bligh was a guest of the governor. The rest stayed aboard the *Resource,* drowning their sorrows and compounding their hatreds. Bligh, on the day of their departure for Batavia, came back to the ship to find them drunk and truculent. As usual, the incident began with the most trivial of issues. A boat crew of his officers — Peckover, Purcell, Elphinstone, Hallett, Hayward and Linkletter — had gone ashore to get provisions. They began drinking as they did so. They refused to pay out of their own pockets the penny or so for the delivery of supplies that Bligh had sent down from the governor's. In the rumpus with the Dutch and dockyard people that followed this refusal to honour a debt, the officers declared that as soon as he got home Bligh would be hanged or blown from a cannon. Now, when Bligh came aboard the *Resource,* both officers and men said openly to him, 'Yes, By God, we are used damn ill, nor have we any right to be used so'. The Dutch harbourmaster and commandant were on the deck with Bligh and heard these things. They also told him what had been said ashore.

His 'character and honor at stake', Bligh immediately demanded an official inquiry. 'It became absolutely necessary', he wrote, 'to convict these fellows where they had presumed to traduce the character of their commander.' He ordered the master, carpenter and the boat crew to be made prisoner and sent ashore for interrogation. He then formally examined Hallett, Ledward and Cole in the presence of Dutch officials. He asked them whether they had any complaint, whether he, the captain, had neglected his duty in any respect, whether he was brutish or severe, whether it was possible for him to have retaken the *Bounty,* whether they had received all their provisions. When they had answered 'no' and 'yes' appropriately, he dismissed them as 'wretches' and 'ordered them on board'. With Fryer and Purcell, he was much more threatening. Fryer in his turn was prepared to offer much more damaging evidence against Bligh. He told the Dutch that Bligh had inflated all his records of provisions in Timor to his personal advantage. The mutiny on the *Bounty,* he said, had been caused because Bligh had given short allowances and skimmed off an inflated purser's surplus. These were telling accusations to the mercantile Dutch, the sort of reprehensible behaviour in a commander they understood.

Bligh caught the true thrust of these charges and denied to the Dutch that he made personal profit out of dishonest provisioning and short allowances. He claimed in any case that his allowances were made on legal equivalents between yams and bread.

As they prepared to sail, the launch people trembled a little at how far they had gone. Fryer apologised to Bligh and begged to be taken, even in irons, and not left at Surabaja. Bligh refused to communicate with him except in writing. Nonetheless, he put the public record of these sad passions aside and did not allow them to surface in the reviews of the *Bounty*'s loss. He permitted Fryer go to Batavia on one of the prows that the Dutch officials assigned to the *Resource* as protection against pirates.

The forced endurance of one another was nearly over. Bligh was to suffer a fever in Batavia, and Elphinstone and Linkletter were to die of one there. There was a final propriety required by the Dutch if they were legally to seize the *Bounty* should it come their way. Bligh saw to it that each man signed a formal affidavit before the governor and his council testifying that the *Bounty* was lost by unforeseeable, unpreventable mutiny, that the loss of the *Bounty* was not of Bligh's causing.

By one of those chances that make us say the world is small and prompts us to muse on the inexplicable interconnectedness of things, Amasa Delano, supernumerary to trading vessels in the East Indies and close friend and shipmate of Mayhew Folger, who was to discover the *Bounty*'s colony on Pitcairn, visited Kupang, Timor, in May 1792. He found the little settlement still talking of Bligh, the *Pandora*'s crew and the escaped convicts of Botany Bay. 'All the boats but one [the launch], in which these different parties of distressed persons came to Timor were left there as a curiosity, and we saw them', he wrote in *A Narrative of Voyages and Travels in the Northern and Southern Hemispheres* (1817). He went on to reflect about the sort of gratification that knowing the history of these events might give. Their principal lesson, he suggested, was that the passions of the inner person were the true determinant of happiness – not dangers, not any kind of external circumstances.

Delano found his story of the *Bounty* and the *Pandora* in a manuscript that Captain Edwards had left with the Dutch governor. But by the time he wrote of these things in 1817, he was much more widely read in the published accounts as well as in letters from his friend Mayhew Folger. He was able to recount the widespread talk about Bligh in Timor. 'The mutineers are not so much excluded from sympathy among these gentlemen at the place', he wrote, 'as they possibly may be among those in England, who have only read the story of one of the parties.'

Delano paused for a reflection on mutiny. Being a master, he knew that no one would be surprised at his horror of mutiny. He knew the sufferings created by unjust commanders. Yet of the twenty mutinies he knew not one should have happened, because the evil mutinies created was greater than the evil they were meant to overthrow. Mutiny, he said, created trails of evils that follow generations into the grave.

Delano's reflections led him to describe what the moral oeconomy of a commander should be. Above all, a commander has to have experience and an immediate and personal sense of the wants, dangers and duties of those he commands. He needs to recognise the part feeling and passion play in all the lives of men on ships. He must know every grade of his

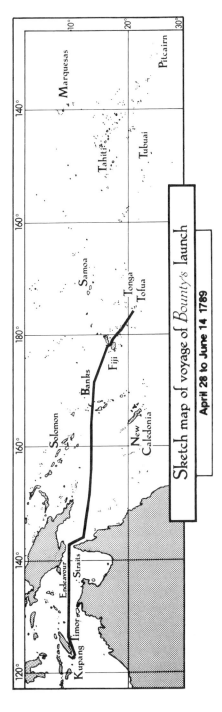

Sketch map of voyage of *Bounty's* launch

April 28 to June 14 1789

Figure 7a.

109

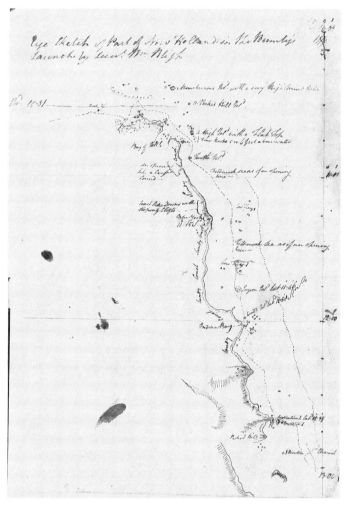

Figure 7b.

Figure 7. The launch voyage. (Art on pp. 109–11)

a. The launch voyage: from Tofua, April 28, 1789, to the Australian coast, May 29, through Endeavour Straits to Kupang, Timor, June 14. b. 'Eye sketch of part of New Holland in the Bounty's Launch' by Lieut. Wm. Bligh in *The Bligh Notebook.* (National Library of Australia. Ref: MS 5393.) c. 'The Flag' in *The Bligh Notebook.* (National Library of Australia. Ref: MS 5393.) d. Kupang. Charles Alexandre Lesueur, 'Timor. Vue de la Rade de la Ville et du fort de Coupang'. Engraving in François Péron, Voyage de découvertes aux terres *Australes. Atlas* by Lesueur et Petit. Paris, 1804, pl. 39. (Rex Nan Kivell Collection, National Library of Australia.)

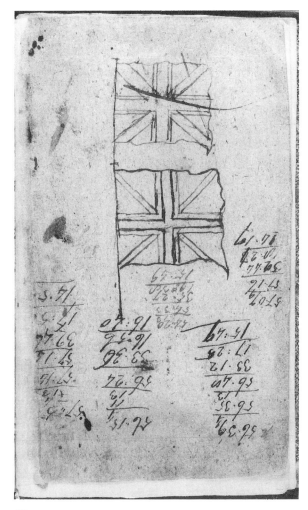

Figure 7c.

Figure 7d.

crew and oblige himself to whatever rule he obliged them. He must be consistent and give no countermand to his own orders. He must frequently seek advice but never receive any that is volunteered. He should reward merit twice for every time he punishes. He will find that justice is never a light thing. Laws must be exact and uniform.

Delano did not say whether he thought Bligh fitted this description of the rightful commander. He suspected that Bligh was still alive (which he was) and was deserving of his good character, as much as Christian was deserving of his. But he gave a context to Bligh's bad language that no other contemporary saw fit to give. It is that which prompts a Reflection on Discipline and its Texts.

Scene ii. *Reflection*

SOME CLIOMETRICS OF VIOLENCE

Suppose Emmanuel le Roy Ladurie was correct in his belief that history is only scientific if its objects of inquiry are measurable. I would hope, Reader, that shortly after being introduced to men such as Francis Pinkney, Jonas Hanway, Herman Melville and John Adams in this reflection on discipline and the unquantifiable propositions they prompt, you would think that supposition of Ladurie's correctness was too much of a concession. All-encompassing or not, scientific or not, statistics do make what Emil Durkheim called 'social facts'. The act of counting and comparing manufactures 'social facts' and gives them the illusion, once created, of reality. Because change over time and the disturbance of random chance seem to call for the play of variables that must be real, if unknown and unexperienced, 'social facts' are 'there' and need to be explained. Statistics give a sense of the industrious historian, too. Reward my industry, Reader, by not going away.

To begin our counting, let us measure the measuring. It is in the way of measuring that we must first establish a domain. Life is not long enough to do all the counting that living contains. We must set a limit. Let us make a domain of all the British naval vessels that entered the central Pacific between 1767 and 1795. There were fifteen of them. Their details are set out in the endnotes. This domain makes something of a 'period'. The period embraces the beginning and the ending of the first British opening of the Pacific to exploration, discovery and exploitation. This gives our measuring discipline a special character. Other sailors in other ships were in fleets, at war, in battle, on station, in foreign ports. We are measuring the discipline on ships whose special purpose was reflected in their special crews. The crews of the fifteen ships were mostly volunteers. Only one of the ships, the *Pandora*, was manned by impressment. She had been sent out in virtual emergency. Sailors — both merchant and navy — weighed the anticipated length of voyage against the anticipated character

113

of the captain. Volunteers negotiated in some sense the limits of their endurance. We have already seen the fourteen who 'ran' from the *Bounty* before she left England. Whatever their reasons for running, it was a sign of their negotiations. The voyages of the ships in our domain were all long, a year and more. Their crews had a continuity under one form of discipline that other crews did not have. Other British naval vessels of the time would have spent as much as 57 percent of their time in port. In a port and in a seller's market of sailor's labour, a sailor could exchange his captain with reasonable ease. The sailors in our domain had to manage the pain of the power over them more cunningly.

My counting of the floggings in the Pacific will leave me with a percentage figure of all sailors flogged. My figure may surprise you into saying 'as many as that!' Or you may shrug and say 'only that many!' My figure is 21.4 percent. I am inclined to say 'as many as 21.4 percent!' One in five of seamen who came into the Pacific experienced the brutalising effects of a full flogging. Of course, this 21.4 percent total includes extremes of variation among the ships. The percentage of men flogged ranges from 8.33 percent on Bligh's *Providence* to 45.15 percent on Vancouver's *Discovery*. The figure also includes the 12.66 percent who were flogged only once and the 8.74 percent who were repeatedly flogged, some as many as nine times. The dubious honour of being the most flogged individual went to George Reybold, a German who joined Vancouver's *Discovery* as armourer. He received a total of 252 lashes on nine different occasions.

It is the way of history to run in fashions. There is a current fashion that claims to run counter to the extravagant earlier descriptions by naval historians such as John Masefield, Christopher Lloyd and Michael Lewis of the details of the harshness of naval discipline. John D. Byrn, for example, has tried to measure the ways discipline was exacted on the Leeward Islands Station from 1784 to 1812 in his *Crime and Punishment in the Royal Navy* (1989). He surveyed seventy-three vessels and found that 'only' 9 percent of seamen were flogged. These percentages were not high, he thought, when compared with the only American figures he had at hand. They showed that one in four American sailors was flogged in 1846–7. N. A. M. Rodger's most thorough study of the Georgian navy from 1755 to 1763 during the Seven Years' War, *The Wooden World* (1986), did not measure floggings but was intent on showing that violent punishment in the navy was not out of keeping with mid-eighteenth-century notions of justice. Extravagant violence on ships, he argued cogently, was seen as undermining true discipline, not supporting it. He offered the interesting reflection that disciplinary violence grew in the last years of the century because contradictions in the structures of class and politics were intensifying. This politics of ships is something to which we shall return.

No doubt contemporaries to our period, 1767–95, would have said 'only 21.4 percent'. *Realpolitik* and commonsense were one on the point. Violence was seen as a necessary instrument of discipline on an eighteenth-century British naval vessel. Violence was seen to be extravagant only if it caused a mutiny. Admiral Lord Collingwood's observation that a captain was the cause of his own mutiny was a cliché of naval etiquette. Such hindsight, however, gave little comfort to those who were hanged or flogged for claiming that somehow a fine line had been crossed between discipline and tyranny. The commonsense logic of the necessity of violence was simple: the sort of people the sailors were and the sort of life sailors led demanded a system of punishment that was efficient, and economical of time. Physical punishment was over in the doing of it. It interfered with the running of the ship in a minimum way. 'Sailors are like granite, hard and lasting', Captain W. N. Glascock (1831) wrote in his often-reprinted manual on command, *The Naval Sketchbook.* 'The hardy mode of life, daring resolution and coarse manners of the lower orders of our island population, particularly in the natives of the seacoast are as essential to the composition of good sailors as their heedless indifference to their future and extravagant mirth and jollity exhibited on occasions of relaxation are requisite and recompense him for his many severe privations.' It was insidious charlatanism, he added, to suggest that the navy could do without flogging. There was no alternative. Confinement was not feasible on crowded ships on long voyages. Sailors liked the fact that flogging left no debt. Those punishments that sought to leave a mark on a sailor's soul rather than his back – mockery, badges of guilt, black books, leg irons – required a dangerous sort of theatre. The ambivalent product of such punishment was guilt. Guilt created that most insidious sort of crime, 'skulking'. Glascock would have agreed with John Delafons, who acted as legal adviser to Peter Heywood at his trial and was later (1805) to write a highly influential book on military law. Flogging, remarked Delafons, was a desirable form of discipline because it was not something done in revenge or for retribution. It was objective, done purely to make example.

There was a science and an art to this theatre of example. Flogging should never be done in anger. It should be administered with aloofness, because aloofness directed the gaze from the man in power to the power itself and its necessity. The occasion should immediately be expunged from memory. There should be no lingering reflections. The execution of the punishment should be done utterly by the rubrics of the Articles of War and the Regulations and Instructions. These texts were the icons of an authority that demanded deference for the punished and the punishers alike. There was to be no guilt for either. The soul would not be touched.

On board the fifteen ships we are considering there were 1,556 men. The boundary line between quarterdeck and lower deck was sometimes blurred when social considerations overrode office and rank, but we can say 16.6 percent of these 1,556 men were quarterdeck. Discipline turned about the way in which this minority managed the large majority, although it was sometimes directed towards members of the quarterdeck as well. Fines, confinement and demotion – never flogging – were their punishment. Bligh punished this category of the quarterdeck more extravagantly than any captain, for example, when he put the midshipman Thomas Hayward in irons for sleeping on watch when Churchill, Muspratt and Millward deserted. It was a mark of Bligh's discipline that we should remember. The least skilled of seamen – ordinary seamen and landsmen – formed an insignificant group in the lower deck of these ships, 4.1 percent. The greater number by far of seamen on these voyages of discovery and exploration were experienced able seamen, 52.2 percent. Another important division of the lower deck was between seamen and marines; the latter were 9.7 percent of the men.

The musters and logs of the ships made these sailors' lives measurable at the time and make them measurable still. Without specifying the myriad qualitative judgements it takes to translate the data of musters and logs into 'scientific' categories, it is possible to make a card for each of the 1,556 men and put on it: the name of each man, his age, place of origin, rank and rating, his promotion or demotion while at sea, whether he was punished and the manner, frequency, extent and cause of the punishment and its time and place on the voyage, whether he was fined 15/- for being with the 'venereals', whether he appeared on the sick list, what debits he had to the purser for tobacco, slops, bedding or dead men's clothes, what advanced wages he had received, whether he died on the voyage, drowned, was discharged or ran. We can know the dimensions of this wooden world, the size of the ships in tonnage, something of their space and time – the complement of the crew, the length of the voyage, the number of days spent at a Pacific island. We can know the personal histories of the commissioned officers.

The forms of physical punishment on a ship were many. 'Starting' – informal beatings with the rattan rope – did not get recorded in official documents. In all likelihood it was not practised where ships were small and the voyages long and the separation of the bosun and his mates from the rest of the lower deck not great. All other forms of physical punishment were officially recorded. But these other forms were infrequent enough on the ships under our consideration for us to say that flogging was the ordinary means of discipline.

Only eight men were forced to 'run the gauntlet', a brutal practice in which a man, pressed from behind by a sword and walking to the slow beat of the 'Rogue's March', passed between two rows of the whole crew and was beaten by the 'knittles' (or nettles, small lines of rope) in their hands. We will come back to one notable example of running the gauntlet. Of the eight examples, six were for stealing and two for sodomy. Sodomy, described in the Articles of War as 'the unnatural and detestable sin of buggery and sodomy with man or beast' was a capital offence with little mercy shown if there was a conviction. Three to four men a year were hanged in the navy for buggery between 1810 and 1816. As many as nineteen men in the whole navy were sentenced to death in the period we are considering, none from the fifteen ships. Running the gauntlet was probably seen as an escape from a worse fate. A few men in the Pacific got away with just a flogging for sodomy, inflicted for 'uncleanliness'.

Confinement was a slightly more frequent punishment, with nineteen cases recorded. On the *Providence* and the *Bounty* Bligh had recourse to confining more than most captains. But Cook, when faced with incidents such as men rushing into the galley to stab the cook or the careless taking of native lives, would confine men in irons, usually for a few days, but in two instances for two to three months.

There was only one incident of 'gagging', the savage practice in which a spike or piece of wood was bound across a man's open mouth. This occurred under Philip Carteret on the *Swallow*, the ship that first discovered Pitcairn – four of the incidents of running the gauntlet were on board the *Swallow* as well.

No examples of 'grampussing' were recorded in the Pacific. In 'grampussing', men had their arms bound in an elevated position. Water was then poured down their sleeves. They would exhale breath, supposedly like the sea mammal, the grampus. 'Grampussing' was often part of the crossing the line ceremonies and was probably more of a device by which the lower deck managed raw justice among themselves.

Fines were very infrequent. Only seven cases were recorded, all for neglect of duty. Mostly the fines amounted to 20/-, or about a month's pay for an A.B. There was much more chance of a man's promotion – 18.2 percent – than his demotion – 2.8 percent.

The reasons why a man was flogged varied greatly. The variety itself is some indication of the arbitrary relationship of the seaman to his institution, a sign that his subordination was thought to be total. Evans-Pritchard suggested years ago (1937) that the incentive to believe in magic came not from a lack of knowledge of the natural world's regularities but from a sense of mystery as to why chance played so much a part in life. That same sense of arbitrariness was at work on naval vessels because so many of the trivial decisions taken in the course of ordinary living were subject to violent reprisal on the personal interpretation of what a superior thought a particular social situation meant. This was the true degradation within the institution. The ordinary right to negotiate what words, gestures, actions meant was taken out of the hands of the participants and given to one man or a group of men who could impose a particular interpretation violently. The easy categorisation of behaviour as 'disobedience', 'insolence', 'mutinous' masked all the ambivalences intrinsic to them. It was in the ambivalences that the pain of power was felt and politics began.

The reasons given in the logs why men were flogged are too many to list in full. Among the most prominent were: 'insolence', 'contempt', 'provoking speech', 'disrespect', 'mutinous expressions', 'quarrelling with shipmates', 'fighting', 'disorderly conduct', 'threatening violence', 'contaminating or refusing or wasting food', 'losing or selling slops', any 'accident' created by 'neglect of duty', 'laziness', 'carelessness', or 'straggling'. Not one of these categories of behaviour was free of what Victor Turner (1982) would have called 'social drama', moments of conflict resolved by ritual performances. They each involved interpretation of complex social signals, before audiences highly skilled in their own interpretations. Making the official interpretation hold and be ritually reinforced was a matter of negotiation. We can catch some of the negotiations if we focus on a few reasons for punishment.

There were 480 occasions when men were flogged within our cliometric domain. Of these, 129 occasions were for 'insolence'. 'Disobedience', 'refusal to do duty' or 'neglect of duty' accounted for 142. 'Insolence' was a notoriously circumstantial offence; as often as not an excuse for the officer's flogging rather than a reason. Real 'neglect of duty' was, as we have seen, an acceptable reason for punishment. 'Disobedience', 'refusal to do duty' and 'neglect of duty' clearly undermined discipline, but there were countless occasions in a seaman's life when commands *should* have been ignored, because the incompetence or ignorance of the officer commanding was dangerous. There were many other occasions when a seaman had to judge whether the command was real or fleeting whim. Indeed, there were times when an experienced seaman would play to the theatre of his own peers and obey a command quite precisely, knowing his obedience would cause embarrassment to his superiors.

'Running' and 'desertion' were crimes for which a man could be hanged by the Articles of War. But as N. A. M. Rodger has written: 'desertion was an elaborate game played by relatively humane rules'. Of the 36,000 deserters he has counted, only 254 were brought to court martial proceedings. Of these men, 176 were flogged and 53 hanged. Being charged as a deserter was in one way an arbitrary act by authority and in another way a gamble by any man who would push his luck. For commanders, discipline could be improved if they played it as a game won and lost. Bligh did not play it as a game. His punishments did not improve discipline. They undermined it.

'Stealing from ship', 'stealing from shipmates', 'stealing from natives'. There were fifty-seven occasions of flogging for 'stealing' in the Pacific: five for stealing from natives. Stealing was an age-old crime in the Articles of War. In so public an institution as a ship, where there was so little space for privacy, trust that the little property personally owned was safe was critical for every man on board. Extravagant punishment for stealing from shipmates was tolerated by the men. Stealing from the ship itself and natives was another matter. In the captain's eyes, the 'ship' might have been a persona due as much respect as an individual's property, but in the seamen's eyes the ship was public and institutional, owned by an Admiralty more in debt to them than they to it. And who knew what it was to steal from natives? The whole basis of intercultural trade and relationships was a 'steal' of goods of incomparable value.

'Drunkenness' was sometimes a cause of punishment in itself. More usually it was associated with 'neglect of duty', or 'carelessness'. There were eighty-seven occasions of flogging for these combined offences. Yet if the navy chose to control men by physical punishment, it also chose to control them by alcohol. A gallon of beer a day while it lasted and a half pint of 'grog' when the beer was gone must have provided a numbing haze to the sharp pains of a sailor's life. Captains were accustomed to add to these portions-by-right. On festive occasions, to reward achievements at some times and to palliate harsh conditions on others, commanders were free with liquor. There was no shyness about it. Temperance was a virtue neither on the quarterdeck nor on the lower deck. Grog lessened the actual alcohol content of drink by being diluted with water. This diluted liquor was always a sign that the drinking was legitimate. The court martial of the *Bounty* mutineers took as sign of mutiny the fact that Christian had distributed 'drams' – undiluted liquor. With all the devious ways they had of beating the navy's systems, seamen could save their grog or trade it. A little extra sent them quickly into drunkenness and punishment. At the same time, such men had no great example from the quarterdeck. It was a rare ship whose officers were never drunk. Yet they went unpunished. Commanders could, of course, punish their men by denying them grog. One of the great ironies of naval reform in the United States in the nineteenth century was that those men who were temperate and refused the grog had no way of avoiding being flogged. For them grog was not a privilege whose deprivation could be an alternative punishment in itself. Thus the men most likely to be self-disciplined could only be flogged. There was too much irony about the role of liquor on a ship not to make drunkenness an ambivalent crime.

It was only late in the eighteenth century that the Admiralty realised how much poor hygiene was costing it in lives and efficiency. It was still later that this realisation was translated into pertinent action by its commanders. Bligh was, as we have seen, outstanding in his attachment to cleanliness, even more so than Cook. (Johann Reinhold Forster, in a comment on the hygiene on Cook's second voyage, remarked that one advantage of ducking in the crossing the line ceremonies was that sailors would get a wash!) In these matters it is not easy to forget Michael Lewis' (1960) estimates of casualties in the British navy through the twenty years of war, from 1793 to 1815. There were 103,660 dead, of whom only 6,540 were killed in action against the enemy: 84,440 men died of disease and accident; 12,680 died in wrecks and fires and explosions. Forcing men to be hygienic to save their own lives does not seem a harsh thing. But it was not easy, and it had to be managed. Hear Cook's problems with William Wedgeborough, whom he confined because there was 'strong presumptive proof of uncleanliness' (Beaglehole 1969). Wedgeborough had eased himself between decks while he was drunk. He had the choice of going to the heads in the netting over open sea at the bow of the ship or of being 'unclean'. He made his choice. That was off Easter Island. Off Erromanga in the New Hebrides he fell overboard and was revived – one wonders why! – with rum. At Tanna he shot a native while on sentry duty, and Cook put him in irons for two months. Off Tierra del Fuego in the terrible seas of Cape Horn, he was drinking with four of his comrades, went up on deck, no doubt to the heads and no doubt now well-disciplined, fell overboard and drowned. Troublesome as he seems to have been, one of his companions wrote that 'he is a fine hearty jolly fellow about 24 years of age and well respected by all his corps'. There are clear signs in the logs of some tension and resentment between Cook and the marine officers over Cook's treatment of Wedgeborough. We can read as well some sense of political management and their subtle alliances in a situation in which Cook's standards of hygiene ran counter to those socially acceptable to others.

These naval vessels in the Pacific were all in a strange environment. Any port anywhere was a place that disturbed the easy running of a ship. Being in port was always an experience that put stress on the relationships within the vessel and occasioned punishment. The punishment was not necessarily meted out in port. That could be dangerous. It would usually be saved for a time at sea. In the Pacific, the disturbing element was the island cultures themselves. The apparent hedonism of the islanders, their invitation to free sexuality, the offer of the comfort of food and climate relativised sailors to a very different experience of life. More importantly in terms of discipline, it brought down to the lower deck level an understanding of all the ambivalences of negotiating through symbols that did not work and of calling on systems that did not apply. The inability of the quarterdeck to control exchanges with the native populations put intense strain on the lower deck. It was they who had to suffer native curiosity. It was they who had to control native stealing and guard native prisoners. Often it was they who had to make instant decisions about the value of the property stolen and the value of the life of the thief. Whatever their decision, it was likely that they would be punished. It was they who had to discover some universal language to establish communications, who had to secure every piece of property against native skills in thieving they could not predict. It was they who had to bolster the reputation of empires by abstaining from sexual intercourse because they had the 've-nereals'.

We find that most seamen, nearly a third (32.7 percent) were flogged for insolence and disorderliness. They were punished for being seen to offer some explicit challenge to the power relationships with their officers. An almost equal number (29.4 percent) were flogged for not performing their duties as seamen properly. Over issues connected with food, clothing and hygiene, 3.2 percent were flogged, as were 1.8 percent for matters concerning the native populations.

There are no outstanding variables in these social facts of our counting. Age had some significance. Those who were twenty-three years old and younger were the most likely to be flogged. But the average age would only have been about twenty-five years. The space of the ship, the size of her complement, the length of her voyage, the year of her departure did not seem to affect the number of men who were flogged. A man's rating was important, however. A man was seven times more likely to be punished if he were lower deck than if he were quarterdeck. It mattered, too, what rating a man had on the lower deck; 47 percent of marines were flogged, 25 percent of able seamen. A man with venereal disease was twice as likely to be flogged as one without such a disease. Similarly, those who deserted were nearly twice as likely to be punished as those who did not try to desert. Irish and Welsh seamen were twice as likely to be punished as English and Scots. Non-British seamen were unlikely to be flogged. In the end, the figures suggest that the disciplinary environment of each ship was different.

Lower deck men must have had some expectancies of their voyage to the Pacific, some sense of the 'deep play' of their lives. We cannot say what that sense was. With the advantage of our hindsight, we could have told them that they might have expected that 15.48 percent would drown or otherwise die before the voyage was over, 5.9 percent would desert, 21.46 percent would be punished and repeatedly punished, 31.85 percent would contract venereal disease, 8.78 percent would be injured or seriously ill. Those returning for more than one voyage to the Pacific would be more likely to avoid punishment. They would have to adjust to the fact that they would likely be members of a crew numbering 104, whereas their seafaring brothers on a merchant ship of the same size could expect to be members of a crew of fifteen to twenty. These lower deck men must have known that there was much lottery in the style of management of these ships. It would have been a matter of urgent inquiry before volunteering. They must have known as well that they would have to manage a world of relationships with their commanders. That world was likely to be quite arbitrary: sometimes extravagantly arbitrary. They would have known that their only cure for that arbitrariness would be somehow to socialise their commanders to their expectancies. If they did not know the limits of their own endurance, they would have been wise to 'run' before they were tested.

Statistics will not explain the mutiny on the *Bounty,* save to show that physical violence by its commander in itself was not likely to have been the cause of mutiny. But the *Bounty* was bigger than its statistics. Unique as it was, it was part of something else. If we would understand it, we must catch in it some of the tension that Europe was experiencing as it changed it systems of social control. We must catch it up in the question of what it took to control an institution of discipline, like the navy, when those subject to that discipline were being relativised by new political experiences around them and new cultural experiences of otherness. It took management, not violence. Officers in new navies and new armies must be 'gentlemen'.

Contemporaries who wrote the first histories of the mutiny on the *Bounty* put its causes in exactly those terms. Bligh was not a 'gentleman'. In the eighteenth century, a naval 'gentleman' was a member of an emerging class meant to manage institutions of discipline. He was the professional within the officer corps of European armies and navies. A 'gentleman' had the social knowledge of how institutions worked and could sort out what was natural in those institutions from what was culturally conventional. A 'gentleman' was a good relativist because he could read the context of every absolute rule in order to know the moment of its application. A 'gentleman' was a modernist. He was the creative spirit in institutions. He made them work. He resolved the contradictions. He managed violence. A 'gentleman' did not use bad language.

Sir John Barrow, second secretary in the Admiralty for forty years from 1805 to 1845 and first historian of the mutiny on the *Bounty,* was not inexperienced in these matters. He happened also to have had connections with the Heywood family. His comments about the gentlemen on the

Bounty were therefore not unprejudiced. He put it this way: 'Seamen will always pay a more ready and cheerful obedience to officers who are gentlemen than to those risen to a command from among themselves. It is the common observation in the service that officers who have risen before the mast are generally the great tyrants. It was Bligh's misfortune not to have been educated in the gunroom of a man-o-war among young gentlemen, which is to the navy what a public school is to those who move in civil society.'

It was only technically true that Bligh rose to command from 'before the mast'. We know only the bare outlines of his early career, but clearly Sir John Barrow, in his *Eventful History of the Mutiny and Piratical Seizure of HMS Bounty* (1831), was simply repeating the gossip of the great cabins and wardroom about Bligh. Indeed, he was plagiarising as well the great naval biographer, John Marshall (1825), who was using the same sources, as much as describing Bligh's actual career. At the age of fifteen, in July 1770, Bligh was rated A.B. on HMS *Hunter* – his only previous experience that we know of was as a 'captain's servant' for a few months at the age of seven years on HMS *Monmouth* in 1762. He was raised to midshipman after six months but then, after three years of that experience, had to volunteer as AB again before being raised to midshipman on HMS *Ranger*. The signs are already there that in an institution that worked by patronage he had none at all. Rather, he was in the marginal group of boys and young men, not strictly forecastle – like Fletcher Christian, indeed – who had to prove themselves in some way to become midshipmen. At fifteen he was not extraordinarily old to begin his career, but he was older by five or six years than most of the boys were who suffered the bruising socialisation of the gunroom. Then suddenly at twenty-two years of age he was master of the *Resolution* under Cook. We do not know how or why that happened. He seems to have been something of an outsider. Much of his bitterness after the *Resolution* voyage must have been resentment of that fact. His marginality would cost him dearly his whole life long.

SOME NON-CLIOMETRICS OF VIOLENCE

The management of the arbitrariness of discipline and the everyday response of seamen to the violence done to them fall outside of statistics. Understanding comes from narrative, from sailors' yarns, if you will. Let me tell you two stories, one of discipline under Captain Samuel Wallis, one of discipline under Captain William Bligh.

Francis Pinkney was twenty-five years old when he was mustered aboard Samuel Wallis' *Dolphin* in August 1766. Wallis was to 'discover' Tahiti on that voyage and by that bring Cook and then Bligh into the Pacific. The *Dolphin's* voyage down the Atlantic was hard, long and uncomfortable. The ship was so packed with stores that the crew had to eat their way through barrels of supplies before they had room to sit down for their messes. By the time they entered Magellan Straits, they were already sick with the scurvy that was to afflict them the whole voyage long. Then the deck caulking of the *Dolphin* failed in the cold southern seas. There was not a dry hammock in the lower deck. On two-thirds allowance, the 'people' did not find the mustard, vinegar and pickled cabbage that Wallis served them palatable. But Christmas pie made of seafowl helped.

By the time the *Dolphin* had reached westward into the Pacific, Wallis had already flogged a half a dozen men for 'mutiny', 'insolence' and 'quarrelling'. Then he flogged Francis Pinkney, 'for pissing on the sails and behaving with insolence afterwards to the boatswain's mate'. What sort of gesture of defiance was that, high in the shrouds? one wonders. Enough to attract some attention to Francis Pinkney if one is reflecting on discipline.

We must return later in our narrative to the violent moments when Wallis first 'discovered' Tahiti. Let us just remark now that this first violent encounter at Tahiti was followed by weeks of blissful peace. Many of the crew, close to death from scurvy, were provided by the Tahitians with the 'most excellent food [they] ever saw'. A small camp for the sick was set up at Matavai Bay. From there the gunner traded with nails and pieces of iron for provisions. The Tahitians had no knowledge of metals. As first the sick and then the fit began to be given shore liberty, there began what the master, George Robertson, described as strictly speaking an 'old trade' rather than a new. The Tahitian women made no mystery of what they were inviting these strangers to enjoy. Nor were they shy at steadily raising the price of their trade as they realised that there were bigger and better nails available as payment. Advanced wages were of little use to the 'Dolphins'. Only larger nails would do. After two or three weeks of such exchange, a twofold crisis emerged. Inflation had depleted the gunner's ability to trade for food, while the carpenter reported that

every cleat (the two-armed metal hooks for fastening ropes) had been removed from the ship, that all nails had been gouged from the ship's side,
that no hammocks could be slung and that all had to sleep on the deck.

Wallis told the men that he would deny all liberties until he was given
the names of the crew who were thieves. Immediately, there was a storm,
'great murmuring among the people'. The lower deck was full of accusations and then declarations that it was better for some to get a dozen lashes
than all to be denied liberty. Finally, Robertson got a name by eavesdrop-
ping in the galley. It was Francis Pinkney's.

Wallis wrote in his journal. 'July 21, 1768. Three of the ship's company, Wm Welch, Taylor and Hugh Steward said that Pinkney seaman
two nights ago drew of[f] with a crow the belaying cleat of the main sheet
under the half deck and then detecting him he begged them not to tell
and he would nail it up again, however it was gone in the morning. This
he could not deny, but said he immediately nailed it in its place and that
some one else must have stole it and that as for the other cleats that were
ripped off he knew nothing of. However as he was detected in drawing it
off and on searching his chest found a great number of country fishhooks
and a collection of large shells which the inhabitants don't part with without nails or iron, which are certain he could not come by honestly. Therefore by way of example made him run the gauntlet three times round the
deck, as a proper reward for his crime. Served fresh pork and fruit.'

It is clear that Francis Pinkney was engaged in several sorts of trades.
He saw a market for whatever he brought back from so exotic a place as
'Otaheitie'. After all, his wages would be slight. If we calculate what
he owed to the purser for clothes, beds, tobacco and advanced wages
(£9/1/2) and to the surgeon for two attempts to cure him of the 'venereals'
(£1/10/0) and place that against the wages (less other deductions) he could
expect for a voyage of twenty-two months (£27/11/6), we find that he
would receive £17/0/4 for nearly two years' work. We know he was from
Neith in South Wales, but we do not know whether he was married.
Francis Pinkney's precise entrepreneurial ambitions are cloudy. But he
would not be the last of the lower deck on Pacific voyages to think he
could make something of a fortune from 'artificial curiousities'.

When Pinkney was made to run the gauntlet, he was asked by the
master, George Robertson, to name the other thieves. He refused. So he
received, by Robertson's estimate, a 'very merciful first round' from his
companions of the lower deck. Not by Francis Pinkney's estimate. Before

he started his second round, he 'began to impeach', but Robertson said it was too late to name his accomplices. This was a bad mistake on Pinkney's part. He got a 'hard drubbing' on his second run, hard enough for Robertson to excuse him from a third.

Robertson read the lesson of this collegially administered discipline to the 'Dolphins', warning them that there would be no liberty if they did not police themselves. There seemed to be no aftertaste to this discipline. Wallis, like Bligh, punished his men at one of the lowest rates (9.67 percent) among the fifteen ships of our statistics. But Wallis' punishing had a different quality to Bligh's and his discipline a different tone. There was mutual engagement of commander and men in the discipline. There was a sense of sporting realism and gamesmanship. Discipline is almost a bargain that both sides will not step over an agreed boundary. The relationship is part joking, part theatrical. The *Dolphin*'s voyage was as harsh as any into the Pacific. Perhaps its bitter and troublesome days are opaque to us, because our view of it is somewhat prejudiced by Robertson's account. His journal is the wittiest, most humane description of any Pacific naval voyage we have. But it is also true that several members of the *Dolphin*'s lower deck wrote a 'Poetic Essay' in appreciation of their voyage. It was not a very good poem, but a poem is not a mutiny.

Bligh's approach to discipline was different to Samuel Wallis'. It was not till the *Bounty* reached Tahiti that Bligh physically punished his men with any intensity. He had flogged Matthew Quintal twenty-four lashes for insolence and John Williams six for neglect of duty in heaving the lead at False Bay, Cape of Good Hope, on the voyage out. In the five months at Tahiti he ordered eleven different lashings. All these floggings, in one way and another, resulted from anomalies in relationships with the Tahitians. They were exchanges that neither Bligh nor his men could control. He, like Cook before him, gave his men a set of rules to work by. The first rule was that 'no one was to intimate that Captain Cook was killed by Indians or that he is dead'. (The Tahitians, however, knew already. The *Lady Penrhyn* from Botany Bay had visited Tahiti, and William Watts, her commander, had seen Cook killed. Someone told the Tahitians the story.) Bligh also instructed his men to treat the Tahitians with kindness and 'not to take from them, by violent means, anything that they may have stolen; and no one is ever to fire, but in defence of his life'. Each man was to take close care of everything in his charge: the value of any item stolen was to be deducted from his wages. No one was to sell goods from the King's stores or trade with the natives for provisions or curiosities except through the gunner who was in charge of all trade. Francis Pinkney's story, we can presume, was often told.

There was an irresolvable dilemma in this. A man could be flogged for having something stolen from his care and flogged as well for trying to prevent its being stolen. Alexander Smith (John Adams) was flogged for allowing the gudgeon of the launch to be taken – the same gudgeon whose replacement fell off at Restoration Island. Isaac Martin was flogged nineteen lashes for fighting with a native whom he believed had stolen an iron hoop from him. Bligh always made didactic theatre with his floggings. He always flogged his men in the presence of Tahitian chiefs, their attendants and the common people. He meant to shock the Tahitians, and he did. They always protested their horror at floggings, and whenever the punished seaman happened to be one of the crew who had formed a special relationship with one of the islanders, the Tahitians reacted in anger. It is difficult not to imagine that a flogging before one's mates and peers would be one sort of humiliation, but a flogging done with studied protocol – almost in slow motion – before a crowd of outsiders who were natives and before whom even a lower deck person held himself in superior self-esteem, was a more complete form of degradation. That sort of humiliation breeds hatred. That extravagant exemplarity is bad language.

Bligh's punishment of Churchill, Millward and Muspratt for desertion makes a useful foil for our consideration of Samuel Wallis' punishment of Francis Pinkney. Churchill was ship's corporal, while Millward and Muspratt were able seamen. Muspratt was sentinel on watch between 12.00 midnight and 4.00 A.M., January 4, 1789. Thomas Hayward, the midshipman, was master of the watch but was asleep when the three made off in the small cutter with a strand of eight muskets and their ammunition. The three had obviously some conspiracy with the Tahitians, because as soon as they landed at Matavai they were spirited away by canoe to Tetiaroa, an atoll twenty-six miles north of Tahiti. For the Tahitian chiefs, Tetiaroa was a sort of playground, where they fished and feasted.

January was the beginning of the rainy season at Tahiti. The deserters made it to Tetiaroa just ahead of a storm that then closed in on them and put them out of reach for nearly two weeks. Bligh was not greatly anxious about them. He was certain that he would get them back. The chiefs asked him nervously whether he would do what Captain Cook had done, take hostages. No, Bligh responded: he simply wanted them to bring back the deserters. His concerns were about his breadfruit plants. Nothing should interfere with their safe collection. If necessary he would have to wait until all the breadfruit was safely on board the *Bounty* and then apply pressure. He instructed the chiefs to surround the deserters in a pretended friendliness and take them.

We cannot be certain what the three men had planned. Taking arms made their desertion more serious than the other extremely common desertions that we know. They soon discovered what every beachcomber in the Pacific was to learn: that it was better to be beached naked than to come ashore with possessions. In any case they must have spent tiresome days and sleepless nights, watching what they owned. They would have had no delusions about islands of paradise. They came – or were brought back – to Tahiti. Bligh went alone to pick them up. Their canoe had capsized on the return journey from Tetiaroa, reminding them how close they lived to death in this place. They were not unhappy to see Bligh. Bligh, for his part, was remarkably calm. He had been raging all these past previous days at the incompetence of his officers. But all his descriptions of his efforts to return the deserters have a still sort of confidence. In his published narrative the desertions were almost an aside amidst his ethnographic interests and his concern to describe the mysteriousness of primitive emotions. He had chanced on a houschold wailing their grief for a dead child, only to see them go into fits of laughter at his presence. He was more concerned to note the stupidity of one of the land party – either Peckover or Christian – in putting a cluster of *tutui* nuts from a *marae* over the trading tent. The intention had been to 'taboo' or forbid entry by the islanders. The effect was to put the whole area under a real *tabu* which could be relieved only by priestly rituals. He did not record anywhere that Churchill had left a piece of paper in his chest with three names on it, that one of those names was Christian's and that Bligh himself had questioned each member of the shore party, finally accepting their ignorance of any reason why their names should appear on a list left by a deserter. In the end Churchill was given only half the lashes that Millward and Muspratt received. That is curious too.

Bligh had careful plans for punishing the three deserters. He was meticulous in all the formal rubrics of a flogging. He flogged Churchill once with twelve lashes and Millward and Muspratt with twenty-four, and repeated these floggings a month later. Thomas Hayward, the midshipman who had been asleep on watch during the desertion, he put in irons for the month between the floggings. At the floggings he added this speech to the reading of the Articles of War: 'An officer with men under his care is at all times in some degree responsible for their conduct; but when from his neglect men are brought to punishment while he only meets with a reproval because a public conviction by trial will bring both into a more severe and dangerous situation, an alternative often laid aside with lenity, and sometimes necessity, as it now is in both cases; it is an unpleasant thing to remark that no feeling of honor or sense of shame is observed in such an offender'.

Bligh had by then had the letter from Churchill, Millward and Muspratt thanking him for not sending them to court martial. It was an important letter in Bligh's eyes, probably because he thought it showed his long-suffering lenience. His speech was directed not so much against the deserters as towards Hayward and all the petty officers. Article 27 of the Articles of War read: 'No person in or belonging to the fleet shall sleep upon his watch, or negligently perform the duty imposed on him or forsake his station, upon pain of death or such other punishment as a courtmartial shall think fit to impose, and the circumstances of the case shall require'. Bligh was warning them that the stakes of their incompetence were high. No doubt the letter was important to Bligh also as a self-serving legalism excusing him from acting beyond his rights in giving forty-eight lashes. But I beg to suggest that his use of it was bad language. It drew attention to Bligh's personal intervention. It invoked gratitude. There was no sense of play in it. Here was no sporting gesture, no engagement of the crew in its own punishment. I imagine that the grievance that Churchill, Millward and Muspratt felt was very different from that which Francis Pinkney felt. Francis Pinkney had nowhere to go for sympathy. Samuel Wallis made all the 'Dolphins' innocent through Pinkney. Bligh made the whole *Bounty* guilty in Churchill, Millward and Muspratt.

IUDICATIO (LAW) AND *COERCITIO* (FORCE)

Edward Gibbon, musing on the success of Roman military institutions, made the frequently quoted remark that 'it was an inflexible maxim of Roman discipline that a good soldier would dread his officers far more than the enemy'. Gibbon found Roman military discipline curiously effective in that it fostered courage and commitment among men who had no virtue – at least, not the sort that came from being citizens with a strong sense of their own interest in the preservation and prosperity of free government. Nor was it the sort that came from class or occupation. Gibbon thought the effectiveness of discipline came from the strong play on honour and religion in the army. Roman soldiers had the conviction, he argued, that glory was not personal but was sublimated to the company, the legion or the army. They took an oath that sacramentalised these sublimations – made them efficacious. The word 'sacrament' comes from the transforming power of these soldiers' oaths *(sacer)*. They knew with absolute certainty that punishment would follow any breach of the rules to which they had sworn obedience.

The editor of Gibbon's *Decline and Fall of the Roman Empire*, J. B. Bury, collected these reflections of the great historian under the annotation 'Discipline'. 'Discipline' is a curious word. The Oxford English Dictionary, in a more discursive note than is its practice, claims that the word's etymology needs to be understood in the antithesis found between 'disciple', who is to be trained, drilled, practised, disciplined, and 'doctor', whose quality is to teach, expound, theorise. There is in discipline the sense that actions and their repeated practice shape the man. External obedience moulds internal spirits. Monks flogged themselves with what they called a 'discipline' – what the navy would call a 'cat-o'-nine-tails'. Self-inflicted pain bowed the will. In military institutions routine, unthinking obedience and coordination forge otherwise disparate individuals into a weapon of power. Discipline is something navies and armies cannot be without.

Embedded in the notion of discipline in military institutions is another set of antitheses. It is the Roman opposition between *coercitio* which, without prejudice to the arguments among Roman historians as to the historical meaning of the word, we can equate with the force of discipline, and *iudicatio,* law. Roman scholars will say that the key to understanding the antithesis is in the terms *provocatio* and *imperium militiae. Coercitio* was the power of the magistrates to compel obedience without appeal *(provocatio)* to some more fundamental power, and was the principle of government in the *imperium militiae,* the army. It was also the governing principle in the provinces, that is, the whole world outside the walls of Rome. The distinction between discipline (*coercitio,* the power to compel obedience absolutely), and law (*iudicatio,* the determination of rights), is one that has teased human ingenuity to describe – to textualise in legislation and constitution – and to act out – to reify in symbol and ritual. Institutions of discipline – armies, navies, religious orders, prisons – sit uncomfortably alongside institutions of law – parliaments, citizenship – because in a modern state, as in the emerging modern states of the eighteenth century, there is no 'outside the walls of Rome'. Citizenship and its politics touch everyone. Institutions that see themselves as 'outside the walls', that rely on *coercitio*, hold a contradiction. They cannot escape a politics, when compulsion is continually negotiated in manufactured sets of rules.

Yet there is a commonsensical character to institutions of discipline that says they can have no politics, no negotiating power within them. The fact of their necessity seems to fill them with natural, even universal, signs. They have, it is supposed, their own intrinsic logic. In principle they must invert the civil order. In military institutions, the individual exists for the group, not the community for the individual.

From the earliest military laws of which we have texts till today's, the 'articles' are much the same. They denounce and punish desertion, straggling, malingering, insubordination, disobedience, theft, conspiracy, sedition, breaking lines, negligence of guard duties. It seems natural that these would be the capital sins of military life. And the principles of human behaviour on which they are based seem just as natural. Masses of human beings are susceptible to the example of single individuals, and, therefore, the fiercest discipline is directed at the weakest. Similarly, rigidities of command need to be externalised, so the institution is carefully landscaped in some way – in the formalities of a Roman camp, in a quarterdeck. Or to take a third example, when men are opened to one another and stand unprotected by ordinary walls of privacy or property or kin, then they are helpless to a hidden enemy in a thief. So discipline marshalls itself savagely against antisocial acts within the group.

But the domains of cultural existence are not absolutely distinct. Even though institutions of discipline, such as an army in its camp, or a navy ship at sea, can win a degree of separation and operate under *coercitio*, they and institutions of law merge. They do so in the cultural persona of the individual. Then power, in the face of being textualised and managed, confronts the contradictions of these institutions.

At the end of the eighteenth century, these contradictions were becoming more marked. Upper classes, fearing revolutionary times, feared politics in their institutions of discipline the more. *Coercitio* and *iudicatio*, always juggled, were now being balanced within a new spirit of management abroad. Now one was expected to be a commander who was at the same time a manager of men under discipline. One must study the science and art of being a true 'gentleman'. There were many dreams and manuals of true discipline to be read.

DREAMS OF PERFECT NAVAL DISCIPLINE

The *Bounty* was larger than her statistics, we have claimed. Understanding her and the events aboard her takes us well beyond her decks. At risk of distracting from the narrative, but in the firm belief that I better understand – and will help the reader understand – the *Bounty* by doing so, I reflect on the language of institutions of discipline and violence. I am impressed with what Peter Stallybrass and Allon White have written in *The Politics and Poetics of Transgression* (1986). 'Patterns of discourse are regulated through the forms of corporate assembly in which they are produced. Alehouse, coffee house, church, law court, library, drawing room of a country manor [and naval vessel]: each place of assembly is a different site of intercourse requiring different manners and morals. Discourse space is never completely independent of social space and the formation of new kinds of speech can be traced through the emergence of new public sites of discourse and the transformation of old ones.' Institutions of discipline were discovering their modernity in the transforming period of the revolutionary age by creating a language that both described and created relations of power. If we would know why Mr Bligh's language was 'bad' we should hear what language was 'good'.

There was one dreamer, at least, who thought that the navy would solve its problems of discipline by being provided with men already disciplined. He was Jonas Hanway. At the end of the eighteenth century, there were manuals aplenty on how to be a midshipman, a lieutenant or a captain. Jonas Hanway dreamed of shaping the souls of ordinary seamen to make them obedient. He was the embodiment and expression of a new episteme of discipline.

Thomas Carlyle remarked of Jonas Hanway that he was a 'dull, worthy man', 'not always so extinct as he has now become'. Indeed, there is a feeling of the fossil in the vast library of Hanway's works, unread, unreadable as they are. He retired from merchant's business in Russia, Portugal and Persia in 1750, aged thirty-eight years, to nurse, he believed, his bad

health for the little time he had left. Then for thirty-six years he laboured
tirelessly on good works of every kind and, even more frenetically, dic-
tated his thoughts to weary clerks: one poor scribe reported ninety octavo
pages in a single forenoon. His works, sometimes four volumes tediously
long, are still to be found tucked into every category of humanity's cosmology that the ingenuity of librarians has discovered. Indeed, even if he
has been extinct for a while, he will have resurrection if modern fads look
for a prophet, for he had much to say on the dangers of tea and of tobacco
smoking, the virtues of wholemeal bread, and of paved, cleaned and lighted
streets, the social evil of giving vails (or tips), the benefits of solitary
confinement in prison, and on the harmful stress created by the repetitive
labours of the poor, especially chimneysweeping. If we smile at the diver-
sity of Hanway's passionate interests, only sampled here, we should also
remember that he was much inured to laughter. For thirty years he had
been the object of derision as he walked the streets of London eccentrically
under an umbrella. London was not yet ready for such novelty.

Jonas Hanway was a man of calculating charity. He was always com-
piling statistics. He had discovered in this era of Adam Smith's *Wealth of
Nations* just how appealing the ironic realism of economics was. Complain
to him that saving a foundling cost the state £86/5/- and he would counter
with calculations showing that with the working expectancy of twenty-
three working years such a foundling would earn £412/7/5. Thus the
nation would profit £326/2/5 on its outlay. 'Political humanity', 'theoretical practice', 'play-game' were favourite phrases of his. They were at the
core of his notions of discipline. They all concerned the relation between
an external world and an internal order. It was Hanway's thesis that sim-
ulation, action, practice created and reflected order at the same time.
Dialectics was not a word he used, but he obviously held that external
discipline and internal order were dialectically related.

Hanway found much to be humane about, much on which to exert his
'political humanity'. Children held an important place in his plans. Suspicious because the mortality rate of infants in parish workhouses was
high, he culled parish records and discovered parishes where, through
twenty and thirty years, the mortality rate was 100 percent or 80 percent.
His 'political humanity' was his long parliamentary battle to create an
efficient parish registration system. Correct figures let him make the politics with which to lash criminally neglectful overseers.

He had begun his charities with 'waifs at sea'. Hanway knew that a naval vessel of sixty guns and four hundred men had a complement of thirty boys who acted as servants to the ship's officers. These thousands of boys in the navy were the 'lice and vermin' of the ship, desperately poor, educated to nothing but vice, pitiable objects of violent carelessness. They belonged with that other forlorn group on a naval vessel – landsmen, who, pressed or volunteered, were scorned by skilled seamen and served as the focus of every tyranny on a ship. Jonas' brother, Thomas, a sea-captain himself, had made a discovery. If landsmen came to a ship uniformly well-dressed, they were much more respected, showed more discipline and learned the seaman's trade in a third of the ordinary time. To Hanway, this was 'theoretical practice'. Dressing in a 'kersey Pee Jacket', a pair of 'drab breeches', 'a seaman's worsted hose', 'a waistcoat with slashed sleeve' itself made order. With these ideas, Hanway helped found, and then sustained with extraordinary energy, the Marine Society. In its first fifty years – he was most active in thirty of them – the Marine Society supplied the navy and merchant service with some 30,000 boys and 30,000 landsmen, each fitted out with a double set of clothing, bedding, needles, threads and knife, a *Seaman's Monitor* and the Bishop of Tuam's *Christian Knowledge,* and a bag to put them all in. It was a massive enterprise of 'political humanity' and was an outcome of Hanway's notions of discipline. Its function was the 'removing of those who are vagrants, pilferers or by extreme poverty and ignorance, are pernicious to the community, to encourage the industrious poor to send their children to sea, and to assist the captains and officers in the sea service in providing them with stout lads as servants'. Just as important in Hanway's eyes was the function of the Marine Society as an active, private charity. 'Instead of continuing means [of the wealthy classes] to pillage a state', the society helped 'to diffuse an active, benevolent, a martial and a concordant spirit which is now become essential to our very being'. Hanway's boast was that in providing efficient and economic organisation, in tapping expertise, and in exercising economies in purchase, he was proclaiming useful virtue. The stipends of the treasurer, commissioners, secretaries, clerks and porters, as well as house rent, entertainment, firewood, candles, paper, pens and ink cost the society less than a hundred pounds a year. The healthy soup he invented made subscription banquets more profitable. The 'gold tickets' that theatre managers donated to subscribers spiced charity with the acquisitive spirit. This was a firm principle of Hanway's utilitarian soul: in order for benevolence to work, it must be self-interested both individually and nationally.

Religion had a critical part to play in Jonas Hanway's 'theoretical practice', in his externalising of principles by action. Uniform clothing, in his eyes, was something of a sacrament of discipline on a ship. Uniformity created order in the signs of it. How much more were the true sacraments of the church 'theoretical practice' of the supernatural. He was much dismayed that taking communion was in such disuse among the poor. Above all communion created deference to an ecclesial order of things. God was mediated by the church in the priest. Obedience to thousands of trivial practices gave discipline to the church, as it gave discipline to a ship. 'No Christian could be a rebel' was one of Hanway's phrases. One of the paths to rebellion in his eyes was Methodism. He took himself one day to Tottenham Court Road to hear John Wesley preach. He was dismayed that 'any man bearing the name of minister should demean himself like an inhabitant of Bedlam'. Wesley, with a 'low kind of language', made cobblers, tinkers and old women 'feel the love [of God] in their hearts as they might do a cudgel on their heads'. Religious experience by that became 'feeling'. Worse, it was unmediated feeling. The poor, the ignorant, full of fancies and wild opinions, were 'determined to take everything in a literal sense'. 'Theoretical practice' required a sense of metaphor and guided interpretation. 'We are not sensible that God does, nor has he told us that he will, usually manifest himself in any extraordinary acts of his power, or display of his presence: he leaves us to discern him in the order of his works and in the regular government of his providence. He has given us his Written Word as the standing rule of our religious conduct. In interpreting and applying this rule, we must make use of our understanding, cultivated in the best manner we are able and furnished with all the helps we can procure. What assistance from his good Spirit he is pleased to give us for apprehending this rule, or living suitably to it will doubtless be given in such a way as is consistent with our liberty, and the free exercise of our own faculties'. Not just a Utilitarian Man, Jonas Hanway, but a modernist as well.

The *pièce de résistance* of Jonas Hanway's 'political humanity', 'theoretical practice' and 'play-game', his 'utmost effort to balance moral and political interest of individual and common welfare' was his

Proposal for County Naval Free-Schools to be built on Waste Lands, giving

such effectual Instructions for Poor Boys as may nurse them for the Sea Service,
teaching them also to cultivate the Earth, that in due time they may furnish their
own food; and to spin, knit, weave, make shoes, etc with a view to provide their
own raiment, while good regulations and discipline diffuse a moral and religious
Oeconomy through the Land (1783).

Hanway published this elaborate vision of how to sacramentalise discipline in 1783 in two editions, one deluxe, the other ordinary. It was, he
thought, the crowning vision of his career. As always, Hanway's arguments began with statistical facts. The navy needed by its own rules of
rating 6,666 'boys' a year to act as servants to officers and perform menial
tasks. If the nation had fifty county schools each of a hundred scholars and
six 'free scholars' (gentlemen's sons who would act as division captains and
pay thirty pounds per year for their tuition), the system would provide
5,000 ordinary boys and 350 elite boys. There were eight million acres of
wasteland in England, of which 5,000 acres could easily be spared to serve
as landscapes that would be exemplary of how the whole land could be
made productive. The nation's naval problem was that it needed huge
numbers of seamen only in wartime. Those seamen needed employment
on land in time of peace. A perfect schooling system would pay for itself
while preparing its scholars for both war and peace. The best preparation
was 'theoretical practice'. So the school needed a garden, a farm, a building where manufacturing skills such as weaving could be taught, and –
it was his proud invention – a 'Land-ship' for learning seamen's skills.
The garden, in order to feed 106 scholars and their instructing officers,
needed 135,500 plants put down in double rows four inches apart and
sixteen inches long. There needed to be seven other farm divisions, one a
nursery of trees, one each for turnips, barley, peas and wheat and two for
clover. All were to be rotated in a five-year cycle. The schoolhouse would
need a Dining Deck, a Working Deck and a Sleeping Deck, all with low
ceilings as in a first-rate ship. He argued, being utilitarian to the last
farthing, that it would also be a less expensive building that way. It
would need suitable mottos on walls, such as: 'Eat like a man: devour not:
and be thankful', 'Cleanliness is Virtue', 'Speak out and be Pardoned'.

Since the poor ate too much meat and drank too much liquor, the diet
of the boys would be exemplary: one-third animal foods, one-third vegetable, one-third farinaceous. The 'Land-Ship' would be a workable model
set on a great spindle, so that it could turn in the wind as the boys set its
sails. Its cannons would be wooden, however. There would be separate

capstan, anchoring and steering machines. There was to be nothing of 'anything that bears the name of science' in the schooling, Hanway wrote. Everything would be _bricolage,_ pottering. The women of the poor, he believed, did the writing in their households. The boys, therefore, needed to learn only to sign their names. But the boys would be instructed to read. Reading would be taught out of the New Testament in order 'to learn the contentment and subordination that are attributes not only essential to earthly government, but also to the hopes of everlasting felicity, and are as necessary to the security of peace, or to the permanence of liberty'. He did not want the boys when reading to put on any affected tones. They must learn to read in their ordinary conversational voices. The playing of drum, fife, as well as jovial songs would 'invite all to lively labour on the earth in handling their spades, houghs, pickaxes, rakes, wheelbarrows and other implements of husbandry', and 'render work as play'.

All these plans were only dreams. They had grown out of Hanway's experience at the Maritime School at Chelsea where he had established most of the institutional rules and customs he elaborated for the Naval Free Schools. But whether Hanway's dreams eventuated or not does not matter. I cite them not for their practice but for their spirit. Anyone will recognise in them the changed episteme of discipline to which Michel Foucault drew our attention. Discipline to be true, Hanway was saying, had to reach into the inner man. Violence was unnecessary and a mark more of failure than an instrument of success. But self-discipline also came from outside, from 'play-games' and 'theoretical practice'. Hegemony came from the seeing, really seeing, the rationality not of discipline but of commonsense.

In Hanway's scheme of things, 'stripes' were to be avoided as much as possible. They were, in any case, the 'least severe' of all punishments. 'They may not operate on a base mind', wrote Hanway, 'because it is base; and on a generous spirit shame will obtain the end'. He offered instead of 'stripes' a series of shaming punishments. First there was the 'Penitentiary Chair', set in the corner of the Dining Room. The 'condemned offender' was to stand on the chair while the rest of the boys ate dinner. In the second level of punishment the offender was to be given a black coat and made to proclaim in an audible voice before grace: 'I am sorry and ashamed of my fault, and promise to be more watchful of my conduct for the future'. Finally, and for serious offences such as stealing, falsehoods and bad language, there would be hours or days in solitary confinement in the

'Penitentiary Room', with the culprit living on bread and water, doing work or reading books and being visited twice a day for moral instruction. Only after that were there stripes and expulsion.

Whatever the punishment, every solemnity was to be observed in order 'that the example may strike'. There was always to be some rhetorical statement made as well. A 'Captain's Harangue' (and every other speech and protocol) was carefully created and printed. 'You are sensible, my boys, that were I to be inattentive to discipline, you could have no school. This boy, who has offended, has acted as if he was his own enemy, as well as yours and mine. Though I perceive by your countenances, your sorrow to see him in this condition may lead you to forgive him, and my compassion inclines me to the same way, but the laws of the school, and the orders of the Directors must be obeyed. There is no departing from this: and it is better that one should be exposed to distress, than the great number suffer for his sake. Learn from his misfortune and avoid falling into the same, and other offences, for they will surely be attended with bad consequences.'

True discipline, as distinct from punishment, was something entirely more positive. It came from rewards and praise and competition. It came from the elevation of 'pattern boys' as shining examples. It came from dividing boys into small groups and creating the conditions of close living arrangements that promoted allegiance, competition and watchfulness of one boy for another.

Of course, 'jovial songs' set to popular tunes and 'cleared of the patronage of Bacchus and Venus' played their role, or so Jonas Hanway – who was utterly tone-deaf – thought.

Song XXXI 'For the Discipline and Concord of the School' went:

> What is man without invention?
> Little better than the brute!
> Sloth's the parent of dissension
> Virtue stops not to dispute.
> And curious eye will find
> Discipline's the path to glory
> Pride the curse of human kind.
>
> Happy then beyond expressions
> Are the pupils of this school
> Where good nature and discretions
> Over willing subjects rule!

> Taught by masters every duty
> That can gild our riper days
> Our confidence in its beauty
> Shews with zeal how we obey.

Hanway was not a man to waste a thought. All the rules of these Naval Free Schools that never materialised were at work in other forms – in his Maritime School at Chelsea, his Foundling Home, his Magdalen Hospital, in the institutions where he collected boys and landsmen for the Marine Society. One naval historian has remarked that these rules were likely to raise 'prigs' and were irrelevant to the true education received in the gunroom and missing, according to Sir John Barrow, in the education of William Bligh. How effectively they created discipline or could have created it, we do not know. It is a puzzle for us to measure Hanway's cliché and rhetoric. His discipline was so didactic it could well have created prigs. Or maybe it would have created 'one-dimensional man'. It would be a mistake, however, to judge Hanway's measures to be ineffective because they were so transparent. There was a seismic shift taking place in the language of power and discipline. The clichés we see from 200 years later were discoveries of a managerial language. Such language, I think, was no cliché for Bligh, and no discovery either.

MIDSHIPMANSHIP

Across two navies, the British and the United States, the midshipmen were the most anomalous figures of discipline. They belonged to the quarterdeck. By that fact their superiors were bound to them. But they had little experience of enforcing discipline upon the ranks below them and little authority for their power. The lower deck could hate midshipmen for the humiliations they imposed, while at the same time the quarterdeck could be embarrassed by the loyalty it had to extend to them. Midshipmen needed to be properly educated to their status. Christopher Claxton offered them (and their parents) one set of protocols in his manual, *The Naval Monitor: Containing many useful hints both for the public and private conduct of young gentlemen in, or entering, that profession in all its branches – in the course of which and under the remarks on gunnery, are some observations on the naval actions with America, also, A plan for improving the naval system as far as it regards that most useful set of petty officers, the midshipman* (London, 1815).

Claxton's advice to midshipmen was full of the commonsense of military institutions. The essence of learning command was to have a Machiavellian prudence on the inside of one's head and shining enthusiasm on the outside. 'Strive to do everything better than everybody else', he wrote, much in the fashion, one suspects, that Dale Carnegie would have written had he been of the eighteenth century. 'Never lose an opportunity of volunteering. . . . The more hazardous and difficult the more credit.' 'Never admit an idea of not succeeding to enter your head. Want of confidence in yourself, if you feel it, will shew itself in your countenance.' 'It is a great blessing that British sailors have no thought or reflection. Men naturally look up to officers, particularly if they know him to be good.' 'To have the real glow of animation and confidence painted on your countenance, it is almost necessary to be in love with the enterprise. A gallant and confident inward feeling will display an animating, bold and encouraging exterior.'

Never walk, always run. Never take the slightest liberty with the men. Never reply to reproofs. Never refuse to dine or breakfast with the officers when you are invited. Never strike a seaman. 'The sting of the blow is felt much longer than the outward pain it inflicts. . . . Nothing can palliate it. It is subversive of good order, discipline and regularity as it is disgraceful.' Be religious, but 'make no outward shew, profess nothing unless you are asked and then with conscious rectitude declare your precepts'. Hear as little as possible and betray still less knowledge. Take bitter pills with a wry face. 'If you say you will punish, abide by your word or your threat will be treated with derision, and be careful in your mode of punishment that you do not allow passion to get the upper hand of your reason.'

For Claxton these virtues of gallantry, enthusiasm and animation were natural. A boy must have some sense of them initially, but they were a learned art as well, dependent on the boy's ability to read the institution around him. There was a fine line between what was the real world and what was theatre in the presentation of self. The successful officer moved easily back and forth across that line without any sign of artificiality. As subordinate to his superiors, he exchanged his own independence for their patronage and approval. As a superior to those he commanded, he allowed them their independence in exchange for their respect. He disciplined himself as much as them.

CAPTAINING

Learning the shades of meaning of captaining at the end of the eighteenth century was both an art and a science. But the accepted prejudice was that the art was experiential – in the gunroom, not the classroom – and that the science was merely reflection on that experience. The captain's was a unique role in the unnatural society of the ship. Distance, solitariness and the flat horizon of the sea in every direction drew that society in on itself. The hazards of the sea were so great, the need for efficiency and system so obvious, that there was always a primitive social contract among sailors to defer to controls that made a machine of their bodies. If the metaphor of sailors as children came easily for captains, the metaphor of captains as fathers came just as easily to sailors. Even in the moments of severest political conflict, the mutineers at Nore were not embarrassed to call the admiral or captain they admired 'father of the fleet' or 'father of the ship'. Richard Dana (1840) put it another way. 'There were no fancies about equality on board ship', 'nor wish that the power of captains be diminished an iota'. Samuel Richardson, a warrant officer who, as James Dugan (1965) notes, sailed on hell ships and happy ships, put it another way still: 'Seamen are greatful for good usage and yet like to see subordination kept up as they know the duty could not be carried out without it'.

Admiral Edward 'Grog' Vernon, famous in the navy of the early eighteenth century for the ways he drilled the captains of his fleet in manoeuvres, tried to describe what others called 'that more gentlemanly spirit' that had been 'gradually gaining ground in the navy'. From the first quarter of the century the 'gentlemanly spirit' had been accompanied by a steady discontinuation of the 'coarseness of language and demeanour which disfigured too many of the old school'. Vernon himself was hardly thought to be temperate in his speech, but he estimated that it was 'necessary that a sea officer should have some natural courage, but it is equally just that he should have a good share of sense, be perfect master of his business, and have some taste for honour; which last is usually the result of a happy education, moderate reading, and good company, rarely found in a man raised on the mere credit of being seaman' (Vernon 1958).

It was an error, he added, to think that all captains needed was brute courage without the 'fine qualities of men'. Such a notion made 'no distinction between the judgment, skill and address of a Blake, and a mere fighting blockhead without ten grains of common sense'. 'Common sense', we can see, was something 'gentlemen' needed; how 'happy education, moderate reading and good company' graced such 'common sense' was left unclear. My guess is that these were Grog Vernon's words for the moderating and liberating consequences of a certain type of understanding; institutions needed to be invented by compromising actions as much as cloned in unthinking repetition. At least that reading fits with Vernon's nickname Grog. Grog was a mixture of rum and ship's water (of the colour of Vernon's grogram green cloak) that he introduced to the navy as satisfying the sailor's institutional right to half a pint of liquor a day, but at the same time compromising its wild effects. It coincides too with the understanding held by heroic commentators on the art of naval discipline, such as Lord Cuthbert Collingwood, who saw that violent tyranny was uncommonsensical and believed that captains brought on their own mutinies. Vernon was writing, of course, of what should be the gentleman's artful enforcement of discipline. His raw view of what discipline actually was in the navy was a little different: 'Our fleets are defrauded by injustice, manned by violence and maintained by cruelty.'

There were others who reflected on the science of managing these institutions of the navy without the violence that could only be counterproductive. Rear Admiral Richard Kempenfelt was one. He drowned in his own great cabin in the harbour at Spithead in August 1782 when the bottom literally fell out of his vessel, the *Royal George*. He was a loss the navy could ill afford as it approached decades of turmoil. Kempenfelt's models for proper discipline in the management of ships came from what he would have called practical reason, but there is a suggestion that he was touching on something more universal in the nature of total institutions. He had a sense of the changing episteme of discipline. Kempenfelt was a reading man. Perhaps his reading included Gibbon. He cited the Roman maxim that 'discipline gives more force than numbers' and went on to argue that 'the only way to keep large bodies of men in order is by dividing and subdividing them, with officers over each, to inspect into and regulate their conduct, and discipline and form them' (Barham 1906). 'At all other times [occasions other than meals, repose, washing and mending] they should be kept constantly employed, and whatever they are exercised about, be particularly careful that they do it with attention and alertness and perfection.' They should be in uniform. Young landsmen should know every rope in the ship within the first six weeks at sea. Religion was essential, especially because British seamen were 'more li-

centious than those of other nations'. Just as the French and Spanish navies had their men observe matins and vespers, so the British should have
morning and evening prayers. 'Don't let anyone imagine that this discipline will disgust the men and give them dislike for the service; for the
very reverse will be the consequence. Sobriety, cleanliness, order and regularity, the conveniences resulting from these to them, will convince [them]
that they tend as much to their particular benefit as to the public service.
. . . With order and discipline you would increase your force; cleanliness
and sobriety would keep your men healthy; punishments would be seldom
as crimes would be rare.'

Kempenfelt stressed division into supportive social groupings, perfection in performance of the most trivial task, uniformity, preoccupation
with cleanliness and smartness, the regular expression of religious belief
and a spirit of competition. We, more knowing in the ways of control of
mass and military behaviour, would count these sentiments as platitudes
of total institutions. He, however, had a sense of discovery – not original,
but new in his making it explicitly relevant to reflections on systems of
control. He was, in that respect, the embodiment of G. Teitler's thesis
on officers in his study *The Genesis of the Professional Officer's Corps* (1977)
as it was being found throughout Europe. The stress on high technical
competence, on esprit de corps achieved through an idealisation of tradition and a code of honour, and on a discourse that repeatedly pointed to
services that navies and armies of Europe were rendering to the state were
the common elements in the evolution of a specialised social group,
'gentlemen', who sought to develop new notions of discipline. This new
discipline depended not on violence but on men accommodating to what
was observed to be 'natural' in human behaviour. In the last decades of
the eighteenth century, when the separate domains of social existence
were becoming less distinct, the essence of the new discipline was to
segregate the institution, to make it apolitical and amoral within itself,
and to focus the gaze of its member on itself.

Physical violence in this discourse and practice of discipline was not so
much the last resort, the final control. Physical violence was the guarantor
of the apolitical and amoral character of the institution. In the hands of
'gentlemen' it was clean, clinical, ordinary, formal. Its function was not
reform or the remission of guilt. It was impersonal, leaving no indebted-
ness to leniency, no distracting anger at excesses. It was theatre of discipline, not of law. One individual being flogged, alone and without allies,

played out the ultimate deference to naked power in the captain on the quarterdeck.

The 'bad language' of physical violence was twofold. Using it often and wantonly as an instrument of social control created politics. Engaging it with moralism opened windows on souls and let hatred and anger escape. It made discipline personal. Bligh's 'bad language' was never the first, but it was the second.

Politics are destructive of discipline. Lord Howe, who successfully resolved the first phase of the Great Mutiny of 1797 by being a 'gentleman' in all the ways we have discussed, saw politics as the greatest danger to discipline. He remarked that he could 'hardly imagine consequences more necessary to guard against than those not unlikely to be expected from the introduction of delegates amongst us'. Delegates were politics: they decentred the system of discipline. The landscape of power within the fleet or on a single ship demanded that no man speak for somebody else, that all individually and separately fix their gazes on the quarterdeck as the real presence of absolute authority. Teitler has argued that the professional officers corps demanded such sublimation to a central state. This need of discipline was mirrored on the ship and was reinforced by the metaphor of the 'king's commission' in the persons of the captain and the lieutenants. The theatre of the quarterdeck was directed at making the ultimate power of the King so nakedly present that inattention and neutrality were, equally with disobedience, acts of mutiny.

A 'gentleman' needed to sustain the drama of that presence without letting it slip into the environment of symbols that passed unnoticed. But equally importantly a 'gentleman' needed to avoid 'crying wolf'. It is an old adage of institutions of discipline that he who needs constantly to claim he has authority has not got it at all. Bligh had little sense of the occasions when he might make signs of the presence of his real authority. At most times the dramaturgies of his power blew away as empty symbols or, worse, they became countersigns. They thrust his own person forward, overshadowed the king's commission in him.

Whenever historians reflect on naval discipline and its breakdown, they always cite the mutinies on the *Bounty* and on HMS *Hermione* and the Great Mutiny at Nore in 1797. The *Hermione*'s mutiny in 1797 was a frenzied massacre of her extravagantly violent officers, and the navy pursued the mutineers until all had been hanged. Bloodily violent, the *Hermione* has been seen as something of an aberration and has been relegated

to a sort of tabloid naval history. About the mutiny at Nore there has
been a more mystifying quiet, if not silence. That the whole fleet should
mutiny not once but twice in home waters in the shadow of a revolution
in France was a shock that the British seem best to have survived by
forgetting. On the political Right among historians, the Great Nore Mutiny is seen as too maverick an occurrence to shake confidence in the belief
that the British had struck happy compromises in their institutions of
discipline. On the political Left among historians, the mutiny's failure is
seen as an embarrassing sign of the 'sub-political' character of the English
working class. Even the genius of E. P. Thompson has not raised more
than a few lines on the Great Nore Mutiny and those only to note that
what was remarkable about it was not the sailors' fundamental loyalty to
the system that controlled them and not their Jacobinism, but the wild
and extravagant nature of their changes of mood. Revolutionary crises, he
argues, are always a conjunction of the generalised grievances of the majority and the more structured aspirations articulated by politically conscious minorities. Among the sailors at Nore the notion of liberties belonging to an English birthright remained vague and was unable to raise
consciousness above a subpolitical level of superstition, irreligion, prejudice and patriotism.

This is not the place either to redress historical neglect or to engage in
debate with historians who have forgotten more about working-class consciousness than I shall ever know. I want simply to complete what I had
begun to argue about the politics of the *Bounty*'s mutiny. If 'gentlemen'
were learning to control their institutions of discipline by managing the
external signs of them, the 'people' were doing the same. What I find
remarkable at Nore – and James Dugan noted it in his fine study. *The
Great Mutiny* (1965) as well – was the seamen's ability to externalise their
social action, to make politics in and to an institution by concocting signs
and symbols. Their commonsense and realistic deferences to the navy as
an institution blossomed into readings of how the system 'naturally' worked.
In an institution in which they were participant audience to a constant
theatre of power, the seamen turned the stage around and played the
actors, directors and producers in a variety of dramatic tropes. They performed with ironic humour, with well-crafted committee procedures, with
a whole landscape of signs. They were 'gentlemen' to their 'gentlemen'.
Their notion of an Englishman's birthright and in that their age-old ap-

peal to a law distinct from tyrannical rule was a classic indication of how they cunningly made politics out of the contradiction between *iudicatio* and *coercitio*. The Levellers had done it before them. What was remarkable at Nore was the form of their politics. The sailors showed that they knew that in the presentation of power the forecastle must be as dramaturgical as the quarterdeck. Alas, in the end, they were too innocent and too trusting in the 'gentlemen' of their institutions of discipline. They mistook the navy's notion of 'gentleman' for that of the gentleman who would honour responsibilities for their welfare. They believed their old metaphors of their captains as 'fathers'. Such innocence cost thirty-six of them their lives.

The *Bounty* mutiny fell midway between the American Revolutionary War and Nore. Those twenty years were more wasteful of the lives of British naval seamen than any in the navy's history. No doubt, like victims in other and even greater holocausts, the British sailors connived in their own suffering by bowing to the power that they maintained by their own deferences. On the *Bounty,* some of them, relativised by experiencing life as it might otherwise be lived, stopped conniving in the sufferings of their way of life. Hedonistic their mutiny may ultimately have been. The navy had little interest in their personal motivation. The theatre of discipline was much more important. It is quite clear from the extravagant response the navy made to these unimportant affairs on an unimportant ship in an unimportant place how political the *Bounty* mutiny really was.

TEXTS FOR DISCIPLINE

Institutions require a memory. A memory creates precedent and order. From the earliest times armies and navies gave a text to their memories in the 'Articles' that governed military behaviour. These 'Articles' established the language of living in an institution of discipline. Like every text, these 'Articles' had the permanence of being written down and the impermanence of every circumstantial reading. But institutions bound so closely to sovereignty and commission as armies and navies put the highest value on unchanging readings. The dangers of war and the sea have justified the rigidities and harshness of military laws but at the same time have separated those bound by them from ordinary living. The real problem came when the extraordinary state of military living became ordinary, when armies became Standing. Then there were two systems, military and civilian, side by side and in some contradiction, and two languages to identify them.

The British, by the end of the eighteenth century, had solved the problem by not solving it. For the army, they had a Mutiny Act that described the army's discipline, but it was an act that had to be renewed annually by Parliament. Technically the army was not standing at all. For the navy they had a brief enunciation of the principles of discipline called the Articles of War, enacted in 1661 and renewed in 1749. But then the navy had a more discursive 'Regulations and Instructions relating to His Majesty's Service at Sea', formulated and adjusted periodically by the Admiralty, acting executively by direct power of the crown, which jealously regarded its rights in this respect. The navy was the King's Own.

This distinction between legislative enactment by Parliament for the Articles and executive direction by the Crown for the Regulations was important. The Articles defined the sovereignly delegated powers over life and death in the institution. These powers came from the Crown and Parliament together and, archaic or modern, were near enough to unchanging. Changing them involved the whole body politic. The Regulations, on the other hand, defined the navy's own management of itself. In its own government, the navy could change itself without having to change other institutions of society. There was relativist and reformist wisdom in this, as we shall see.

In the Articles of War the British had an historical text for their system of military discipline that arose out of their own experiences. Part of being a 'gentleman' was in knowing the poetics of that text, in knowing how to match a reading of it to changing circumstances. 'Gentlemen' had to be participant observers of how it actually – as distinct from how it rhetorically or literally – textualised daily life in the navy. There were many anomalies to which they had to adjust. No anomaly was so great as that between the rhetoric of disinterested loyalty of fighting for the Crown and the self-interested possibility of making private fortunes in that fighting. For officers and men alike, the prospects of prize money were an instrument of discipline in their own right. Every rank had its right to a proportionate share of the value of a captured enemy ship. It was legalised piracy. It was the deep play of a seaman's life, the lottery that took some of the pain of discipline away. The language of the King's Own men could have a gusto that came from greed as much as from loyalty. The arithmetic of prize money was as regulated as shares of pirate plunder or as whalers' lays, and was as much a subject of yarning as food. Prize money bound the men to the institution, but it meant that they knew what the honour of gentlemen was with a knowing wink.

There really were two texts for discipline pertinent to our considerations: the British Articles of War of 1661 (13° Car. II St. 1.c 90) and their revision of 1749 (22° Geo. II c. 33). There is not much doubt that both these sets of Articles were directed at officers of the British navy rather than ordinary seamen. The Act of 1661 was meant to counter the 'baseness of spirit' and cowardice among officers that had led to the disgrace of Dungeness in 1652 at the hands of the Dutch. The Act of 1749 was intended to reinforce and reiterate this earlier set of reforms by putting officers, even those on half-pay, permanently under Admiralty control and by removing the privilege of courts martial to lessen penalties for breaches of the Articles. Courts martial, being in the control of officer peers, were unlikely to be instruments of discipline, unless the self-interest of the officer group was affected by the crime. The political storms that followed this act of 'tyranny' of 1749 showed how clear the poetics of the Articles were on those on whom they imposed. Admiral Byng, indeed, was executed because the Articles did not allow a lesser penalty for the crime for which he was executed. His execution demonstrated how dangerous it was to legislate discipline with any great specificity. This certainly, to use Voltaire's famous phrase about the issue, 'encouraged the others' to change the Articles.

The revolution in France, which gave a political edge to all questions of discipline in the British navy, followed, of course, the rebellion of the American colonies. These rebellious colonies, bound together loosely and uncertainly in their Continental Congress, had to create military institutions. Neither a standing army nor a permanent navy was palatable in their republican circumstances. Indeed the ambivalences of revolution made it difficult to create texts for their institutions of military discipline. There was a strong privateering spirit abroad against which the rhetoric of loyalty and sacrifice faltered. There was as well a severe distrust of the moral calibre of ordinary men who would need to be disciplined. Unlike the British, who institutionally were preoccupied with the officers and left those officers to manage the discipline of the men, the Americans were preoccupied with the moral calibre of the men. They wanted a morally upstanding military as much as a disciplined one. It was a fundamentalism that would create much pain.

In 1775, John Adams was given the task of writing the rules and regulations for a navy that was still more a glint in the eye of some members of the Continental Congress than a reality. He cut short his search for these rules with his customary philosophical aplomb and trust in historical certainties. 'There was extant', he explained, 'one system of Articles of War, which had carried two empires to the head of mankind, the Roman and the British, for the British Articles of War were only a literal translation of the Roman'. He concluded that 'it would be vain for us to seek in our own inventions and in the records of warlike nations for a more compleat system of military discipline: it was an observation founded on undoubted facts that the prosperity of nations had been in proportion to the discipline of their forces by sea and land. I was therefore for reporting the British Articles of War *totidem verbis.'*

Well, not quite *totidem verbis.* In fact, Adams mixed the statutory Articles of 1661 with some of those of 1749, together with the executive regulations of the British Admiralty, and added a number of inventions of his own. He did reduce the number of causes for the death penalty from twenty-two to three (the Sixth Congress brought the number back to twelve: as late as 1940 there were twenty-five causes for the death penalty in the U.S. navy). Making one text out of two texts so different in structure was done, perhaps, with the lawyer Adams' tidying eye, but institutionally it tended to blur the characteristics of discipline and law. The thrust of the British Articles was to control all naval men under one law of majesty so that *coercitio* threatened all, but that law was managed distinctively by role and by different forms of punishment. Adams, however, distinguished the functions and obligations of officers and men so that *coercitio* did not threaten officers as it did men. He limited by law the power of commanders to punish their officers, except by court martial. He would create by that an officer corps of inflated self-consideration. He defined the ideal relations of officer to men and did not leave them to circumstantial management. He introduced the notion of flogging into the fundamental law of the navy (it was further enshrined by the Sixth Congress). Flogging in the U.S. navy became a matter of law, not, as in the British navy, a matter of regulation. It would prove very difficult to eradicate. Fundamentally, Adams confused the notion of the 'gentleman' officer as a manager of coercion with that of the gentleman officer born and educated to civilisation. This led to contradictions that inevitably made the U.S. navy an object of social reforms. Its discipline would be seen to be in conflict with law and with the republic's ideals.

Certainly John Adams enjoyed his role – in retrospect at least – as founding father of the United States navy. Those evenings in Philadelphia, when the Naval Committee met in a tavern at 8:00 P.M. after the Congress' debates were over, lingered long in Adams' memory. Then as the Jamaican rum began to flow, the members talked of Greek and Roman and British history, and of Pope and Milton. They spoke too of the Articles of War they were planning, and the price of frigates. The seventy-year-old Samuel Hopkins, liquor not having passed his lips all day till 8:00 P.M., enlarged the evenings till midnight. 'The flow of his soul made all of his reading our own and seemed to bring recollections in all of us of all we had ever read', remembered Adams. Adams' own experience as a lawyer at Plymouth, Barnstable and Martha's Vineyard among codfishers and whalers had given him a high opinion of the 'assiduity, patience, perseverance, and daring intrepidy of our seamen'. How he viewed that other class of seamen, the riotous, blasphemous and drunken sailors in Boston has to be inferred from the rules he made for them. The fact is that Adams saw a New England navy in character and strategy – small ships making swift sorties – and a United States navy in name. In the politics of an unsettled revolution, of course, that view roused 'loud and vehement opposition', 'formidable arguments', and 'terrible rhetoric' from non-Yankees. The rivers and harbours of New England were too numerous and too small to be blockaded by a British navy, they argued. But a British navy challenged by the very existence of an American navy could blockade Chesapeake and Delaware Bays and destroy the trade of the southern colonies. Small, dashing expeditions cutting off the smaller British vessels trying to get inshore would be effective on the New England coast, but not in the open waters farther south.

There was an entrepreneurial and private side to Adams' vision of the navy. It also contradicted the more public character an institution of discipline needed to be. Privateering was a much more appropriate embodiment of the natural 'virtues' he saw in seamen. Yet George Washington was already cursing the notion of privateering and the contradiction it presented to military efficiency and discipline. The very first sally of the American 'navy' had ended in a mutiny of the *Hannah*'s crew, because the crew's expectancies of prize money had been unfulfilled. As it happened, the punishment of the mutineers by flogging had to be cancelled (except for the ringleader): such discipline was not to be suffered by the American community, who shared the conviction that private profit was a legitimate expectancy for public causes.

There were many men in the nascent U.S. navy who saw the need of 'gentlemen'. John Paul Jones, perhaps because he came to suffer most from the lack of a true institution of discipline, was the most reflective: 'None other than a gentleman, as well as a seaman, both in theory and practice, is qualified to support the character of a commissioned officer in the navy, nor is any man fit to command a ship of war, who is not also capable of communicating his ideas on paper in language that becomes his rank.'

Jones did not define what a gentleman was, but in his various complaints about the new navy he indicated what sorts of characteristics a gentleman should have. He should be a 'free citizen of the world' and, by that, be committed professionally to an institution. He should be examined for entrance and promotion by an outside body, and, by that, be free of patronage and be dependent on the system itself for the allocation of positions. He thought the British system of seniority the best. There needed to be absolute confidence in the skills of officers and their ability to manage their own behaviour. An appeal against a court martial sentence, he complained, simply intruded politics and law. As for men, a body of seamen was made professional by enlisting them 'during the pleasance and giving them all the prizes'. Such professionalism created a binding association of seamen with their officers. This was not a moral relationship – as Adams was seeing it – but one of mutual respect institutionally created. 'Military science', he wrote, 'is only acquired by dint of study, of reflections and combination'; 'birth, patronage, solicitation, intrigue sometimes win employment and rank; but they do not secure success and credit'. 'Courage alone will not lead to renown.'

Jones' definitions of 'gentlemen' were, like Vernon's and Kempenfelt's, full of practical reason. He proved to be correct. He predicted that without a system of seniority, the navy would be full of conflict. Indeed, duelling was to plague the U.S. navy for sixty years. The number of officers killed in duels equalled two-thirds of those killed in wars till 1848. United States officers struggled to formulate a code of honour that was more social than professional. Jones predicted that without a profession for seamen of the lower ranks as well, the navy would draw only the social dregs of the ports. From the perspective of some, at least, that is what the navy came to get. United States seamen, according to one commentator, were 'reckless, profligate, intemperate, profane, creatures of impulse, slaves of despotic masters at sea, dupes of rapacious landlords and greedy harpies on shore, no commanding motives to improve, yielding to pleasures of the moment, in daily peril yet drowning reflection with resilient gaiety'. Until the middle of the nineteenth century the ordinary seamen of the U.S. navy were looked upon neither as professionals of the sea nor as respected yeomen of the land. They were seen to be and were treated as marginal men, exploited by a large range of parasites on the land and violently abused at sea. Jones understood, where Adams had not, that the complexities of military knowledge, the modern experience of bureaucratic forms and new definitions of patriotic duty had changed the nature of discipline.

WHITE JACKET

The contradiction between *iudicatio* (law) and *coercitio* (force) in institutions of discipline becomes apparent and dangerous when political consciousness is raised by broader social expectancies – a revolution, say, or the political consequences of a period we know as an Enlightenment. I have a witness for that proposition. It is Herman Melville. Any study of seamen's lives under discipline in the Pacific is blessed by being able to draw on three experiential works of art: Herman Melville's *White Jacket: or The World in a Man-of-War* [1850], Richard Dana's *Two Years Before the Mast* (1840), Charles Nordhoff's *Man-o-War Life: A Boy's Experience in the United States Navy During a Voyage Around the World in a Ship-of-the-Line* (1883) [1855]. A kindly reviewer wrote of *White Jacket* what might have been written of all three: *White Jacket* is a 'union of culture and experience, of thoughtful observation . . . the sharp breezes of the forecastle alternating with the stillness of the library, books and work imparting each other mutual life'. Any historian would rise in self-esteem if he or she would write an ethnographic history of seamen's lives such as Melville's or Dana's or Nordhoff's.

White Jacket was Melville's witness to the excessive violence of the U.S. navy and his reflection on its causes. Critics tell us that the book was many other things as well, notably an ironic blow at a family deeply conservative, proud of its own naval connections and somewhat appalled at this beachcombing kin of theirs. We can be less Freudian and more political than that. Melville was an astute and indefatigable reformer, and he was convinced that the essential contradiction in the American navy was that the officers were sustaining aristocratic privilege within an institution chartered under a republican constitution. The violence of the officers to their crews had little to do with the necessary efficiency of a ship or the unwillingness of the men to be disciplined. It arose largely from the officers' concern to establish class and status, to make small island kingdoms of their ships. The officers were violent because they had no authority. They had power sustained only by constant ceremonialism.

The white jacket in *White Jacket* may be thought, in some anachronistic presumption, to be the officers' dress uniform. It was not. Blue was the dress colour of the time. The white jacket was that untarred, carry-all, absorbent, handmade coat that made 'White Jacket', the narrator, look like a ghost in the shrouds, that was nearly the death of him in the yards, that he laughed at and was laughed at in, and that he threw into Norfolk Harbor to end what he saw as his cruel bondage to the navy. The white jacket was a sort of Joseph's coat, a symbol into which Melville bound all the stories of his experience on board the USS *United States* – or the 'Neversink' as he called it – as he returned home from Hawaii after his whaling and beachcombing experiences in the Pacific, fabulised in *Typee* (1846), *Omoo* (1847) and *Moby Dick* (1851).

We have some measure on Melville's fictional imagination in *White Jacket*. We have the logs and journals of the *United States*. Like the British, the Americans measured sailors' lives carefully. We can count American floggings, too. On the *United States,* Melville witnessed 163 floggings, inflicted by her captain, Thomas ap Catesby Jones. Of all twenty-five voyages of American naval vessels in the Pacific from 1812 to 1845, Jones' was the second most ferocious. A typical American captain would flog on the average six men a month while on tour, although captains such as John Aulich on the *Vincennes* could tour the whole Pacific and flog only one man. American naval vessels were much larger in complement than the British, carrying up to 500 men. They sailed under individual orders, not as part of a fleet. Their crews were taken from a level of society already much put upon by landlords, loan sharks, agents and tavern owners. They came aboard their ship with a deep sense of wrong and were put to meaningless labour in overcrowded conditions. The cause of the floggings that

soon began was generally drunkenness. Rejecting the bonds of their pur-
poseless institutional lives, they engaged in orgiastic drinking and exploited every imaginable system to acquire liquor. Thomas ap Catesby
Jones, cranky and eccentric in violence, was nonetheless a fit subject for
allegory and parable. Melville made him a parody of all U.S. naval captains.

On the other hand, Melville had no romantic image of ordinary seamen. 'The navy is the asylum of the perverse, the haven of the unfortunate. Here the sons of adversity meet the children of calamity and here
the children of calamity meet the offspring of sin', was his comment.
What he was concerned to show was that, debased as sailors were, no man
should be stripped of his human and civil rights in the name of expe-
diency. There was not, nor could there be, anywhere 'beyond the walls of
Rome' in a true republic. A sailor's life was different but it was not grotesque. Nothing – not even efficiency, or a peculiar need for order – could
justify the violence of a flogging. 'Blind and crawling servility' was no
substitute for reasoned subordination in duty. Military power must recognise civil liberties. For the sailor Melville encountered in the Pacific, however, 'our Revolution was in vain; to him our Declaration of Independence
is a lie'.

For Melville the anomalies that John Adams had written into the texts
of discipline for the navy were the causes of the violence. By congressional
legislation one man, a lower deck man, was flogged for an offence while
another man, his officer, was fined for the same crime. By law one man,
a sailor, could be arbitrarily punished without protection of the judgement or even the testimony of his peers, while another man, his officer,
had his rights preserved by all the legalisms of a court martial. And to
take matters back to where we began, Article XV of the U.S. navy's code
of discipline forbade quarrelling, provoking or reproachful words. The
people were flogged unmercifully for their bad language. 'Officers of the
navy, answer me!' Melville charged. 'Have you not, many of you, a thousand times violated this law, and addressed to men whose tongue was tied
by this very article, language which no landsman would ever hearken to
without flying to the throat of his insulter?'

In the end, Melville recognised that the *realpolitik* of violent power in
the navy was nothing more than the rationalisation of the status, class and
privilege of one set of men over another. By this lucid perception, the
commonsense argument that physical violence as an unfortunate necessity

gets revealed for its social self-interestedness. The violence done to seamen in both the British and the U.S. navies sustained privilege, comfort and wealth. Sublimations of officer gentleman into the Crown and of the sufferings of ordinary seamen into the general welfare of the navy and the nation did not change the fact that the true beneficiaries of the violence were the officers themselves.

So our reflection on discipline and its texts leads us to a final thought. The violence of discipline was not inevitable. Any captain could have known how to be a 'gentleman', how to manage the symbolic environment of his wooden world. Any captain could have been relativised by experiencing the otherness in his men's lives. Any captain could have discovered some social contract with his people, could have known how far his own person intruded on his role. Any captain could have known what Admiral Collingwood knew: that he would be the cause of his own mutiny. Any captain could have known how much he was the cause of the pain of those he flogged, how much he was the hangman of those that mutinied.

ENTR'ACTE
Sharks That Walk on the Land

When Bligh heard the clacking of stones in the gloom on the beach at Tofua, he remembered where he had heard that sound before. It was at Hawaii in the hours following Cook's death.

That day, unforgettable for all who shared it, was for Bligh a reminder of his distance from the men around him on the *Resolution*. Bligh had fired the first shots that day. He fired them on the far side of the bay in which Cook was killed, but they were cause enough in the eyes of some to have raised the alarm and fear among the Hawaiians that ended in Cook's death. Then Bligh was sent to guard the mast of the *Resolution* being repaired on the raised stone platform of an Hawaiian *heiau* (or temple). Lieutenant King, later to be Bligh's commander and author of the official account of the *Resolution*'s voyage that aroused Bligh's disgust and anger, instructed him to remain calm, to guard the mast but not to fire on the Hawaiians. But the Hawaiians began to cluster out of sight around the *heiau* and started to clack their stones, throwing some from places of surprise. Bligh's men killed six or eight Hawaiians in the *mêlée*. King, enraged, was forced to rescue him and pull them all back with the mast to the *Resolution*.

King, in his published account of the day, was full of the mystery of the events and of his efforts to stop the bloodshed. Bligh, scribbling marginal notes in his copy of it, was full of angry rejection of any mystification. Cook had died, according to him, because of the cowardice and incompetence of his officers and of the men who were expected to protect him. The Hawaiians had to be punished savagely. Only their fear of naked violence would quieten them. To attempt to remove crosscultural misapprehensions was an 'old woman's story'. The day of Cook's death in Bligh's memory of it was associated with dangerous incompetence and the necessity of being firm and violent with natives.

Cook, alive or dead, was never far from Bligh and his *Bounty*. We will understand something of the way they were connected in Tahiti if we

know the meaning of the Hawaiian proverb: 'Chiefs are sharks that walk
on the land'.

The Polynesians are those people who some two or three thousand years
ago spread to all the islands of the Pacific through the great triangle that
reaches from Hawaii to New Zealand to Easter Island. That was their
great cultural triumph. They had mastered the immense ocean. They had
discovered all the islands of the Pacific and then in turn were discovered
by European explorers from the sixteenth to the eighteenth centuries of
the christian era.

In their different island worlds the Polynesians developed separately,
playing variations on their common cultural themes. They held in common, however, an understanding of themselves – call it a historical consciousness – expressed in the mythical opposition of 'native' and 'stranger'.
This opposition of 'native' and 'stranger' was prior to and independent of
the European intrusion. The Polynesians were native and stranger among
themselves and to themselves. They saw themselves as made up of native,
those born of the land of their islands, and stranger, those who had at
some time come from a distant place. 'Tahiti' is, in different forms, the
Polynesian word for a distant place. Strangers came from Tahiti. Typically
in their myths the first stranger, a chief, came many generations ago in a
canoe from a distant place. He found the natives of their island and either
overthrew the existing chiefly line by violence or married the highest-
born women of the natives and established his stranger's line.

In myth and in ritual this opposition of native and stranger was a constant metaphor of Polynesian politics and social organisation. Political
power was thought to come through usurpation by the stranger and was
given legitimacy by the native. A reigning chief would trace in genealogy
his line to a hero who had come from a distant place and conquered the
native inhabitants of the island and their chief. It was not just an event of
the mythical past, however. The reigning chief, even if he had come to
power by the natural death of his father, would have played out a usurping
role in the rituals of his accession and would have married into that line
that connected him most closely with the original natives of the land. So
the opposition native and stranger was both history and cosmology. It
offered an understanding both of the past and of the present: the conqueror, the stranger, came from the sea; the conquered, but founding
force, the people, were of the land. So Land and Sea had the oppositions

of Native and Stranger. And because Polynesian cosmology imagined the sky as a great dome reaching down all around the island to the circle of the horizon, those who came by sea came from 'beyond the sky'. They were *atua,* gods. Being called *atua,* gods, as they almost universally were, the European Strangers who came to Polynesian islands from beyond the sky were both flattered and reinforced in their judgements of savage simplicities. We may hazard a guess that the Polynesians, just as they saw in their own Stranger Chiefs the incarnation of usurping power, so they expected the European Strangers from beyond the sky to play out their mythical usurping roles. Native was to Stranger as Land was to Sea. There were other associations as well. Strangers from the Sea, from Beyond the Sky, Usurping Power were chiefs; they were also man-eaters, sacrificers. That Hawaiian proverb caught it all: 'Chiefs are sharks that walk on the land.'

In Hawaii, as elsewhere in Polynesia, the structural opposition of Native and Stranger was played out in an annual cycle of rituals. Eight months of the year belonged to the Stranger Chiefs, and were the time of human sacrifice and war, the time of *kapu* (taboos), and of those protocols of the dominance of chiefly power. It was the time in which the chiefs walked on the land like sharks and the people of the land, the commoners, obeyed all the *kapu,* or suffered death as *kapu*-breakers. These eight months of the year belonged to Ku, the god of war and sacrifice, the ancestral deity of the Strangers.

These were the ordinary months of the year. But there were four months beginning October–November that were a sort of carnival time, when the ordinary was overturned. These four months belonged to the people of the land, the commoners, the natives. It was a reversed world in which the chiefs ritually lost their power to the people, when *kapu* and protocols were put aside, in which there were no sacrifices or wars, in which the god of the land, Lono, returned to the islands. The chiefs went into seclusion, locked themselves away on their own individual lands. The time of Lono was called *makahiki (ma-tahiti,* voyage from a distant place). *Makahiki* followed a strict calendar. It began with a procession of the priests of Lono right-handedly around the island. That is, the land was always on the right and the sea on the left. Right hand, life, land: left hand, death, sea. The procession of Lono was a symbolic act of his possession of the land. At the same time there were left-handed processions, counterclockwise, around the lands of the chiefs, symbolic acts of dispossession. In the

time of their seclusion the chiefs lost that power that they had usurped
from the people of the land. Lono's procession was led by Lono's symbol,
a crosspiece of wood from which hung bannerlike pieces of white cloth
made of bark, and bird skins. At all stages of the procession the common
people came forward with abundant gifts. It was a time of feasting and
games. There were great boxing matches, sledding, running races, javelin
throwing and dancing. Like carnivals everywhere it was a time of freedom, sex roles were reversed, *kapu* were overthrown and none was sacrificed for breaking them. When the island had been encircled, the procession ended at Lono's temple. Then at the end of the four months of *makahiki,*
the first or second week of February, the chiefs returned. They confronted
Lono on the beach in front of his temple in an act of ceremonial violence
in which the chiefs re-enacted their usurping role. Lono's temple was
dismantled, the new year of Ku was begun with a human sacrifice and the
kapu were reimposed. Once again the sharks walked on the land.

In November of 1778, James Cook's *Resolution* and her consort the
Discovery appeared off the northwest coast of the island of Hawaii. It was
Cook's third voyage. He was a world-famous man. His voyages of discovery had captured the imagination of Europe and America. He was also a
tired man. It was his tenth year at sea on Pacific explorations. Historians
of Pacific explorations in hindsight, and indeed Cook's colleagues in reflection on what happened on this third voyage, have agreed that even at
this stage all was not well. Cook's temper, never good, was less in control,
and he flogged more than 37 percent of his crew, and many of them more
than once. Cook's cool judgement with native peoples seemed awry and
his patience thin. He was sick with years of the strain of leadership in
dangerous places and the horrendous food of voyaging. His poor stomach,
kidneys, bowels and lungs would offer a grim picture for any 'Body Programme'. Sir James Watts, a medical historian, has played on the irony
that, in saving himself from scurvy and a vitamin C deficiency, Cook lost
out on vitamin B, and he may have had worms that deprived him of niacin
and thiamin. For those who do not read boxes of breakfast cereals seriously, Sir James has a grim warning for what a lack of niacin and thiamine
can bring: fatigue, headache and insomnia, breathlessness, irritability and
depression, painful mouth and tongue, digestive disturbances, loss of interest and initiative, constipation or diarrhoea, loss of concentration and
memory, psychoneurotic personality change, sensitivity to sunlight. 'Historians', Sir James warns, 'have ignored for too long the serious effects on

decision making from vitamin B deficiencies, which could help to explain some otherwise inexplicable actions of the great naval commanders'. Be that as it may, the *Resolution*'s men went to the northwest coast murmuring among themselves at their commander's ill temper and wondering at his imprudences.

Indeed, as the *Resolution* approached Hawaii he was crankier than ever, because his crew, conservative as ever, would not drink the spruce beer he had substituted for their grog for the sake of their health. And his crew were cranky at him, spoke 'mutinously' as the phrase went, because instead of stopping at anchorage where they might have enjoyed the pleasures of the islands, he had, for the sake of manipulating the market on supplies, decided to keep at sea off Hawaii and to drop in only at selected bays. They had spent hard months mapping and surveying the northwest American coast in a vain effort to find a passage through to the Atlantic and had comforted themselves with dreams of wintering in the islands. Instead, for nearly two full months in the winter seas of December and January off Hawaii, since made famous for their enormous surf and commented on by Cook as the largest he had ever seen, they made their slow clockwise voyage around Hawaii, beating constantly against the wind, tacking endlessly, the whole crew angry at Cook and he at them.

When they came close to land to do a little marketing, they noticed several things: there were only commoners and no chiefs to visit them; the offerings made were extraordinarily generous; the islanders all called Cook 'Lono'. Finding none of the usual versions of Cook's name – 'Tuti' or 'Kuki' – would satisfy the Hawaiians, Cook's officers also began to refer to him as Lono when they spoke of him. The two vessels with the crosspieced masts and sails proceeded on their right-handed procession around the island till on January 17 they anchored at Kealakekua Bay on the south coast of Hawaii. They received a welcome there the like of which they had never seen in the Pacific – a thousand canoes and ten thousand islanders in complete jubilation.

Kealakekua is a large, sweeping, half-moon bay. High cliffs in the centre drop to the water's edge and divide the low-lying point on the western edge, where there were the many huts of a settlement, from a shallow valley in the southeast corner, where there were a few huts and a large stone structure. This last was a temple or *heiau*. It happened to be Lono's temple at which the annual *makahiki* procession began and ended. It came as no surprise to the priests of Lono and all the people of Keala-

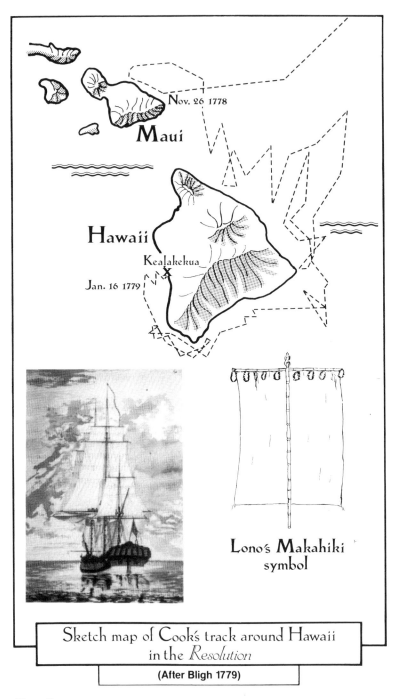

Nov. 26 1778

Maui

Hawaii

Kealakekua

Jan. 16 1779

Lono's Makahiki
symbol

Sketch map of Cook's track around Hawaii
in the *Resolution*

(After Bligh 1779)

Figure 8a.

Figure 8b.

Figure 8c.

kekua that the two vessels with Lono's symbols displayed and seen off-
shore early in the *makahiki* season should have slowly made their way to
where it all began and ended.

There were no chiefs in all that welcoming crowd, and the priests of
Lono led Cook immediately to their temple where he let them do with
him ritually what they wished. They took him to each of the images of
lesser gods and he heard their denunciations of them. He let them hold

Figure 8d.

Figure 8.   Processions and landings. (Art on pp. 164–6)
a. Processions and landings. The *Resolution* tacked its way around Hawaii to Kealakekua, where the right-handed processions behind Lono's crossbeam symbol began and ended. (Henry Roberts, 177–?. Watercolour. Mitchell Library, Ref: ZPX D11, f34; Map after Bligh 1779; E. S. C. Handy and Elizabeth Green Handy, *Native Planters in Old Hawaii.* Honolulu: Bernice P. Bishop Museum, 1972.). b and c. Anchored at Kealakekua between Kalaniopu'u's village (left background) and the *heiau* (right foreground), Cook and his crew were drawn into the *makahiki* rituals that marked the end of the season of Lono and the beginning of that of Ku. (James Cook, *A Voyage to the Pacific Ocean.* London: G. Nicol, 1784. Baillieu Library, The University of Melbourne.) d. A feathered image of Ku. (Art Gallery of NSW.)

his arms like the crosspiece of Lono's symbol and offer him sacrificial food. He sat through the long litanies as they chanted 'Lono, Lono, Lono'. He then asked the priests whether the small enclosure beside the temple might not be his to erect a tent for astronomical observations. He needed to watch the stars. So the sailors erected a strange little temple of a tent and talked stars and sun to the priests of Lono who knew all about stars and were watching them themselves because the *makahiki* feast was determined by the rising and setting of the Pleiades and the setting was nearly upon them.

The high chief of Hawaii, Kalaniopu'u, did not appear for several days. When he did come on January 25, he came with a ceremony and majesty that the sailors had not seen before. He came in the great feather cloaks of Hawaii and invested Cook in one of them, still in the British Museum. There is no evidence of the ceremonies of opposition, although Kalaniopu'u would not meet Cook on the *Resolution,* only on the beach in front of Lono's temple. The Englishmen thought it curious that Kalaniopu'u immediately and anxiously asked when they were going. The Englishmen left on February 4. It was, as far as computers can calculate it, the last day of *makahiki* in that year. They did not go before two more unnerving coincidences. The Englishmen wanted firewood and asked for the fences, scaffolding and wooden images of Lono's temple and were surprised that the priests of Lono readily agreed. The priests demurred at only one statue. It was the image of Ku. That one stayed, the priests said, and busily helped the sailors dismantle Lono's temple at season's end.

Also a much-loved gunner on the *Resolution,* William Watman, had a stroke and died. The chiefs asked that he be buried in the temple. Old William Watman was buried with ceremony he could hardly have foreseen. 'As we were filling the grave', the *Resolution*'s journal reads, 'and had finished reading the ceremony (during which they preserved the most profound silence and regard) they would throw in a dead pig and some coconuts, plantains, etc.; and indeed were inclined to have shewed their respect for the dead by a great quantity of these articles, they also repeated some ceremonies, and although they were in some measure stopped from going through their funeral prayers, yet for three nights and in one it lasted the best part of it . . . [they] surrounded the grave, killed hogs, sang a great deal, in which acts of piety and good will they were left undisturbed: at the head of the grave a post was erected and a square piece of board nailed on it with the name of the deceased, his age and the date, this they promised should always remain and we have no doubt but it will as long as the post lasts and be a monument of our being the first discoverers of this group of island.'

So the Hawaiians made the Englishmen's sacrifice their own. And while the season of Ku was thus begun, they had no qualms that it be marked with the cross and sign of Lono. As it happens, William Watman's death is remembered there still with a sign that has lasted longer than his wooden cross. There is a plaque there now celebrating this as the first Christian service on Hawaiian soil.

Makahiki was over and on those last days the people constantly asked when Lono was going. When Cook said his goodbyes and said he would be back next year in the winter from his search of the northwest passage, the priests said they expected him.

So Cook went, and he would have been back next year, except that a few days out the foremast sprung on the *Resolution,* and he was back in ten days. There was no welcome this time. 'It hurt our vanity', the Englishmen said. The people were insolent and the chiefs sullen and questioning. There were immediately thefts and confrontations. The Englishmen could not believe that the atmosphere could change so rapidly and put it down to the strains that nearly 300 extra mouths brought. Truth was they were out of season and out of role. They were not of the land: they were of the sea. They were not Native come to power for a season: they were Stranger, usurping power, sharks that walked on the land. The change in the Hawaiians brought changes in the English, and they say as much in their journals — that they displayed power and violence much more overtly to get their way. There were several incidents of violent clashes, and on February 13 Cook himself alone except for a marine, was involved in a strange pursuit, running several miles, pistol in hand, after a thief. That night a cutter was stolen, and on the morning of February 14 Cook closed the bay with armed men, sent Bligh to stop a canoe leaving the bay and went ashore looking for Kalaniopu'u to take hostage for the return of the cutter. Kalaniopu'u was asleep and was obviously ignorant of the cutter's theft. He came willingly enough with Cook down the pathway in his settlement till some of his relatives said something to him and he looked frightened and sat down. Then came news, first to the crowd and then indirectly to Cook, that another chief had been killed in a clash on the other side of the bay. Lieutenant Rickman was responsible. The crowd around Kalaniopu'u became threatening, and Cook fired shot out of his double-barrelled gun at a man who was about to strike him. The shot was ineffectual against the warrior's protective matting, and when Cook fired a ball to kill another assailant it was too late. The crowd rushed forward and, with daggers that the Englishmen had given them, killed four marines and Cook at the water's edge. There was nothing that the waiting boats and the more distant ships could do. They saw their captain lying face down in the water with three or four Hawaiians beating him about the head with rocks. Then they saw his body being carried off in triumph.

The English were enraged and dismayed, unbelieving that they could have shared in so awful a moment for a man of destiny such as Cook. They looked for a reason for it all, and found it in the cowardice of Lieutenant Williamson, who they thought had withdrawn the boats too early, or in the imprudence of Cook in carelessly exposing himself and being too precipitate, or in their own carelessness at not having demonstrated the power of their guns before it was too late. Clerke, Cook's successor, acted calmly enough and refused to allow wholesale retribution, but there was fighting and slaughter nonetheless. They do not describe in their journals acts that they say are better not described. But the sailors mutilated those they slaughtered, carried back their severed heads in the bottom of their boat, hung them around the necks of those they captured. It is difficult to know whether these actions were shocking to the Hawaiians or whether they fitted fairly well the expectancies of those who knew that in the time of Ku there would be sacrifice.

Certainly everything that the Hawaiians did was a mystery and a contradiction to the Englishmen. They could not reconcile the savagery they had seen with the nonchalance with which many of the Hawaiians now treated them. Cook's body had been carted up the cliffs to a temple of Ku where it had been ceremonially divided among the chiefs. It is something a conqueror would do to the defeated or the successor to his predecessor – bake or waste the flesh from the bones so that the bones could be distributed. 'Every chief acts as a conqueror when he comes to power', the Hawaiians say. The priests of Lono who had been so friendly got their share of Cook's remains, and, mystified that the Englishmen should be so disturbed, brought a parcel of bones and flesh to the ships to placate them. When would Lono come again, they asked as they gave over Cook's bones. Return, of course, he did. *Makahiki* came every year, and for forty years and more the right-handed procession of Lono at *makahiki* time was led by a reliquary bundle of Cook's bones. It did not mean that the annual coming of Lono was more real because of it: Lono's coming was always real. It did mean – it is Marshall Sahlins' (1981) joke – that god was an Englishman.

E. H. Carr has scandalised his historian colleagues by enunciating the principle that a historical fact is not what happened but that small part of what has happened that has been used by historians to talk about. History is not the past: it is a consciousness of the past used for present purposes. In that sense the death of Cook immediately became historical. Those on board his ship began to write down what they thought had happened. An interpretation of what had happened mattered to them. They blamed one another for negligence or incompetence or cowardice. They examined the inconsistencies of their most consistent captain to excuse negligence, incompetence and cowardice on their part, to find a cause of his death in his weariness, his bad health, his crankiness. They searched their understanding of the uncivilised savage and of the treachery of natives. Clerke and King, at least, if not the rest of the crew who thirsted to be savage to the savages, sensed that what they had seen in their way the Hawaiians had seen in ways incomprehensible to them. None of them could comprehend why the Hawaiians seemed to presume that nothing had changed. The women still came to the ships at night even after the slaughters of the day. Old friends among the priests and chiefs and people came forward and inquired for Lono as if he had never died.

There were two strange scenes in those confused days after the killings. One on the side of the mountain in the temple of Ku, Cook lying there dismembered but resurrected in those who possessed him. The other in the great cabin of the *Resolution,* the gentlemen of the two ships observing the proprieties of the navy in dividing up the clothes and possessions of their late commodore and buying them in a small auction.

We will never really enter the minds of those in the temple of Ku. It is hardly likely that they had killed Cook in order to make actual the ritual death of Lono at the hands of the high chief Kalaniopu'u. But when it was done they understood what had happened because their myths gave them a history and that history was necessary for the maintenance of all that they were. They were Native and Stranger to one another: Kalaniopu'u was the greatest Stranger of them all, the usurper, shark that walked on the land. He was who he was because in the season of sacrifice and war, in the season of Ku, he was conqueror of the land, of the people, whose god was Lono and whose season was *makahiki.* All Cook's gestures and threats, done in his eyes for the sake of property and discipline, were gestures out of season. It was as if the right order had not been played out and Lono had not been conquered for the season. Cook was not Native now, but Stranger, a shark that walked on the land. In those circumstances the killing was easy and the death made everything come true again. So they kept asking when Lono would come again.

The gentlemen in the great cabin auctioning their captain's goods had their own proprieties. They had to find the correct balance between the pragmatism of navy men a year and more from home, making use of things their owner no longer needed and making sense of their own emotions. They had to cope with wearing the captain's shirt and britches and the growing realisation that they had lived with a hero. They had difficulty in knowing the line between their own experience and the growing reality of their myths. They knew they had been present at a moment of some destiny. And they tried in their journals and logs to make sense of it. They cursed the corruption of the Deptford naval suppliers who gave them a bad mast whose splitting brought them back. The venality of some small merchant had killed Cook. They remembered all the imprudences of Cook – in landing at low tide when the ships could not get near enough to protect him, in not listening to his marines who told him to get out, in not showing the Hawaiians the real force of their arms. They blamed Lieutenant Williamson, commanding the boats, for not doing something, anything. Williamson was disliked: they easily made him something of a scapegoat. They blamed Lieutenant Rickman for his inopportune killing of an Hawaiian chief. The gentlemen auctioned off Cook's clothes in the Great Cabin as the chiefs divided up his bones in the temple of Ku. They all – gentlemen and chiefs – had some sense of how great men find resurrection in their relics. Even the lower deck had their eyes on the value of souvenirs. All the Hawaiian artefacts they had collected went up in value, and you can find them now in the museums of the world – spears, axes, feather cloaks and beads – marked with the note that they belonged to the men who had belonged to Cook and had seen him die. They all had a clear sense that they were making history. And they knew that making history is a very divided thing. They knew all the chances and circumstances of the event – they knew crankiness, cowardice, carelessness; they knew the accidents of timing. They knew the inscrutability of heathen savages and their own civilised ignorance. They knew that if they had *not* done this or *had* done that, it would not have happened. But they knew, or they were coming to know, that what really had happened was that a hero had died. How it happened was not the accidents of it at all: how it happened was the heroic meaning of it. All the rest of their lives, in wardrooms, at dinner tables, in pubs, they would be asked how it had happened. It would not matter that they were like valets who have no heroes. Whatever they said about what actually happened, what really happened was that Cook had died a heroic death.

If Captain Cook found resurrection among the Hawaiians in the spirit of Lono, he also found resurrection among his fellow countrymen in the spirit of hero, discoverer and humanitarian. It did not matter whether he was really Lono for the Hawaiians. It did not matter whether he was truly hero, discoverer and humanitarian for his fellow countrymen. When news got home to Britain and spread, the British, the continental Europeans and the Americans made myth of it in poetry, drama and paintings. And the myth has had a sustained relevance in continually changing environments for 200 years. This has been not just in a proliferation of histories, but in continual rounds of as many metric moments of centenaries, sesquicentenaries and bicentenaries as the birth and death and all significant moments in between can provide.

In every corner of the earth there are wayside shrines to Captain Cook – cairns to say he was here, plaques to remember the remembering of him there. His relics are in glass cases on shelves, in safes of five continents. A day does not pass without bacteria, humidity and dust adding to the worries of the caretakers of his things. A year does not pass without some document or artefact or painting from his voyages of discovery joining the fetish commodities sought by governments, galleries and libraries. There is a world army of security guards and guides possessive of his relics, roting his history.

Two hundred years of celebrating Captain Cook may seem a lot of hero-worshipping, but it is not enough. 'Ways of seeing' Captain Cook in libraries, articles and museums have taken on a life of their own. Exhibitions, publications become a performing art in themselves. Why Captain Cook became a hero will not necessarily be the reasons why he remains one. The value of the cargo of his relics grows with time and itself sustains his cult.

But Cook has touched some other cultural nerve as well. If the myth of Lono sustained the realities of chieftainship and power, the myth of hero, discoverer and humanitarian expressed in rituals, monuments and anniversaries sustains our own image of who we are and who we should be. How the civilised mythologise themselves in possessing the Native, and how the British did this in Captain Cook, is the point of the reflection on possessing others below.

One can walk from the water's edge where Cook died, through the tangle of undergrowth that covers Kalaniopu'u's village along the path they both walked February 14, 1779, up to the temple of Ku. Here in 1826 Lord Byron set a monument when he brought back the bodies of Liholiho and his queen from Britain. The royal couple had gone to secure the aid of King George IV but had died of measles. Liholiho was laying claims on a special relationship that had begun with Cook's death and resurrection. Lord Byron set a cross on a cairn in Ku's temple. Its replacement is there still, always the *double entendre* that it ever was when different eyes see the same symbol as sign of the cross and sign of *makahiki*. When the world is full of sharks and gods as well as heroes and discoverers, who can write the history of them all?

.

ACT TWO.
The Beach

T HAT MOST FAMOUS of anthropologists, Claude Lévi-Strauss, in that most famous of his books, *Tristes Tropiques,* mused on the landscapes in which he felt most comfortable. Not high mountains, he wrote, they are too formal and abstract; not beaches, there is too much commotion and passing. He liked pastured mountains, lofty balconies, undomesticated landscape, easily imagined sights that humankind caught forever in its beginnings might have seen. It seems appropriate that Lévi-Strauss' structural anthropology may have been born on pastured mountains. I think history is more likely to be born on beaches, marginal spaces in between land and sea. Anyway this is where I would take you, to beaches where everything is relativised a little, turned around, where tradition is as much invented as handed down, where otherness is both a new discovery and a reflection of something old.

The words Native and Stranger, capitalised, may seem a little romantic and abstract. They are not meant to be, and they are not. Polynesian Native and European Stranger initial encounters were violent. Capital letters will not make the blood go away. The Polynesian words that describe this opposition of Native and Stranger are certainly not romantic: *kama'aina/haole* in Hawaii, *maohi/papaa* in Tahiti, *enata/aoe* in the Marquesas, *tagata/papalagi* in Samoa, *maori/pakeha* in New Zealand. These Polynesian words of opposition are always strong, expressive of both pride and degradation, of dominance and fear, of boundary and status. They are never neutral words. They damn and praise. They abuse and boast. They are words with history. They change their meanings and their tone with the changing relationships and oppositions they describe. It is difficult to find translations that do not have their own changing context and history. Call *kama'aina* 'native', and we are caught with the overtones of wildness and subordination that have been the cultural accretions on the word 'native' from a century of empire, mission and exploration. Look for transformations of the concept 'native' in historical usage, and we find images that are skewed by false geography, religion and racist power — 'indian', 'heathen', 'kanaka'. Look for a synonym that affects a neutrality — 'indigene', 'aboriginal', 'inhabitant', then the word acquires the unreality of all formal constructions and still does not hide the prejudices.

We can soften the noun 'native' with a little adjectival dignity and talk of 'native-born' and 'native land', and by that hope to leach out empire and implant roots. 'Stranger' already seems a softer word than 'alien' or 'foreigner' or 'intruder' or 'invader', too. It does not catch the ridicule or laughter or hatred that lay at different times in *haole* and *papalagi*. And it holds a contradiction. We use it now as if it has a meaning out of time only to discover that we need some algebra of its changing meaning to apply it to the past.

But I choose to let the words Native and Stranger stand. Until this moment the history of the *Bounty* has been 'ours', the Strangers'. We understand the Ship and recognise its history because in some way it mirrors ourselves. We are joined to it by language, by a sense that the questions we ask about it are questions about ourselves. But now as we step onto a beach at Tahiti that past of the *Bounty* is also somebody else's. We will not altogether understand it. The Native in it will be partly irrecoverable, partly so other that we will understand it only dimly. But because the *Bounty* Strangers stepped onto a Native's beach then, we the Strangers are now bound together with the Native by that contact. There is now no Native past without the Stranger, no Stranger without the Native. No one can hope to be mediator or interlocutor in that opposition of Native and Stranger, because no one is gazing at it untouched by the power that is in it. Nor can anyone speak just for the one, just for the other. There is no escape from the politics of our knowledge, but that politics is not in the past. That politics is in the present. There are men and women killing one another in the Pacific now because Strangers stepped on Natives' beaches. We have to write our history of the Pacific as the history of Native and Stranger Bound Together because we are bound together by that past reaching into the present. Who can change what was done? Who can return life or punish the dead? The only world we can change is that of the present of which we are a part. That world now has been encompassed by Native and Stranger alike. That world encompassed, the ways in which Native and

Stranger possessed and possess one another is the object of our mutual and our separate histories.

The beach at Matavai on Tahiti is of black sand. In Marlon Brando's film, *Mutiny on the Bounty,* the beach at Matavai was of white sand, transported by the ton from the New Jersey shore. Hollywood has a heightened sense of the appropriate props for South Seas islands, so white sand was dumped on black sand for the filming of the movie. It was nothing new for the beach at Matavai to be thus renovated according to outsiders' proprieties. The French had seen the whole island of Tahiti as New Cythera – Venus' birthplace. And the English, eyes blinkered by classical aesthetics, had seen Apollo and Hercules there too among the Tahitians. A beach from the sea, from a ship, from a camera lens is full of fiction. The beach itself, however, is a much more marginal space, where neither otherness nor familiarity holds sway, where there is much invention and blending of old and new. Tahitian beaches were special places of invention and discovery.

In Tahiti, the island people made beaches the mythic meeting places between Natives and Strangers. Their beach became enclosed in the ritual space of their places of worship, consciously set between land and sea. These temples, called Taputapuatea (Sacrifices from Abroad), were placed on promontories of land abutting the sea opposite a passage in the reef. Taputapuatea were theatres for the Tahitians' deepest plays about the origins of their power and authority. They had had such theatres long before the arrival of the European strangers in 1767. Their plays turned around the balance of legitimate authority vested in the natives of the land, and the violent, usurping power of strangers who came from the sea. There were two sacred places in these temples. One, on the edge of the sea, was the place of sacrifice where power was quietened and controlled: the other, on the side of the land, was a place of archive and preservation, where the symbols of authority's continuity were kept and community celebrated. The beach at Tahiti had a grammar. Its meaning came out of the paradoxes of violence and quiet, sea and land, stranger and native, politics and cosmology. No one met on the beach at Tahiti without bending to that grammar.

When the mutineers landed on the beach at Matavai in September 1789, there had already been twenty-two years of meetings between the islanders and European voyagers. The meetings had been cosmological:

the grammar of the beach had always been brought into play. The meetings had been historical: they were circumstantial in character and in time. Samuel Wallis' 'discovery' of Tahiti in 1767 had begun a period that by 1789 had not ended. So the beach that the mutineers landed on had its history as well as its cosmology. Our task is to blend them.

Tahiti looms out of the sea in two great massifs. One massif is the core of smaller Tahiti, called Taiarapu: the other is the larger Tahiti, called Tahiti-nui. The two massifs are joined by a low-lying isthmus known as Taravao and are skirted with rising ridges, a narrow plain and, beyond, an apron of reefs. The island of Moorea is closest to the south, near enough to be always part of the Tahitian political and social landscape. Away to the north-west, a hundred miles, are the leeward islands of the group – Huahine, Raiatea, Taha'a, Bora-Bora – out of sight but having a presence nonetheless. Matavai Bay was on the western side of the northern reach of the island of Tahiti. It was in the lee of the prevailing winds and by that was attractive to the strangers' ships. It was the strangers' alien presumption that the importance of Matavai to their needs was a sign of the social importance of the place. It was not.

The people of Tahiti, perhaps 35,000 in 1767, lived on the narrow coastal plain, more scattered in hamlets than concentrated in villages. Seen from the sea, their houses set in gardens and trees looked like plantations to the Europeans. Their social divisions were complex and volatile. A social map, taken out of time, does not describe their changing dominances, but at the end of the eighteenth century there seem to have been three main groups struggling for power and calling on changing alliances with three or four other groups. The three struggling for hegemony were, first, the Seaward Teva (Teva i tai), who occupied all of Taiarapu; their chiefly line shared the name Vehiatua. Second, there were the Landward Teva (Teva i uta), who consisted of four local divisions in the southeast of Tahiti-nui, but were centred on Papara; their 'queen', Purea, was understood by Samuel Wallis to be queen of Tahiti. Third, there were the Porenu'u, who occupied Pare and Arue on the edge of Matavai; their chiefly line shared the name Pomare. The lesser groupings were the Araroa, who lived on the windward side of Tahiti from Matavai to the isthmus; the Fana, who preserved a shaky independence at Fa'a'a; and a group, whom it has always been a puzzle to describe, at Pa'ea and Puna'auai. These last people were the custodians of the critically important temple or *marae* of the god 'Oro at 'Utu'aimahu-

rau. Why the god 'Oro was critically important belongs to our cosmological history.

There were four *marae* of the god 'Oro on Tahiti. The map shows their
sites. The first *marae* was established on Tahiti from Raiatea at Tautira
in about 1730; the second, 'Utu'aimahurau', was established in the
1750s in Pa'ea. A third *marae,* Mahaiatea, was being built by 'queen'
Purea and her husband, Amo, for their son, Ter'irere, about 1767–8 in
Papara.

The fourth temple was established at Tarahoi near Matavai by the Pomares, in their ascendancy. It was established in the time the mutineers
were in Tahiti, and with their aid. This *marae* had been at Tarahoi much
longer than that. It was in fact the first part of the Tahitian cultural
landscape that the European Strangers mapped. From 1767 it was called
'Morai Point'. After that, and because of the morbid interest in its bones
and the remnants of sacrifice, it was visited and sketched and painted by
Sir Joseph Banks, and, among others, by William Bligh and by young
George Tobin, a lieutenant with Bligh on the *Providence.*

Consider Tobin's watercolours of the Tapu'apuatea at Tarahoi (p. 186).
They are the cosmological beach we are describing. They are not pano-
ramic of the whole *marae,* but focus on two sections. The one looking
seaward – the *Providence* and the *Assistant* can be seen anchored in Matavai Bay – depicts the stepped stone *ahu* on the water's edge and the
remains of human sacrifice buried there. The other, looking landwards,
over the ceremonial pavement with its kinship stones or monuments,
shows the various treasure-houses of sacred paraphernalia and offering
platforms that would hold the god's share of postsacrificial feasts. On the
boundaries between the seaward part with its violence and the landward
part with its communion, the chief would play his mediating rituals in
all the guises of his human godliness.

Samuel Wallis in the *Dolphin* 'discovered' Tahiti on June 21, 1767.
He anchored at Matavai and then held off an attack by the Tahitians,
killing great numbers with canon and musket. He took possession of
Tahiti and Moorea for Britain and then left after an idyllic month-long
interlude of intercourse of every sort. There is some debate whether the
Dolphin was the first European vessel that the Tahitians had seen or of
which they had heard. Bougainville, commanding the *Etoile* and *Boudeuse,* arrived nine months later, in April 1768, fresh from giving the
Falklands back to Spain. He anchored for ten delicious days at Hitia'a,

called Tahiti 'New Cythera' and returned to France with Aotourou, the
first Tahitian to 'discover' Europe. The British, teased by Wallis' report
that he had seen the Great South Land to the south of Tahiti and, in any
case, looking for a place to measure the transit of Venus across the sun,
sent James Cook in the *Endeavour*. With him went Joseph Banks. The
Endeavour arrived at Matavai on April 13, 1769, for a three months'
stay. When the English left this second time, they took away Tupaia, a
priest and chiefly adviser, but he did not survive Batavia. The Spaniards,
anxious about what both the British and the French were doing in the
Pacific, sent four expeditions to Tahiti between 1772 and 1775 and set
up a mission at Tautira, where two friars and a young helper, Maximo
Rodriguez, spent ten miserable and unsuccessful months. Rodriguez's
account of their miseries survives in part. A number of Tahitians were
taken to Peru and some were returned to Tahiti.

The Spanish visits bracketed Cook's second visit in the *Resolution* and
Adventure, in August 1773 and April 1774. This time, Johann Reinhold
Forster and his son Georg were among the 'experimental gentlemen' on
board. The *Adventure* took to England a middle-ranked Tahitian called
Omai, but Cook brought him back on his third visit in the *Resolution*
and *Discovery* in August 1777. This third time, Cook had only professional naval observers with him. He and the Admiralty had become wary
of 'experimental gentlemen'. Cook established not only a British hegemony at Tahiti. He established a hegemony of his person as well. On all
of his visits, Cook had anchored at Matavai.

Eleven years followed, with no ships visiting Tahiti. Then, between
1788 and 1793, came a flurry of visits – those associated with the establishment of the convict settlement at Botany Bay, the two breadfruit
voyages of Bligh, the search for the *Bounty* mutineers in the *Pandora,* a
new survey expedition led by George Vancouver in the *Discovery* and
Chatham, and the beginning of whaling and trading in the Pacific.

Figure 9.   The beach and island of Tahiti. (Art on pp. 183–6)

a. Tahiti – Socio-cultural divisons. (After Kling, 1971.) b. Tahiti – The Strangers come.
(After Kling, 1971.) c. Matavai after Bligh's survey on the *Providence,* 1792. (After Bligh,
1792) d. The seaward section of the Taputapuatea at Tarahoi. (George Tobin, *The Morai
at Oparrey, Island of Otahytey . . . looking towards Matavai.* Watercolour. In *Sketches of HMS*
Providence. Mitchell Library, State Library of N.S.W. Ref: ZPXA 563, f 39.) e. The
landward section. (George Tobin, *Morai Point.* Mitchell Library. Ref: ZPXA 563, f 42.)

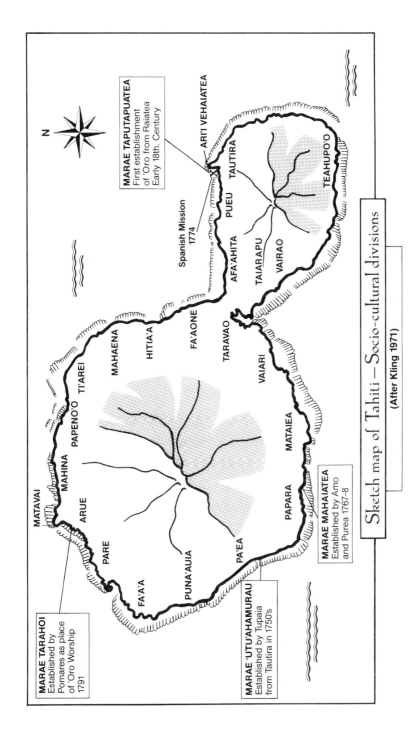

MARAE TAPUTAPUATEA
First establishment
of 'Oro from Raiatea
Early 18th. Century

ARI'I VEHAIATEA

TAUTIRA

PUEU

AFA'AHITA

Spanish Mission
1774

TAIARAPU

VAIRAO

TEAHUPO'O

MAHAENA

HITIA'A

FA'AONE

TARAVAO

PAPENO'O TI'AREI

VAIARI

MAHINA

MATAVAI

ARUE

MATAIEA

PARE

PUNA'AUIA

PAPARA

FA'A'A

PA'EA

MARAE MAHAIATEA
Established by Amo
and Purea 1767-8

MARAE 'UTU'AHAMURAU
Established by Tupaia
from Tautira in 1750's

MARAE TARAHOI
Established by
Pomares as place
of 'Oro Worship
1791

N

Sketch map of Tahiti – Socio-cultural divisions

(After Kling 1971)

Figure 9a.

183

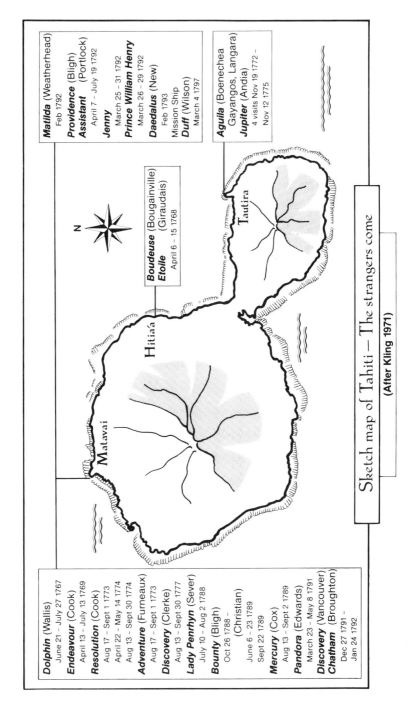

Dolphin (Wallis)
June 21 - July 27 1767
Endeavour (Cook)
April 13 - July 13 1769
Resolution (Cook)
Aug 17 - Sept 1 1773
April 22 - May 14 1774
Aug 13 - Sept 30 1774
Adventure (Furneaux)
Aug 17 - Sept 1 1773
Discovery (Clerke)
Aug 13 - Sept 30 1777
Lady Penrhyn (Sever)
July 10 - Aug 2 1788
Bounty (Bligh)
Oct 26 1788 -
(Christian)
June 6 - 23 1789
Sept 22 1789
Mercury (Cox)
Aug 13 - Sept 2 1789
Pandora (Edwards)
March 23 - May 8 1791
Discovery (Vancouver)
Chatham (Broughton)
Dec 27 1791 -
Jan 24 1792

Matilda (Weatherhead)
Feb 1792
Providence (Bligh)
Assistant (Portlock)
April 7 - July 19 1792
Jenny
March 25 - 31 1792
Prince William Henry
March 26 - 29 1792
Daedalus (New)
Feb 1793
Mission Ship
Duff (Wilson)
March 4 1797

Aguila (Boenechea
Gayangos, Langara)
Jupiter (Andia)
4 visits Nov 19 1772 -
Nov 12 1775

Boudeuse (Bougainville)
Etoile (Giraudais)
April 6 - 15 1768

N

Tautira

Hitiaa

Matavai

Sketch map of Tahiti — The strangers come

(After Kling 1971)

Figure 9b.

184

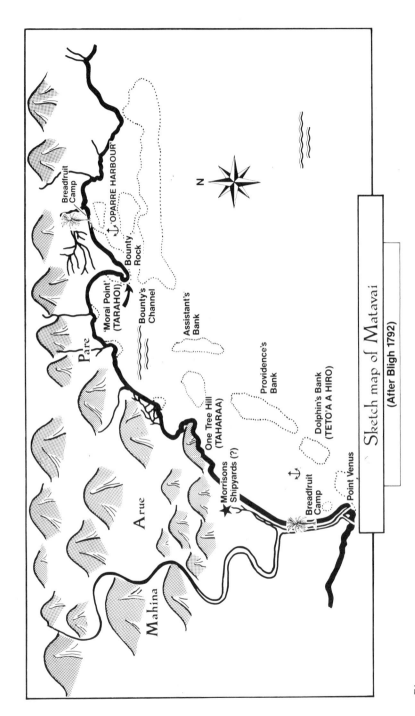

N

Breadfruit Camp

'OPARRE HARBOUR'

Bounty Rock

'Morai Point' (TARAHOI)

Bounty's Channel

Pare

Assistant's Bank

One Tree Hill (TAHARAA)

Providence's Bank

Morrisons Shipyards (?)

Arue

Dolphin's Bank (TETO'A A HIRO)

Breadfruit Camp

Point Venus

Mahina

Sketch map of Matavai
(After Bligh 1792)

185

Figure 9c.

Figure 9d.

Figure 9e.

William Bligh spent nine months in two visits in the *Bounty* and *Providence* at Matavai. When the mutineers returned to Tahiti in September 1789, there began a period after which Tahiti was never without European residents.

Matavai was in the shadow of Tahiti's highest mountain, Oro-Hena, which pressed close to the sea. The bay bent around from its east point, Teauroa (Point Venus), to a high promontory, Tahara'a (One Tree Hill). In Tahitian eyes, Matavai had some association with Hiro, a trickster, a god of thieves and a rival of 'Oro. Hiro grew up at Matavai and was schooled in sacred knowledge there. He played with the sand and made the dunes. Teto'a a'Hiro, his rock, was the reef on which the *Dolphin* stuck in 1767. It has been called Dolphin's Bank ever since. Out of all those thieves whom the Strangers flogged and killed, those who got away no doubt blessed Hiro for their skills. If the Strangers had something of 'Oro in their violent power, then there was also something of the trickster in the thieving. A river, Vaipopo'o, paralleled the curve of the bay and divided Point Venus. The spit thus formed made a place of boundaries, where Cook set up his observatory, Bligh his tent for breadfruit, and the London Missionary Society their first mission.

The separation of the district of Mahina in which Matavai lay and of Pare, where the Pomare family ruled, lay just west of Tahara'a hill. Beyond that was 'Oparre Harbour', as the British called it. Further still was Taunoa, an anchorage to which Bligh moved the *Bounty* when he found Matavai too open to north-west weather. At Taunoa, in some isolation because of his sacredness, lived the firstborn of the Pomare line. This western point of Matavai Bay, Tarahoi, was called by the British 'Morai Point'. This stretch of the island from 'Point Venus' to 'Morai Point', was something of a back bay to indigenous politics but it was essentially 'Otaheite' to European strangers. It was the Beach to which the sixteen men of Christian's *Bounty* returned.

Scene i. *Narrative*

BETWEEN LAND AND SEA

Whatever drove the sixteen men to leave Christian and return to Tahiti in September of 1789, it could not have been a sense of settlement. Tahiti, to them, was a Beach, a place in between mutiny and ordinary living. It was not unpleasant for that, of course, either in anticipation or in fact. They returned to a life that, by many measures seamen might have had, was blissful. It was ambivalent and threatening, nonetheless. They knew, from their previous five months' stay, that life was cheap on Tahiti, and that their lives would be under siege for what they owned and for being on land now and not shipboard. They knew that this symbolic environment was full of mysteries and that the only natural sign they could be sure of was violence, to which they had the key in their muskets and pistols. They knew also that Tahiti was a place of sacrifice. The debris of sacrifice – skulls and bones and corpses – was everywhere to be seen and smelled. Their beach was between gallows and altar.

Tahiti was a place of sacrifice. Spanish friars in 1775, themselves whispering priestly invocations over bread and wine to commemorate the sacrifice of Calvary, were the first to see human sacrifices at Tahiti. Cook, and then Bligh, were both fired by Joseph Banks' ethnographic zeal and became eager participant observers of sacrifice. (Indeed, they were incorporated into the ceremonies more than they knew.) The European strangers were entertained by a sense of their own civilised superiority over savage natives by nothing so much as their discovery that the Tahitians made human sacrifice. Although the strangers themselves sacrificed human lives – naturally, ordinarily, frequently – to the abstractions of *realpolitik* – the law, the Crown – to their God they offered symbols of a body and blood in bread and wine, or they devised other metaphors of atonement. Nothing scandalised them so much in Tahiti as the fact that natives seemed to do things the other way around. Natives seemed to have real gods and make-believe polity.

What is more, the natives sacrificed lives carelessly. Natives did not eke out symbolic meanings in their sacrifices. They did not seem to make 'victims' or dramatise the victims' destruction. There were no social acts of deference or proclamations, no correct forms. As lore began to accumulate about who the victims might be, and as the strangers watched more intently in their visits, they learned that the victims were the wretched of society. Victims were said to be thieves or violators of some *tapu*. Potential victims lived in fear of a rumour of war or a promise of peace or any of the great social moments of their chiefs (*ari'i*) or of any other *ari'i* whom their own chief cultivated. Victims – they themselves knew who they were – had only to know of the trances and tremblings of a priest possessed by the gods for them to flee to the mountains until the appropriate number had been taken. The potential victims were said to be a pool of wretches fatally related in their nothingness, but equally they could be pushed into that pool by politics, as families lost their social footing and showed their powerlessness in the loss of a member as a 'victim'. Stories about the taking of victims were all about stealth and subterfuge and speed: a wink, a nod, the doubletalk by an *ari'i* of 'taking this crab' or 'that pig', a sudden blow from behind, a quick parcelling of the body in fronds and leaves, then the familiar sight of temple attendants loping by with the enveloped flesh stretched on a pole between them. The gods did not demand that their meat be fresh. The parcels could lie about in a rotten stench for days or weeks, waiting for the ritual occasion. Being victim was a male privilege. In times of sacrifice, nothing female or anything touched by a female could intervene. Nor was the time of sacrifice a time for anything domestic or ordinary, such as cooking or harvesting or fishing. The catching and killing of the victims, to civilised observers, seemed to resemble the distracted and cavalier behaviour of savages towards their idols – careless, superficial, irreligious. It did not fit the civilised image of what proper sacrifice should be. For the civilised, biblical metaphors of sacrifice ran culturally deep. A sacrificial altar was the proper stage for killing, and it required all the external signs that real transformations were taking place – even as happened when Abraham prepared to sacrifice Isaac and when the Romans sacrificed Jesus. The eyes of witnesses and participants should be bent to see the significances behind the appearances. All those involved should be leached of personality and circumstance, in order to play their roles as victims, executioners and representatives of power. Sacrifices displayed order starkly. They tamed wildness. When natives made them, sacrifices seemed only quirky pantomimes of power and order.

The sixteen mutineers had to be inventive about the ways they tamed the wildness around them. Individually, they had learned to profit by the exchange in the Tahitian relationship of *taio,* or 'friend'. 'Tayo' and 'taboo' were the first words to cross stranger/native cultural boundaries in Tahiti. In *taio,* Tahitians exchanged names and, with names, the rights and obligations of personality and role. 'Tayo', in translation on the strangers' side, was something else. Strangers had no eyes to see the nuances in the Tahitians' relationships and obligations. Yet all the crew of the *Bounty* had made 'tayos', and now the sixteen men returned to theirs and, separately or in pairs, made residence with their old 'tayos'. Ordinarily a 'tayo' would not be a woman except occasionally, when such a 'friend' might be a very high-ranking woman. The mutineers' 'tayos' were mostly male relations of the women with whom they cohabited.

The 'tayo' exchange was personal. But the mutineers felt the need of a corporate existence as well. Indeed, on the beach, the Tahitians did not let them escape their identity as strangers, as British. The mutineers found it, and the Tahitians gave it, under the same symbol: the British flag. The mutineers, a day or so after they landed, marched behind the flag to visit the boy 'king', Pomare. Then later they erected a flagstaff in the small compound of their houses, raised the flag and hauled it down before an ever-interested cluster of Tahitian spectators. They even began to hold Sunday's divine services beneath it. They needed some sign on their beach of their civilised otherness.

In Tahitian affairs, the British flag had come to have an important place on *their* Beach. To know how important it was, one must know how the Tahitians tamed the wildness within their own polity. It has to do with feather girdles and flags and sacrifices.

Captain Samuel Wallis of HMS *Dolphin* was in bed when he took possession of what he was pleased to call King George's Island in honour of His Britannic Majesty. Wallis and many of his men were sick — they thought fatally ill — with scurvy and its many complications. In the scurvy's painful lethargy, the island they stood off taunted them. Its sweet smells wafted to them, and they knew it to be more beautiful than any island they had ever seen. For five days they had slowly moved along its northern shore, probing the reefs for an entry and an anchorage, looking for a beach where they could land without wetting their muskets. Their contacts with the islanders had been good and bad. The islanders who had come to the ship had been full of antics, had made speeches at the sailors, had thrown plantain branches into the sea, had made small gifts of food. But when the ship's cutter went closer to survey the bottom, the canoes crowded in threateningly. Already the 'Dolphins' had killed and wounded some islanders to show the force of the musket and to drive off the great double-hulled vessels that could easily overwhelm their cutter. In the wardroom the officers deliberated whether they should risk a landing or hurry on to Tinian, 4,000 miles away, and let the Pacific do its worse to them in the shortest possible time.

They really had no choice. Their bruised bodies, their suppurating gums, their swollen faces told them that. They had to stop their own rot with fresh food and get water in quantity before they went on. Matavai was their saving. The bay lay calm and deep behind the reef. A river curved behind the bend of the black sand beach.

'Port Royal' they called it, with half a dream for a British Pacific Main that never was to be, but Matavai, its native name, in the end held the day. They had a scare as they ran aground on a reef inside the bay, but once off they were soon at anchor undamaged except for a scrape on the *Dolphin*'s new experimental copper sheathing. Around them stretched a panorama engraved forever as paradise on the European mind. The 'Dolphins' saw the panorama more pragmatically. Their cannons could sweep it all, from off the port bow at what was to be later known as 'Point Venus', for the planet observed there, to 'Skirmish' or 'One Tree Hill' or Tahara'a, two miles around on the starboard side.

At Matavai the score of the first meeting of European stranger and Tahitian native came to its counterpoint. The fugitive moments of contact became dramatised, staged for the understanding it gave them of one another. In the calm of the bay, the ship's people and the land's people could organise their confrontation and in that sense make it meaningful. Captain Wallis could have simply fed his men and watered his ship, and gone on. But he needed to 'make history' by 'taking possession' of the island he had 'discovered'. For that, proprieties needed some play. The Tahitians, to believe their later legendary memory, saw fulfilled their prophecies of being visited by canoes without outriggers, but they also began to collect themselves in Matavai for a more dramatic reception with even more mythical meaning.

The 'Dolphins' prepared their ship with the suspicion that they might be attacked and the expectancy that if they were to get food and water they must discover a trade. Their preparations for fighting were well practised. They divided into four watches, loaded the great guns with shot and grape, and armed every man with a pistol and cutlass. They later varied in their count of the canoes around them, but they were generally agreed that they numbered between four and six hundred. Perhaps 8,000 natives manned them. No doubt the 'Dolphins' were apprehensive, but they had also smarted a little under the captain's instructions to remain quiet and 'test the temper' of the natives in the days before. They had suffered the indignity of cuffs and rough treatment and uncomprehending exchanges and now were not averse to teaching the natives a lesson.

There was, as well, an ambiguity in the situation. The 'Dolphins' had an etiquette for killing when they fought. They fought with rules – about prisoners and prizes, about surrender and the niceties of chivalry. But on the edge of this battle, the natives were other. Their otherness was nowhere so marked as in the wanton antics of the girls who stood on the prows of most of the canoes. The girls lifted their wraps and flaunted their nakedness. They made unmistakable gestures and responded to ribaldry of the seamen as if sex had its own language of natural signs.

In the middle of this sea of sexuality, and in a canoe that everybody noted for its magnificence and for the 'awning' over the platforms that joined its double hull, was some sort of native director. The 'Dolphins' guessed he was one of the 'principal inhabitance'. He was wrapped in red-stained *tapa* cloth. He offered bunches of red and yellow feathers. It was he, someone later said, who gave the signal with the wand in his hand. With that action thousands of natives pulled pebbles from the ballast of their canoes and showered the *Dolphin* with painful accuracy. The *Dolphin* responded with awful effect. 'It would require Milton to describe', her master wrote. The canoes were smashed with round shot. When the natives rallied after the first shock and seemed to be returning, the three-pounders were loaded with seventy musket balls apiece and when the canoes were within three or four hundred yards they were sprayed, with 'considerable loss'. The great guns concentrated on the large canoe. It was the 'King of the Island', the 'Dolphins' thought. They admired the courage of those in the five or six canoes who stayed with the king even though he became the target of their firing. They will think us gods, some of the crew said, and others worried what revenge the natives might take if they came with firebrands. By nightfall the powder smoke had gone, and the

Figure 10.
The struggle between the Tahitians and the *Dolphin* at Matavai, as represented in an engraving in Hawkesworth's account of British circumnavigations. (From John Hawkesworth, *An Account of the Voyages Undertaken by Order of His Present Majesty for Making Discoveries in the Southern Hemisphere.* London: W. Strahan and T. Cadell, 1773. Baillieu Library, The University of Melbourne.)

officers discussed whether it was spices they now smelled on the warm heavy air. They would marvel later how little effect all this killing seemed to have on the natives. It seemed to justify their own carelessness. The *realpolitik* of discovery and possession meant the native was not owed the ordinary etiquettes of war. The Dolphins could think of nothing better to do in the aftermath of the slaughter than to 'act haughty' to the natives and teach them to trade more sensibly.

How the natives saw the strangers is, by any standard of objective discourse, nothing more than informed guess. Yet to say that the meeting on the part of the natives was a coordinated and dramatised reception seems certain. That it was invented for the novelty of the conditions also seems certain. Their invention was suffused with their own old cosmological familiarities. It was not a 'natural' scene just because the strangers saw it suffused with their own familiarities. The coordination of the natives' 'attack' was not at the hands of the 'king of the island'. There was no 'king of the island', and later there was a strange silence about this incident of violence among those who had ambitions to be 'king of the island' when the European visits became more frequent.

It made no sense in the Tahitian way of things to see the 'king of the island' as a chief performing a political or territorial role, no matter how natural it seems that they should have been defensive against an invading 'other'. The 'other' of their wars and battles had always been territorially specific – other alliances, other islands. The 'other' of this encounter was much more generic to their categories of identity. The women performing 'wanton tricks' in the canoes were a clue that something other than battle or ambush was in their minds. We know something of Tahitian war at sea. Like the English, they had their etiquettes of killing. They had their ceremonies of engagement and disengagement. In none of these were women performing 'wanton antics'. But in other circumstances, especially in the rituals of 'Oro, women's dancing was sacramental to the presence of the god. Like the tufts of red and yellow feathers, women caught the eye of the divine to focus it on prayer or an offering. Indeed, failing these entrapments, abuse and aggression towards the gods were not unknown. Tahitian gods were not so distantly divine, even 'Oro, that they could not be tested and contested. There was no great contradiction seen in raising the attention of the gods by arousing their lust or making them angry.

No doubt it is commonsensical on our part to read the hurled pebbles and signalled attack as ordinary ambush. And, we may think, a keen perception by the Tahitians of the lust in the seamen's eyes could have led to a strategy of subterfuge in staging the women's dancing. The Tahitians had no experience of cannon and were not necessarily convinced of the power of the musket. Native greed, strangers' callousness, misread signs are thus the commonsensical history of the event. But they are not, and it is commonsense that is the deceiver. Greed, callousness and misread signs have their play, but the 'king of the island' was likely to have been an *arioi* master of a lodge or a priest of 'Oro. His double canoe was no battle ship. It was likely to have been 'Rainbow', his sacred transportation. The awning he stood on was likely to have covered the ark of 'Oro's accoutrements. What the Tahitians saw on the *Dolphin* was Tahitian gods, divine in the Tahitian way. Their agnosticism, their religious relativism was still in the future, long after the *Dolphin's* going, long after the supposedly humanising effect of the 'Dolphins' ' very predictable behaviour.

Tahitians were adept at seeing the divine in the human, whatever the contradictions. It is a stranger's view, not a native's, that there is a necessary contradiction between commonsense realism and mythical understanding. Missionaries would later be scandalised at worshippers' irreverences to their idols, as if reverential piety were a measure of belief. Both Cook and Bligh were cynically convinced of the superficiality of native beliefs because each had seen the natives' distracted, formalistic behaviour in rituals. Natives as well as strangers, ourselves as well as others, easily bridge apparent contradictions between myth and commonsense. The insider knows that myth and commonsense answer different questions.

What always embarrasses the stranger's effort to understand the native is the stranger's insistence that the native perceptions should be literal, while the stranger's own perceptions are allowed to be metaphoric. So the Tahitian natives' supposed belief that the European strangers were gods 'from beyond the sky' is seen as a belief of literal equivalence between man and god, easily dispelled by the very ordinary behaviour of lusty, cantankerous seamen. Whereas the strangers' more typical understanding of themselves is that they hold things in their varied meanings, so that there is for the stranger no difficulty in taking 'he is a god' into any number of metaphors about perfection in physical beauty or intelligence or morality without any necessary incarnational literalness. So that if one argues that the native Tahitians received the *Dolphin* in a dramatic play that made sense to them out of their cosmology of 'Oro, there is a half expectancy that the illogicality or contradiction in the experience should have destroyed the literalness of their understanding. Their consequent makebelieve in the face of contradiction is seen as either a sign of native simplicity or as evidence that they were by this forced into a cultural agnosticism that was the seed of change.

History, myth, sacrament, ritual do not work that way. They all serve to colligate the past and make understandings that bring order to the present. They make sense of what has happened by economising the wealth of possible causes of events down to principal determinants that really matter. They do not predict what will happen, nor do they give a rubric for future behaviour. This, from another perspective, is the issue that Marshall Sahlins addressed in *Historical Metaphors and Mythical Realities* (1981). The Hawaiians had a mythic understanding of Cook as the god Lono. They did not, because of that, act out the narrative of their legends with predictable literalness. Nonmythic factors in the event – fear, anger, imprudence, pride – had their effect. But those factors, like all the other inconsistencies and contradictions and novelties surrounding the events, did not matter beside the simplicities that came from a few recognisable clues. To suggest, as I do, that the Tahitian natives put the arrival of the European strangers into the context of their beliefs about 'Oro with all the resonances those beliefs had in politics, religion and society is not to write the history of their contact. What 'actually happened' is inevitably reduced in the story of it to a finite mixture of infinite actions and meanings. What significantly happened for the Tahitian natives was much simpler. The arrival of the *Dolphin* was the occasion of another 'Oro incarnation or materialisation, and all the Tahitian associations of sovereignty and sacrifice, of colony and coming from 'beyond the sky', of alliance and title, were at work. It did not matter that the Tahitians were soon to discover in the 'Dolphins' the very flesh-and-blood qualities of deified chiefs and the man-made quality of deified things. Their transformations of their past and present experience were about a much more real and immediate world beneath the appearances of things.

The *Dolphin* had sailed into Matavai by what may always have been, but certainly by her entry became, a sacred passage off the *marae* Tarahoi. She was, by any measure the Tahitians had, a special ship, of the quality of 'Rainbow', even perhaps of the quality prophesied when news of similar vessels that had visited other islands reached Tahiti. She streamed with the magnificent decoration of white sail and bunting and flag. The Tahitians offered her plantain branches – *ta'ata meia roa*, 'man-long-bananas', 'Oro's token human sacrifice – from the moment they saw her. The plantain branches they offered her, the inducement of naked dance and sexual gesture by which 'Oro's presence was attracted to his sacred *marae*, spoke the metaphors by which they grasped the novelty of her arrival. Slain pigs, the bunched red and yellow feathers – which no doubt meant that at some Taputapuatea a human sacrifice was lying – made the novelty familiar. If the tone and direction of myths of 'Oro collected later are any indication, the *Dolphin* came like one of the marvellous canoes of old from afar, and Tahitian expectancy would be that she would make a landing, be the centre of sacrifice, be the occasion for reinstatement and investiture of the *ari'i rahi*, be the circumstance for alliance and treaty, and the establishment in them of some hegemony. The arrival at Matavai was true to the myth of how 'Oro would arrive to colonise a new place. It had happened at Taiarapu long ago and more recently at Atehuru. The novelties did not matter, nor even the contradictions. The Tahitians were entertained and wholly satisfied by its simple meaning.

On the day following, the violence was quiet. All day the Tahitians used 'a great deal of ceremony'. They stood in their canoes, peered hard at the *Dolphin,* made long speeches, held high their plantain branches. They clearly watched every move of the 'Dolphins', and if a sailor 'looked surly' or if there was any gesture that seemed hostile, quickly the Tahitians raised their branches high. In the end they threw their branches into the sea and came towards the *Dolphin.* Pointing to the shore and talking to the ship all the while, they threw a plantain branch on board. By this they had made a sacrifice and in their eyes made the situation manageable, for they then began to trade quite freely. The trade that afternoon was interrupted briefly when a seaman defrauded a Tahitian and the native made as if to strike him and created a great commotion. The seaman, already bruised by the stones of the day before and no doubt remembering that he had tried to kill these same natives, was given a dozen lashes by Wallis. For him, it was a rueful token of the ambiguities of every meeting of native and stranger.

June 26 was the day for possession – the first of many such days for Tahiti, as it turned out. Wallis took possession of Tahiti in the name of George III with a pennant and a pole, a turned sod, a toast to the King's good health and three British cheers. Nine months later, Comte Louis Antoine de Bougainville buried an oak plank inscribed with the message that Tahiti belonged to the French. He also left the names of all his men in a bottle. Then the Spaniards, when they came, set up a Holy Cross, processed to it with lighted candles, sang their litanies, said a mass, fired their muskets and guns, wrote a solemn little convention to themselves. Elsewhere it was different and the same. Three crosses on Easter Island for Spaniards, cairns and inscriptions in New Zealand for the British, white flags in Tonga for the Dutch. Turning the sod, depositing pennies in a bottle, throwing sand into the sea, raising loyal toasts, carving messages on trees, scratching words on pieces of paper, showing the colours, nailing copper and lead plates to a post – ancient ceremonies of 'turfe and twygge' the English called them – or solemn acts 'to bring faith and testimony in public form', to cite the Spanish phrase.

Wallis, being in bed ill, sent Tobias Furneaux, his second lieutenant, to take possession of Tahiti. When Furneaux lined up eighteen able seamen, a sergeant with his twelve marines and three 'young gentlemen' or midshipmen on the black sand of Matavai bay, he was making ritual. He was making signs about authority and power, dominance and proper order; and each was established in the making of the signs of it. Presumably Captain Wallis could have shouted out from his sickbed, 'this island belongs to us' but that was not 'the right way of doing things'. That did not contain the doubletalk of snapped orders, of straight lines, smart appearances, silence in the ranks, reverences to the flag. The ritual occasion is marked off from everyday actions by special languages, formal postures, the slow motion of meaningful gesture, the fancy dress of formal occasions, careful etiquette. There is always a 'priest' at ritual moments, someone who knows the established ways of doing things, someone who plans and marshalls the actions. Or there is a book of rubrics, a permanent record of the order of things. Of course in social actions of a symbolic kind it is always, in the phrase made famous about the 'thick description' of them, 'wink upon wink upon wink'. The actions are a text in which the abstract realities are mythically read, certainly, but the participants are also observing many levels of meaning. A ritual about possession may be at the same time a ritual about the hierarchy of authority between seamen, midshipmen, sergeant and second lieutenant, or, as in the case of the possession of Tahiti, it may have been a play telling the sailors about the wardroom divisions of their superiors. As it happened, the first lieutenant of the *Dolphin* – 'Mr Growl' they called him – was absent, not for the first time, and the running of the ship had fallen to the young and willing Toby Furneaux. Standing at attention, looking with a fixed gaze, feeling the ambience of sight and sound, even perhaps sensing the irony between their bedraggled condition and the solemnity of the symbols, Furneaux and the seamen made ritual with meanings of never-ending amplification.

Tobias Furneaux had marshalled his guard on the beach. Behind him in the bay were three boats, under the charge of Mr Molyneux. The boats' musquetoons were trained on the small crowd of natives gathering on the far side of the stream. Behind the boats was the *Dolphin,* cannons trained on the same target. The guard set up a pole and a pennant, or 'pendant' as was the navy's word. The pole was nothing grand or permanent, a spare spar, but tall enough to let the tapering colours stand free, and firm enough to hold them stiff in the breeze. The colours were red. James Cook saw them years later and simply called them 'British Colours' and, as we shall see, William Bligh sketched them and called them 'red buntin'.

Whether red, or why red, may seem an idle interest, but being curious about symbolic action is being more meticulous than idle. Prior to the ceremony, Furneaux would have asked his wardroom colleagues and then his captain which was the correct flag for acts of possession, or he would have known that British colours were more appropriate than naval colours on such occasions. And if accidents had affected the proprieties — say, that they had none of the proper bunting to spare — its replacement would not have been made carelessly because only the 'indians would see'. The real viewers of the ceremonies were themselves, and the proprieties observed were a currency in their relationships, about being responsible, about being a good officer.

There is a phrase we use when we see other people doing something memorable or beating some record or doing things for the first time. We say they are 'making history'. Contained within the phrase is a sense that what is remembered will change the environment in which others will act. They will have to respond in some way to the history that has been made. Samuel Wallis and Toby Furneaux were 'making history' in taking possession of Tahiti. They did not impose any system of ownership on Tahitian land. They did, however, leave an historical marker. Their acted-out events would leave a public memory of an act of possession that was meant to change the relations of other sovereignties to this land now possessed. When James Cook came to Tahiti later and found that the Spaniards had written *Carolus Tertius Imperator* on their Holy Cross, he scratched it out and wrote *Georgius Tertius Rex* instead. The Spaniards were furious for years. The Viceroy of Peru constantly tried to get another expedition together to scratch out Cook's inscription. It was not as if Wallis began British Empire in the Pacific: he left no delegates, he built no forts. He simply 'made history' with the presumption that the history he made would hold others to the efficacy of his symbolic acts.

Wallis left a more concrete historical marker at Tahiti. He left his flag on its pole. By the time Furneaux had read his proclamations and hauled the pennant to its place, a crowd of four or five hundred Tahitians had gathered on the bank of the river that divided them from the beach. They each held a plantain branch, a forest of a crowd, a crowd of sacrifices. If a flag for the Europeans might stand for something else — for nation, for legitimate power — and if gestures around a flag might stir moods and sentiments of loyalty and pride, then so might a plantain branch rouse as strong sensibilities for the Tahitians. Cook remarked three years later how omnipresent was the symbol of the plantain, and how effective. It was a sign of peace, of deference, of sacrifice. *Ta'ata meia roa,* 'man-long-banana', it was called when a branch was offered to a god or to a chief as substitute for a human offering. Abstracted out of its natural environment where it abounded in rich variety, the plantain branch could calm an angry man, placate a god, legitimate a chief – given the conditions in which the sign could be read. As a flag could stir a manly bosom, given martial music, a solemn tread and a supportive crowd, so a plantain branch could raise reverential awe, given the smell of rotting sacrifices, the shade of sacred trees, the beat and tone of a temple drum, the call of sacred birds, and the deferences of bared torsos and averted faces. It was the ambience of ritual action that created an environment in which the symbols worked. This was not easily experienced by strangers. Instead of being entertained – catching the meanings of the actions and being preoccupied with interpreting them – the strangers were the observers, catching the symbols but not the signs, translating the outward formalities of the other's signals but not their meaning. To the strangers the forest of sacrifices looked like a Palm Sunday procession and was depicted as such in Hawkesworth's (1773) publication of Wallis' voyage.

Meanwhile the Tahitians had found their own layers of meanings, their own 'wink upon wink upon wink', in discerning in the strangers' ceremonies on the spit of land between sea and river. Tahitians were intrigued for more than twenty-five years at the symbols of the strangers' flags and their ceremonies about them. During Cook's stay at Tahiti as well as Bligh's, the Tahitians became bored with the exotic behaviour of strangers, but they would collect nonetheless for their evening parades and their ceremonies around the flag. Even the *Bounty* mutineers erected their flagpole and on Sundays would have large crowds to see them haul their flag. Before such fundamentalisms of authority Tahitians never ceased to have an anthropological wonder. On the occasion of the *Dolphin's* arrival in 1767, whatever else the Tahitians saw, they interpreted the flag-raising as a moment in which sacrifices were owed, and they came with their forest of plantain branches to make them.

When the 'Dolphins' left the beach and returned to the ship, they saw the crowd of natives approach the flag tentatively. With many gestures of deference, the islanders laid plantains and an offering of pigs at its foot. They were startled at the movements of the flag in the breeze. Then an old man came out to the *Dolphin* in a canoe and made a formal speech.

The sailors did not know its meaning, but it seemed to concern the flag. He threw a plantain branch into the sea and made an offering of pigs to the people on the ship as he had done to the flag, as if he had struck an agreement. With others he took the flag down and carried it away. That night the 'Dolphins' saw many large fires along the shore and on the sides of the hill.

Early next morning, a crowd of several thousand processed along the coast. In the midst of them a young man held the flag aloft on a pole. They seemed to be making for a cluster of canoes near the *marae* of Tarahoi. The 'Dolphins', worried that it augured a repetition of the day before, broke up the crowd with a few cannon shots, then harassed them with grape, and destroyed the canoes. When the remnants of the crowd collected at Tahara'a, 'Skirmish Hill', the 'Dolphins' fired their cannons again, so that the crowd could see the balls bouncing across the landscape, ploughing through the trees. The cutter was sent in to land among the canoes, and its crew smashed with axes what the cannons had not shattered.

Perhaps the 'Dolphins' were correct in surmising that the flag was being taken to the canoes. We cannot know. It was unlikely that there was to be another attack, however. In all probability the Tahitians were making for some canoe, some other 'Rainbow' of 'Oro. We know they were soon to take the flag to the other side of the island, to the district of Papara, to a *marae* called Mahaiatea then being built or about to be built by the chief of the Landward Teva, Amo, and his wife, Purea. Amo and Purea were about to invent something. Amo's name meant 'Wink'. They were indeed about to put 'wink upon wink upon wink'.

Purea, or 'Oberea' as a much wider English public began to know her, was about to enter the stage of history as the 'Queen of Tahiti'. She was not queen, of course, but a royal personage was needed to make Englishmen's fantasies work. How they invented her and she invented them belongs to the story of how native and stranger became symbiotic to one another, how they possessed one another. Indeed one has to say that, even if the complications become confusing, the inventing of Purea did not end with the eighteenth century. Inventing Purea has been part of a long historical process and is illustrative not merely of the ways native and stranger become environmental to one another but also of the ways the past becomes environmental to the present.

Purea entered the stage modestly enough. Two weeks after the rituals

of possession, George Robertson, the master of the *Dolphin*, saw a small
fleet of ten or twelve double canoes, all bearing streaming pennants of
red, white, blue and yellow, land near the *marae* of Tarahoi. Then Mr
Pickersgill, the surgeon, 'on a walk in the country' ten days after that,
came upon a great house, the 'palace' as it came to be called. There he
was entertained by the queen, and she in turn was fed hand to mouth by
her 'ladies in waiting'. On July 11, or perhaps July 20 — there is some
conflict in the records — Purea came on board the *Dolphin*. The captain
treated her royally and there began a series of mock-social occasions in
which Wallis and his officers displayed their civilised ways and enjoyed
the gaffes that showed the satire in savage queens. They laughed at her
simplicities in handling telescopes and cutlery and mirrors, but they were
of divided opinion on whether her extravagant show of sorrow at their
departure was a subterfuge (to ambush them again) or whether it was
native childishness — or perhaps they actually were something special. On
the whole they seemed to take pleasure in their relations with this queen-
but-not-a-queen: she gave them after all some control over their own marginality.

In the way of things, the day-to-day relations of Purea with the officers
of the *Dolphin* were less important than the history made of them. That
history was to compress Purea into a single fiction out of two ethnographic
encounters. No sooner had Wallis returned to England than Cook was
sent out to Tahiti to check on his supposed sighting of the Great South
Land and to measure the Transit of Venus across the sun for the Royal
Society. The young Joseph Banks went with him. Cook and Banks found
the politics of Tahiti changed. More correctly, they found they had to
change their suppositions about the politics of Tahiti. Purea and Amo had
been defeated in their plan to establish their son Teri'irere as the most
highly titled and the most politically significant figure on Tahiti. The
Seaward Teva had broken away from Taiarapu, massacred many of the
people of Papara and destroyed any hopes Purea and Amo had of making
Mahaiatea the ritual centre of the island. Purea was no longer 'queen'.
The politics of the island, in so far as it concerned the strangers, was in
the hands of a man called Tu and his line, the chiefs of Pare-Arue, near
Matavai.

There is now a ceremony performed at Tahiti each year during the
Bastille Day holidays. At the *marae* Arahu Rahu, reconstructed for tourists and 'folkloric' celebrations, the 'king' and 'queen' of Tahiti are in-

vested with a *maro ura*, a wrap or girdle of red feathers. It is a symbol, like a crown and sceptre, of their sovereignty for the duration of the celebrations. Thousands are there to see the ceremony. The royal couple 'fly' on the shoulders of attendants, as the high chiefs of old 'flew', lest their sacred feet touch the ground. 'Priests' are there, decked out fantastically in improvisations of what priests used to wear. Sacrificial offerings of food and cloth are made. All process to the sacred stones where the couple stand before the altar for the investment. It is a carnival of monarchy in republican days. It is not peculiar for that, of course. If clowns could be kings in the topsy-turvy world of carnival, then native citizens may well be kings in republics-on-holiday commemorating the overthrow of a stranger monarchy 10,000 miles away.

These ceremonies in Tahiti have the familiar quality that we experience in our weariness with the ritualistic. They seem meaningless, empty actions, performances distanced from the realities of living, forms without structures. Ritual robes become fancy dress, symbols become mere decoration. It is a syncretism of a make-believe past and a fatuous present. We are familiar with it: Hawaiian dancers in Kodak shows at Waikiki, Mickey Mouse as King of Disneyland, Dale Carnegie as Sincere Man, the blank face of *Homo touristicus,* Advertising Man, Plastic Man. Our world seems puffed up with emptiness. Who can make sense of signs that do not signify, of symbols that crush with their weightlessness, of sacraments that leave no mark?

In a postmodern culture such as ours, in which the researcher is bent on learning our mythic nature in order to sell us soap and underwear, it is difficult not to be sceptical about the appearances of things. We see the manipulation and declare the manipulation to be the reality. One could imagine, for example, the organising committee of the Bastille Day celebrations in Tahiti wanting a 'divertissement' in the 'folkloric' mode. To choreograph the ceremony they call on the cultural memory of 'experts', who, by all the complex modes of the transmission of historical consciousness, have their translations of 'how things used to be done'. But one could not now describe all the syncretisms and translations, the extensions and changes in Tahitian cultural perceptions of the *maro ura,* of 'flying', of investitures and sacrifices. These signs and symbolic actions enjoy some continuity with the past and they have some cultural presence, yet they establish different realities. Certainly they are 'Tahitian' in character, but they present distinct expressions of what being 'Tahitian' might be. In a metaphor of the Pacific, the symbols of the past are *cargo* to the present. The present possesses the relics of its past with all the inventions and conservation with which cultural artefacts out of time and out of place are received across a beach.

The *maro ura* of Pomare is very pertinent. If young George III of England needed to wear a crown and to sit on the Coronation Stone of Scotland and Ireland in order to be King in 1760, then a twelve-year-old Pomare of Tahiti needed to wear the *maro ura* to be *ari'i nui,* chief, in 1791, and to stand on the robing stone of his *marae,* that sacred preserve of his titles. His *maro ura* was a feather wrap, five yards long and fifteen inches wide. The brilliant red head feathers of the parakeet and the whitish-yellow feathers of the dove were sewn to a woven backing. The black feathers of the man-of-war bird bordered the wrap, top and bottom. The *maro ura* has come to be called the 'feather girdle' in the way archaic words get some establishment in the history of things. The girdle was always unfinished. The bone to sew it was left in the weave. All the social moments of chieftaincy, sacrifices, wars and peace found their register on the girdle with added feathers and folds. In the feathers was a history of sovereignty, more mnemonic than hieroglyphic, capable of being read by priests, who had the custody of the past.

Tahitian politics turned around the feather girdle. There are uncertainties about the wrap. There were two of them; maybe Pomare's was a third. Perhaps there were more. The two we know from legend and myth were the *maro tea* and the *maro ura,* the yellow girdle and the red girdle. We know of Pomare's girdle from a number of descriptions of European visitors who saw it and from William Bligh, who drew it. The descriptions are all agreed that it was made of both yellow and red feathers. That Pomare's girdle may have been a third sacred *maro* and meant to be syncretic of both *maro tea* and *maro ura* belongs to our later story. In any case its distinction from a traditional sacred *maro* would not have put it outside the paradigm of Tahitian politics. That paradigm allowed a distinction between power and authority. Power was recognised to rise and fall independently of authority. The feather girdles were the currency of authority. They conferred title and rank that it was the consensus of powerful and weak alike to recognise.

Feather girdles were the sacraments of authority because they were signs of the god 'Oro. 'Oro, the god of sacrifice, had always been part of the Polynesian pantheon, but in the eighteenth century 'Oro had begun to play a special part in Tahitian politics. He had begun to emerge from his island of Raiatea, first to Bora-Bora, then to Tahiti.

There was an element of mission or colony in 'Oro's expansion. His priests would establish a new sacred place always with a stone transported from an original temple. Places sacred to 'Oro shared the common name, Taputapuatea, and always focused on canoes and their arrival with sacrificial victims. Tahitians, like all Polynesian peoples, had some preoccupation with the origins and voyages of their ancestors and with strangers who came from beyond the sky. Their legendary memory of Taputapuatea told of grander days when the Friendly Alliance of the islands would send processions of canoes in double file through the sacred passage to the beach of the temple. Each canoe bore on its prow the paired sacrifices of men and fish. The canoes would be beached at Taputapuatea and would be rolled up the shore over the bodies of sacrificial victims. Tahitians remembered the names of 'Oro's priests in phrases like 'Persistent Growth', 'Steady Growth', 'Extension of Power'. 'Oro himself was incarnated in a log or a clublike basket of sennit covered in feathers, more abstract in his representation than anthropomorphic. He himself was a voyager around their islands in a sort of an ark or feathered basket coffer set on a canoe called 'Rainbow'. He had first come to the Tahitian islands on a rainbow that joined sky and land. As the *ma'ohi* – the native islanders of the whole Society Group – saw it, the great celebration of 'Oro at his birthplace of Opoa on Raiatea was a time of commitment to alliances that stretched beyond the bounds of their individual islands.

Under 'Oro's patronage functioned the only group in the islands who called on loyalties wider than tribal and local divisions. They were called *arioi,* a privileged company who travelled and played. 'Comedians' was an old missionary word for them; it caught the topsy-turvy carnival that was structured into their role. They would play the clown to established authority: they overturned the rules of proper behaviour, and danced and played without responsibility. The masters of the different *arioi* lodges wore their own *maro ura* of red-tinted *tapa* cloth. They travelled with 'Oro in his canoe. 'Oro, present in his wand and feathered basket, would travel with his priests and his court of *arioi.* The grand sight of their fleet, its largest canoes decked with streamers, each vessel beautiful with their every valued decoration, belonged to the annual cycle of Tahitian experiences.

The Taputapuatea were places of sacrifice. They were also treasure-houses of the sacred paraphernalia of 'Oro. The representations of 'Oro were kept there in special feathered containers, as were the sacred *maro* and the other accoutrements of priests and chiefs. Pomare kept his *maro* in a sacred spot to the southeast of Matavai. Pomare's *maro* had been brought there in 1791. It had come from other sacred places, firstly the *marae* Mahaiatea in the district of Papara and then *marae* 'Utu'aimahurau in the district of Pa'ea. In the *maro's* voyages of twenty-five years is a whole history of Tahitian politics. In 1792 when he returned on the *Providence,* William Bligh saw Pomare's *maro* at Tarahoi near Matavai. His drawing is our only relic of it. He also drew 'Oro's canoe, 'Rainbow', with its brilliant ark. Joined to the huge streamer of bark cloth that flew from the canoe's stern was a 'St. George's Ensign'.

Bligh was intrigued to discover that the Tahitians had sewn into the feather girdle a thatch of auburn hair belonging to Richard Skinner, one of the *Bounty* mutineers who had elected to stay at Tahiti when Christian went on to Pitcairn. Poor Bligh, he was always sensitive as to his relations with the socially elite. So he was mystified that somebody as insignificant as Skinner should be remembered in so sacred an object as the girdle: 'an ostentatious mark of [the Tahitians'] connection with the English and not of respect to the Person it belonged to', he remarked by way of explanation. Skinner was the ship's barber. He had astounded the Tahitians on the arrival of the *Bounty* by producing a barber's model head and wigs styled in the latest fashions from London. In Tahitian eyes, Skinner was somebody special. As a barber, he had a special power to touch *tapu* places. And his own head was red – *tapu,* as special as a parakeet's feather. One could wave a red feather to catch 'Oro's attention in prayer: one could sacrifice it to Pomare's sovereignty: one could do it with a lock of a stranger's auburn hair as well.

Collected in this sacred place of 'Oro where Bligh saw the girdle was other cargo. There were the skulls of two *Bounty* mutineers. One of the men – Churchill, as we shall see – had been raised to be chief at Taiarapu before his death. The other skull was that of Thompson; he had murdered Churchill but had been killed in his turn. Pomare's family had conquered Taiarapu, won the skulls and, temporarily, sovereignty over all of Tahiti. At the *marae* at Tarahoi were also drums and carved statues of gods that the mutineers had brought back from Tubuai. There was also a portrait of Cook painted by John Webber and given by Cook to the Pomare family. Like the *maro ura,* the portrait was an unfinished document. The Tahitians would take it to each ship that visited the island and ask each captain to sign a message on the back. The portrait was wrapped in red cloth. Everyone who approached it bared his shoulders and all made deferences to it when it was uncovered. For years after they had received the portrait – and a huge box with lock and key to keep it in – the Pomares, father and son, took it with them on important expeditions, unveiled it on special ritual occasions, and had it present whenever they offered formal hospitality to stranger captains.

Bligh saw something else in the *maro ura* in addition to Skinner's auburn hair. It was the most famous object of all. He saw a British red pennant sewn into the body of the girdle, as a lappet or fold of its own. 'Red Buntin' he described it on his drawing. It was the pennant that Tobias Furneaux had erected on a pole on June 26, 1767, when he took possession of Tahiti for King George III. The Tahitians had taken down the symbol of English sovereignty and incorporated it into a symbol of sovereignty of their own.

Tarahoi was, in fact, a Tahitian museum of the people's contact with the European stranger. The hair, the skulls, Cook's portrait, the red bunting were cargo. They were strangers' things remade to Tahitian meanings and kept, as in some archive, as documents of past experiences that were repeatedly read for their meaning in all the ritual actions that displayed them and preserved them.

Pomare's *maro ura* was a parable in feathers and red bunting of the translating process. Its expression was Tahitian; its language was 'Oro's; its discourse was of sacrifice. In 1789 the boy chief of Pare near Matavai, Pomare, had the right to wear the *maro ura,* but he did not own it. The *maro ura* was kept at Taputapuatea, in the territory of his enemies. Pomare had the authority to wear it but not the power to retrieve it. He had to make deferences of his own to get the deferences of others. If he were to be paramount chief, he needed both authority and power. The mutineers would allow him to fulfil this requirement.

Each of the sixteen mutineers at Tahiti had his equal lot of weapons and three gallons of wine. (No doubt the wine was the good fortified Madeira wine that Bligh had purchased at Tenerife for Sir Joseph Banks' cellar and his own.) They had only a few goods in common store – an anvil, a grindstone and some kettles. They decided, out of shrewd experience, that their most desirable wealth from the Tahitian point of view was none of these: rather, it was the icons and sacred drums they had stolen from

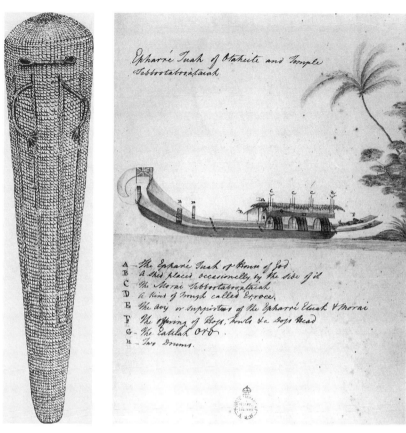

Epharré Tuah of Otaheite and Temple
Sebbootaboonataiah

A — The Epharré Tuah or House of God
B — A shed placed occasionally by the side of it
C — The Morai Sebbootaboonataiah
D — A kind of trough called Erroce.
E — The avy or supporters of the Epharré Etuah & Morai
F — The offering of Hogs, fowls &c dogs Head
G — The Eatilah Oro
H — Two Drums.

Figure 11a.   *Figure 11c.*

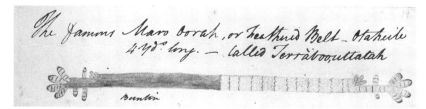

The Jammi Maro oorah, or Feathered Belt — Otaheite
4 yds long. — Called Terràboouttatah

Figure 11b.

Figure 11d.

Figure 11.   The god 'Oro and the paraphernalia of his presence. (Art on pp. 209–10)

a. The 'Oro of Taputapuatea rituals. (Courtesy of Douglas Oliver, *Oceania*. Honolulu: University of Hawaii Press, 1989.) b. The *maro ura* as Bligh drew it. (William Bligh, *The famous Maro Oorah, or Feathered Belt*, 1791–3. Watercolour. In his *Drawings*. Mitchell Library, Ref: ZPXA 565, f 19 lower image.) c. 'Rainbow' as Bligh drew it. (William Bligh, *Epharre Tuah of Otaheite and Temple Tebbootabooataiah*, 1791–3. Watercolour. In his *Drawings*. Mitchell Library, State Library of N.S.W. Ref: ZPXA 565, f 18.) Bligh was careful to note the names and functions of the parts of 'Rainbow' he drew. (A) *Fare Atua*, or god house, where the clublike representation of 'Oro and other sacred paraphernalia were kept. (C) The icons of birds that he called *marae taputapuatea*. Bligh saw 'Rainbow' as a mobile *marae*. Sacrifices (F) of hogs are on 'Rainbow's' prow and a 'St George's Ensign' left by Cook on the stern. d. 'Rainbow' as Tobin drew it. (George Tobin, *A double canoe with the Eotooa (God) and provisions on the prow . . . Island of Otahytee*. 1792. Watercolour. In *Sketches of HMS* Providence. Mitchell Library, Ref: ZPXA 563, f 41.)

Tubuai and the red feathers and clubs they had bartered for in Tonga on the last days before the mutiny. A week after they landed, they marched in a body from Matavai to Pare and the *marae* at Tarahoi. Their *taio* were with them. A Tahitian marched before them with the Union Jack on a staff.

The boy 'king', Pomare, was waiting for them in the precincts of his *marae*, outside his *Fare Atua*, his sacred treasure-house. He was 'flying' on the shoulders of a man: everything his feet touched was *tapu*. He was wrapped in a great swathe of white *tapa* cloth, and his head was garlanded with red and black feathers. It was a time of formalities, and the Tahitians negotiated with the mutineers on the beach quite differently and more soberly than with sailors on a ship. The mutineers would not bow to Tahitian custom by stripping to the waist in the 'king's' presence. Nor would they remove their hats, protesting that they would have been expected to wear headgear when under arms in the presence of King George. The Tahitians invented a solution. They put a piece of *tapa* cloth on the shoulders of the mutineers and invited them to remove *this* Tahitian dress in the presence of Pomare. In the speeches and gift giving that followed, the Tahitians addressed the Englishmen only by the name of each one's *taio*. In exchange for their gifts to Pomare, the mutineers were granted two pieces of land, one from which they might harvest coconuts, the other for breadfruit. The ceremonies ended with volleys of muskets 'in three divisions', but probably not carried out with the precision in military manoeuvring that the Tahitians, with a remarkably critical eye, had come to appreciate and demand. Then Tu, the father of Pomare, told the mutineers to 'follow [their] own Country's fashion in everything and take no heed of their ceremonies'. The mutineers may not have seen it, but the Tahitians had made a beach for them between Land and Sea. The *taio* in them would tame their strangers' violence.

It must have been difficult for the mutineers not to take heed of the Tahitian ceremonies and, for that matter, for the Tahitians not to take heed of theirs. First, there was the *heiva* or dance to honour Captain Cook. In addition to the portrait of Cook painted by John Webber, Tu owned another. In September 1789, Captain John Henry Cox of the *Mercury*, the vessel that had so nearly sighted the *Bounty* at Tubuai, had been mystified at the garbled stories told him by the Tahitians about a ship returning without its captain, and a man who had stayed at Aitutaki with Captain Cook. Cox told the Tahitians that Cook was dead and left them with a picture of the event, a print of Johann Zoffany's famous painting of the killing of Cook in Hawaii. The mutineers may have felt a little uncomfortable that Zoffany's picture was also in Pomare's *Fare Atua*. It showed the hero as sacrificial victim, the 'fixed expression of suffering' etched on his face as he lay before an Hawaiian warrior. What the Tahitians would have made of the Hawaiian warrior posed as a neoclassical thug caught in the suspended action of sculpted Roman discus throwers, we cannot know. But we know that they certainly knew, when they displayed Cook's portrait and danced for hours before it, that Cook was dead. We have to think they wished him some resurrection. We have to think, as well, that somehow this wish for resurrection joined them to the mutineers. Between land and sea the Tahitians gave Cook resurrection in the flag that bound them and the mutineers together.

The Tahitians paid homage to the portrait of Cook whenever they displayed it. Sacrifices were made to it: not human sacrifices in the instances we know of, but surrogates of human sacrifice, in plantain branches and suckling pigs. Then there were endless chants. One was translated by Morrison (1935) as 'Hail, all hail, Cook, Chief of Air, Earth and Water, we acknowledge you Chief from Beach to the Mountains, over man, trees and cattle, over the Birds of the Air and Fishes of the Sea, etc. etc.' Of course, it has to be said in a parenthesis to which we will return that Cook had other apotheoses. On the stage at Covent Garden and not long before the *Bounty* had sailed, choruses paid homage to another portrait of Cook. In a setting designed by John Webber, the choruses sang:

> The hero of Macedon ran o'er the world
> Yet nothing but death could he give.
> 'Twas George's command, and the sail was unfurled
> And Cook taught mankind how to live.
>
> He came, and he saw, not to conquer, but save.
> The Caesar of Britain was he;
> Who scorned the ambitions of making a slave
> While Britons themselves are set free.
> Now the Genius of Britain forbids us to grieve,
> Since Cook, ever honoured, immortal shall live.

Certainly, the Tahitians did their best to give Cook a real presence, though they expressed it in a different way. The relationship between themselves as natives and the mutineers as strangers was mediated by their common bond to Cook. They now called the mutineers *metua,* a kinship term that even the most expert of Polynesian scholars would hesitate to be precise about. Morrison (1935) translated it as 'uncles'. It could be 'fathers', it could be 'brothers', it could be all of these. Whatever it meant, it indicated some claim on obligations owed by their bond in Captain Cook. The Tahitians quickly made the claim explicit by calling on the mutineers to help them in their political struggles.

AN ICON OF THE BEACH

Only Morrison, among the mutineers, showed signs that he came to Tahiti with a plan. He was *taio* to Poeno, the *ari'i* of Matavai. He returned to Poeno's household with Millward, who was *taio* to Poeno's wife. Morrison had plans to build a sailing vessel. He would call her *Resolution* – not a bad name for a vessel built on a beach where Cook was the bonding element. The *Resolution* would indeed be a resurrection. To build her, Morrison needed land on which to construct her, labourers to collect materials, and the patronage of authority. Matavai offered him the best opportunities.

The remaining fifteen men re-established relationships they had made earlier. George Stewart went with Peter Heywood to the house of the woman whom Stewart had invited on board the *Bounty* every night the ship was at Tahiti. Bligh tells us of this relationship in describing an inspection he once made of Peter Heywood's house, set in its avenue of shaddock trees at the foot of the hill that was Heywood's lookout. Bligh could see in the house's peaceful comfort how the men had been 'happily entrapped through their own seduction'. Meanwhile a group of five other men – Muspratt, McIntosh, Norman, Hilbrant and Byrne – went off to Pare to live with Ari'ipaea, the uncle of the young 'king'. The rest went in twos and threes, Coleman and Thompson, Sumner, Burkitt and Ellison, all usually dependent on the *taio* of one of them. Ominously, Churchill was alone. He would not be tamed until he was dead. Richard Skinner also lived separately, in the house of his 'wife's' father. Skinner was the red-headed barber made into a historical artefact.

The first dispersal of the mutineers around Tahiti favoured the districts of Matavai and Pare and the congregations of the kin and title of the Pomares. Within a few weeks and when invitations came from rival *ari'i*, notably Vehiatua at Taiarapu and Temari'i at Papara, the mutineers realised how much of a capital their residence was. Inevitably the two men who threatened the internal discipline of the mutineers most dangerously, Churchill and Thompson, went off to the camp of Pomare's strongest and

bitterest rivals, the Seaward Teva, then in the last days of the chieftancy
of Vehiatua.

Morrison first broached his plan to build a sailing vessel large enough
to reach Batavia or the northwest coast of North America or even South
America to McIntosh and Norman. They pledged themselves to secrecy
as to the vessel's ultimate purpose. They would get no help from the
Tahitian if its purpose of escape were known. They would also get opposition from those among the sixteen who would think that the escape of
some would mean a death warrant for the rest. So they spread it around
that the purpose of the ship was merely to sail around the island.

Morrison was a serious man and, in the matter of boatbuilding, well
aware of his limitations. He needed the carpenter's skills of Norman and
McIntosh, the coopering of Hilbrant and the metalworking of the armourer, Coleman. But Morrison was an autodidact too. His first thoughts
were for books on how-to-do-it, and where to go and how, when the vessel
was finished. Christian had taken Bligh's books and charts with him.
Thompson, however, had claimed midshipman Hayward's quadrant and
books. He traded the quadrant with Morrison easily enough for a gallon
of wine and one ninepenny hatchet. Books were another matter. Not that
he could read or write: he wanted the paper for cartridges. Finally Morrison was able to wheedle out of him the book he most wanted, John
Hamilton Moore's *The Practical Navigator and Seaman's Daily Assistant,
Being an Epitome of Navigation,* by exchanging empty pages of a log for it.
Not that any of them, in the end, would trust so important a matter as
sailing to a book-learner: they let Morrison read the Scripture and the
Book of Common Prayer; they let him organise their liturgical lives. But
at every step of this extraordinary voyage of theirs, they showed that the
domain of their experience and skills made real boundaries around their
personal authority. In the seven hard months that it took them to construct their schooner, Morrison had to be more the humble diplomat and
willing labourer than captain or potential navigator of any sort.

Their achievement was great. This thirty-one-foot, clinkered, half-decked
schooner, to be called *Resolution,* was to be taken as a prize from the
'pirates' when the navy found the mutineers at Tahiti. She was then renamed *Matavy* and made a tender to the *Pandora* in its search for the
Bounty. She was subsequently forced to accomplish her own extraordinary
voyage of discovery through the Fijian islands when she was separated
from the *Pandora.* Then she was given as a gift to the governor of Timor

for the services he rendered to both Bligh and Edwards. Edwards distributed 300 guineas to the *Pandora*'s crew as 'prize-money' for this capture from the 'pirates'. How galling that must have been to Morrison in his irons! Then she left Timor and entered the sea-otter trade on the north-west coast of North America. Then she made a record-shattering voyage from China to Hawaii, and ended her days somewhere in the China trade.

The *Resolution* was a *bricoleur*'s dream, an icon of the beach. Everything in her was a compromise of invented tools, experimental methods and material novel to her purposes. Tahitians were constant visitors to the makeshift yards, marvelling at the energy of the labourers and the slow carefulness of their labours. One blind old man fingered every piece of the hull and declared that Tahitian canoe builders' ways were stupid in comparison to these strangers' efforts. The builders had no drills or planes. They had only small handsaws to work one thirty-foot plank, eight inches wide and one inch thick, from a single tree. Each plank took two days' work. 'Itia, the wife of Tu, gave them a saw that Cook had given her ten or more years before. It still looked as new and would have been worth five shillings in London, wrote Morrison, remarking on Cook's expensive gifts.

The mutineers built themselves a shed on the land Poeno had given them. They needed it. The wet months of December and January were upon them, and the heat was excessive. Their shed and yards were near Point Venus, about three-quarters of a mile from a launching spot. They had few suitable nails and no forge or bellows at which Coleman could do the ironwork. Nor did they have moulds to shape the frames. The cheap adzes and hatchets, especially made from Sir Joseph Banks' design for exchange with the Tahitians, were not nearly good enough for the delicate scarfing and edging they must do. In a natural environment that had no oak, elm or pine, but only *purau* (hibiscus), *toa* (ironwood) and *mape* (chestnut), they had to reinvent a shipbuilder's kit of knowledge about the stress and flexibility of these woods and their endurance against rot and insects. They had to discover resins (breadfruit gums) and the means of tapping them in large quantities, and they had to find the appropriate fats that would make a kind of pitch that would caulk and not crack. They needed hoops for their barrels, and knees that would not straighten. They needed materials in quantities unheard-of on the island. A day's firing and boiling would render them only a pound of salt from sea water. They could get a hundred pounds of salt pork into a barrel that they had made out of *faifai* (*Serianthus myriadenia*), but it took many months even to accumulate ten barrels of the meat. How did one join *toa* and *purau* woods to make the hard centre and shaped rims of a pulley? Some things the islanders made efficiently and easily for them, such as 400 fathoms of rope. They had no sails. Christian had taken them all in the *Bounty*. Matting was a poor substitute. When the Tahitians realised that they had control of something essential, such as matting, that the strangers needed but could not make, suddenly such an item became an important instrument of diplomacy. It was hidden away and promised to them – not in so many words – if they were prepared to do certain things, such as fight for Pomare. The *Resolution* was truly an icon of the beach. The more the men invested in this means of escape, the more they were bound to the systems of the island.

It was not easy for the men to cooperate in this venture. There was not much of paradise in their hard work. Hilbrant and McIntosh grumbled in their German and Scots accents at being forced to be stopgap artisans. Coleman was factious and continually spelled out the conditions of his involvement. Norman carped about the causes of their troubles.

Many of the planks, fired in order to be bent properly, cracked in the process, and all the work had to be repeated. The different woods required were high in the mountains. They were difficult to drag down as logs and yet impossible to work on the site because of poor tools. The men had to engage large numbers of lower-class Tahitians to collect all sorts of materials and had to reward them with feasts. There was not much of paradise in either the daily grind of the 'skilled' artisans or the heavy labour of those who had to axe and carry the wood. Indeed there were times, in the seven months of its building, when they simply walked away from the *Resolution,* and Morrison was left to potter at the things he could do.

Came July 1790 and the eighteen tons of their masterpiece needed to be shifted the three-quarters of a mile from the yard to the water. The Tahitians did it for them, with ceremony and efficiency. The strangers' icon was now the natives' icon also. Poeno, as chief of Matavai, and Tu, as father of the young 'king', made it clear that anything as important as a boat should be launched in a Tahitian way. Priests, having been feasted and given gifts, spent a day and night chanting and praying in a secret, sacred language. What they said we do not know. But they would have directed the attention of specific gods – Tane, Ta'ere, Te-fatu and Ta'aroa

– to portions of the boat and dedicated each part in turn. They then would have taken some relic of the boat or of the tools used to make it and 'put them to sleep', as their phrase was, in the *marae* at Tarahoi. While three or four hundred Tahitians rolled her to the sea, a priest co-ordinated their efforts from the deck. Once she was on the water, plantain branches were thrown out to her, even as these substitutes for human sacrifices had been thrown out to the deck of the *Dolphin* at the first arrival of European strangers to the island. They 'made the canoe drink' in the waters of Matavai Bay. Perhaps its builders then drank a cup of Madeira and christened her *Resolution.* Perhaps the Tahitians called her *Resolution* also. Certainly, the Tahitians saw her as something of their own, a product of the beach, mediated in their relationship with Cook. They sailed their canoes in company with her, flying their imitations of the British flag then flying over 'Oro's canoe, 'Rainbow', as well.

FLAGS AND FEATHER GIRDLES

In the months of the boatbuilding, the lives of eight or so of the mutineers were made routine by their labours. The 'young gentlemen', Heywood and Stewart, had a more arcadian existence in their cottage at the end of an avenue of shaddock trees. Churchill and Thompson, meanwhile, were the epitome of the licentious and roguish beachcomber. All the mutineers were well protected by their *taio* and the chiefs. They would not have had much doubt, however, that it was their relationship to the highly ranked Tahitians that kept at bay much ordinary envy and anger at their presence. There were at least two thefts. In the first, the thief took, among other things, the halyard of their flagstaff. They gave him 100 lashes. Then Brown (a beachcomber left by the *Mercury* – the sixteen had been alarmed to find him on their return to Tahiti) cut off the thief's ears. Poeno, Morrison wrote, had urged them to kill the culprit. They likewise flogged another thief with 100 lashes.

In February 1790, Morrison tells us, Thompson 'ill-used' a young girl for which her brother knocked him down. 'Ill-used', we must presume, was Morrison's euphemism for rape. Thompson then shot a man dead, together with the infant he was carrying. The man was a visitor from another island, totally innocent and ignorant of what had happened in relation to the girl. In the disorder that followed, Churchill proposed a pre-emptive strike against who knows whom, just as they had planned to carry out the killing of all the men at Tubuai. He volunteered to be the general of their army and the men's captain. It was an offer that the others refused, and, by gifts and diplomacy, they quieted the situation. As a result, Churchill went off with Thompson to Taiarapu, at the other end of the island. There his ambition to be a leader of some sort, a passion for command that had bedevilled them since the day of the mutiny, was fulfilled. His *taio,* Vehiatua, the *ari'i* of the Seaward Teva, died and, in some way, Churchill was made *ari'i* in his place.

Almost immediately Churchill acted as an *ari'i* might. He killed a young boy who had frightened off a duck he was stalking. Aware that Thompson was bitterly jealous of his honours and fearful of the dangers in that, Churchill had Thompson's weapons stolen. Thompson then returned to Matavai, persuaded the others to lend him a musket and returned to Taiarapu, where he killed Churchill. Enraged that he had killed their chief, one of the Teva, Hitihiti, who had gone with the *Bounty* to Tubuai, stalked Thompson, knocked him down, held him flat on the ground under a plank and battered him to death. Morrison, who later acted as coroner, identified from a scar that the head, which had been severed and sent as sacrifice to the Taiarapu *marae,* was Thompson's. As we have seen, both Churchill's and Thompson's skulls ended up at 'Oro's *marae* at Tarahoi, together with the Tubuai icons, Richard Skinner's red hair − and, of course, Captain Cook's portrait.

Wars were perennial on Tahiti, so it was inevitable that the mutineers would become involved in them. They were part of the systems of the beach to which the men were bound. The wars on Tahiti were cruel and destructive but, to a stranger's eye, the hatred that should have been in them was badly organised, and peace was bizarrely resilient. The causes of war also seemed mysterious and childish. They seemed part of the make-believe of native polity. So, the first actions the mutineers took when the Pomares invited them to join their wars was to change the face of battle. If they were to go to war, then let it be 'real' war.

War was perennial on Tahiti because there was always an imperfect match between power and authority (or rank). Tahitian commonsense bowed to metaphors of rank in kin − titles won by birth and symbolically expressed in the *maro ura* and in the establishment of 'Oro's *marae.* But often those with lesser title were more powerful or, as happened in September 1790, the young 'king' Pomare, who had the highest title, was allowed to visit the *marae* where his *maro ura* was preserved only when there was peace with the people of Atehuru – traditionally his enemies. Moreover, the Seaward Teva, as well as their allies, did not recognise the legitimacy of his birth, from which his title derived. The various alliances on which his power depended were precarious, always threatened by the ambitions of other *ari'i* and the internal politics of each congregation of kin.

We may remember that when Wallis left Tahiti he thought that Purea ('Oberea') was the queen. Cook, the next Englishman, after Wallis to come to Tahiti, came with the expectancy that he would find Purea queen. Cook was a man for maps. He made what he modestly or professionally called a 'Plan or Sketch' of Tahiti and, on a circumnavigation of the island to make this 'plan', came upon the *marae* at Mahaiatea. He discovered that Mahaiatea belonged to Purea. To Cook's eyes, the *marae* at Mahaiatea looked a little unkempt. But there were 'altars' with sacrifices of pigs and fruits rotting on them, and some of his crew saw that the place was in current use. The *ahu* towered higher than any other 'pile of stones' he had seen – it was forty-four feet in height, ascending eleven steps in a pyramid two hundred and sixty-seven feet long and eighty-seven feet wide. Hewn stone, 'very agreeable to the eyes', served as a facade for the stone filling. Reddish rocks made the foundation. On the top were two carvings: one of a bird and a broken one of a fish. All was enclosed within a stone wall that Cook meticulously stepped out, 360 feet by 354 feet. By this time, he had seen a number of *marae* on their promontories, and he knew what to look for: the pavements, the high pillared wooden platforms on which the sacrifices were laid, the stone uprights in the court of the temple, the wooden carvings that leaned, usually crazily, against the *ahu* or protruded from the topmost step. At Mahaiatea, human bones were scattered on the beach between the sea and the *ahu*. Cook noted their presence only passingly, no doubt presuming that they had eroded and fallen from their burial place on the seawall of the *marae*. Other sources, those of Tahitian memories, however, talked of the land around Mahaiatea being covered with the bones of those killed by the Seaward Teva as they swept over the isthmus to defeat Purea's people. The huge *marae* was a monument to Purea's grand but frustrated ambition, the bones a headstone to their delusion. Purea and Amo, her husband, had either built Mahaiatea to house the *maro ura* with the Wallis pennant sewn in it or had housed it soon after the *marae* was built for their son. Wars swept their ambitions for paramountcy away, and the *maro ura* – this single one or perhaps two – was beached by this tide of Tahitians' affairs among the people of Atehuru.

Pomare's first call on the mutineers' services came in March 1790 while they were still preoccupied with building the *Resolution*. They were asked to do little more than clean and repair Pomare's muskets. But that was enough to allow his ally, Hitihiti – the same man who had gone with Christian to Tubuai and had killed Thompson – to defeat, as a 'general', a 'rebellion' on the island of Moorea. It was an important victory for the Pomares. It established the rule of close allies in Moorea and freed them to focus their attention on Tahiti.

In September, the people of Atehuru and Fa'a'a tested the Pomares' strength by staging a raid on Pare. They took two human sacrifices. It was a disturbance too close for the mutineers to ignore. More importantly, it provided an opportunity to bargain with the Pomares for matting for their sails. Accordingly, eight of the mutineers marched on Atehuru and Fa'a'a in the middle of a large rabble of warriors. They found the face of battle as ethnocentric as any other cultural act with which they had to deal. When they came upon the ritual symbols of set battle – a bark cloth *maro* and sacrificed pigs tied to trees – it became clear that the conventions of Tahitian battle were inhibitive of what they conceived to be the purpose of a battle – the defeat and submission of the enemy, the occupation of his territory. A warrior's response to challenge for the Tahitians was more important than any tactical or strategic advantage. Tahitian champions needed to dazzle in their performance. The snatching of a sacrificial victim from the field of battle was a victory in itself and a reason for ending the fighting.

Priests and warrior leaders and exhorters (*rauti*) who would 'animate the troops by recounting the deeds of their forefathers, the fame of their tribe or chief, and the interests involved in the contest' also played their allotted roles. To the mutineers, it was senseless, nothing like real fighting. There were not even lines of battle or uniforms to distinguish enemy from friends. They all looked alike! Dismayed, they marched home, hardly having done a thing.

It was a mistake. Tied to conventions that could win them nothing, they looked like losers. In the next days, the people of Atehuru and Fa'a'a came boldly to the mutineers' residences and boatyard at Matavai. They shouted that they would burn the schooner and soon have each one of the mutineers' skulls as a sacrificial trophy in their *marae*.

Now there was something universal in the signs. It was basic *realpolitik*, whatever its ethnocentric guise, that the mutineers should not be seen to be losers. So they tried again. They marched on Fa'a'a. This time, the people of Matavai, who had over the years witnessed and appreciated the strangers' various military manoeuvres, such as changing the guard and raising the flag, marched in a phalanx behind them, dressed in a ragbag of European clothing and jealously defending Matavaian privileged position against the rest of the warriors. This time the Atehurans and Fa'a'ans fled before them into the mountains where they had a fortress of some sort, behind a defensible narrow pass, and an arsenal of stones. The mutineers succeeded in killing several men with musket volleys. Despite the barrage of missiles, they then broke into the Atehuran stronghold and let the Matavaians plunder at will.

On a small stage, the victory was awesome. A balance of power had been destroyed. But it was not enough. The Atehurans, those farther away, had to be taught a lesson. Atehuru was too far away from Pare and Matavai for the mutineers to march in the heat. They had the *Resolution.* She was without sails. The expedition would provide the perfect reason for insisting on them. This was an occasion of some triumph. The mutineers sailed *Resolution* to Tarahoi. There a great fleet of canoes collected, all with British ensigns of painted *tapa* flying from their sterns. The canoes towed the *Resolution* down the coast and inside the reef, to Papara. It was like a regatta of 'Rainbow', of 'Oro in his violent trope, coming to the land of Papara from the sea.

At Papara, the large army left the canoes and immediately began destroying houses and plantations of trees. The mutineers were not particularly sensitive about killing natives, but destruction of property touched a nerve. So they moved quickly to prevent it. Their troops were in a high pitch of excitement of being organised in the strangers' way. Through spyglasses, they saw that the enemy had retreated to a mountain fortress even stronger than the one they had overrun at Fa'a'a. It was fronted by a growth of reeds from which the Atehurans could sortie out in surprise attacks. So the mutineers organised a disciplined siege. They put the reeds to the torch and encamped on a nearby plain. In the night, they set a watch. On the half-hour, Hitihiti would strike a piece of iron loudly and his men would call the watch around, shouting out what their Tahitian tongues could make of 'All's Well'. Morrison, with some pride in his achievement, had mended a watch and made an hourglass. The Tahitians did not know it, but time, with its economics, was upon them.

The Atehurans, imprisoned in their fastness, read the signs and, on the next day, came out behind a white flag to negotiate. They would give up the *maro ura,* the ark of 'Oro and 'Rainbow'. These were to go to Tarahoi. But not before one of their chiefs, attempting to bypass this intrusion of the strangers, tried to take the sacred objects directly to Pomare. He was caught and brought to the *Resolution,* trembling in the certainty of his fate. But he too was given a little lesson in the conventions of strangers' war. 'Englishmen did not kill prisoners', the mutineers told him. It was time for sacrifices, nonetheless.

INTERLUDE: ON SACRIFICE

We began this narrative of the mutiny on the *Bounty* with a representation of sacrifices – the execution of Millward, Burkitt and Ellison. On Tahiti we have seen how all-pervasive sacrifices were. There is an otherness in both these sets of killings that is difficult to understand. I have tried to begin some understanding of them by invoking concepts such as ritual, sacrament, sign, symbol. Such concepts, however, add debate as well as understanding. Who will agree on what these concepts mean? Who will even agree that they add to understanding? Should not history, we have been asked, be about the realities of 'who rides whom' rather than the appearances of such realities? Should not history be about power rather than the signs of power? History, I think, should be about both. Power and its signs in our experience of them are not really distinct. Yet we know that both those who exert power and those who bow to power manipulate its signs. We know the freedoms as well as the constraints of power. We have a sense that there is nothing so determined that it could not be otherwise. There seems, however, nothing so absolute as the taking of life. Sacrifice is the ultimate exercise of power. I am drawn to sacrifice like a moth to flame. The dialectics of constraint and freedom, of appearances and reality, of sign and signified are at the heart of sacrifice and any history of it. I would understand them better.

I have to confess that I have offered sacrifice. I have been a priest. I have whispered over bread and wine that they were something else, body and blood. I have entered the liminal space of ritual, putting on vestments, speaking a special language, adopting formal gestures and demeanour, scrupling for rubrics. I have followed the dramaturgical patterns and the culturally 'natural' structures of sacrifice – of purification in symbolic washing and penitence, of preparations of the offerings and of the altar, of staging the mediating role of the victim in communion of people with the divine, all embellished for their meaning by reflections on and prayers out of a sacred history that is both timely and timeless. And I know the troughs and peaks, the schizoid character of that experience. I know how symbolic worlds are fogged out by the meaninglessness of distraction and by boredom and by all the other lateral pursuits of a social mind and a reluctant body. I know, as well, how ordinariness can be swept away in a moment, and how symbols, in time and space, can lose their separateness to be distilled in one sweet moment of simplicity.

I do not apologise for what may seem, in this special discourse, so scandalously a personal note. That is where everyone begins, even those who deny most vociferously that they do so. There is no other way to 'do' history and anthropology than by participant observation, than by blending a foreign and a familiar experience into something new. There is no past that I describe that is not joined to my present: there is no other that I describe that is not joined to myself. I have not made my knowledge less certain for that, or more relative. Its persuasiveness aside, my knowledge has all those certainties of being human and being cultured. It does what we do in every pragmatic moment of our lives – balances the system in our signs against the idiosyncrasy of their expression. If I were looking for a definition of the present moments of which the past has been made, I would offer this: the present is the creative product of our readings of the system in our signs and the occasions of their expression. If I would write ethnographic history, I must re-present the actuality of those creative readings for their systems and their accidents.

Of course, in a matter of symbols, where are the systems – in the signs, or in the reader of them? Is there anything 'natural' about sacrifices that join us, in our present moments, with the priests on Tahiti – with the Franciscan friars, with Tutaha the Tahitian priest? For us, the systems that we see in sacrifice are inextricable from our experience and our discourse. That discourse has been shaped in ways we can scarcely describe by scholarly reflections we may or may not have read – by William Robertson Smith on 'Sacrifice' in the *Encyclopaedia Britannica* (1892), by Henri Hubert and Marcel Mauss in their essay on *Sacrifice: Its Nature and Function* (1964 [1898]), by E. E. Evans-Pritchard distilling a catholic past into an anthropological present in his *Nuer Religion* (1956), and Victor Turner doing the same in *The Ritual Process* (1969). How many times through how many generations have those of the Judaeo-Christian tradition had to make cosmological sense of the history of Abraham and Isaac, and the contradictions of a Providence that would demand a father's killing of his son? How many would have read or heard in ritual circumstances the Epistle to the Hebrews and been teased by its cosmology of priesthood? The writings of the exegetes among the Fathers of the Church have trickled into our minds. They puzzled with the contradictions of a God who died on a cross and a Victim who was at the same time Priest. Thomas Aquinas and John Calvin have been born again in schoolhouse catechisms as they queried how bread and wine could be surrogates of body and blood, how the actual killing of Jesus in time, by Roman authority, could have symbolic representation out of time, time and again, and still be real. In the piety of youth, how many have made sacrifices – in Lent, out of fear of Hell, for 'pagan' babies, for a bleeding Sacred Heart? Mythic souls stir still, no matter how distantly and stiltedly, as the young are married and the old are buried and friends celebrate the seasons with the outward signs of giving and the naturalness of communion and fellowship. Aesthetic souls tremble a little at antiphons, at a *Kyrie* and an *Agnus Dei*. If long ago most of us were relativised by both history and anthropology to the fictions of institutions, who does not still feel an awe for the sacred spaces of sacrifice, be they a cathedral or a Vietnam memorial, and, given the proper combination of circumstances, feel what we are meant to feel by grandeur, separation and the ambience of holy things? All around, when we have eyes to see, when they are made dramaturgically present, are symbols of sacrifice – crosses, Easter holidays, Lenten appeals, war monuments. Even in these postmodern days when we are tourists to our soul, the metaphors of sacrifice belong to our persons and our public cultured selves. They belong and they do not belong. The symbols make us, but we make the symbols, too. In their presence, we create, as much as we respond to, their meaning. We can never find a fundamentalism in their meaning that is not changed by the circumstances of our reading them. Even sacred history, when it is presented with the institutional certainty of Revelation, is never static in the meaning of its words, but, moved by our changing relationship to it, is always parable of something larger and more encompassing. And when we try, as we now do in this study, to discover the roots of this metaphor of sacrifice, we find that there is not a symbol, not a sacred history, not a theological reflection on a symbol that is not larger than itself in the meanings given to it. Who will tell us that in this we do not participate in a widely human experience, that our personal present is not joined in some way with a Past and an Other?

Well, with the Franciscan friars at Tautira, anyway! They were two rather petulant priests – 'jesuits', the English called them for years, in token of their indiscriminate Protestant suspicion that all priests were conspirators. Their names were Geronimo Clota and Narcisco Gonzales. They had been dumped on Tahiti in 1774 by Don Domingo Boenechea as a sort of 'lay-by' on empire. The friars built a mission at Tautira, on the isthmus between Greater and Lesser Tahiti, south of Matavai. They called it, La Sanctissima Cruz, Most Holy Cross. They inscribed on their cross, 'Christus Vincit, Carolus Imperat', 'Christ Conquers, Charles Rules', and set it in a small compound made of their house, their chicken coops, their pigsties and their garden. On a hill overlooking the settlement, they had put a flag of native cloth in the King of Spain's colours and with his coat of arms. Their house was a two-roomed box that they had brought, prefabricated, from Lima. Around it and over it, they had had a Tahitian hut built. In this strange little temple, while native priests offered sacrifice on sacred stones on the outside, stranger priests offered sacrifices on sacred stones on the inside. Natives and strangers both whispered and sang their prayers about the power of flesh and blood to change their destinies.

In July 1775, Vehiatua, the *ari'i* of the Seaward Teva, whose son Churchill was to succeed as 'chief' fifteen years later, was dying. There was uproar in the valleys around. The *to'ere* drum beat in the *marae*. The 'big bellies' (*opu nui*) stalked victims for sacrifice, and Vehiatua's people brought surrogate victims of plantain branches. The friars, with their servant and an interpreter, an enterprising young man called Rodriguez who wrote down all he experienced, trembled at the possibility that they might be the victims. They had come to Tahiti fully provided with the paraphernalia to make sacred places and do sacred things. There was a portable altar, a chest that locked away the vestments and sacred vessels but unfolded to be a table on which to commune, an altar on which to make offerings. The friars, in being friars, were spiritual nomads in their own religious tradition. But they were as well, sent out, missioned, and they took their tabernacle with them. Their tabernacle was a lead sheath encased in linen, made to hold the unleavened bread of their 'host'. In a leaden sheath, in a box within a house, they would have the Real Presence of their God. Each morning, in the dark and long before dawn, they said their masses secretively, lest the natives become too curious. Each morning, they made little adaptations to a liturgy designed for cathedrals and the symbolic environments of establishment. They had privileges, after all, as travellers. To all the rules and rubrics that prescribed their priestly offices – 'taboos' we would call them, if talking of native priests – they added new ones that described how they could behave out of reach of bishops and in a make-believe church. For the accident of being outside some ambience controlled by a hierarchy, they had rubrics to make them official. They must have been very sensible of their isolation and their missioned character – in the crumpled vestments that came from their chest, in their 'church' without its trace of incense and candle smoke, in their sacred space without the still heaviness of worshipped treasures, in the chalice made light for travel.

All their sacred paraphernalia was symbolic, and each piece held a history. In the way of cultural things and because they were trained to reflection and parable, the friars could have told a history and described the meanings of their symbols. The prayers they said as they vested told significant stories about girding their loins and being chaste, about a kerchief or maniple and being diligent in their labours, about a simple alb and being humble. Perhaps – again, because they were priests but also because the history of things accrues popularly and the priests must describe significances to their acolytes – they would have had some notion of the evolution of their sacred 'vestments' from the ordinary daily clothes of centuries ago. It would have been a comfortable sort of history, explanatory but antiquarian. It would be like explaining the origins of a handshake in the distrust of the knights of old of each other's sword hand. The stories, in the prayers and comfortable histories, would have been notional symbols, part of the bric-a-brac of a meaningful environment. The effective signs probably had no substantive content or story at all, and their meaning, if humanly conscious at all, was tucked away in the priests' reflective core. The signs were in actions done in relation to others – in putting on the vestments, setting themselves apart, knowing their priesthood in its outward show.

On their portable altar, the friars performed their priestly tasks over a small squared piece of linen that, in established churches, would have been the altar stone. Altar stones and their linen substitutes contained relics of martyrs, certified as such in some way – bone fragments, cloth that had touched a martyr's bones or tomb. There is history in altar stones. They were signs of the church's universality and hegemony. The martyrs' tombs from which the martyrs' relics had been taken became cathedrals where the faithful worshipped and held the eucharist outside the spaces controlled by kin and tribe. By extension and delegated authority, they symbolised in the altar stones other lawful places of worship. The linen altar stones of the friars made a church of their house within a house.

We cannot presume that the friars incorporated their altar stone into their symbolic environment with the sense of history we have described. They doubtless could evoke, out of their own theological training and innumerable sermons, the symbolic meaning of offering the sacrifice of Calvary over a martyr's bones. The martyrology that they daily read would identify the historical sacrifice of life that their relics represented. In the litany of the saints, in the reading of the divine office, in the psalms they recited, the friars translated words that were old and perennial into meaningful phrases that quieted their fears, relativised a sacred past to their present needs. In that dialectic of past and present, the history they made of their symbolic environment was informed by all the dramatic images of what sacrifices naturally and appropriately should be. The genuflections and graceful turnings of their gestures, their carefulness about the crumbs that escaped the confined sacred space of their altar stone, their separation of 'blood' in a chalice and 'body' on a paten, all combined with readings and prayers that, by rote and routine, cleared the spaces of their mind for interpretation and were dramaturgies of a notion of sacrifice that was properly and naturally ordered into purification, offering and communion. The pervasive consistency of all their actions stamped priesthood on them 'as if' they had slaughtered a lamb and made of it a whole burnt offering. Their make-believe sacrifice was more real than real, as all its parts, even its contradictions, made sense in their ordered history of it.

As well as this constant renewal of meaning in their dramatic representation of sacrifice, the friars' altar stone, like their vestments, was a cultural artefact of an ecclesial system. The stone had meaning in the history they could tell of it and in the ways it conformed with their sacrifice. But it also had meaning in the rules that bound them to its use, in the sanctions that reached into their eternal souls if they did not obey a rubric. The stone was a document of their universal priesthood and their institutional character. They might not read all its meanings as they daily bent over it but, like everything else that was sacred around them, it narrowed their choices and mirrored very clearly who they were in what they could and could not do. They bowed to power as they bent to make sacrifice.

In sacrifice, human actions – in the destruction of a living thing – are transformed by being given meaning. What is destroyed – a man, a pig, a plantain branch, a piece of unleavened bread – becomes something else: a victim, an offering, a gift, a scapegoat. The instruments of that transformation are always dramaturgical. There is always a play, a ritual, to present the meaning. There are always words to tell the story, to make the meanings explicit. There are always things that, in their colour or shape or in their association, make an environment of signs. The sequence of actions draws their elements together, like a melody of notes. The environment of signs makes an ambience, like a harmony of notes. But the significance of these plays is never automatically effective or static. The rituals are conditioned by all the circumstantiality of human existence and all the endless creativity of meaning construction. Above all, they are always historical: the meanings of the signs are always being changed by being read, by being interpreted.

In one sense, there needs to be an element of otherness for the signs to be seen. Outsiders – ethnographers – see signs and structures: insiders are too much engulfed in the speech (*parole*) of them to see their language (*langue*). When everything is customary in this theatre, the mind goes backstage. Bligh and Cook, for example, were scandalised that, in awesome circumstances, the Tahitian priests played distracted, careless roles, showing the distance between the words they spoke and the meanings they extracted from them. But Bligh and Cook would have known the contempt that familiarity brings in all the stages of their own lives – among judges, grave-diggers, in the throne room, in the sacristy and on the altar, even on the quarterdeck. How often, we might have asked them, had they laughed at some muffed symbolising of power and yet joined the conspiracy of its meanings? The otherness that makes us see the signs is very often the challenge that the symboling not be done. It is rare that we do not bow to the power that bends us to sacrifice. We may say that we see the emptiness of the signs or that we hold our distance from their meanings but, for whatever reasons we proclaim, we bow to the power of their expression. We are socialised to their properties and, by that, are slaves to them for the disturbance we are loath to create.

Otherness can relativise too. It can reduce signs to symbols, make meanings notional and, by that, free us from their power. The native Tahitians easily absorbed the strangers' symbols into their own signs. For every play of power and authority of the strangers, the natives had a counterplay. The outside world made little difference, only giving a new currency for their customary exchanges. The strangers' plays of power, status and hierarchy, their signs of state and delegation of authority, were narrowly mirrors of the natives' own staging. They could easily absorb a flag of possession into their *maro ura* of sovereignty. They could invent a role for the Union Jack in their ceremonies of incorporation and submission. They were confident that they possessed the stranger: the stranger did not possess them. Inventiveness has a liberating effect. They should not have been so confident.

The same Pomare, whom the *Bounty* mutineers helped to inaugurate as *ari'i nui* and whose investiture with thirty sacrifices they witnessed, later became a Christian king, under the influence of London Missionaries whose venture the mutineers also inadvertently helped to initiate. Bligh had remarked of the old Tu, this man's father, that he had grown in astuteness and energy in learning many things about the strangers – their mechanics, their manners, their artisanship. The son was no less astute. When he threw away 'Oro's *maro ura* to become king, he built himself a new *fare atua,* sacred treasure-house. Cook's portrait was gone, and the Tubuai drums as well. The pride of place in this new treasure-house was Pomare's collection of writings and what he had printed at the mission printery. Whatever Pomare wrote, he archived in this *fare.* The key to his sovereignty this time was not so much a pennant or a Union Jack as the artefacts of literacy. By this time, too, the missionaries had written him a Book of Laws and a Constitution, a sort of altar stone, shall we say? of state. In them, the missionaries had laid down the death penalty for sedition. When 1820 came, there were traitors to his kingship. Tahitians born in the old restlessness against the family's hegemony, and with some sensitivity to what was changing, burnt Pomare's *fare atua* to the ground and destroyed his writings. Asked for their counsel, the missionaries believed it was better that two Tahitians should die rather than Pomare indulge in a war of reprisals. They agreed to sanction the execution of two culprits. When the missionaries visited them in their confinement, the prisoners were in a state of 'manifest repentance'. The missionaries could only 'hope it was to life'. They were as sceptical as always, and as unseeing, of native sincerity. In any case, the culprits could be coached to be victims. The condemned sang hymns at the foot of the gallows and on the gallows itself. They appeared to die without a struggle. The judges and attendants needed to be persuaded not to wear the feathered bonnets of priests of sacrifice, and Pomare needed to be told that, in this form of sacrifice, the victims would not be laid at his feet. However, the bodies were transported, presumably on a pole, back to Pare. Taputapuatea at Tarahoi was gone, but this seat of Pomare's government needed relics nonetheless. And the sacrifices were worth the awkwardness of missionary men of god directing its theatre. 'Peace was proclaimed. Thus we were preserved from the horrors of war.'

ANOTHER SORT OF ALTAR STONE

The *maro ura,* with 'Oro's ark, was brought to Tarahoi in early October 1790. The mutineers and their schooner played their part in its welcome. Many of the enemies of Pomare made their submissions and, at the same time, became *taio* of the mutineers. But there was much more ritual significance to eke out of the occasion, and October marked the beginning of six months of ceremonies that would last through the remainder of the mutineers' stay at Tahiti. Indeed, what may be thought to have been the last of the these performances was played out in the presence of Bligh, on his return to Tahiti in July 1792.

Throughout October the mutineers worked on the schooner. The *Resolution*'s mast, made of breadfruit wood, had been carried away in the course of their military expeditions, and now they searched for a replacement and a spare. They continued boiling sea water for salt, but they had to be satisfied with eight hundredweight of salt pork in barrels, because their overworked pot cracked and became useless. Then there was all the carpentry to complete – on oars, gaffs, booms, rails and yards. At the same time, their brutality towards women was raising an edge to their relationships in the immediate neighbourhood. Coleman was seized by a man who said he had raped his wife while the *Bounty* had been at the island collecting breadfruit. Coleman was ransomed with a gift, but the other mutineers returned to the man's house and shattered it with gunshot, then plundered it. To make amends, the local chiefs turned the man off his land and brought gifts to the mutineers. In this there were signs, made elsewhere as well, that lower-class Tahitians had a perception of the strangers that was different to that of the chiefly classes. Coleman, soon after this incident, declared that he would not sail with Morrison. They still had only a few mats for sail. Suddenly the grand ambitions for sailing to Batavia or the northwest coast of America were gone. They hauled the *Resolution* out of the water for the wet months of December and January, divided up the salted pork, and watched the Pomares stage the theatre of their hegemony.

The first act of that theatre was a procession of the 'king's flag' around the island. The 'king's flag' was a Union Jack, a present to Pomare from Captain Cox of the *Mercury*. Whether the procession was clockwise around the island, with left hand to the sea and right hand to the land, is difficult to say. In Hawaii, the point would have been of great significance. Left-handed processions were signs of some dispossession of the violent power of the chiefs. More confidently, we can surmise that the procession began and ended at Taputapuatea at Tarahoi and that it stopped at each of 'Oro's *marae,* around the island. Certainly – because the sources tell us so explicitly – the procession made its way quite precisely along the boundary between land and sea, not just on the beach but on that truly liminal space where the water of the lapping waves sank into the sand of the beach. As the flag arrived at each *marae,* it was set atop the *ahu* with the other icons of 'Oro's worship. Sacrifices were offered and lengthy prayers recited by the priests. The flag bearers were feasted and the congregation of the local *marae* offered some show of allegiance to Pomare. At Papara, where the mutineers had collected, there was a request that a volley of musket fire be added to the ceremony. The mutineers obliged and this 'thunder from the sea' was well received. 'Oro's voice was expected to be heard in thunder at times of sacrifice. That he might be incarnate in a musket blast was as fitting as being incarnate in a flag.

When the 'king's flag' returned to Tarahoi, it was clear that the Seaward Teva at Taiarapu had not made their obeisances. Neither were they to appear at Pomare's investiture. Although the afront indicated that there was some unfinished business in the matter of hegemony, remedying it was put aside for the moment. The mutineers began to conspire as to how they might make politics happen. They were under some delusion that their beach had become their island; that they were masters rather than marginals.

February 13, 1790, was the first day of Pomare's investiture. It inaugurated weeks of extravagant feasting. The landward section of the *marae* at Tarahoi had been renovated and enlarged. The landward section was where 'Oro's sacred paraphernalia would be kept and his sacrifices set aside. The local congregation of the *marae* would be feasted there. The symbols of continuity and legitimacy were established there. The seaward side, marked by the stepped *ahu* at the water's edge, was dominated, on the day of the investiture, by two large canoes brilliantly decorated and laden with immense quantities of food. Rows of human sacrifices, thirty of them, lay like rollers on the ground, in their envelopes of matting and leaves. The space was crowded with garlanded and bonneted priests, temple attendants, and *ari'i* bearing their offerings of plantain branches. Pomare was carried – 'flew' – from the sea and placed on the only space where so sacred a person could touch the ground. It was his own sort of altar stone, a small beach between landward authority and legitimacy, and seaward power and violence. *Tepa,* this stone was called. On *Tepa,* Pomare stood naked until the *maro ura* was wrapped around him and a wicker shade, covered in feathers, put on his head. The human sacrifices were brought to him, the envelopes about their heads peeled back like banana skins. The priests scooped the eyeballs out with bamboo spits and held them before Pomare. He, open-mouthed, 'ate' the eyes, which were then put on 'Oro's offering stand. The *ari'i* from different *marae* congregations then brought forward their victims – in proportion to the size of their districts – and their gifts of pigs and cloth as well as food for the feast. Although there is no mention of it in the accounts of Pomare's investiture, a ceremony would have begun that turned his world topsy-turvy for a moment. He had been raised to divine heights and shared the food of the gods. The world of the young *ari'i* was then turned upside-down. Semen and faeces were 'poured' over him, no doubt in the same way as he 'ate' the eyes. The beach on *Tepa,* his altar stone, was indeed a liminal space and thus full of contradictions and reversals.

In the midst of these ceremonies, Morrison, as interested as ever in things religious, asked a question of the priests. What did it mean that the young king ate the eyes of the victims? In all the descriptions we have of Tahitian beliefs we have little theological reflection, and the answer the priests gave to Morrison will have to do. 'The King is the Head of the People for which reason the Head is sacred; the Eye being the most valuable part is the fittest to be offered, and the reason the King sits with his Mouth open, is to let the Soul of the Sacrifice enter into his soul, that He may be strengthened thereby, or that he may receive more strength of discernment from it, and they think that his Tutelar Deity or Guardian Angel presides to receive the Soul of the Sacrifice.'

All over Polynesia the native peoples suffused their religion and culture with a fascination for images and metaphors of mediation and transition. Birds and canoes featured strongly in their symbols. Birds and canoes were in between — in between land and sky, in between land and sea. They were natural instruments or vehicles of the divine. Gods were in birds, and mythical heroes travelled to their islands in canoes. A feather could serve as a sacrifice. The call of a bird in a temple tree could be the voice of a god. 'Oro could come on a rainbow. 'Rainbow' could be his canoe. His 'Rainbow' canoe could be peripatetic. Polynesians wanted the signs of their sacraments to show some passing between. That was their realism. Their chiefs were divine and human at the same time. Their symbolic landscape had a particular expression and a general abstraction.

With their 'kings' it was the same. 'Oro, the god of power, was reached only by human sacrifice. The only bridge to 'Oro comprised those like the boy Pomare who had the right to wear the sacred *maro*. They were divine — befeathered: they were human — 'smeared' with shit. They were for a time the god to whom sacrifice was made: they were, by 'eating', the victim being sacrificed.

The answer the priests gave to Morrison was that it was so, not how it was so. The priests could not tell how it was so, anymore than Lord Hood, president of the court martial board who made a sacrifice to the Law of the mutineers, could tell how it was that George III's majesty was offended by a mutiny or how it was atoned by taking a life.

Bligh, as keen an ethnographer as Morrison but perhaps not as imbued with as empathetic a spirit, was the next to describe the boy Pomare mediating sacrifices to 'Oro. He was at the same Taputapuatea at Tarahoi, just fourteen months later. It happened to be on April 28, 1792, the third anniversary of his mutiny. He does not mention this, although it will be seen that it is not far from his mind, as he realises that the sacrifices he is witnessing were due in part to the military interventions of his 'pirates' in the lives of the natives.

At Sun rise I set out in my Boat with Tynah [Tina, Pomare I] and Orrepyah [Ari'ipaea] for Oparre [Pare], where Hammenne, manne [Ha'amanemane or Tutaha the principal priest] was waiting our arrival at the Morai at the entrance of the Harbour. He was at Prayers at the Temple, the Etuah [*atua*, the god] laying before him, wrapt in Red Cloth as I had seen it at Tepippee. To the right of it lay the body of a dead Man wrapt up in the Platted branch of a Cocoa Nutt Tree, and tied to a Pole by which means the Body was carried about. To the right of the Priest were two Drums very different in size, and at a distance of 20

yards in the same direction was the 'Eva'tah [*fata*], or Altar, on which were
twenty nine dead Hogs, and a middle sized Turtle. On nine stout posts was
erected an Ephare Tuah [*fare atua,* house of a god], and there were two others
on Cannoes. Two other priests assisted Hammennemanne besides two or three
inferior people of the order. I had scarce been seated a quarter of an hour by the
Priests, when the Sun having risen above the Trees, caused such a violent stench
from the dead Body, as forced me to quit the place and take a seat out of the
direction of the Wind, where our friend Tynah had placed himself under a
spreading Tree. Otoo [Pomare II] was carried about on a Man's shoulders talking to us and playing his tricks during the whole time of the devotion. After
the first prayer upon our arrival, the Bundle which they called the Etuah [the
god] was untied and exposed. The Marro oorah [*maro ura*], or feathered Belt,
was also taken out of another bundle and spread out, so that I had a view of
every sacred thing that belonged to them. Hammennemanne now began another Prayer, it was very long, but had many repetitions in it, so that it is not
so extraordinary, as Strangers imagine, the retentiveness of this Mans Memory.
Taking up his prayer in all its various changes and repetitions, the whole
amounted to this. We have sacrificed a Man – we have presented his Eye to
thee as a token of thy power, and unto our King, because it is thy will he
reigneth over us, and knowing that everything belongeth unto thee. We display
our feathers. We present our hogs; and all this we do oh Oro, for we know
thou delightest in it – and our hope and wish is to do as thou desirest, prosper
us therefore in all our undertakings, let us conquer our Enemies and live in
Plenty.

  After this prayer, a Hog which had been strangled was scorched his hair
taken off, and the entrails taken out and burnt except the liver. After smearing
the Hog over with its blood, and broiling the liver, the whole was brought to
the Morai, (or Temple) the place of Prayer. This appeared to me to be particularly the offering of my Friend Tynah, and Hammennemanne pronounced another prayer, which was in favor of King George, Myself and all the People who
were with me in the Ships. The Drums were beat at intervals, and the Hog
being laid on the Evatah and the Corps buried by the side of the Morai; the
Marro was made up in one bundle, and the Eatuah in the other, carefully covered over with a piece of English Red Cloth (as I have observed before) and the
Ceremony ended.

  There were not many people present, and among those that were, I saw no
grave or serious attention. The Priest himself the moment he had done prayers
began to joke and create fun in an obscene manner.

  Tynah requested I would not return immediately to the Ship, as he had ordered a Turtle to be killed for us; it was about 20 lb in Weight and baked as
they do their hogs. While it was dressing we went to the Morai on the Point of

the Harbour; and there I observed that two Bodies had recently been deposited under the Coral Rocks, Men who had been sacrificed at the beginning of the War. The dead Body we saw was brought from Moreah [the island of Moorea] four or five days back – it was a sacrifice made by the people of that Island and sent to Otoo. The Ceremony of presenting the Eye was not performed at this time, it was done when the body was first landed.

In War time these Sacrifices are common – on being defeated; a Man is Sacrificed to their God to implore assistance and success. On a Victory, is their most sacred way of returning thanks. The Wretch on whom the lot falls is of no estimation, and is always called a bad man. On my return to Tynah, the People showed me a large Drum in one of their houses, that Christian brought from Toobooi [Tubuai]. It appears that this Wretch had gone to Toobooi to settle, but on finding the inhabitants inimicable, he was forced from it and returned to Otaheite, where part of his Gang left him as I have before related.

The Turtle being near ready, our repast was to be taken on the Ground which was covered with fresh leaves for that purpose under the Shade of a fine tree. When we were all Seated, Tynah desired the Priest to perform a Ceremony called Errow,wow,ah [*aroha*]. This Ceremony is a token of Friendship and intercourse with all those who the Ereeahigh [*ari'i*] shall be pleased to Name – it gives all the Chiefs great pleasure to know of it being performed and feel themselves highly honored in having their Names called over. It is performed thus – the Priest collected a number of leaves and standing up, he called every name as Tynah directed him or he knew to be his wish, and each set of names he numbered with a leaf. These leaves were then given to Otoo (who was by on a Mans Shoulders) and he held them until all the friends were called over, among whom were ourselves and the Ships. Part of this Ceremony Myself, Mr Bond and James Harwood the Surgeon who was with me assisted in, by the help of Tynah, who told us alternately what we had to say. The first Word was Errow,wowah [or in Hawaiian, *aloha*], which signifies the Kings good Wishes to the person whose name follows.

The Morai or Temple where the Ceremony was at, is an oblong pile of Stones about 10 yards long and four feet high (a Pavement was in the front where the Priests Sat and leaned their backs against the Stone Posts for that Purpose), on the top of which was, stuck about fourteen rude ornaments, on some of which was a resemblance of a Man and on others a Bird. The whole range of them they called Tebbotaboo,ataiah [Taputapuatea], as they did also similar Ornaments on the Ephare Tuah that were in the Cannoes. The only interpretation I can give to Tebbotaboo ataiah is, that it is their Great Temple or principal place of Worship.

The Red Bundle their Etuah (which they called Oro) was nothing more than a number of Yellow and Red feathers, and four rolls about 18 Inches log platted over with Cocoa Nut fibres, to which they gave the Name of some inferior Deities. Captain Cook calls this lump of superstition the Ark.

The Marro Oorah, or feathered Belt, which is put on the Erreerahigh when the Sacrifice is first made and the Eye presented, is about 12 feet long, and about 14 inches wide, one half is made of Yellow Feathers stitched on Cloth, and the other half is some Red English Buntin without any feathers. The ends are wrought, with feathers, in divisions, which give a change to the form of it, and are the parts which hang as ornaments when worn by the King. The Yellow-Feathers are diversified by narrow stripes of red feathers, it is however not remarkably elegant or neatly made.

We took our repast very heartily, and with the most attentive and kind Welcome ever Men had. Our conversation turned various ways. They spoke in a very reprehensive manner of Christian, and said they were very happy that Captain Edwards had carried so many of them away. Coleman the Armourer they said cried when he spoke of me and had told them that he was not concerned in the busyness, and had declared so to me when I was drove away from the Ship, on this account they said they had considered him as a good Man, and were glad to hear I had forgiven him. Churchill and Thompson they said lived at Tairraboo [Taiarapu], where being jealous of each other, Churchill induced the Chiefs to Endeavor to steal Thompsons Musquet and Pistol, the Friends of Thompson informed him of it, he therefore on the first sight of Churchill shot him through the Body. This produced an utter averson in the Chiefs to Thompson, they laid hold of him in return and beat his Brains out, thus two Villains affected their own destruction, and avoided the punishment that awaited them.

I was particular in my questions to know how it was, that the Marro which we had known to be kept at Attahooroo [Atehuru], together with the God Oro and Temple Tebboo-taboo,ataiah, would be now at Oparre. The General answer was, that they had been at War with the Attahooroo People, and had seized their God and brought him to Oparre. This I find really to have been the case, and that the Bounty's People assisted with their Musquetry.

Before the present Otow's [Pomare I] time, it appears that Attahooroo was the principal residence of the Erreerahigh. In my last Voyage, I have given an account of the Principal People as far back as Otow's Father, which I find perfect, and from this and the information these People give me the Power of Tootahah, who was a great Chief and Otow's Uncle, was the Cause of the Marro and Tebboo,tabooataiah remaining at Attahooroo; but as he had been a long time dead, and those people having injured them, they went to War and Conquered the whole District.

The Moon was now nine days old. I asked the Name of the Month and Tootahah [Ha'amanemane] told me as he had done in 1788 that it was (Ahounoonu or) [*Auunuunu*, 'suspension', the stormy period in which the fisherman's paddles are put away], April.

About noon we all returned to the ship.

The next investiture in the Pomare kingly line occurred thirty-three years later, in 1825. Pomare III, Pomare II's only son, had been born with a missionary assisting as a midwife at his delivery. He was an infant of three years when he was crowned king of Tahiti. Again missionaries were mid-wives, this time to his kingly power. He walked to his coronation in the royal chapel near Papeete covered by a canopy, behind a procession of girls strewing flowers. There were newly appointed judges of the realm and governors and magistrates to act as witnesses. The Protestant missionaries planned the ceremony. Theologically, perhaps, they were more interested in sacraments of the Word than in sacraments of sacrifice, but they put great store on sign just the same. The Reverend William Henry anointed Pomare; the Reverend Henry Nott crowned him; the Reverend Daniel Tyerman gave him a Bible and the Reverend David Darling preached to him. They all shouted 'Long live the King' when investiture was finished, and the day ended with a proclamation of amnesty and a coronation din-ner.

A phial of oil, a code of laws, a Bible, a crown and a sceptre, these were the sacred things that made Pomare III king; they were the cargo that made him 'king'. These were the cultural artefacts of strangers from across the beach. 'Regents', 'governors', 'judges', 'church', 'people', these were the personifications of his 'kingdom' and the extensions of his sovereignty. From this distance they have the look of litter of a beached civilisation. One wonders what would turn their empty symbols into signs, what would make their metaphors into metonyms, what would make their rituals work in the way they wanted them to work. In these borrowed services of the civilising process, did the natives see themselves or did they see the strangers?

Back in February 1791, when the weeks of feasting following the inves-titure of Pomare II were over, the young *ari'i* came to pay his dues to the mutineers. He came amidst a happy, dancing procession, seated on the shoulders of his bearer and borne to the beach at Matavai. Held over his head, like a panoply, was his Union Jack. His people crowded under it with him. It was not big enough for them all, of course. So they had enlarged it with a huge piece of *tapa* cloth, painted like a flag. In a long undulating and swaying line, under this stranger's flag made in so many ways their own, they paraded before the mutineers and called out to them, '*Metua*', 'uncles'. During all these days since February 13, the mutineers had gone inland from the beach only by way of the Taputapuatea at Tarahoi. The natives demanded that the strangers move from sea to land across the ceremonial beach of sacrifice. It was as if the sacrifices that controlled the violence of 'Oro in Pomare were expected to control the mutineers as well. Thus transformed the strangers were truly *metua*.

The mutineers were now consciously plotting to bring the Seaward Teva under Pomare's control. They again launched the *Resolution* and agreed to sail her all the way around the island to Papara. Temari'i, the *ari'i* of Papara, had planned to invite many warriors to a great feast. The mutineers were to be invited as well. A considerable army would be thus collected. They would attack neighbouring Taiarapu by surprise.

On the night of March 23, ten mutineers assembled at Papara. Heywood, Stewart, Coleman and Skinner remained at Matavai. Next morning a messenger sent by Hitihiti arrived from Matavai. A sailing ship had arrived at the bay. They had not much doubt, and soon learned for certain, that it was a naval vessel come for them. Suddenly each man had to decide his own future. Most wanted to make a gesture of innocence by presenting themselves freely, but they soon learned that between them and the naval ship, the *Pandora*, were two cutters already sent out to capture them. One of the cutters, they also learned, was under the command of midshipman, now lieutenant, Thomas Hayward from the *Bounty*. He was 'angry', the natives told them. Their true danger, however, lay in the natives themselves. The chiefs sensed immediately that the mutineers were a lost cause and plundered them of weapons. They then seized the *Resolution*. Three of the mutineers were simply thrown overboard and nearly drowned. The Tahitians then stripped the *Resolution* of everything that could be moved. In the end, Hayward rounded up most of the mutineers and brought them aboard the *Pandora*. There they found that Captain Edwards had no time for any of them, whether they had surrendered freely or been caught. Each of them was imprisoned indiscriminately. A couple of the mutineers had escaped to one of the natives' mountain fortifications. But they had helped to change the face of battle on Tahiti, and now the Tahitians winkled them out easily and exuberantly.

MANAGING THE SUBLIME

Each of the fourteen 'pirates' on the *Pandora* was put into irons and led below to the airless, stinking half-deck that was to be their prison till Edwards built 'Pandora's Box'. They were objects of curiosity but no great sympathy from the crew. Twenty-three percent of the 'Pandoras' had been pressed for the voyage. Many were unskilled landsmen and marines. They had all been sent on a dangerous voyage not yet completed. Whenever things went wrong, the fourteen 'pirates' would be reminded that they were the cause of it.

Edwards was fearful that his prisoners would escape. He had seen how well they could swim. He had seen how sympathetic many of the Tahitians – although not the chiefs now – were to them. He was even more fearful of what intercourse they might have with his crew. Even when Pandora's Box was finished, and Lieutenant Larkan, who was to be their tormentor, had strained against their chests to clamp their manacles and leg irons tight, Edwards was still fearful. So he forbade their visits to the heads, where there might be whispers to the forecastle, and let them live with buckets of their own excrement and urine.

While the *Pandora* was being fixed of the leaks it had developed and Edwards was deciding where he would go in search of the *Bounty*, the prisoners were enclosed in their box for nearly two months in Matavai Bay. They were also subjected to the constant wailing of their women as they paddled in canoes around the stern of the *Pandora*, lacerating their heads in grief. Edwards was happy to oblige when the prisoners requested that the women be kept away. Their box was not so closed that the rain would not pour in or that seaspray or the water used in washing the decks not drench them. Utterly naked except for the irons, standing or sitting, they would slip and slide into one another as the ship moved. Finally, Edwards ordered that boards be nailed to the floor against which they might lean or strain.

Is it too fanciful to see a comparison between these mutineers enveloped in their box and Tahitian sacrificial victims bound in their matting on their poles? Certainly the only care for their lives came from the orders that the Admiralty had given Edwards. He was to 'keep them as closely confined as may preclude all possibility of their escape, having proper regard to the preserving of their lives that they may be brought home to undergo the punishment due to their demerits'. Their gaolers were already fussing like priests over the rubrics of their sacrifice. The members of the court martial would do the same.

Edwards had driven the *Pandora* hard round Cape Horn and across the vast emptiness of the Pacific to Tahiti. By that route he came as close as he would ever get to the *Bounty* at Pitcairn. When he left Tahiti looking for the *Bounty* he had only eyes to the west. Christian had left hints that he would go west, and Edwards' orders were to sail home by Endeavour Straits. (Before the *Pandora* sailed, Bligh had warned whoever would listen that Edwards was not a good enough navigator to get through the straits.) The mutineers' schooner *Resolution,* now a prize because the 'Pandoras' had taken her by force, was renamed *Matavia* (or *Matavy*) and became a tender for the frigate. In the unknown waters they would sail, a tender to guide them and search out passage was an important asset. But into their search, the *Pandora* and the *Matavia* would get separated, and for the rest of the westward voyage the *Pandora*'s search would be as much for her tender as for the *Bounty*.

The lottery of life that made the 'Pandoras' look at the mutineers with blame for their hard times began early. At Palmerston Island, a low atoll lying behind a dangerous reef, they found the *Bounty*'s spar. Morrison and Heywood had cut it adrift at Tubuai in a faint-hearted effort to get away. The spar had drifted nearly a thousand miles to Palmerston. In making sure that none of the *Bounty* men was on the island, the *Pandora*'s cutter was sent out with five men aboard. It never returned. The sailors did not know whether the cutter was smashed on the reef or whether it had been blown into the vast sea to the west. The *Pandora* searched for it for five days and went on.

The lottery of life worked in other ways. For two natives, whose island the *Pandora* visited on her search, encountering the ship brought death. They were killed for thieving small items. To what sorcery the natives may have thought they owed their bad fortune we cannot say. We can leave the final count of all these incidental sacrifices of native lives to strangers' notions of order and property until a little later. *Realpolitik* is costly and has not much of a memory for these easy killings that were the consequences of it.

There was another sort of lottery, that of discovery. From Bligh's *Bounty* voyage, from his escape in the launch and from Edwards' search for the mutineers came a number of 'discoveries'. Perhaps listing the names of

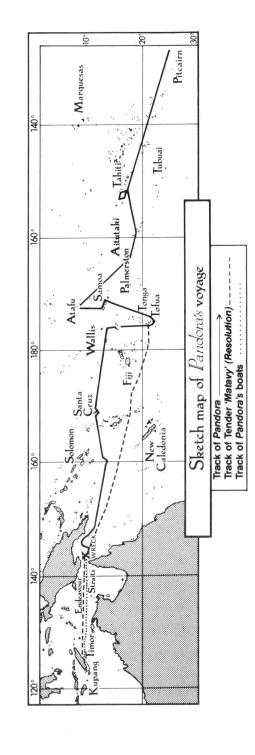

Figure 12.

Pandora's last voyage: November 7, 1790 left Portsmouth; 136 days sail to Tahiti by Cape Horn; May 19 left Tahiti to search for *Bounty*; August 28, wrecked on reef; September 15, boats arrived at Kupang, Timor.

the islands put on strangers' maps by these voyages will not make as much an impression as seeing the first maps made of them. Let us do both: Bounty Islands, Aitutaki, Yangasa, Mothe, Noau, Nairai, Viti Levu, Koro, Yasawa, Motu, Saddle Island, Reef Island and Vatgamai. Bligh's 'Sketch of Part of New Holland in the Bounty's Launch by Lieut Wm Bligh' from his Notebook (Figure 7b) will give us some sense of his commitment to navigation. These sketches are not usually seen as his major 'discoveries', but picture the launch filled with all sorts of sad passions making its way up the coast within the reef and discover something of Bligh himself. Edwards in the *Pandora* added Tureia, Nukuonu, Rotuma, Fataka and Anuta to the world's maps. The *Bounty* under Christian also made some discoveries of its own, as we shall see.

On August 25, 1791, four and a half months after leaving Tahiti, the *Pandora* encountered the Barrier Reef, the edge of the continental shelf of Australia as it reaches up to New Guinea. Edwards was running south, tacking to get away from the reef, sounding all the time. The boat had been out all afternoon looking for a passage and had come back in the dusk with the men saying they had found one. Before the ship was under weigh after hauling the boat aboard, however, there was a shout from the leadsman that he had found bottom. It was not warning enough. The swell and the fierce current pouring through the passage seized the *Pandora*. There was no wind in her sails to hold her off the coral. Within minutes they were on the jagged wall of the reef. There was nothing they could do to get her off, because there was no bottom on which to anchor out from that great wall in the sea. Nine feet of water poured into her from the very first breaches in the hull. The waves simply ground her over the reef till she was thrown into the still and shallow water on the far side. There she began to settle quickly. The surgeon's watch – found nearly 200 years later by underwater archaeologists – stopped at 11.12. That was near enough to her last moment.

From the minute it had all begun, the mutineers, confined in their box, were in terror. In the dark, still in their irons, the scuttles bolted above them, thrown about in the wild motion of the ship, they could hear the fearful cries and the panic. They screamed to be taken notice of and clanked their irons. Three were pulled out to man the pumps. Finally, they managed to pull off their manacles. But Edwards, despite his intense engagement in saving the ship, was also watching them. He ordered the master-at-arms to go into the box and replace their irons. The master was to stand over the bolted scuttle with a musket and fire on them if there was the least sound. The mutineers could see the four boats aft the ship and the feet of Edwards and the other officers who were actually standing on top of Pandora's Box. The water began to surge into it with the heaving of the ship. The last lurch threw the master-at-arms overboard leaving the scuttle bolted. The screams of the mutineers now attracted the attention of William Molter (A.B. in the muster roll, and quartermaster's mate and 'Moulter' in other records). He opened the scuttle and then, in the phrase of the court martial report that gives us the incident but does not help us imagine how he did it, 'pulled the long bars through the shackles saying he would set them free or go to the bottom with them'. It must have been a scene of nightmarish proportions as they struggled for a turn at the key to their handcuffs and as they scrambled through the tiny scuttle against the water pouring in. Hilbrant did not make it. He drowned in Pandora's Box. Underwater archaeologists have found a half-opened padlock and a skeleton in the stern of the sunken *Pandora*.

The sea was now calm, though it boiled with stores and equipment surging to the surface from the sunken ship. George Stewart and John Sumner were killed by a gangplank that sprang out of the water and fell back on them. Richard Skinner, the barber with the 'auburn hair' preserved in the *maro ura,* had been too eager to get out of the scuttle and was still in his handcuffs when he jumped into the sea. He was the fourth of the mutineers to drown.

The sea was calm, but it could not have been quiet. Thirty-four men drowned that night. Shouts and wild cries must have filled the air for some time. There were men pinned by loose cannons and fallen masts and others clinging injured to floating debris. They caught the gleam of the white sand of a cay or low sandbar in the moonlight. Ninety-nine men made the two or three miles to reach it. In nice irony two of the mutineers were saved by the roof of Pandora's Box, which had floated free.

The bare white sand of 'Pandora's Cay', humped like the back of a whale out of the coral sea, was no great comfort. It rose only six feet and measured ninety yards by sixty. Any change of weather could easily wash them off. The sun rose to broil them. For the mutineers, six months naked in Pandora's Box was no preparation for the equatorial sun. Their tattoos mocked their nakedness. Edwards erected tents of sails to shelter the officers and crew. He sent the 'pirates' off by themselves. They were flayed by the sun and shivered in the nights. In the end they could think

Figure 13.
The wreck of the *Pandora*. Peter Heywood's drawings for Nessie in his letter describing his calamitous *Bounty* voyage. (Nessie Heywood, 'Correspondence'. Courtesy of the Newberry Library, Chicago. Ref: Case MS E 5. H5078.)

of nothing better to do than bury themselves to their necks in the sand. For three days, Edwards kept the men on the cay, preparing the boats for their voyage to Timor, making trips for supplies to the *Pandora,* whose masts were visible above the sea. The ship's cat had saved itself in the mast, no doubt temporarily in the face of men with little or nothing to eat. They tried to fish but were as luckless as the survivors in Bligh's launch.

A pinnace, a launch and two yawls had to carry the ninety-nine men. Edwards distributed the prisoners, assigning two and three to a boat, and taking Morrison, Ellison and McIntosh with him in the pinnace. In whatever way the men were divided, each boat was more crowded than the *Bounty*'s launch. They made a sort of deck of oars along the thwarts (or traverse seats) and stacked themselves in a storeyed way, lying either in the bilge of the boats or along the ridge of the oars. It was a desperate thousand miles to Timor that they faced. The pinnace held most of the supplies, so the four boats sailed in tow in a long line lest they get separated. Their food was a few bags of ship's bread, some wine and a little water. Two pieces of bread measured against a musket ball was their daily ration. Maybe Thomas Hayward, making this voyage a second time, told them of Bligh's trick for a fair division.

As they left the cay, the line of boats filed passed the *Pandora*. Her mizzenmast and the poop still broke the surface of the sea. She is still there on the ocean floor, mapped out by the larger objects not yet corroded away – cannons, anchors, stoves, storage pots. The multicoloured fish of the reef ballet eerily over her with their sharp turns and pirouettes. In Greek mythology, Pandora was one of the most beautiful women created. She was meant to be Zeus's instrument of vengeance against Prometheus and humankind. She had opened her box and released all the evils of humankind. Only Hope, it was said, remained inside. We cannot say how much hope the prisoners left in their Box. They must have felt somewhat bewildered by a providential god who had saved their lives but was still inexorably leading them to their deaths. They must have had some sense of being victims.

Why Edwards singled out Morrison, Ellison and McIntosh to be with him in the pinnace we do not know. We may suppose that Morrison looked the most dangerous, not for his violence or for any evidence that he had been a leader in the *Bounty*'s mutinous conspiracies, but because he had discovered an inner freedom that was bad for discipline. It is plain that Morrison was a religious man, but in disturbing ways. Perhaps he had a touch of Methodism, always disturbing in the fleet. Methodism seemed to give institutional men an unreachable strength. Ten days into their escape from Pandora's Cay, Morrison was conducting a small prayer service with McIntosh, Ellison and several others of the *Pandora*'s crew in the pinnace. Actually he had led those around him in prayer for at least four and a half years. Edwards, seeing them at such unestablished and spontaneous prayer, was enraged. He did not know to what dangerous purposes God might be invoked. He ordered that Morrison be taken aft and pinioned with cord and put in the bottom of the boat. He then ordered the same punishment for Ellison. When Morrison 'attempted to reason' with him, Edwards shouted 'Silence you murdering dog, are you not a prisoner? You piratical dog what better treatment do you expect?' Morrison then showed his true freedom and courage. He told Edwards it was a 'disgrace to the captain of a British man-of-war to treat a prisoner in such inhuman manner'. The words enraged Edwards still further and he took up a pistol and threatened to shoot Morrison. When Morrison began to answer again, Edwards declared he would 'heave the log with him', throw him overboard. Morrison saw that Edwards would 'bear no reason' and, beside, Morrison's mouth was parched. He would not waste his strength in argument. It is too much to say with any certainty, but let us say it all the same: at that moment hope came out of Pandora's Box. Morrison had called on an Englishman's birthright. He had become courageously political. Trussed up now so that he resembled a 'man-long-banana' on 'Oro's canoes even more, Morrison had nonetheless won.

Fourteen days of painful sailing saw them at Kupang, Timor. The prisoners were thrown into the Dutch gaol and put into stocks on the floor. For six days their bodies reacted diarrhoeatically to new forms of nourishment. They were made to lie in their own excrement. The stench eventually sickened the Dutch doctors who were responsible for them and who ordered that they and their cell be washed down. They were then put in irons so that they could at least walk a little. Remarkably, the prisoners could not be said to have been a despairing lot. They began a sort of cottage industry, making straw hats that they sold to buy food and clothing. It was work they continued virtually the whole voyage home. It was their small triumph that when the 'Pandoras' got some spare cash from the sale of the prize of the *Matavia* – miraculously its crew had also survived and made it to Batavia – the prisoners were able to make a considerable profit.

They themselves wore their straw hats all the way to Portsmouth. In fact, their sales were so lucrative on the British man-of-war that took them from the Cape of Good Hope to Portsmouth that one wonders what sort of badge these hats made by the mutineers of the *Bounty* came to be. It would have been the sort of political joke that seamen were apt to make – here were these sacrificial victims to the Law being brought back wearing straw hats that were badges of their independence, just like their tattoos.

Peter Heywood, pressured to draw a self-portrait by his loving sister Nessie, chose to pose wearing the straw hat he himself had made. He did not wear it for the court martial, of course. There he worked his symbols more discreetly. He wore the uniform for mourning. Make no doubt. Each of the men was arranging the symbols of this sacrificial moment meticulously. It was plain that the authorities meant to slay them ritual-istically, meant to make a sacrifice of them. It mattered, in this scheme of things, that someone should actually die, but, more importantly, it mattered that he (or they) be 'killed' in the same way that Pomare 'ate' the eye of his sacrificial victims. Peter Heywood's naval connections – notably his uncles Captain Thomas Pasley and Captain T. M. Heywood – knew this well. They knew that Heywood was innocent and would appear innocent. They also knew that innocence would not win anyone an acquittal. The mutiny, wrote Captain Heywood, preparing Peter for the inevitability of his 'killing', had been a 'crime which, viewed in a political light is of the blackest dye'. 'Every true friend of his country' would know how much King and Country 'depended on the prosperity of the navy'. He must endure the sentence of death – yet with the almost certain knowledge that His Majesty would offer him mercy. He was in his inno-cence the perfect sacrificial victim. His 'killing' and the clemency sacra-mentalised the arbitrariness of power.

Peter Heywood's connections plotted endlessly over the ways in which he should enter the conspiracy of his victimhood. They needed a lawyer, and first chose a leading orator of the Bar, Mr Erskine of the firm of Mingays. But they quickly backed away from someone whose renown might trigger naval prejudice. They chose instead a younger, less 'smart' counsel, Mr Const, who would simply help Peter by setting him ques-tions to ask witnesses and assist him in writing his formal declarations. And they sought out Aaron Graham and John Delafons, lawyers who were both well versed in naval ways and able to manage the campaign while keeping Mr Const in low profile. They spent long hours coaching Peter in his role, practising him in dress, language and deferential tone. They never entertained the slightest doubt they would succeed, but they knew how conniving such charades all must be. Their letters and notes are full of cautions to the family about the dangers of appearing to know all the winks and whispers that told them the Law was being managed.

Everyone who saw the 'pirates' in these last weeks before their trial remarked how calm they were. The filth, confinement and terrors were gone. They were hedged about with the quiet inevitability of their fate. Their returning sparkle made those that witnessed it feel all the more confident that their social systems were working properly. They had come back to an England changed by the events in France. There was hardly a day in which the newspapers did not report some action charged with significance for systems and law. It was above all a time to reflect on what it meant for governments to kill and to 'kill'.

Edmund Burke was reflecting on the ways in which signs and symbols worked for the purposes of government. He had, in his earlier days, worked out an aesthetic theory on the difference between the Sublime and the Beautiful. 'Whatever is fitted in any sort to excite the ideas of pain and danger, that is to say, whatever is in any sort terrible or is conversant about terrible objects or operates in a manner analogous to terror is a source of the sublime', he had written. 'I call beauty a social quality . . . inspiring sentiments of tenderness and affection'. His *Reflections on the French Revolution* had appeared as Bligh returned to London, in March 1790, and at a time when the determinations were being made that the mutiny would be atoned at no matter what cost. To Burke, the Revolution was sublime. All its events and actions were an awful mimesis symbolising the terror of dismembered order. But in distinguishing the sublime and the beautiful, he made a famous analogy. Suppose, he wrote, that there was a theatre crowd experiencing the sublime on the stage – King Lear or Macbeth, say – and there was a public execution outside the theatre. Would not the crowd rush out of the theatre to see a man hang? They would, because public execution was full of natural signs of terror and of the sublime.

If he had read the London *Times,* as no doubt he did in those disturbing days, Burke might have had some reason to doubt how natural the signs of terror were or at least to wonder what it was that was seen in an execution. In July 1790, the *Times* reported that three thieves – Read, Jenkinson and White – were hanged in London. All three were full of contrition, the report said, their faces full of dread. White and Jenkinson were instantly motionless when they were hanged. Read, for more than five minutes after being suspended, showed signs of life by his convulsive struggles. 'While the flesh was still quivering with life', the *Times* noted, 'a woman of genteel appearances had the hand of Read applied by the executioner to her neck for a quarter of an hour; at the same time another man applied the hand of Jenkinson to the face of a child about two months old. It is a notion entertained by many, that persons afflicted with the protuberances called wens will infallibly receive a cure by having the hand of a hanging criminal passed frequently over the affected part'. There was much unaccountable invention, one would have to say, in the meanings attached to these sacraments of power.

Had he an ear for it, Burke would have learned much about executions from the language that was used to describe them. Cant phrases for hanging were many. Even a quick perusal of the *Dictionary of the Vulgar Tongue* (1811) will show that, although it is not easy to discover cant phrases for a naval hanging. Perhaps the hegemony in the navy was too complete, and the terror too close, to foster a joking relationship about it. 'Cant' itself was a nautical word – to angle away. Those lower classes who bore the brunt of public executions and those lower-class crowds that attended them indeed 'angled away' their meaning. To them a hanging day might be a 'Beilby's Ball', a 'Paddington's Fair', a 'Morning Drop', a 'Scragg'em Fair', a 'Wry Necked Day', and a man might be 'jammed', 'scragged', 'stretched', 'noozed', 'tucked up', 'twisted', or 'die of hempen fever', 'kick the clouds before the hotel door', be 'choked by hempen squinsy', 'dangle in the Sheriff's frame', have a 'wry mouth and a pissen pair of breeches'. With terror and majesty 'angled away', there was not much sublimity in that language. Remember how disturbed the naval lieutenant who witnessed the mutineers' execution was at the picnic spirit of the thousands at Portsmouth gathered to see Millward, Burkitt and Ellison hang. Sublimity can be socialised away by all sorts of 'angling'.

When it came to the practicalities of executions, Edmund Burke himself stressed not so much the natural qualities of the signs in them as their manageable character. He wrote of these matters in 'Some Thoughts on the Approaching Executions humbly offered to Consideration'. Burke was prompted to put his considerations in writing when dozens of rioters were convicted and their punishment posed the question how to execute them to the greatest exemplary effect. He favoured giving the whole episode a dramaturgical unity. The condemned should not be executed singly but should be put to death in one didactic moment. 'Nothing will make government more awful than for those to see that it does not proceed by chance or under the influence of passions.' Therefore there should also be a judgement made as to the appropriate number of men to be executed. Burke thought six would be most fitting and that they should 'be brought out and put to death on one and the same day in six different places and in the most solemn manner that can be devised. Afterward great care should be taken that their bodies may not be delivered to their friends or to others who may make them the object of compassion or even veneration'. The 'lower and middling people of the city' should be managed with the greatest finesse and delicacy. Since excesses in executions only roused tenderness, the sense of necessity for the punishment must appeal to commonsense. Thus the signs of justice and sovereignty for Burke were absolute, but their application prudential and circumstantial. What was done was just if the signs of what it meant were effective.

These were the politics of justice. Expedience ruled. The navy conjured endlessly with expedience to make its sacrifices of the *Bounty* mutineers work. They had in the end a perfect victory for commonsense. The victims, too, played to the same theatre. One or two newspapers betrayed that tenderness that Burke was frightened of, but they were a manageable minority. There were plenty of 'cant' views of what happened at the execution – so there was not unblemished sublimity – but, as we have remarked, sacraments and sacrifices are like that. It really was a perfect ending, and the whole event could then be forgotten. Four men – Norman, Coleman, McIntosh, and Byrne – who were terrorised for nineteen months as if they were guilty were acquitted. Three – Millward, Ellison and Burkitt – were slain and declared it was proper that they should die. Two – Heywood and Morrison – were seen to be 'killed', and reborn as paragons of naval virtue. One – Muspratt – was 'killed' and exquisitely saved on a point of law.

Let Edward Christian have the last word. In 1819, as Chief Justice of Ely, he wrote a treatise entitled *Charges to Grand Juries in the Isle of Ely upon Libels, Criminal Law, Vagrants, Religion, Rebellious Assemblies, etc. for the use of magistrates and students of the law.* 'The people of England', he wrote, 'have always manifested a far greater dread of tyrants than of robbers and murderers'. So, in order to teach the people how heinous were the crimes of robbery, he advocated much more extensive use of the death penalty especially in regard to that 'most important Act of Parliament in the whole Statute Book, 12 Anne c.7' which 'makes it a capital crime to steal 40s in a dwelling house'. He was offended at 'effeminacy and tenderheartedness' in regard to the death penalty and quoted his cousin the Chief Justice of England, Lord Ellenborough. 'The passing [of] sentences of death, a ceremony than which nothing can be imagined more awful, nor as I firmly believe, more effectual for the purpose of restraining crimes by terror, and as it were, crushing them in embryo, has been treated with unpardonable levity, as a judicial mummery.' It was the same Lord Ellenborough who said of Edward Christian that 'he operated in the full vigour of his incapacity', but we have them together in this case proclaiming a fundamentalist commonsense in the literalness of their signs of power.

In 1809 Peter Heywood thought he saw Fletcher Christian on Fore Street, near Plymouth Dock. The man whom Heywood saw face and back ran away when Heywood confronted him. We have to suppose that any man might run away if he was thought to be Fletcher Christian, but the rumours that Christian had somehow returned to England have never ceased. Prudence suggests that the rumours have been wrong, but prudence also suggests that the narrative we are about to enter on concerning what happened to Christian and the *Bounty* after they left Tahiti may be based after all on a false premise. Reader, the years are too long already for me to spend more on being certain. Let me transfer the burden to your shoulders. Read my narrative. It will be then for you to decide how different my story would be if none of it was true.

Scene ii: *Reflection*

IN THE NAME OF THE REVOLUTION . . .
OF THE KING . . . OF THE PRESIDENT

Possessing others in the Pacific has been bloody. Possessing others has been ugly. There has not been much cultural relativism in possessing others, not much sense of the good in the other. James Morrison and Peter Heywood had a rare sympathy for the natives who possessed them. Before I tell that rare story in the bleak history of the *Bounty*, let me tell another just as rare in an even more bleak history.

My story begins on a Frenchman's last night in Polynesia. The Frenchman was Etienne Marchand, and it was June 1791. Bligh was in the *Providence* on his return to Tahiti. The fourteen *Bounty* prisoners were in Pandora's Box, Christian's lot were on Pitcairn. American merchants were celebrating the new freedom of their revolution, and the first traders were in the Pacific looking for skins and furs that they would sell to China. The French King had lost his freedom and was on his way to prison and death.

Etienne Marchand was in his cabin on the small vessel, *Solide*. The ship was off an island that his men had insisted he call 'Marchand' for himself, and anchored in a bay that he had called 'Fine Welcome'. The island was in a group he had called 'The Islands of Revolution', the northern Marquesas. He was reflecting on what he had done that day. He had raised the *tricolore,* was proud to have been the first to show this flag of freedom and equality in the Pacific. He had deliberately cut short the usual ceremony of taking possession by omitting the volley of muskets, and he was proud of that as well. He would not be the first to introduce an instrument of violence to islanders whom he thought to be a people of peace. He made some reflections in his journal. He wondered what it meant to take possession of islands that were already possessed by those who had truly discovered them. It was a fair question – about sovereignty and power, about the meaning of symbolic acts, about language and useful gestures in a discourse about ownership and first rights.

Marchand felt squeamish about 'possessing' these people. 'Protect' them was a better word, he thought, although he did not say from whom they should be protected. He might have asked to whom it was that he made these gestures of possession. Not to those possessed. They saw the gestures in other ways. They carried off the flags to sacred places, made their reverences to monuments as if they were vindication of old stories about strangers who came 'from beyond the skies', and fitted all they saw into their own calendars. Sometimes they stood around and watched the ceremonies, not really part of them and never able to let the rituals make the reality they signified. They never dreamed that they were owned or that their acts now had new dimensions, joined as they were to empire and subject to expectations of loyalties they could never know. Sometimes they made their own plays. These were as ineffective as messages as were the strangers' plays to them. They embodied the meanings of their world in things like banana stalks, palm leaves, pigs and feathers, and said things about the sacrifices they were making, the *tapu* that bound them, the cosmologies that made sense to them. There they were, native and stranger, each making plays about themselves that the other could not see, but bound together by an environment that now for each included the other.

It was good for the peace of Marchand's romantic soul that he could not see ahead fifty years to the brutal scenes when France took possession of these same islands again. Empire could not have been more miserable or more callous. It was a May morning in 1842, the feast of St Louis, the name day of the French King, Louis Philippe. Admiral Dupetit-Thouars disembarked from the *Reine Blanche* at Vaitahu, a valley on the island of Tahuata in the southern Marquesas. The admiral brought a guard of sixty infantrymen in ceremonial dress and formed them into a square around a flagpole they had erected on the dancing place behind the beach. At 10.30 he read a statement declaring that he had taken possession of the Marquesas in the name of the King of France. He then struck the soil with his sword three times, and, with three volleys and a rumble of cannon from the ships, the band began to play 'Domine Salvum' for the King and the 'Marseillaise' for all the unexpected changes that had undermined his kingship.

The Marquesans were quite excited. They responded by producing a half-buried cannon from an old wreck and detonated it with a double charge and a satisfying roar. Then there was Solemn High Mass, which ended in a downpour, and natives and strangers crowded into a tent. No doubt the strangers in their sweaty uniforms smelled bad to the natives. No doubt the natives in their rancid coconut oil smelled bad to the strangers. The chief of the valley, Iotete, signed the cession of his land to the French in a spidery scrawl – in triplicate. The French Ministre de la Marine had insisted that all cession of land be signed in triplicate to be sure of their legality. Iotete was dressed in a large red shag coat decorated with massive gold epaulettes and covering white pantaloons. He wore a pasteboard crown as 'king' of the valley. Someone remarked that if the black tattoos and the strange coiffure could be forgotten he would look rather like a Bourbon. Dupetit-Thouars had previously given him a flag – of red and white squares – and the French officers laughed to themselves that they had given a cannibal king the signal flag that summoned sailors to their evening meal.

The comedy did not lessen the tragedy that followed. Within months the French strangers were at war with the Marquesans. Trying to find allies, the French made and remade kings. They bombarded villages. They moved populations. They killed natives by the hundreds with their weapons and by the thousands with the diseases that came from their poor hygiene. 'Ecological imperialism', Alfred Crosby has called this suffusion of disease throughout the world's environment. Disease and death came with ships, as did power and trade and religion. They made the world one system, a World Encompassed, Native and Stranger Bound Together.

What would Etienne Marchand have thought of a scene on the afternoon of Good Friday, three years later, in 1845. It was 3.00 P.M. – think, even if you are not a christian believer, how heavy with cultural meanings that moment would be – of seven last words, of a 'man of sorrows', of crucifixion, of death before resurrection. The French chose that moment to execute by firing squad a petty Marquesan chief, Pakoko, for his resistance to their rule. It was an illegal act, even by French official perceptions, but who is to say what is moral, let alone legal, when there are necessities of empire?

The Spaniards had taken possession of these same islands nearly 250 years before the French. The scenes were just as bizarre and just as cruel. There was a touch of Calvary in them too. Taking possession, the Spaniards said mass and sang their 'Te Deum'. But their solemn rituals were preceded, interrupted and followed by savage rounds of killings. 'What did it matter', one of the Spaniards said, 'if the devil took these heathens a little earlier than was expected?' In the end, to score the point of their power, the Spaniards hung the bodies of three natives on stakes. One of the soldiers pierced the central body with a lance. As a sign of their possession, they erected three crosses and called the place where this had been done 'The Valley of the Mother of God'.

Americans took possession of these islands after the Spanish and before the French, in 1813. Lieutenant David Porter had come to the Marquesas to escape the British. In the USS *Essex* he had devastated the British Pacific trade during the War of 1812, and was now recuperating from these raids, with the prisoners he had taken, on Nukuhiva in the northern Marquesas. There he set up Fort Madison and built a small village called Madisonville. But he soon discovered than the Marquesans were more preoccupied with fighting among themselves than with providing him with necessities, especially with pigs. And worse, the Taipi (Herman Melville's 'Typee'), who were the enemies of the Teii, the people of the bay in which he established Madisonville, strode to the tops of the ridges above Madisonville and there made gestures that indicated – in Porter's words – that 'the Americans were the posteriors to the Teii's privates'. That, Porter judged, was a clear insult to the American flag. So he attacked the Taipi and killed five of them. He was a little disturbed that his allies, the Teii, did not enter his diplomatic wars, but, rather, took the five dead off, sacrificed them and ate them, instead. However, the Taipi were still recalcitrant with supplies of pigs for the hundreds of sailors, marines and prisoners of war in Madisonville. Worse, his allies were making jokes about it – about Porter's lack of courage, about how easily the Taipi were getting away without paying tribute. So Porter launched another attack. But he made an error. He attacked by marching over land. The Taipi killed one of his marines in ambush in the thickets and drove the rest off. What would his allies say of him now? He made a second attack from the sea, driving his men up the valley, burning houses, destroying breadfruit trees, killing, he said, 'great numbers'. Satisfied with his victories, he then collected the chiefs and forced them to put their marks on a petition to President Madison. Porter wrote of that petition: 'Our rights to this island being founded on priority of discovery, conquest and possession, cannot be disputed. But the natives to procure to themselves that friendly protection which their defenceless situation so much required have requested to be admitted into the great American family, whose pure republican polity approaches so near to their own.'

These posturings on behalf of Spanish, French and American empires – and English, too: James Cook's men had killed a Marquesan in these same valleys for stealing a penny nail – were, to use a phrase of C. Wright Mills of twentieth-century generals, 'crackpot realism' run wild. They were parodies of treaties and alliances, rhetoric of national politics, talk of alarums and excursions, sensitivity to honour and image, symbolic acts of punishment. It was 'crackpot realism' smeared with blood, nonetheless.

Such crackpot realism left little room for the sort of softness Etienne Marchand displayed. It allowed very little sense of the virtue in native culture. In fact, the greatest threats to civilisation, as seen by crackpot realists, were those who 'went native'. Beachcombers in the Pacific have been a great scandal to the civilised – to naval captains, to colonial administrators, to missionaries. Hidden in all the anger at the mutiny on the *Bounty,* we have to see the scandal as well; so many men 'went native'; so many men did not possess natives so much as they were possessed by natives.

GOING NATIVE

The mystery of Peter Heywood in the story of the *Bounty* has always been how cunning was his ingenuousness. How was it possible for him to have been so innocent? How could his too-honourable poses be unaffected? With Christian and the guiltiest mutineers eluding the navy, Peter Heywood, the only senior officer on trial, bore the brunt of public suspicion. He knew it would be so from the first shock of Edwards' treatment of him in the *Pandora.* His first letter home, written from Batavia, acknowledged how dangerous his position was. But it was not until he saw the letter Bligh had written to his mother, but which his family had kept from her, that he knew that Bligh's malice was lethal. He lost his private innocence on reading that letter, too. He would never forgive Bligh for what he saw as wilful malevolence. His public declarations of loyalty to Bligh were something else. Let us distinguish the overt manipulation of the legal system, the manoeuvring of patronage, the public displays of virtue from the question of his innocence. Some historians, knowing the gulf between Heywood's personal feelings towards Bligh and his public statements, have declared him dishonest and therefore his protest of innocence of mutiny a sham. But we have to understand that he was engaged in theatre of

life and death. I have no difficulty in believing that Heywood was innocent of the mutiny of which he was accused but that he knew perfectly
well why there was one.

Heywood's relationship to Christian was close. Christian had been
teaching him Latin, Greek and navigation on the voyage out. Heywood,
in the end, was Christian's confidant, and Christian clearly sheltered him
from overt participation in mutinous acts. Through all the events at Tubuai and Tahiti, Heywood's calm confidence that he would be seen as
innocent is patent. When the *Pandora* arrived at Matavai, Coleman, the
man whom Bligh requested to stay on the *Bounty,* was the first to reach
her. But that was only because Heywood had sent Tahitian friends to tell
Coleman of the *Pandora*'s arrival and to take him to her. Heywood, prepared and anticipating what he would do, went out in a double canoe
paddled by a dozen of those friends. He was so innocent that he could not
see how offensive his figure was to the naval officers of the *Pandora*. He
stood on the canoe, wrapped in a barkcloth *maro,* tanned and tattooed,
'gone native' and virtually indistinguishable from them, deviant to system
and rule. It must have been a cruel realisation to stand in Edwards' great
cabin and, under his knowing gaze, explain that his midshipman's logs,
his eighty-odd drawings, his description of Tahitian life and all the trappings of his official life were in a chest in the house of his *taio*. 'Tayo'! We
can almost see Edwards' savage look.

Living in Tahiti, Peter Heywood had made a discovery of native virtue.
His was not a discovery of the Noble Savage or of the Primitive. It was
much more simple and less a culturally centred image than that. It was a
realisation that their hospitality and generosity were genuine, that he
could not find the limits of them, that the greatest gift he could give
them in return was to let them make him like themselves – to endure the
pain of the tattoos, to speak their language, to know the subtleties of
their thinking. It was a beachcomber's discovery that there was more joy
in being possessed than in possessing. It was a sense of cultural relativism
that not many could share from a ship. The beach was the only proper
spot for such exchange.

Peter Heywood's 'going native' in dress, language and custom encouraged presumptions of his guilt in the mutiny among the quarterdeck of
the *Pandora*. Explanation was of no help. He had, however, to explain it
all to his family as well. The seventeen-year-old midshipman may have
been possessed by the Tahitians. He was most certainly possessed by his

sister Nessie. The Heywood household on The Parade, Douglas, Isle of Man, could have been Mansfield Park. The drama of Peter's role in the mutiny, then of his capture and return, raised Nessie's emotions to an intensity worthy of Jane Austen, or at least raised emotions that were expressed in the language of Jane Austen's heroines' world. There is extant still in the Newberry Library, Chicago, a collection of Nessie Heywood's correspondence with all the actors in this drama and many of her poems. She was a modest but extensive 'poetess' – her description of herself – and there was not much of her life – her invitations, her thank-you notes, her moments of emotional crisis, her gifts to others, the visits of naval gallants to her parlour – that was not transformed into verse. Peter was her Lycidas. John Milton had said it before her:

> For Lycidas is dead, dead 'ere his prime,
> Young Lycidas and hath not left his peer.
> Who would not sing for Lycidas? he knew
> Himself to sing and build the lofty rhyme.
> He must not float upon his watery bier,
> Unwept, and welter to the parching wind
> Without the need of some melodious tear. ['Lycidas' I:i]

The tide of Nessie's possessing literature rose with the mounting drama of Peter's trial.

> The best of brothers. Friend, Companion, Guide
> Joy of my youth, my Honor, and my Pride.
> Cruel Time. How slow thy lingering pace
> Fatal voyage – rob'd my soul
> Lov'd Lycidas
> Thy face expos'd to slanders wound
> And fell suspicions whispering ground
> Hopes of prevention urg'd thy stay
> Or Force which thou resistless must obey.

This plaintive verse was written February 25, 1792. Peter had not yet returned on the *Pandora,* and the family had no real news of him other than Bligh's cruel letter to his mother. On March 2, Nessie added more verses to her diary: 'Damon's gone. Adieu to love', and then, – 'Ex tempore on a party by Lord Harris in his pleasure boat' – 'Verse on the Langrade to Lt Js Bruton' – 'Loss of a wager of gloves that it would not rain between 10–8'.

Nessie took her role to be something more than simply being inspired by the gentle muses. She poured the intensity of her concerns over everyone who, she felt, needed to hear them – on Peter himself, of course, then the Heywood naval kin, then the captain friends of that kin who would be part of the court martial panel, then the lawyers and the vicars and parsons who would bear witness to a wider world how upstanding a lad Peter was. Above all, when it became clear that he would sculpt the defence's strategies and posturings, she poured herself on Aaron Graham. It is clear from the responses of all these people to Nessie that her audience rose to her virtue and were titillated by it. While the deadly theatre of the court martial was being played out, she presented another theatre of manners offstage. There she possessed her audience with her maidenhood, and they were stirred by it to an affected sort of chivalry. How intensely and with what sincerity she played her role can be seen from the fact that not twelve months after Peter's liberation, Nessie died of consumption. Sir John Barrow was among the first historians of the mutiny to make great use of Nessie's correspondence. He said of her: 'This impassioned and most affectionate of sisters, with an excess of sensibility, which acted too powerfully on her bodily frame, sunk, as is often the case with such susceptible minds, on the first attack of consumption'. Perhaps so. Aaron Graham and Thomas Pasley were possessed by Nessie's sensibilities only for a short time. Graham played a sordid, unchivalrous role in helping to defeat the Great Nore Mutiny. Vice-Admiral Thomas Pasley sat as president of the court that hanged Richard Parker, leader of the same mutiny.

On Peter's return to England, his family and friends discovered that he too had a poetical streak. In fact he revealed that his most inspired moment at Tahiti had come on February 6, 1790, when he did:

> Sit down upon the fruitful oroo's root
> To ruminate in Meditation mute.

The *uru* was the breadfruit tree. So it was truly a place to inspire some thoughts on why he was there and what had happened to him. And the date, February 6, 1790, was the day, unknown to him, when his father had died on the other side of the globe. If it was telepathy, it was not theirs to wonder how datelines and naval time reckoning affected it. In Tahiti, Peter was already convinced of the importance to him of the poem, which he called 'A Dream'. Later, the coincidence with his father's death added marvel to it. The poem is easily mocked, but not many beachcombers expressed in verse their puzzlement at their situation. The clichés do not make a lie of the experience. They show another sort of cultural possession.

The 'Dream' is one of those poems a man could write at a critical point of life to express in an unfamiliar medium profundities that ordinary words will not bear. It is the sort of poem by which a man will etch his possession of a moment in his memory. In Heywood's poem the generosity of the thoughts was remarkable, given that the boy had experienced mutiny, murder and now cultural isolation. His puzzle, as he sat beneath the breadfruit tree on the side of a hill looking out over Matavai Bay, was why he was so welcome in these 'fertile islands whose ancient source / cannot be trac'd or Origins found'. He found a deep contrast between the artificiality and rhetoric of his own cultural values and the natural virtues he saw displayed on Tahiti. He wrote: 'We pretend. They duly practice'.

> Sure friendships there, and gratitude and love
> such as ne'er reigns in European blood
> In these degen'rate Days, tho' from above
> We precepts have and know what's right and good
> And tho' we're taught by laws of God and Men
> How few there are who practice what they know.
> Yet they from Nature's dictates use each man
> As they could wish to them all Men should do.

It is not that Heywood was happy. He lived with a 'secret melancholy and miserable mind', but his dream gave him a 'dawning wisdom'. He could recognise in the otherness of these natives their 'simplicity' and 'beauteous morals'.

> On this far distant shore! and tho' received
> By these most generous Indians with joy
> And Friendship such as scarce can be believed
> Vying together, how each shall employ
> His Time with most alacrity to please.

He recognised this 'dawning wisdom' as a sort of providence that made sense of his condition.

Heywood was to be in need of a sense of providence. No matter how re-assuring his lawyers were of his eventual safety, he was young and

inexperienced enough to feel the deadly danger of it all. To hear the death
sentence shook him deeply, and again he turned to verse to gain possession of himself.

> I have gain'd on this important day
> Victory consummate o'er myself
> Birthday to eternity.

Heywood's imprisonment on the *Hector* waiting for his trial was another
sort of beach and his calm another sort of control of two cultures. In the
end, he was marked for life by his experience of his beaches. He became
a favourite of admirals and possessed by them as a sort of medal to their
commonsensical naval justice. But that only drove him away from them
all. He was to record at the end of his naval career that of twenty-nine
years, seven months and one day of service, he had spent twenty-seven
years, six months, one week and five days at sea. He was forever in distant
places, Tahitis with other names, mapping foreign shores. In the end he
surveyed more coasts than William Bligh.

POSSESSING OTHERS WITH A LAUGH

The Tahitians, I have suggested, possessed their strangers through 'Oro,
and then in Captain Cook. True possession by the British came, I am
about to argue, through complex processes of representation. Notably the
British possessed Tahitian otherness by laughing at it.

Cook had returned to England from Tahiti after his first expedition in
the *Endeavour* with Sir Joseph Banks in July 1771. Within five months he
was on his way to the Pacific on his second voyage. He had remained too
briefly at home to publish an account of his first discoveries. Joseph Banks,
who might have been expected to publish the brilliant science of his voyage, was in a huff at not being allowed to dominate another Grand Tour
of the Pacific. In any case Banks was involved in the harum-scarum of his
social-scientific life. So the task of presenting the Pacific discoveries of
Byron, Wallis, Carteret and Cook was entrusted by the Admiralty to Dr
John Hawkesworth. Hawkesworth was a savant, more a moralist than a
geographer. The Admiralty authorised Hawkesworth, but the publishers,
William Strahan and Thomas Cadell, made sure his book would be entertainment for the public by giving him £6,000 for the copyright, the
largest payment in England for the whole of the century. Hawkesworth

completed *An Account of the Voyages undertaken by the order of his present Majesty for making Discoveries in the Southern Hemisphere, And successively performed by Commodore Byron, Captain Wallis, Captain Carteret and Captain Cook, in the* Dolphin, *the* Swallow *and the* Endeavour: *drawn up from the Journals which were kept by the several Commanders, And from the Papers of Joseph Banks, Esq.* (London, 1773. 3 vols.) but did not live to enjoy the money. Within months of publishing his volumes he had died, killed by the anxieties that the jealousies, scandals and criticism of his work had raised.

Hawkesworth was a reflective man, very conscious of what he was about when he was translating other men's ethnographic moments. Was *Voyages* his book? he asked himself and the reader. Who was the *I* that joined the navigators' different experiences? What did it mean to join not one but dozens of logs and journals together? What was the real experience – the dull data of sailing or the moral issues of their encounter? He had a sense that if his book was about Pacific discoveries it was also a vehicle for something else. That something else – his sense of the universal significance of totally particular events – is what got him into trouble. His critics were loud. The sailors, whom he purported to represent, said he was not like them at all. Dr Samuel Johnson, always cantankerous about natives and foreign places, was totally dismissive: there were better things for Hawkesworth to write about and for Banks better things to do. Horace Walpole got into a fluster. John Wesley disapproved. Many of its loudest critics did not read the *Voyages* at all because it was an 'attack against religion and an outrage against decency', and £6,000 was just too much to pay for what many believed they could do better.

The extravagance of the critics' rage concerned almost everything about Hawkesworth's book, but they reserved a special sense of scandal for the fact that a moralist, someone who had been given a Doctor of Letters for his uplifting thought, should have titillated the public by displaying the gross sexuality of the Tahitians and the randiness of Mr Banks. There was horror as well that Hawkesworth should have denied what everybody knew to be a 'particular Providence' in the saving of Cook's *Endeavour* after its shipwreck on the Australian coast. 'A Christian' who hounded Hawkesworth in the press for months said it all:

Our women may find in Dr Hawkesworth's Book stronger Excitements to vicious indulgences than the most intriguing French Novel could present to their imaginations – and while our Mariners no longer look up to the Almighty for

Deliverance from Shipwreck – or feel Gratitude rise in their Breasts on being
saved from impending Evils – our Libertines may throw aside the *Women of
Pleasure,* and gratify their impure minds with the Perusal of infinitely more lascivious Recitals than are to be found in that scandalous Performance!

Actually, Hawkesworth was a disturber on two counts. His exposition of
native sexual customs was history, a story of what happened, not a fantasy. To tell his history, he needed to affect a neutrality that, in his critics'
eyes, he did not have. His suspension of judgement was seen as a judgement. He also disturbed in his relativist stance. He had written that he
did not think it was by a particular divine intervention that the *Endeavour*
was saved when the wind dropped as she ran aground on a reef off the
New Holland coast. It was no more specially providential, he said, than
the sun rising every morning. It was his comment on an old and unfinished debate about the efficacy of prayer and the problem of evil. But in
the dramaturgy surrounding his contentious publication it was transformed from a theologians' squabble into a confrontation about myths and
heroes. The fever of excitement about Pacific discoveries, the fever of excitement about a book that had earned an author £6,000, the fever of
excitement about the gossip concerning famous people, all transformed
private theological opinions that did not matter into a public declaration
of faith on which civilisation was seen to turn. People who would never
have read Hawkesworth berated him for undermining the confidence of
the masses who prayed daily for helping intervention by a loving God.
European culture was on the edge of a revolution in its own myths about
the relationship of the supernatural and the natural. Hawkesworth's view
on a 'particular providence' became an occasion on which many, in being
forced to look at the other, were entertained by ambiguities they discovered in themselves.

Purea, or 'Queen Oberea', the woman who took Wallis' flag of possession and sewed it into the *maro ura,* appeared in Hawkesworth's *Voyages*
in an engraving entitled 'A representation of the surrender of the island
of Otaheite to Captain Wallis by the supposed Queen Oberea'. She is seen
presenting a plantain branch as if it were a palm branch of peace. Behind
her come a procession of her people, bowing and making deferential gestures. Wallis is holding his musket like a sceptre and is supported by his
guard looking like a troop of Hessian mercenaries. A large crowd of Tahitians look on, peering out of a pavilionlike grass hut, which is Purea's
'palace'. It is, of course, a 'representation' of a 'surrender' that never took

Figure 14.
Wallis takes possession of Tahiti from 'Queen Oberea,' as the engravers of Hawkesworth's
Voyages saw it. (John Hawkesworth, *An Account of the Voyages . . .* 1773. Baillieu Library,
The University of Melbourne.)

place,with gestures that could never have been made. Being history of
something that never happened, it went on to abstract a truth whose
accuracy did not matter: 'Tahiti belongs to us'. But Purea became famous
in England for other reasons altogether. Purea entered English imagination because she had, it was said, a tattooed bum, because she orchestrated
a public copulation, because she watched while a young girl danced naked
before Banks, and she slept with Banks while he had his clothes stolen.
She entered the English imagination not as something other but as something familiar in an argument about morality and corruption. Knowing
Purea, the English could laugh at Banks and at women too.

The British possessed Tahiti by compressing the complexities of all the
ethnographic moments experienced in encountering the island into a few
experiences made memorable because they displayed Tahiti as a mirror for
themselves. Beginning with Hawkesworth's account, descriptions of Tahitian ways and the Tahitian environment began to accumulate in books,
magazines and newspapers, in notes and programmes for museum collec-

tions, in caches of letters and journals, in the memories of a myriad of conversations with those who had been there. There is no way of measuring their full effect, no way of knowing whether the infinite variety of experiences was drawn together in any one image of Tahiti. There was, however, a compression of these experiences into a set of simplifications. These simplifications emerged not so much out of philosophical systems concerning soft primitivism or out of a romantic mood. They arose out of dramatic ironies in which the appropriation of the natives allowed the strangers to be entertained by themselves.

To judge from the constant guffaws, one of the principal dramatic ironies turned on Queen Oberea's 'pinked bum'. Perhaps there had been a British preoccupation with the lower anatomy over the centuries, but at the end of the eighteenth century there was clearly something very delicious in seeing the courtly dignity of a 'queen' shattered by the revelation of a 'tattowed breech'. Hawkesworth's *Voyages* was followed by the publication of an extraordinary series of poetic and satirical letters. They purported to be written by many people – by a 'Professor of the Otaheite Language in Dublin and of all the languages of the undiscovered islands of the South Seas', and by a 'Second Professor of the Otaheite and every other unknown language'. 'Oberea' herself supposedly wrote two letters to her lovers, one to Banks, one to Wallis. Omai, supposedly her plenipotentiary, wrote to her and then to the 'Right Honourable the Earl of XX, Late XXXXXXX – Lord of the XXXXXXX'. 'An officer at Otaheite' wrote to 'Lady Gr**v*n*r' a 'poetical epistle (Moral and Philosophical)', and a 'Lady of Quality' wrote to Omai. The 'Injured Harriet', Banks' jilted fiancée, wrote to the 'presumptuous Indian' and 'savage usurper' 'Oberea'. The publications jabbed and jibed at Banks, stuck like a butterfly on his own collection board by the pin of his own naïveté. They caught others as well, Lord Sandwich and his various ladies, 'the English arioi' of Pall Mall, venal bishops and ambitious bishops' wives, Methodist preachers with their 'bagpipical drawl' preaching messages 'dangerous to society'. And always there was the 'luscious Hawkesworth' who 'scenes obscene . . . painted best'. These poems and letters cannibalised one another in their glee; they came back again and again to the same incidents on the voyage; they made simplicities by repetition. They were redolent with classical and literary allusion: Dido and the *Aeneid* as representative of real high culture mocked the spurious charm of savages. They played the ironies every way – of English courtly cultivation seen through innocent primitive eyes, of raw savages seen by exquisite sophistication. 'Here painted faces bloom on every strum / In Otahiete we tattoo the bum.' 'Vain Oberea will in vain beseech / And to the bawdy winds betray her painted breech'.

Banks' botanical interests were the subject of every conceivable *double entendre* as critics explored the metaphorical field around his *plant*. 'Oberea' was a 'hapless fair one' for losing both her crown and her lover Banks. But she was also a 'hotty-tooty queen' for her easy morals. Nothing gave an edge to their satire more than three sexual incidents in which Banks and Oberea played a part. One concerned a small Tahitian girl whose public copulation was apparently marshalled by Oberea and observed by Cook. The second was the stealing of Banks' vest and pistol while he slept on Oberea's canoe. There was a third whose context we have already seen when we reflected on Francis Pinkney and his running of the gauntlet. It was the subject of forbearing humour rather than satire. No doubt this was because promiscuity of the lower classes was less pornographic than dissipation among the aristocracy. This was the incident of the nails and the 'old trade' of Tahitian women's sexual favours for the new currency of spikes and iron. Francis Pinkney was widely known, if not by name, then from what he did. The inflation in the 'trade' as the Tahitian women found there were bigger and longer nails was full of poetic license. In these circumstances a *nail* was also a *plant*. One contributor to this soft pornography wrote:

> With nails we Traffic for the blooming maid
> And the ships planks supply the dangerous trade.
> At last the fair ones see with strange surprise
> Some nails produced of more than common size.
> The happy females with this treasure grac'd
> Display their triumphs and our coins debased.
> In vain we sue, the Nymphs comply no more.
> 'Give us large nails', reaches from the shore.

There was a fourth interest that shows how the discovery of the Tahitian other was translated into more self-centred concerns of the Europeans and was made memorable because of that. A furious debate began to rage as to who introduced the 'venereals' to Tahiti, Wallis or Bougainville? British versifiers credited the French. They were sure that 'pining Venus mourns the gift of France'. One was confident that when 'a Frenchman gave, a Briton heal'd the wound' — with Harry's patent venereal medicine. Beyond the scruffy verses, whose attention to venereal disease was slight, there were louder and more official protests of British innocence in spreading the disease. The matter was quickly transformed into an issue of national honour and international diplomacy, the continued memory or history of which affected Europe's relations with Tahiti for decades.

The English took a prurient interest in Tahitian dancing. 'Timorodee', the word describing it, came into common usage at the end of the eighteenth century. We are uncertain whence the word came. J. C. Beaglehole, editor (1967, 1968) of Cook's Journals, suggested that 'timorodee' was Cook's version of the Tahitian *te ai maro iti,* meaning mock copulation, but the renowned scholar of Tahiti, Douglas Oliver, measuring his certainties more precisely, is noncommittal. In any case, 'timorodee' was taken to mean lascivious dancing of the sort that was performed for Banks by a young girl who ceremoniously, by his account, 'displayed her naked beauties' in making a present to him of the white bark cloth in which she was voluminously wrapped. One of the poetical pamphlets described the scene:

> While, as she turns her painted bum to view,
> With fronts unblushing, in the public shew,
> They search each crevice with a curious eye,
> To find Exotics – where they never lie.
> O Shame! Were we, great George, thy gallant crew,
> And had we – damn it – nothing else to do,
> But turn thy great design to filthy farce
> And search for wonders or an Indian's a . . . ?
> But then to print our tale!
> O, curse the thought.

Cook had commented in his journals on the public copulation of a young man and a girl of ten or twelve years at the gate of Fort Venus under the direction of Oberea. In Cook's interpretation, the act was done 'more from custom than lewdness'. But Cook's niceties of judgement did not stop the howls of derision at such incipient cultural relativism. With barbarism so blatant, the notion that the savage was soft or noble was a mockery. The lesson to be learned was that there were no lessons to be learned.

Then the image of the young Banks crying 'thief' in the middle of the night for the loss of his silver-frogged waistcoat and pistol while he lay naked beside his 'old friend Oberea' on her double canoe was a gift beyond price for the satirist.

Didst thou not, crafty, subtle, sunburnt strum
Steal the silk breeches from his tawny bum?
Calls't thouself a Queen? and thus couldst use
And rob thy Swain of breeches and his shoes?

It was a scene out of pantomime, a farce parodying savage kingdoms and the malapropism of scientific gentlemen. 'Great Alexander conquered boys and belles', wrote the supposedly 'Injured Harriet' of her fiancé Banks, 'Mine sailed the world around for cockle-shells'. What Wallis, Cook and Banks saw and what Hawkesworth described were not 'exotics' at all. Banks' romantic effort, Cook's more puzzled attempt, and Hawkesworth's tentative tries at discovering the Tahitians in their otherness were denounced as insufferable licence. The Tahitian were not Other at all: they were the same only worse. Even the most tenuous cultural relativism in understanding the Tahitians as they were threatened this commonsense realism. In the *realpolitik* of a joke all the world is the same. Strangers possess natives in a laugh.

Purea had another sort of incarnation. She appeared as 'Oberea The Enchantress' in a pantomime at Covent Garden, December 1785. The pantomime was a staged version of Cook's voyages to the Pacific. It was called *Omai or a Trip Round the World* and proved to be entertainment in all the senses of the word that we have used. While pantomime at the end of the eighteenth century had not settled into all its conventionalities and still awaited the skills of such actors as Joseph Grimaldi to fix the prominence of such characters as Clown, nonetheless its rubrics were clearly set into formal structure. It was always a tale of a virtuous young love thwarted by authority or rivalry, and the whole transformed magically into a romping charade of Harlequin, his lover Columbine, his rival Pantaloon and Clown interacting through successive scenes until all was resolved in a splendid finale. The timeless inevitability of the harlequinade was a setting for a vaudeville of topicality in which current events, personages and scenes were made comically present. The ritualistic and unequivocal formalities of the pantomime made the relevancies of the current topics the more dramatic and simple. There was no narrative, no masque in the topicalities, only scenes, the more real for the unreality of the magic and the make-believe. But that did not mean that the pantomime was insignificant, without meaning. It was not just puff and glitter. 'Omai', wrote

Figure 15.
'Oberea The Enchantress'. P. J. de Loutherbourg's costume design for the pantomime
Omai, after John Webber's advice. (Philippe Jacques de Loutherbourg, *Obereyau Enchant-*
ress. 1785. Watercolour. National Library of Australia.)

the critic in *Rambler's Magazine,* was a 'school for the history of Man'. The
Times critic, who reviewed nearly every performance, said:

The stage never exhibited such a combination of superb and various scenery –
enchanting music and sheer fun. The scenes, characters and dresses being, except a few, novel and foreign to this country, contribute much to heighten the
delight, for what can be more delightful than an enchanting fascination that
monopolizes the mind to the scene before the eye, and leads the imagination
from country to country, from the frigid to the torrid zone, shewing as in a
mirror, prospects of different climates, with all the productions of nature in the
animal and vegetable worlds, and all the efforts of man to attain nourishment,
convenience and luxury, by the world of arts. It is a spectacle worthy of the
contemplation of every rational being, from infant to the aged philosopher. A
spectacle that holds forth the wisdom and dispositions of Providence in the
strongest view.

The pantomime, other critics wrote, was a 'beautiful illustration of Cook's voyages'. It was a translation into entertainment of ethnographic moments in which the European strangers confronted the otherness of the Pacific island natives, tried to describe that otherness and in that description possess them.

The genius of this translation was Philippe Jacques de Loutherbourg, and with him the Irish playright, John O'Keeffe, and the musical composer, William Shield. They were joined by the painter of Cook's third voyage, John Webber. Their genius was to make appealing theatre and to make their translations seem real. De Loutherbourg was recognised as the great technological innovator of the eighteenth-century stage. In *Omai*, his brilliance was on full display. It caught up the simplicities of being native in an exhibition of civilised technology. He even re-created the latest technological advance – the flying balloon, invented only two years before – to help audiences sense they were seeing history as it happened. In the madcap farce of the pantomime, they applauded and gasped at realities, both experienced and unexperienced, masterfully represented.

John O'Keeffe, the playwright, did not have to write a script. Pantomimes were sung and mimed. It was against the law for them to have spoken dialogue. But in all his lyrics O'Keeffe verbalised the British mood of satisfaction at its humanism towards savage peoples. He also mixed Tahitian words into the lyrics, solemnly translated their meaning in footnotes in the printed programme. In his memories of later years, he singled out, as an example of the realism of the pantomime, a scene in which the actor Ralph Wewitzer played a Tahitian prophet. Wewitzer made his obeisance to Cook in extempore nonsense patter. This 'tahitian' speech was also carefully 'translated' in the programme. The language of natives is always gibberish to the civilised. The 'as if' was just as good as the real.

There was much praise for William Shield. He caught, it was said, the 'vernacular airs of Otaheite' in his music with remarkable accuracy, imitating conches and mimicking wild beasts 'to make the performance as characteristic as possible'. Shield was fresh from composing his version of the *Marriage of Figaro*. He was later to become Master of the King's Musick. *Omai*'s music was as comforting as Wewitzer's gibberish, and just as possessive. The music crossed a cultural boundary, put order on disorder, 'as much as science can approach barbarity', the critics said.

John Webber contributed the greatest sense of authenticity of all. He could paint what he had seen. He was the expert adviser for props and scenery on what Tahitian landscapes and native sacred places were really like. He could reconstruct weapons and native crafts. He drew the costumes for the procession of Pacific nations that worshipped the hero Cook, in the final scene. A giant painting of Cook's apotheosis or divinisation descended on the stage. Webber was impoverished because he was forbidden to exhibit any of the paintings from his expedition with Cook until the official accounts of the third voyage were published. He could make a few pounds painting a few backdrops and giving directions to the dozen or so painters who worked for three months to put the sets together. Sir Joshua Reynolds, who had completed a portrait of the real Omai when he was brought to London, sat in the orchestra seats at the pantomime to get the best possible view. He solemnly pronounced the painting of the scenery very real indeed, although he had not got closer to the South Seas than his own studio.

The relics surviving from the pantomime are few – reviews and descriptions in a dozen newspapers and magazines, the published lyrics of John O'Keeffe and a narrative programme, two maquettes or scene models in a museum and a private collection, sketches of the costumes by de Loutherbourg and Webber, de Loutherbourg's sketch of the apotheosis of Captain Cook, a painting of the large canvas that had descended to the stage, and the original engravings of Cook's voyages that were the inspiration of the scenes. The names of the characters in the pantomime were, like the Tahitian words in O'Keeffe's songs, snatched from the public accounts of the European encounter with the Tahitians. There was Omai, the living curiosity and sample of noble savage, who had come to England and returned to Tahiti with Cook. Omai retained his name, but in the pantomime character was transformed into the son of 'King' Otoo (Tu, or Pomare I) and made heir to the Tahitian throne. Oedidee (Hitihiti, whom we have met) was made a rival of Omai and the protégé of Oberea. Oberea (Purea), in some token of what had happened to her reputation in all the satire and laughter, was now a menacing sorceress bent on raising Oedidee to the throne of Tahiti. Her goal in the pantomime was to foil the marriage of Londina to Omai. Yes, Londina, the beauteous daughter of Britannia, was promised by her mother to Omai in order to join the two kingdoms of Britain and Tahiti in lasting harmony. Omai's rival to Londina's hand was a Spaniard, Don Struttolando. It was the Don's pursuit of the lovers that set up the helter-skelter trip around the world that provided the continuity of the pantomime – to Kamchatka, to the 'Ice

Figure 16.
Cook's second apotheosis, which critics thought a little bland, but which seems dramatic enough for the hero. (Philippe Jacques de Loutherbourg and John Webber, *The Apotheosis of Captain Cook*. British Museum Ref: 1849–10–3–88.)

Islands' (Arctic or Antarctic did not matter) – to the Friendly Islands, to the Sandwich Islands, to Tahiti.

In Tahiti, the climax and denouement take place. Omai is finally rescued from Oberea's evil spirit. Her famous palace – we have seen it – is burnt down. Omai is installed as king. Then to Matavai, 'the Great Bay of Otaheite', comes a grand procession of all the peoples of the Pacific islands that Captain Cook had discovered or visited – Tahitians, New Zealanders, Tannans, Marquesans, Tongans, Hawaiians, Easter Islanders – and Tehutzki Tartars, Kamchatkars, Eskimos and Indians of Nootka, Oonalaski and Prince William Sound. The peoples of the procession, carefully identified in the programme, are 'dressed characteristically' according to Webber's advice and de Loutherbourg's design. They acclaim Omai as King. A Mad Prophet steps forward and congratulates Omai for paddling [!] to the 'Country of the mighty George whose great sword in the hand of Elliott [General Elliott, Governor of Gibraltar – Bligh had been with the *Cambridge* when she helped relieve the besieged Garrison at Gibraltar in 1782] keeps the Strong Rock from the Rich King of Lima, even in his own land'. (The Mad Prophet, at least, knew the significance of Don Struttolando, the politics of Gibraltar, and why an English audience might get special entertainment at booing Don Struttolando!) He continued, no doubt with farcical intensity: 'Know all that Omai is the master of fifty red feathers, master of four hundred fat hogs; he can command a thousand fighting men and twenty strong handed women to thump him to sleep!' (Tahitian massaging was a curiosity. Cook himself had been 'thumped'.) An English captain then steps forward, gives a sword to Omai and initiates a grand lament for Cook:

Captain: 'Accept from mighty George our Sovereign Lord
          In sign of British love, this British sword'.
Oberea: 'Oh joy! Away my useless spells and magic charms
          A British sword is proof against the world in arms.'
Captain: 'Ally of Joy! Owhyee's (Footnote: The island where
          Captain Cook was killed) fatal shore
          Brave Cook, your great Orono (Footnote: A Demigod or hero
          and distinguished title with which the natives honoured
          Captain Cook) is no more.'
Indians: 'Mourn, Owhyee's fatal shore
          For Cook, our great Orono, is no more!'

At that moment the giant painting of the *Apotheosis of Captain Cook* begins to descend on the stage. Cook, looking a little anxious it has to be admitted, rests in fluffy clouds over Kealakekua Bay where he had been killed and sacrificed and is now being crowned by Britannia and Fame. The voices of the people, now so firmly part of the British family, well into a great chorus:

> Ye chiefs of the ocean your laurels throw by
> Or cypress entwine with a wreath.
> To prove your humanity, heave a soft sigh
> And a tear now let fall for his death!
> Yet the Genius of Britain forbids us to grieve
> Since Cook ever honour'd immortal shall live.
>
> The hero of Macedon ran o'er the world
> Yet nothing but death could he give

'Twas George's command and the sail was unfurl'd
and Cook taught mankind how to live.

He *came* and he *saw,* not to *conquer* but to save.
The Caesar of Britain was he:
Who scorn'd the conditions of making a slave
While Britons themselves are so free
Now the Genius of Britain forbids us to grieve
Since Cook ever honour'd immortal shall live.

It was a very satisfying moment. O'Keeffe thought the finale the high moment of his pantomime. The critics felt a little cheated that, after an evening of extravagant spectacle, the apotheosis of Cook was represented rather blandly in a painting. After all, they said, a deification was something special and deserved a little drama of its own. But it was enough for most. George III came to see the pantomime on many occasions and was tearfully happy when seeing it. It was performed fifty-six evenings in all.

It is a folly at such a distance and with such sparse evidence to say what was happening, what social realities were being established by these dramaturgies. But surely we can say that, in the ambience of entertainment, mood and meaning were being reduced to simplicities. In *Omai* the absurdities and make-believe of the pantomime were blown away by the reality of the truth of the last scene. With music and chorused voices and staged solemnity to set the soul a-quiver, the humanism of Civilisation was set beside the quaintness of the Other. In that humanism was known the benignity of power, the good intentions of the end that will justify the means. It was (as it always is) the *realpolitik* of empire grandiloquently expressed that properly bound native and stranger together. On the other hand, the natives were more quaint than threateningly different. There was the Mad Prophet's quiet put-down of the new 'King' Omai's power in fifty red feathers, four hundred pigs and twenty thumping women. But the quaintness of make-believe kings was heightened by being staged in a form of entertainment in which the audience was meant to be convinced that it was watching something authentic because it was technologically brilliant and scientific. De Loutherbourg's talent was to make illusions realistic. The whole night long the audience saw fantasised historical characters – Omai, Oberea, Otoo, Oedidee – in the authentic environment of their houses, their ornamentation, their language, their music. The authenticity of the realisms of this unfamiliar native environment was made the more convincing by the realisms of a more familiar environment, also meticulously restored in every detail – Kensington, Margate and Plymouth. That is why the audience could come away certain that they had been at a 'school for the history of man' whereas, in the history of men and women, the pantomime was an extravagant hocus-pocus.

The inventions of Purea did not end with her dying or even with the demise of contemporary interest in her. I tell Purea's story as if our meeting with her is somehow direct, as if the events of the past are disconnected with the present. We know that is not so, of course, but we are adept in seeing the past as if it were unmediated by its relics and our questions of them. Like physicists who blinker themselves to see through the material characteristics of the world around them to its nuclear structure, like botanists who blinker themselves to see a tree in its classification, not in its poetry, we too impose a discipline on ourselves to see not the present, but the past. For us all, the ambiguities are too many, the lateral pursuits too tedious, the operational judgements too complex for us to be anything but pragmatic in our blinkered view. Yet it is the present with which all of us who love history – who write it, who read it – are in touch. We possess the past directly only because we are in supportive agreement that the tone of our narrative and the tenses of our language make the past present. The past is really mediated to us by all the inventions that have happened in between.

You, the reader, are mediated by me, the writer. One has to suppose that you have heard of Purea at this moment for the very first time. There will be some among you who you will have heard of Purea before. They will know that what I write belongs to a discourse that has already engaged the attention of highly respected Polynesian scholars, such as John C. Beaglehole, Colin Newbury, Niel Gunson, Douglas Oliver, Roger Green, Roger Rose. Their works are displayed in my bibliography. These readers will know the problematic that has been shaped by these scholars' discourse: whether the hegemony of political power that was eventually established in Tahiti evolved out of Tahitian potentialities or whether it was effected by the European arrival, or whether some combination of evolutionary and external forces prompted change. These scholars ask whether the Pomare dynasty's victory at the cost of Purea's family's defeat came from political violence or from manipulation of accepted legitimating symbols. Those readers will know that my own or anybody's entry into that discourse would be by way of both removing and increasing the ambiguities. I justify my right to tell the story of possessions by submitting my statements to the test of accuracy, by having read all the extant sources, by warning about their contradictions, by elaborating on the grades of my sense of certainty, by argument and extension of argument. I could not tell the number of times I have 'met' Purea – in undergraduate essays I have corrected, in researches for something else in all the books that I have read. There is not a sentence that I write of her that could not take a page or a chapter to balance its probabilities, to make explicit the meandering trail by which I come to it. And you, the reader, are in any case a figment of my imagination. I write for you, making decision on decision about what I select, what I leave out, wondering what you would know, what would tease you to read more. It cannot be that I write just for Douglas Oliver or Niel Gunson or Colin Newbury or Roger Green or Roger Rose, although they will know my licences. It cannot be that I write to make my readers equally expert as they or I about Purea. I write to have my inventions join my readers' inventions. Poor impossible-to-reach Purea is not the mutual goal of our knowledge but the vehicle for our joined understanding. Her exemplarity is surely our shared invention.

Purea and the whole context of her life come to us through a chain of inventions and possessions by an infinite number of strangers and by Purea's own native descendants, who in time became strangers to her as well. The inventions of the strangers came by way of their own historical reconstruction and out of many references, direct and indirect, made by later seamen and missionaries. Mostly these were a jigsaw of references to Tahitian men and women connected to Purea by marriage and descent. Much was in the way of reflections by the likes of Cook, Forster and Bligh, correcting the misinterpretations of one another. Its history, like all history's inventions, was made by what has been called colligation, the drawing together of the bits and pieces of many pasts, of many discoveries.

Among the many small inventions and possessions of Purea made to accommodate her to different presents has been one large one. It came a hundred years after her death, and it came from an unexpected pen, that of Henry Adams, the American historian. There are many reasons why men have been driven to the Pacific and to possess others. Henry Adams had been wounded by his wife's suicide and inspired by Robert Louis Stevenson's wanderings in the Pacific. Looking to be possessed by and to possess something primitive, Adams arrived in Tahiti in 1891. There he found himself more bored than enchanted, but in his last days, as he looked for a ship to escape in, he met with an old woman of nearly seventy years, Arii Taimai. He met her, as it chanced, at the ceremonial opening of a bridge. The bridge had been built with the stones of the dismantled *marae* Mahaiatea, the sacred place that Amo and Purea had built for their son about 1767 in the days of their high ambitions. The old woman was pleasantly garrulous, full of the legends her father had taught her. Arii Taimai was of the Teva clan. Her great-grandfather had been Amo's brother. She had, in her own name, title to more than thirty Tahitian *marae*. She had also been adopted by the widow of Pomare II, had spent nearly the whole of her life suspended in the web of rhetoric about dominance and legitimacy of Tahitian lines and titles.

Day after day in 1891, Arii Taimai talked to Henry Adams through an interpreter, her daughter Marau. Adams had to leave before he made sense of it all, but Marau forwarded further notes to him in Washington when he returned there in 1892. Tati Salmon, the son of Arii Taimai, visited Adams in Washington later in the same year. Adams returned the hospitality he had received in Tahiti and used Salmon as informant to enlarge an interest that had come to preoccupy him greatly. Now surrounded by his books, Adams soon absorbed the history of Tahiti that had accumulated through the journals of Wallis, Cook, Bougainville and Bligh, as well as the publications of the London Missionary Society. With the extravagance of the wealthy and the fastidious, he had a few copies of his researches privately printed in 1893. Then, aware of the uncomfortable feeling that he had discovered his own American cultural commercialism through Tahitian simplicities and idealism, he abandoned his American history researches and went looking for his spiritual roots in medieval Europe. In 1908 he edited a version of the *Memoirs of Arii Taimai*. In it he maintained the fiction that it was Arii Taimai's pen that had written the memoirs. It is, in fact, a relatively simple exercise of criticism to trace Adams' hand as he interwove an English text with Tahitian memories interpreted to him in French by Arii Taimai's daughter. Every element of the *Memoirs* is a translation. But in translation it was a version of Tahitian history established long before Adams had written the first pages. Arii Taimai and Marau had given him a Teva understanding of the past. It was a Teva narrative of possession that Adams projected, a story shaped from the experiences of the waxing and waning fortunes of Purea who had lost, and of their enemies the Pomares who had lost and won and lost.

Henry Adams, the historian, we know to have been somewhat fixated on women and their relationship with power. Speaking in Arii Taimai's voice, he wrote of Purea: 'If a family must be ruined by a woman, perhaps it may as well be ruined thoroughly and brilliantly by a woman who makes it famous'. As the Teva clan remembered her, Purea upset proprieties by demanding acknowledgement of her social superiority in symbolic ways. Her son, a boy of eight or nine in 1767, was the most highly titled person in Tahiti, the possessor of both the *maro ura* and *maro tea*. In their policy, Tahitians had no difficulty in distinguishing the deference they owed to those with higher titles because of genealogies and the deference they owed to the politically dominant. Deference to those with high titles they paid at the sacred places of these titles, at the Taputapuatea in the case of titles that were owed sacrifice. Deference to political dominance they showed in submissive ceremony to symbols of extended authority. Submission ceremonies surrounded the acknowledgement of some sign of dominance as it was processed around the island. Political power was expressed not so much by the person and the presence of the *ari'i* as by the extension of their persons in their symbols and by their messengers. It was acknowledged by gift and sacrifice. Purea's downfall occurred over her effort to equate the titled dominance of her son with her own political dominance and that of her husband, Amo. As the Teva told it, it was an affair of women. Purea, in building the *marae* Mahaiatea, imposed a *rahui,* a prohibition of food and certain behaviours that was the right of *ari'i rahi,* or high chiefs, alone to impose. To obey it was to acknowledge superiority. Two women, Purea's sister and her brother's wife, challenged the *rahui* by paying formal visits to her. These formal visits demanded hospitality and therefore the lifting of the *rahui* between equals. The rift that followed Purea's refusal to acknowledge the women's equality and raise the *rahui* was said to be the cause of battle and of the defeat of Purea that followed.

Other sources put the matter differently. After the investiture of Teri'-irere at Mahaiatea, they allege Amo and Purea demanded the ceremonial submission that came with the procession of symbols around the island. We have seen exactly that sort of procession after the investitute of Pomare II. The Seaward Teva refused to submit, and in the battles that followed, Amo and Purea were defeated and the *maro ura* of Teri'irere moved to a new (but older) sacred place in Ahuru, Papara. This attempt by Amo and Purea to establish political hegemony over the whole island

of Tahiti followed the Tahitian possession of the Wallis flag and its incorporation into a *maro ura*. The sources say quite explicitly that it was not
the Wallis flag that was paraded around the island but some other symbol.
There is some debate among scholars whether the Wallis flag was added
to an old *maro ura* or whether it became the establishing element of a new
maro ura. The most knowledgeable of modern historians of ancient Tahiti,
Douglas Oliver, says that he favours the view that the British flag was
incorporated in an already existing *maro ura*. It is, let there be no doubt,
a question of guess and probability. Who knows? Perhaps the old *maro
ura* was destroyed by Wallis' cannons when he sank what I have suggested
was 'Rainbow' in Matavai Bay. In any case, let me invent another sort of
past out of what I see as a different set of likelihoods. It is pertinent to
our understanding how people possess one another.

That the *maro* with British colours was a new symbol has some supportive argument. Descriptions of those who saw it say it was made of both
red and yellow feathers, not just the red of the *maro ura* or the yellow-
white of the *maro tea*. It seems logical that combined colours meant that
it had the qualities of all the others. The drawing Bligh made of it showed
the bunting to be at one end. It seems finished because the rounded tassels
that were essential to the sacred wrap were attached to the bunting. If the
bunting had been added to an existing *maro,* one would expect twenty
years of sacrifices (from 1767 to 1788) to have enclosed the bunting with
further lappets of feathers.

Let us suppose that the British flag, possessed by the Tahitians in the
context of their 'Oro beliefs and seen by them as a symbol of political
dominance and sovereignty after their violent disaster with the English,
was taken by the people of Amo and Purea to Papara. There the flag was
constructed into a *maro ura* (the term was used generically by the Tahitians as well as specifically). There is no evidence that they made it a sign
of their deference to the English. I think it is possible that they saw it as
a sign of overarching sovereignty that was outside and above local politics
but was imbued with all their metaphors.

Their translation was certainly some extension of the potentialities of
their own symbol system. It was neither a totally new nor a totally old
way of doing things. This new *maro ura* was in itself a history of the first
native encounter with the stranger. It was a document, a text to be read
by those with immediate knowledge of its meaning. It gave institutional
continuity with all the structures and roles of its preservation and its ritual

re-presentation. Perhaps Amo and Purea had already begun to build their new *marae* Mahaiatea before the *Dolphin* had arrived. Perhaps the new *maro* demanded a special place. Certainly Mahaiatea was grander and more ambitious than any other sacred site on Tahiti and could have been something new for something new. The procession around the island arranged by Amo and Purea demanded submission to a new sort of authority. It was an authority that claimed to exercise hegemony over all other authorities. The Wallis flag gave it some external sign, some reification. That the Wallis flag itself was not processed in these first ceremonials is of little significance. They had only one flag. When they possessed more than one flag they did process with it, as they did at Pomare II's investiture. When they had several flags they attached them as well to their most sacred vessels, such as 'Rainbow', 'Oro's canoe. It makes sense to see the British possessing Tahiti in their flag and their violence, and Purea inventing an interpretive document of those events and making it symbolic of the hegemony she claimed.

Possessing Tahiti was – and is – a complicated affair. Indeed, who possessed whom? Native and stranger each possessed the other in their interpretations of the other. They possessed one another in ethnographic moments that got transcribed into texts and symbols. Each archived those texts and symbols in their respective cultural institutions. Each made cargo of the things collected from one another, put the cargo in their respective museums, remade the things they collected into new cultural artefacts. They entertained themselves in their histories of their encounters. Each reading of the texts, each display of the symbols, each entertainment in the histories, each viewing of the cargo enlarged the original encounter, made a never-ending process of it in the production of a narrative. Each possession of the other became a self-possession as well. Pantomimes in this respect were no less significant than ceremonies, or acts of possession, of processions of hegemonic signs. While English audiences possessed Tahiti and themselves by laughter, Tahitian audiences enjoyed the grotesque nature of the English as well, by mocking them in their *heiva* dances, by mimicking their stranger posturings. Possessing the other, like possessing the past, is always full of inventions.

ENTR'ACTE
Ralph Wewitzer:
The First 'Captain Bligh'

Men of power have a sense of history. In their triumphs they 'make history'. In their failures they foresee themselves 'vindicated by history'. Bligh's urgent concern, once the mutiny had happened, was for the history that would be made of it. His mutiny, as he knew, would become what it would be represented to be. His *Narrative of the Mutiny* (1790) was well formulated before his return and was quickly in the press. His *Voyage to the South Seas* (1792), the broader account of his breadfruit voyage by which he had hoped to make a fortune, he had to leave to a friend, James Burney, a companion on the *Resolution,* to polish for publication while he went off in the *Providence.* Sailing down the Atlantic in the *Providence* and about to succumb to a physical and nervous breakdown that would nearly kill him, Bligh was nonetheless full of an author's afterthoughts. He posted back suggestions for Burney on how to gloss his story and make it sell.

The first theatre for Bligh's representation of his mutiny was the London newspapers. There were fourteen daily and fifteen tri- and biweekly newspapers at the time. They were a theatre. Theatre owners were newspaper owners. Actors were journalists. The newspapers were overtly committed to oppositional and advocacy politics. Seven dailies and six tri- and biweeklies were committed to 'Government'. Seven daily and nine other newspapers were committed to 'Opposition'. News was an undifferentiated mixture of information and gratuitous comment, with large-scale inventions of a participatory readership and outside correspondents. There was open conspiracy in the fantasy of some sort of correspondence between a world outside the newspaper and a world made by the newspaper. Who could define the difference between advertising and newsmaking when the 'puffs' of persons and institutions, and self-congratulatory stories, were bought at annual or piecemeal rates and presented as news? Abusive 'paragraphs' were managed in the same way. Blackmail belonged more to the comedy of life than the tragedy. Libel, with the collusion of the courts, was an instrument of social control. Stables of writers, permanently or occasionally employed, cloaked the politics of every event or relationship with a stage-whispered knowingness and a salacious sense of novelty and fashion. The strangeness of this to us, well accustomed as we are to the manipulation of news, lies not in the fact of it, but in the open gamesmanship of it. Authenticity claimed in such high hyperbole and theatre became a continual satire that was not just the metaphor of politics but its soul.

Bligh was quite intent on making his own puffs and paragraphs. He had his narrative to make public. His timetable was impressive: March 16, 1790, arrival in London; April 1, announcement of the publication of *A Narrative of the Mutiny on Board His Majesty's Ship the* Bounty *and subsequent voyage of part of the crew in the ship's boat from Tofoa, one of the Friendly Islands, to Timor, a Dutch settlement in the East Indies;* May, excerpts of the *Narrative* published in the *Gentleman's Magazine;* June, the *European Magazine* reviewed the volume with large extracts, introducing it with this satirical wink and nudge:

> The high sense of courage and fidelity which fills the bosoms of British officers renders them tremblingly alive to the least suspicion derogatory of their professional character, and every endeavour that truth will justify or spirit can achieve is immediately adopted to rescue their fame from the apprehensions of jealousy and the prejudices of opinion.

Bligh had returned to England in the middle of one of the most extraordinary twelve-month periods in European history. The Bastille had fallen on July 14, 1789. Englishmen were at first supportive in a self-congratulatory way. 'France is blest with English liberty' boasted one ditty. The London theatres were quick to represent the dramas of revolution. By August 31, Sadler's Wells was presenting a series of dramatic actions called *Gallic Freedom or Vive La Liberté*. Among the actions played were the assembly of the bourgeoisie, the assault on the Bastille, the massacre of the citizens, the cannonade, the general attack and a 'descent into subterranean dungeons in discovery of unfortunate objects'. But the Lord Chancellor was keeping watch on too much popular exuberance at antiauthoritarianism and began censoring several other portrayals of the revolution. When, on January 21, 1790, King George was attacked in his carriage by a madman, there was public outcry and suspicion that the madman was a French agent. So in July 1790 the Royal Circus was particularly careful in performing *The Triumph of Liberty or the Destruction of the Bastille with Mr Capon's Views of the Pont Neuf in Paris, Outside the Bastille and Drawbridge, Inside of the Bastille various instruments of torture. Place du Dauphin, near the Pont Neuf.* The theatre took pains to conclude the spectacle with 'Britannia seated in her triumphal Car, supporting two Grand Transparent portraits of the King and Queen of Great Britain'. London was thus entertained both by the news from France and by the joys of British loyalty.

Making history of current events was an industry of newspapers and theatres alike. Only seven weeks after Bligh's return, on May 3, there appeared the following advertisement in the London dailies:

ROYALTY THEATRE
Well Street, near Goodman's Fields
To continue every Evening during the Summer Season, with
a Variety of Entertainments.
This Evening, May 3, will be presented
a new Musical Piece, called
Tar against Perfume:
Or, The Sailor Preferred.
a new Dance, called
The Merry Blockmakers:
by Mons Ferrere, Mad. Fuozzi, Mad. Ferrere, Mr Bourke etc
A new Musical Piece, called
A Pill for the Doctor
or, The Triple Wedding.
A Favourite Song by Miss Daniel
The whole to conclude with (never performed) a
Fact, told in Action, called
THE PIRATES
Or, The Calamities of Capt. Bligh
Exhibiting a Full Account of his Voyage, from his taking
leave at the Admiralty, and shewing the Bounty falling
down the River Thames – the Captain's reception at Otaheite, and exchanging the British Manufactures for the Bread
Fruit – with an Otaheitian Dance – an exact representation
of the Seizure of Capt. Bligh, in the cabin of the Bounty
by the Pirates, with the affecting scene of forcing the Captain and his faithful followers into the Boat – their Distress
at Sea, and Repulse by the Natives of Timur – their miraculous arrival at the Cape of Good Hope, and their friend-

ly reception by the Governor.
Dances and Ceremonies of the Hottentots on their Departure,
and their happy arrival in England.

The advertisement did not have it quite right. 'Timur' should have read 'Friendly Isles'. But this was corrected on May 5 and further care for authenticity indicated by the addition of the phrase 'under the Immediate Instruction of a Person who was on Board the Bounty storeship'. Probably John Samuel, Bligh's clerk, gave the 'immediate instruction'.

Ralph Wewitzer was the first 'Captain Bligh'. William Bourke was the first 'Fletcher Christian'. William Bourke's only claim to fame had been that he danced a mean double hornpipe, but Ralph Wewitzer was better known for his 'low humor' and 'whimsical but just' impersonation of Frenchmen and Jews. Wewitzer was a Jewish jeweller become – somewhat by chance – comedian-actor when his sister asked him to fill in as Ralph in *Maid of the Hill* at Drury Lane. He was said to have had 'tolerable wit', although one Scottish punster was reported as remarking that he was of 'wee wit, sur'. Now, in May 1790, he was manager-owner of the Royalty Theatre.

It had been Wewitzer who had stopped the show with his presentation of a Tahitian prophet in the pantomime *Omai*. It was he who had spoken the gibberish with persuasive realism. He had that special ear and eye for otherness that persuaded audiences that he had got differences right. These caricatures are, we know, a feature of cross-cultural representation – the presentation of self in louder and slower charade, the reduction of the other to some nuance in voice or gesture. Otherness becomes a cartoon. Cultural operators, to use Jim Boon's phrase, render some ritual or drama to a radical simplicity of meaning. They catch authenticity in an instant, and vindicate a sense of essence in something alien.

Wewitzer's *Calamities of Captain Bligh,* as it was publicised, was a 'Fact, Told in Action', a series of scenes with no spoken text. There was an overlay of music and songs, but the action was mime. The reason was that Wewitzer did not have a licensed theatre. He was manager-owner of the Royalty Theatre, the only nonlicensed theatre at the time within the City of London. The theatres that were legitimate by the Licensing Act of 1737 were Covent Garden, Drury Lane and, in summertime, the Haymarket, all in the City of Westminster. Wewitzer, at the Royalty, had to present ballet, mime, vaudeville, songs and pantomime because he was denied

Figure 17.
The Tahitian Prophet, drawn by P. J. de Loutherbourg and played by Ralph Wewitzer in the pantomime *Omai*. (Philippe Jacques de Loutherbourg, 'Prophet's Dress'. c. 1785. Watercolour. National Library of Australia. Gift of Dr Niel Gunson.)

the right to perform textual plays by English law. The realism of his 'Fact, Told in Action', then, depended on a stage setting that held the action of the mimes in perspective with the scene. The puppetry, sound, lighting, correlated with the actors' movements to give total perspectives to the scenes. Continuity depended on the audience's constructing a narrative out of some crib in the programme, such as in the advertisement for *The Pirates*. Facticity depended on the formulaic character of the history. The spectacle was the unthinking man's narrative, an animated cartoon.

There were other Facts Told in Action that London theatregoers could have taken in during the same weeks as Ralph Wewitzer was performing as 'Captain Bligh'. They could have gone to the Royal Circus and seen

Siege of Quebec
P.I. a Grand Picturesque: View of the Isle of Orleans, situated a little below Quebec
P.II. View of General Wolfe's Tent and the English Camp
A View of the French Forces, Headquarters, Camp etc.
P.III. A View of the Heights of Abraham and Part of the Town of Quebec
The general engagement between the English and the French Army
Manoeuvres of the Highlanders with their Broad Swords
The Death of General Wolfe
The whole forming the most Interesting Spectacle ever presented to the Public
The scenery, decorations and dresses entirely new.
The music composed by Mons. Rochefort and brought from Paris by Young Astley
under whose direction the whole of this Capital Entertainment has been brought out.

Indeed, there was heavy competition for the public's gaze on English heroics. Bligh, on the *Bounty,* had fallen in with HMS *Guardian* under Captain Edward Riou at the Cape of Good Hope, in December 1789. The *Guardian* was taking stores and convicts to Botany Bay. Twelve hundred miles south-east of the Cape, the *Guardian* grounded on an iceberg while trying to replenish its water. She was holed so badly that Riou put as many men as he could into launches and set them off to the Cape while he and the rest, pumping for their lives for five weeks, took the *Guardian* back to the Cape. At Sadler's Wells, patrons could see 'A Living Picture' rather than a Fact Told in Action. The advertisement in *The Gazetteer and New Daily Advertiser,* June 19, 1790, read:

English Heroism
In which is particularly and correctly given
A Living Picture of the Guardian Frigate
(Commanded by Lieutenant Riou)
In her very perilous situation in the South Seas, employed amongst stupendous Floating
Islands of Ice: descriptive of the several agitations among the Crew on her first striking
on the Ice, the full Discovery of their imminent Danger, the uncommon exertions of the

officers and crew, the magnanimity of the Commander, the final departure of
the boats,
with the providential arrival of the launch, and afterwards the Guardian, at the
Cape of
Good Hope.

These 'Interesting Spectacles', 'Living Pictures' and 'Facts Told in Action'
were performed in a nonfictional space that gained its seriousness by being
enclosed in performances that were clearly set against fantasy and imagination. *The Calamities of Captain Bligh* was introduced by 'a new Musical
Piece', the *Tar against Perfume,* and a new dance, 'The Merry Blockmakers'. On other occasions there were different preludes:

Mr Lee Lewes
will appear for the first time in three years at
this theatre in an Entertainment called
Laugh, If You Like It
In which (for that night only)
He will exhibit Characters and Caricatures
with several entire new subjects and others
selected from those of approved
Wit and Humour
the whole conveyed through a Medium never
before attempted by him, and prepared at
very great expence.

And *Calamities* itself was embellished with

A Naval Overture
Capt. Bligh   Mr Wewitzer
Fletcher Christian   Mr Bourke.   Marine Mr Rees
Dutch Captain (Song To relieve a fellow creature)
Mr Matthews
Greenwich Pensioner (Song) Mr Cook
Lt Dreadnought (Song) Mr Birkett
Song, in character, Loose ev'ry sail. Miss Daniel
A Scene from
True Blue or Press Gang

Wewitzer's history of the *Bounty* was set firmly against froth, triviality
and make-believe. Fantasy was its foil. The chimerical gave perspective to
realism and responsibility. Audiences, in the end, would be able to ap-
plaud their own seriousness. Perspective allayed the disturbing nature of

theatre as well. Sympathy, admiration, horror and gratitude were unquestioning and presumptive sorts of emotions and reactions. The spectacles left little room for doubts or a sense of alternate interpretation.

We are not in a position to know exactly what Ralph Wewitzer meant
by his 'Fact Told in Action' He was not likely to have been making a
philosophical statement. He was not likely even to have believed that *The
Calamities of Captain Bligh* was free of interpretation. His whole theatrical
livelihood was dependent on 'puffs' and 'paragraphs'. His peculiar talent
was a mimicry that unmasked social shams. Indeed, he was to lose his
fortune because the Royalty Theatre could not survive the established
forces of legitimate theatre. In June 1790, he was to stop the unsuccessful
run of his 'Fact Told in Action' to go to Paris for the celebration of the
first anniversary of the Fall of the Bastille. He anticipated that the spectacle on the Field of Mars would be dramatic material for the stage. His
living continued to turn around the sense of display and self-conscious
authorship of 'facts'. In 1829, he died in poverty, aware that the social
eminence of his patron, the Duchess of Albany, was no guarantee of her
word or her promised care. No doubt he would have got a thespian's joy
out of the dismay of his landlady, who had made a similar presumption
about the Duchess' word and bought a splendid coffin for Wewitzer, only
to find that nobody would pay her for it. She transferred Wewitzer's body
to a 'shell' instead, and sent him to a pauper's grave. We may safely
gamble on a belief that, after all, Wewitzer had an actor's sense that
history is not so much fact as a performance.

Nonetheless, Wewitzer's 'Fact Told in Action' played a small part in a
movement. Walter Benjamin was to write much later of modernism that
'the history that showed things "as they really were" was the strongest
narcotic of our century'. The theatre that, like Wewitzer's, purported to
show 'things as they really were' was a part of this illusion. I would like
to take you back to de Loutherbourg and *Omai* to show how this was so.

The pantomime *Omai,* first performed at Christmas in 1785, was still
being revived in part or in whole through the 1790s. De Loutherbourg's
stage settings made many resurrections in new presentations. More importantly his revolution in stage perspective and his insistence that a plot
be carried forward with visual consistency had changed the expectancies
of audience and critics alike. De Loutherbourg had been made a member
of the French Academy as a twenty-two-year-old painter of genius in 1762.
His annual exhibitions of paintings in the Salons of Paris were of historical

and mythological tableaux of battles, storms and landscapes that had attracted Denis Diderot's attention. It was not just the realism of his paintings – 'Don't the cows live, ruminate . . . let's stop in the midday sun' – that Diderot admired. The paintings also approximated Diderot's ideal of the theatre. 'The whole of Diderot's aesthetics rested', Roland Barthes has noted, 'on the identification of theatrical scene and pictorial tableau: the perfect play is a succession of tableaux, that is, a gallery, an exhibition; the stage offers the spectator as many real tableaux as there are in the action moments favourable to the painter. The tableau (pictorial, theatrical, literary) is a pure cut-out segment with clearly defined edges . . . "a whole contained under a single point of view, in which the parts work together to one end, and form by their mutual correspondence a unity as real as that of the members of the body of an animal: so that a piece of painting made up of a large number of figures thrown onto the canvas, with neither proportions, intelligence nor unity no more deserves to be called a true composition than the scattered studies of legs, nose and eyes on the same cartoon deserve to be called a portrait or even a human figure" '.

When de Loutherbourg went to Drury Lane in 1772, he demanded artistic control of the whole stage – its settings, the costumes upon it. The stage was to become his composition, a consistent whole. The more bizarre anachronisms – Alexander in a Ramilles wig and helmet, Lady Macbeth in hooped petticoat – were banned immediately. His triumph was to coordinate the visual and auditory appreciation of the audience to the foreground and background of the stage. Critics marvelled at his genius in the production of such pieces as *The Wonders of Derbyshire or Harlequin in the Peak,* in which he persuaded an English public eager to be reassured of their own worth that their landscape was as wild, romantic and inherently dramatic as any foreign spot. William Gilpin may have invented the 'picturesque', but de Loutherbourg discovered to the English that they had a story, a history, in their sublime landscapes. Their appreciation served him well. The Duke of York, to name only one admirer, invited him to witness his action at the Battle of Valenciennes, the better to catch the rhetoric of the moment with his brush.

While critics raved over *The Wonders of Derbyshire,* de Loutherbourg's real love was his eidophusikon. In his eidophusikon was a miniaturised stage six feet wide and eight feet deep on which he reproduced images. It was his shrine to the belief that space was movement and light, that seeing was a multivalent experience. It was a shrine as well to his growing alchemist's belief that nothing disappears: everything is a transmutation of form and texture. So water in unseen glass tubes became hail and rain: vast tambourines became thunder: shells and peas in balls became the rush of waves: changing transparencies hot and cold light: the emotion and mood of seeing something the effect of a Schubert sonata: distance a fading sound: sky the oblique movements of two and three painted veils: time the changing reflection from screened lights. Antitheatricals, one would think, would have been dismayed at such transmutations and illusions. But to de Loutherbourg these were natural facts in action, conferring reality, not disturbing it.

De Loutherberg's scenes also calmed the sense of otherness by contriving familiarity. His eidophusikon sessions were made up of a series of scenes: Aurora over Greenwich Park, Noon at Tangier and Gibraltar, Sunset near Naples, sun in the fog, setting sun after a rainy day, rising of the moon and waterspout. He made his histories with a different level of illusion. Between these natural scenes he would have transparencies of incantations, of conversations of sailors of different nations, or the arrival of French and Dutch prizes at Portsmouth, of Satan and his troops.

Victor Turner, fascinated through all his scholarly life by the theatricality of human behaviour, in his last days turned his attention to the actor's performance and the wider cultural issue of perspective. Jean Gebser's monumental work on perspective had influenced him to agree that perspective was the key to modernity. 'Perspective spatializes the world: it orients the eye in relation to space in a new way . . . it represents a rationalization of sight'. By perspective the whole world is measurable. That was the true scientific excitement of the late eighteenth century. Galileo had given them the ambition 'to measure everything measurable and to make what is not measurable capable of being measured'. Newton had given them the means to measure. 'Navigation' was taught in the smallest of schools around the country. The orderliness of time and space that came from astronomy made measuring the lodestone of understanding. Measuring was cosmological: a mathematician was as much a divine as a theologian: the measurability of the world was a demonstration of its God-given order and telos. Measuring was a political economy: Jonas Hanway was only one example of the joy of statistics to those who would measure the world. Measuring was social control: the navy, Britain's outstanding model for mass bureaucracy, was measuring endlessly.

The essential requirement of measuring is to see the world in a blink-ered way. To cut out the irrelevant, one needed discipline. So disciplines proliferated – optics, mechanics, hydrostatics – becoming separable do-mains, comfortable and confident in their different perspectives, each its own eudophusikon on the world. This power of discipline to satisfy view-ers with their own conventionalities as if their exclusions made a world more real than real had a very theatrical quality. The theatre is the great-est blinker of them all. 'The relationship between geometry and theater', Barthes called it. 'The theater is precisely that practice which calculates the place of things as they are observed: if I set the spectacle here, the spectator will see this; if I put it elsewhere, he will not, and I can avail myself of this masterly effect and play on the illusions it provides. The stage is the line which stands across the path of the optic pencil, tracing at once the point at which it is brought to a stop, and, as it were, the threshold of its ramifications. Thus is founded – against music (against the text) – representation.'

These perspectives of discipline – neither in systems of knowledge nor in the theatre – are not 'natural'. Participants require a great deal of socialisation to believe that their conventions are without convention. In-evitably this is dialogic. The stage makes the audience: the audience makes the stage. There were signs at the end of the eighteenth century that theatre audiences were becoming more disciplined. There was still an occasional price riot. There were still catcalls. The pits and boxes and galleries still had their separate expectancies according to class and wealth. But it was a time in which the audiences enjoyed their own education. It was a time of prologues: it was a time in which the audiences saw them-selves as good, sentimental and moderate, glorifying the nation's triumphs, ridiculing individual failures, in which the theatre loosened the inhibi-tions against tears and laughter. When *The Death of Captain Cook* – a French ballet received in Paris with 'uncommon applause' – played at Covent Garden in 1789, there were tears and hysterics at Cook's fatal stabbing. (Actually, on one occasion an actor called Ratchford, playing a marine, was run through by a real sword left out by accident by the prop man. His death throes received particular applause by an unknowing au-dience.) And, lest we miss an opportunity to thrust home our argument that the stage made otherness familiar and made the history-that-ought-to-have-been like history-that-had-actually-been, see the description of the ballet and know that its 'original music, its new dresses and scenery, machinery and decorations' added realism by their fashionable modern mode.

April 13   The Death of Captain Cook

Pt 1. The Nuptial Procession, with the Performance of the Marriage Ceremony according to the customs observed at O'Whyhee. The manner of combat between two Nations.

Pt II. The arrival of the Resolution. The disembarkation of the English, with the ceremonies observed at entering into a Peace with the Natives. A preparation for a Human Sacrifice. The Assassination of Captain Cook.

Pt III. A Representation of the Naval and Military Honours observed in erecting a Pile to the Memory of Captain Cook, by the officers of the Resolution. The ceremony performed on the same occasion, according to the manner of the Natives of O'Whyhee. To conclude with a representation of a Burning Mountain

A 'Fact Told in Action' became a fact, authentic, by the perspectives to which an audience was socialised. Ralph Wewitzer used all de Loutherbourg's tricks of realism – storms at sea, the *Bounty*'s movement through familiar places on the Thames, the 'exact representations of the mutiny', stereotypical Tahitian customs – their dance, their exchanges, display of civilisation in the penetration of 'British manufactures', various foreign landscapes, idealised emotions – loyal obedience, distress, savage violence, friendly welcomes, triumphant returns. And who can tell at this distance the hidden meanings of apparently so ordinary a thing as a 'Hottentot dance', when Hottentots were the object of such prurient curiosity at the time for the difference of their sexual organs? His narrative was a sequence of tableaux that linked a commonsensical history to a seen perspective. By that the story with the scenery was factual, disciplined, modern. There were no paradoxes.

I use the word 'paradox' advisedly because it was Denis Diderot's famous contention that there was a *Paradox of Acting* (1958, 1964). Diderot's paradox was that the more a great actor appeared to be overwhelmed by the emotion of his role, the cooler he was and the more in command of himself. In an opinion that has shocked generations of actors – mostly, I think, because they have not heard what he was saying – Diderot argued that 'It is extreme sensibility that makes actors mediocre. It is middling sensibility that makes the multitude of bad actors. And it is the lack of sensibility that qualifies actors to be sublime.' 'I require of this man [actor] a cold and tranquil spectator. Great poets, great actors and perhaps in general all the great imitators of nature . . . are the least sensitive of beings . . . they are too engaged in observing, in recognizing and imitating, to be vitally affected witnesses. All [the actor's] talents consist not in feeling, as you imagine, but in rendering so scrupulously the external signs of feeling, that you are taken in.'

Diderot was not attacking the actor's moral and aesthetic awareness of the world around him, from which alertness he learned the external signs of the inner man. David Garrick's genius, which sparked Diderot's reflections on acting, came precisely from that tenderness. Diderot was saying what another genius of stage directing was saying much later: 'Never lose yourself on the stage. Always act in your own person as an actor. You can never get way from yourself. The moment you lose yourself on the stage marks the departure from truly living your part and the beginning of exaggerated false acting'. That was Constantin Stanislavski (Hapgood 1958).

Diderot demanded a distance between the actor and the role. 'Performance consciousness' is the modern phrase. Acting should be in the subjunctive, Richard Schechner has written. What sort of mimesis is that? What sort of representation? Diderot had an answer to those questions, too. 'Reflect a little as to what, in the language of the theatre, is being true. Is it showing things as they are in nature? Certainly not. Were it so, the true would be commonplace. What then is the truth for stage purposes? It is the conformity of action, diction, face, voice, movement and gesture to an ideal type invented by the poet, and frequently enhanced by the player.' Representation, for Diderot, was not the replay of set forms. Representation was always creative. The audience was not being asked to see its commonplace self in the mirror of the stage. The audience was being asked to be inventive, to be interpretive of the relationship of particular expressions to an ideal type. Mimesis is thus a process, not a replication.

David Garrick had transformed the English stage with an acting praxis of this theory. Garrick was the enemy of formalism and caricature, the reduction of characterisation to formulaic narrative such as 'tragic struts, elaborate gestures, chanting declamation'. 'He realized the fiction', 'his business was not to methodize words but to express passions' was the high praise of one witness, the theatre critic Charles Dibdin. It was not that Garrick's acting was without convention – how can anything expressive or cultural be without convention? His audiences enjoyed the conventions he invented. He always exited with a bridled head and with exaggerated alertness. Could he have told us why he did, we may wonder. Would not it have been that he wanted to leave a sense of anticipation at the ending of something? Would it not have been a signature to the authorship of the role he played?

Garrick was not one much for words about acting, but he had this to add to something of Diderot. 'The greater strokes of genius have been unknown to the actor himself, till the circumstances and the warmth of this scene has sprung the mine, as it were, as much to his own surprise as that of the audience.' That genius in acting is not simple imitation, since every expression of passion is idiosyncratic and acting can never be so particular, but the observation of what it is that the actor is representing should be 'cherished by the genial warmth of his conception, translated by his judgment, raised to perfection and made his own'. We can hear Garrick saying two things about mimesis in this. One was that acting was not the mimicry of signs but the transformation of them. The other was that in representation the theatre is a dialogic experience, and there is an uncertainty principle created by that dialogic element. Representation includes the audience: the text includes the reading. That audience must be socialised, acculturated, educated to the transporting conventionalities that make for entertainment. This induction of the audience invokes not merely the grammar of the dramatic representation of the play itself, not merely the forms of behaviour of the audience (their attentiveness, their silence, their cued response and engagement, the dress they wear, the class they come from, the seats they sit in), not merely the coded signs of their appropriate interpretive mood (green carpet on the stage for tragedy, entry from a stage door complete with its windowboxes for the prologue), but adaptiveness to the changing poetics that the physical environment of the theatre required. (Theatres were getting larger at the time, forcing a caricaturisation of gesture and speech that had to be seen and heard from a distance. De Loutherbourg and Garrick changed the angle of lighting from below in the proscenium to above and from the side. The changed shadow effects were a revolution in realism in themselves and changed audiences' expectancies.) Garrick in his day was the great exponent of the prologue. The prologue filled that liminal space between the end of everyday living and the beginning of theatre in which the audience was primed to look at itself as much as the stage. In the prologue, the audience was educated to be interpretive and reflective.

Ralph Wewitzer's *Calamities of Captain Bligh* was no great success. It seems to have run through a dozen or so performances. Then on May 18 there appeared an ominous note in *The Times:* 'the Royalty Theatre does not meet with the success that was expected, as the house has in general been but very indifferently filled'. Then Wewitzer closed the theatre down altogether for a few weeks, till at the end of June there was a final flurry of benefits – for Wewitzer himself, then for the actors and singers. The final performance of *The Pirates Or, The Calamities of Captain Bligh* was on June 30, as a benefit for Mrs Angel Lee, housekeeper, and Mr Burrell, the Box Office Keeper.

Of Bligh's reaction we know nothing. We cannot even say whether he went to see his 'Fact Told in Action'. He must have felt some disappointment and some sense of being used in that this representation of his triumph reached 'King and Country' through the Royalty Theatre. His chief rival for the attention of the King and Country at the time, Captain Riou, was being represented in legitimate theatre with all its proper associations. Riou would be in the public eye for many years. Being on the edge of things, being used, being dependent on incompetents, having to strain for opportunities – maybe Bligh thought, too, that these were his true calamities.

Bligh's history was to be staged, at least in part, once more in his lifetime. On April 25, 1816, at Theatre Royal, Drury Lane, was presented

A New Romantick Operatick Ballet Spectacle
founded on the recent Discovery of a numerous Colony, formed by
and descended from, the Mutineers of the Bounty Frigate called
Pitcairn's island.

'Vivant Rex et Regina – No Money to be returned' the advertisement ended, and there was a promise of 'Encreasing effect on every representation'. 'New and Selected Musik, new Scenery, Dresses, Embellishments.' (As it happened, Ralph Wewitzer was on the stage at Drury Lane that very same evening, but in another play, *A Trip to Scarborough,* as Probe, the Jeweller.) There were nearly forty natives in the ballet chorus and there were familiar names among the cast – 'Otoo', 'Oberea' – but now become grandson and granddaughter of Fletcher Christian. There are plenty of signs in the playbill that enthusiasm for the project outran knowledge of what had happened at Pitcairn.

This was April 1816. Bligh was in the last months of his life. Elizabeth, his wife, was dead. The sea and the navy had cost her dearly. She could never be persuaded in all these years to put a foot on a ship's deck, but she and Bligh were a loyal and loving pair. With all the things that she had collected in the years of his absence around him, Lambeth became a lonely house. He left it for the care of his daughters. Whether they told him of the discovery of Pitcairn we cannot say. It is difficult to believe that there was not somebody eager for his reaction to the news.

Bligh had not been in his grave five years, however, before Lord Byron gave him the importunate invitation: 'Awake, Bold Bligh'. *The Island* was Byron's last completed poem. It was not, by estimate of generations of critics and his own, his best. There were murky depths to its motivation in the ways in which the Christians, the Wordsworths and the Coleridges were joined to the hatreds that had begun to preoccupy Byron's personal life. Except for the fact of the mutiny and its chief protagonists, Bligh and Christian, *The Island* paid no attention at all to what 'actually happened' after the mutiny. There are footnotes almost of a hallucinetic character, in which Byron claims on good authority to have some historical detail – that Christian, for example, just before committing suicide loaded his musket with a vest button and with it killed the marine about to capture him. But it is clear that in Byron's mind that true historicity lies in the mythic significance of a revolt against properly constituted authority, which can have no peaceful end, and the embracing of native simplicity, which ends in ecstasy. To make that happen, Byron makes of Bligh a 'Gallant Chief', whose true island is 'Old England's welcome shore', and whose discipline, self-control and perseverance made him a true hero. Christian is dark, brooding, melancholic, 'in hell' with guilt at having taken men to their death. His island is the stark rock in the sea where he makes his last stand and from which he throws himself in self-destruction. 'Torquil' is the innocent young mutineer, whose passion for the native girl 'Neuha' redeems the mutiny. While Christian makes his last stand against the British sailors sent to bring him back, 'Torquil' and 'Neuha' escape by diving into a secret cave. It was 'a night succeeded by such happy days / as only the yet infant world displays'. Torquil's own island was the Hebrides. One might have expected from him a more rugged response to Nature and the Native. Indeed, when Torquil tried to explain the mysticism of his union with Neuha, Byron has one of the other mutineers, 'Ben', say 'Right, that will do for the marines', and adds a solemn little footnote that 'tell it to the marines' is 'one of the few fragments of former jealousies which still survive (in jest only) between these gallant services [of seamen and marines]'. Ah, indeed, tell it to the marines!

Byron, by this time, was a strong antitheatrical. He had declared he would never subject himself to theatre critics or theatre audiences. Perhaps, by this time, too, he was so despised in public that his work could be pirated with impunity. In July 1823, there appeared at Sadler's Wells 'one of the most successful Aqua Dramas ever produced'.

The Island

or

Christian

and

His Comrades

Embracing the principal events of the Mutiny on Board the Bounty Armed Ship on her passage from Otaheite in 1787, the incidents of which have become interesting for being the origin of the singular and romantic population of Pitcairn's Island, lately discovered.

The music and overture by Mr Nicholas: the Scenery by Mr Greenwood and Mr Mildehall; the Dances by Mr Eller; the dresses by Mr Townley and Mrs Balding; the Machinery by Mr Copping; the properties by Mr T.G. Flower; the Fireworks by Signor Mortrain; the Melodramatic Business arranged and the whole produced under the direction of Mr Vining.

Capt Bligh, Mr Lewis; Lt Christian, Mr Campbell; Jack Skyscrape, Mr Renaud; Will Blunt, Mr Elliott; John Adams, Mr Strickland; Tom Transit, Mr Webber; Jack Grogan, Mr Lacante; Peter Pink [a botanist from Covent Gardens Market] Mr Vale; Moodai, Miss Johnstone; Blowoke, Miss Treby; Zoastro, Miss Adcock.

NEUHA, by Mrs EGERTON

Mutineers, Crew, Native Dances, Divers, Marines, etc.

Programme of the Scenery, etc.

Sections of the Deck of the Bounty

With appropriate Rigging, Sails, Guns Mounted, Capstan, etc.

Time – Midnight – immediately previous to the breaking out of the Mutiny, when she became guilty of

'*Young hearts which languish'd for some sunny Isle*'. '*Where summer years and summer Women smile*'.

Success of the Mutiny, Bligh and Officers forced into Boat,

The Sails Set, the Anchor weighed, and

'*Huzza for Otaheite is the cry, As stately sweeps the gallant vessel by*'.

During the progress of which the Scene gradually changes from Moonlight to
Sunrise.

General View of Otaheite

*'The soil where every cottage seem'd a
home'.*

Interior of the Islands

*'Kind was the welcome of the Sun burnt
sires
Kinder still their daughters gentler
fires'.*

Habitation of Neuha

*'The gentle savage of the wild
In growth a Woman, but in
years a child.*

Breadfruit Plantation

Characteristic Ballet
by Mr Eller, Miss Adcock, Miss Collison and the Corps
de Ballet

Bay of Otaheite

'A strange sail in the offing, fore and aft'. 'Egad she seems a wicked looking craft'.

Otaheitian Landscape

*'What e'er may have us now in chase
We'll make no running fight, for that
were base'.*

Sea Beach

*'Beside the jutting rock the few ap-
peared'.*

Black Rock of Toobonai

CHRYSTALLIZED BASALTIC CAVERN

*'Where all was darkness till day
through clefs above let in a sober'd
ray'.*

*'As in some cathedral glimmering
aisle
The dirty monuments from light
recoil'.*

*'Thus sadly in the refuge submarine
The vault drew half her shadow
from the scene'.*

Retreat of the Mutineers, general attack on the

REAL WATER

Overthrow of Christian and his Comrades, Victory of the British Flag over
Mutineers and deserters.

ALLEGORICAL FIREWORKS

With Captain Bligh's Ship in the Offing

BRILLIANTLY ILLUMINATED

*'And from that hour a new
tradition gave'.*

*'The sanctuary, the name of
Neuha's Cave'.*

The most magnificent effect is produced by the State with its attending scenery,
etc ascending to the roof of the theatre in sight of the audience, removing the

delay of more than 20 minutes for so many years complained of in preparing the last scene of Aquatic Dramas. The machinery invented by Mr Copping.

It is respectfully intreated that the Ladies and Gentlemen in the Pit will keep their seats during the Water Scene.

To conclude with a grave comic Pantomime

Gil Blas

or Harlequin Everywhere

Montagne

Russe.

ACT THREE.
The Island

THERE ARE MORE than 25,000 islands in the Pacific. Yet any one of them can be lost in an immense ocean that covers a third of the globe. Remarkably, in the central Pacific where a canoe or a ship could sail for months or for 5,000 miles and never make a landfall, every mountaintop that had pushed from the ocean bed, every coral reef that had grown above the ocean surface had been discovered before the European strangers had had the courage or the knowledge or the technology to discover the sea. Every island in that 'Many-Island' triangle of Polynesia that stretches from Hawaii to New Zealand to Easter Island had been visited or settled in a great spill of people through 3,000 years. Some of these islands were too dry or barren to sustain life, and today the mark of a visit lies in relics or bones or tools. Some islands were lush yet, for some reason, were abandoned. One of these was 'Matakiterangi'. It is a surmised name. No one lived to tell its name. 'Matakiterangi' is known to us as Pitcairn.

Philip Carteret, in his slow and painful trek across the Pacific in the *Swallow* in 1767, having lost his commander, Samuel Wallis, in the *Dolphin,* came across 'a small, high inhabited island not four or five miles round', 'scarce better than a large rock in the ocean'. The island was covered in trees and he and his crew saw a stream splashing down the cliffs. The surf was violent, but they thought that 'in the fine summer season' a ship might land. Carteret named the island Pitcairn after the midshipman who had discovered it. That had been Carteret's promise to the young gentlemen if they should keep a good watch. 'The common men' had been promised the reward of a bottle of brandy. Carteret passed on. Pitcairn was virtually the only Polynesian island he saw in his circumnavigation of the globe. But John Hawkesworth recorded this single success in his *Voyages.* Fletcher Christian found a copy of Hawkesworth in Bligh's cabin.

Islands lie behind the screen of the sea. A screen as large as the Pacific Ocean thoroughly sifts the life that reaches an island. The few species of plants and animals that survive the sea, now without competition, play many variations on their own themes. All living things come to an island with only the capital of their minds, their instincts and their genes. In the case of human beings, they can also bring with them a select cargo of natural and cultural artefacts. Nothing is transported whole, however. The webs of significance are always darned.

The surprise, indeed the miracle, of Pacific islands is how much of what now seems natural to rich and easy South Seas living had to be transported. Of the fruits and vegetables that fed newcomers – coconut, breadfruit, taro, plantain – of the trees that clothed and housed them – paper mulberry, palms, hibiscus – of the animals of their feasts and sacrifices – pigs, dogs, chickens – all had to come with them in their canoes. There is enough randomness in the fullness of these transported kits to puzzle theorists about the purposefulness or accidental nature of the voyaging. At 'Matakiterangi', the settlers had come and gone, leaving a nearly full kit of culturally significant vegetation. Either they did not bring animals, or they took them away with them. They left, on a platform at the cliff edge overlooking the only landing spot on their island, their stone gods, resembling more the *ahu* on Easter Island than the Taputapuatea *marae* on Tahiti. Yet the platform marked a beach, and is a reminder that an island is a place of symbols and of processes in symbol making, of the mind and heart caught in transported systems yet making something new.

That making islands should touch in us some mythic nerve is suggested by our perennial interest in Robinson Crusoe in all his guises. Add to that the fascination when the building process is not just out of disordered nature but is in some relation to disordered otherness – the Savage, 'Man Friday', Caliban – then there is something at work in us more than island romance.

A narrative that tells how someone constructed and furnished a house, not a makeshift dwelling, but a permanent home, using, with ingenuity, new materials and new designs to catch nonetheless old metaphors of security and comfort and status, or a story that tells of reinventing technologies to manufacture dyes, clothes and medicines out of foreign plants and minerals creates a liberating wonderment at how much else is building block in life. Island making sublimates a sense of alienation. Pitcairn holds those stories in its being, together with the paradox that it was both paradise and hell.

Scene i. *Narrative*

A MURDEROUS SETTLEMENT

Christian had slipped the cable of the *Bounty* at Matavai Bay late on the night of September 22, 1789. That he had notions of where he was going seems clear. He had seeded in the mind of Henry Hilbrandt the idea that he was off to the Duke of York Island (Atafu) in the Tokelaus, 1,400 miles north-west of Tahiti. He had already been studying Hawkesworth in Bligh's cabin. The Honourable Captain John Byron's frustrated note was there in Hawkesworth. Byron had been looking for the Spanish discoveries of Mendana and Quiros but, he wrote, 'the only person that ever pretended to have seen them was Quiros, and I believe he left no Account behind him to direct any other person to find them by'. Christian sent his pursuers north-west of Tahiti. But he sailed south-west in search of the Solomon Islands where Quiros had sought to establish a 'New Jerusalem'. South-west took the *Bounty* below the usual low-latitude tracks of British discoveries. No doubt Christian hoped to benefit by British scepticism about Spanish navigation.

The first islands the *Bounty* came upon were Rarotonga and Mangaia in the Cook Islands. To the natives, at least as legend has had it, the ship appeared as a floating island with two rivers of water and a taro plantation. And indeed the *Bounty* was by now cranky, with her pumps at work and her decks still a garden farm of plants and livestock for the mutineers' future home. The Rarotongans benefited by being given some orange trees and bits of iron, and they thought their prayer that the stranger 'Cookies' might visit them had been granted. They had heard of 'Cookies' from a native party that had drifted from Tahiti. The Mangaians had a taste of the less predictable quality of these 'Cookies'. One man had been delighted at the pearl shell buttons on Christian's jacket, and Christian had made him a gift of the jacket or given him the chance to wear it for a moment. The native stood on the *Bounty*'s gunwale proudly flourishing his acquisition. One of the mutineers shot him dead.

It was Teehuteatuanoa ('Jenny'), one of the Tahitian women aboard, who later told the story. She related that 'Christian was highly indignant. He could do nothing more, having lost all authority, than reprimand the murderer severely'. The *Bounty* left Mangaia to the sound of loud lamentions as the islanders took away the corpse, still perhaps in Christian's jacket. Perhaps there was one other relic of the *Bounty*'s visit – the 1784 edition of Nicholas Culpepper's *The English Physician Enlarged*. It was inscribed 'March ye 10th 1786', perhaps by Thomas Huggan, and was purported in much later days to have come to Mangaia from a *'papaa*—ship like a garden'.

Out of Christian's moodiness and overreactive response to tensions that Bligh caused in him, later English commentators, such as Lord Byron, made a melancholic, guilt-ridden figure. Rumours were strong that Christian had made his Island in this deep mood of depression. And reports were as strong to the contrary. He began, said others, with confidence and faith. The religiosity for which Pitcairn was later famous, they said, came from him, not from John Adams. The prayer of the Prodigal Son that Christian was said to have made a compulsory recitation by his community can take us either way – was it a prayer of confidence? was it a prayer of guilt? – 'I will arise, and go to my Father, and say unto him: "Father, I have sinned against Heaven, and before thee, and am no more worthy to be called thy son." '

Samuel Coleridge was an eclectic sort of knower and a vicarious voyager in his poetic experiences. How his imagination was sparked eclectically and vicariously in the composition of *The Ancient Mariner* was long ago masterfully described by J. L. Lowes in *The Road to Xanadu* (1927). How the tale and its voyager may have been connected with Fletcher Christian has been intriguingly explored by Charles S. Wilkinson in *The Wake of the Bounty* (1953). Let us displace two books with two sentences on the subject in order to make a simple point about Fletcher Christian's iconic character. Coleridge – like Byron – took Christian out of history and transformed his story into a mystery play about how a heinous act perpetrated against society but done in ignorance might be redeemed. For that Christian need not be a hero, or be right or wrong, nor need we be the judge of either. Trivial persecution *can* make a man desperate; unthinking acts *can* change the world. However, he was, by his act, an object of universal sympathy. That the inconsequential should be so consequential is an albatross around all our necks.

Just as the English public were to be titillated by Oberea's 'pinked bum' and Sir Joseph Banks' 'plants', they also had a prurient interest in the figure of a man, Christian, who could sacrifice everything for the 'ladies of Otaheite'. Edward Christian, in his defence of his brother Fletcher, tried desperately to play down his sexuality, but most people were more knowing than to believe that. In this respect, Bligh's strangely lame response to Edward Christian's *Pamphlet* defending Fletcher had only one good scoring point in it. He could quote Edward Lamb, who had been with them both on the *Britannia*: 'In the Appendix [of Edward Christian's *Pamphlet*] it is said', testified Lamb, 'that Mr Fletcher Christian had no attachment amongst the women of Otaheite; if that was the case, he must have been much altered since he was with you [Bligh] in the *Britannia;* he was one of the most foolish young men I ever knew in regard to the sex'. Prurient interest was instantaneously fired. In 1790, just weeks after the publication of Bligh's own account of the mutiny, there appeared from the publishers Robert Turner, London, *An Account of the Mutinous Seizure of the Bounty with the succeeding hardship of the crew. Secret Anecdotes of the Otaheitian Females.* The anonymous author had scoured Hawkesworth and all the voyaging literature to leer at the temptations posed by Tahiti all over again. It was soon known that Christian and eleven others on the *Bounty* had had the 'venereals'. Coy remarks about how this would have put him into the hands of Thomas Huggan, the surgeon, would have been a standard joke or innuendo. Certainly the *Letters of Mr Fletcher Christian containing the narratives of the Transactions on Board His Majesty's Ship Bounty Before and After the Mutiny with is subsequent Voyages and Travels in South America* (1796) played on all the usual *double entendres* and portrayed Fletcher Christian as 'candidly acknowledging' his intercourse with the women of Otaheite, who were 'constitutionally votaries of Venus'. The *Letters* were a fraud, but they played on credulity successfully enough for William Wordsworth, his old school friend, to issue an authoritative denunciation of their authenticity. It hardly mattered. Christian, the mutineer, had already escaped them all and has ever since.

This elusive and plastic character of Fletcher Christian comes from the fact that we have so little of him of his own making. There is a signature of his against the bill of credit made at the Cape of Good Hope. There is a Bible, again inscribed only with his name. But nothing else. That does not mean there have been no surprises in the discovery of things about him over the past 200 years, or that there will not be surprises still. A sense of belonging and roots will always inspire historical inquiry. Glynn Christian, descendant of Fletcher by five generations, has surprised every scholar with his interest in the *Bounty* and with his discoveries. As I have not seen what he has seen, I am dependent on him, and happy to point any reader to his *Fragile Paradise* (1982) for further detail.

It was not Fletcher so much that Glynn Christian discovered as his elder brother, Charles. Charles had a somewhat unstable personality, and in 1811 he wrote an unpublished autobiography in the form of a series of letters defending his character and professional standing. These letters are described by Glynn Christian as paranoiac in their response to attacks on Charles' reputation as a surgeon and accusations that he forged banknotes. (One could be excused for being paranoid at being accused of forgery – it carried a death penalty.) Charles had graduated from Edinburgh University after two years of medicine to become a surgeon aboard vessels of the East India Company. In 1787, he had been assigned to the *Middlesex* on its trading voyage to Macao and Madras. Remarkably, the *Middlesex* crossed paths with the *Bounty* at Spithead in November 1787. The *Bounty* was delayed there three weeks, with Bligh fuming at the incompetence of the Admiralty in causing these delays. The two brothers, Fletcher and Charles, spent a night together at Spithead. Charles had an extraordinary story to tell Fletcher. He had been involved in a mutiny on the *Middlesex*. The captain, John Rogers, had survived the mutiny, in which the first officer had pointed a loaded pistol at him and the second officer had struck and abused him. Charles Christian was accused of being part of the conspiracy. The *Middlesex* was not a naval vessel. There would be no court martial, no hangings. In fact, for some reason, Rogers did not even report the mutiny to the company. The directors of the Company, discovering the mutiny, punished the captain with a £500 fine and suspension, and censured and suspended the mutineers. The two brothers, Charles coming home in some uncertainty as to his future, Fletcher leaving home on a long voyage, must have talked long into the night. We can only wonder whether Fletcher told Bligh the story and, if he did, what effect the story had on their relations.

Fletcher Christian was and is a nubilous figure. Such haziness befitted his iconic mould. He has easily conformed to his makers' images. Peter Heywood, the moment he was free of the constraints of appearing innocent, wrote to Edward Christian that he would prove to him face to face that Fletcher 'was not the vile wretch void of all gratitude, which the world had the unkindness to think of him: but on the contrary, a most worthy character: ruined only by having the misfortune, if it can be called, of being a young man of strict honour, adorned with every virtue, beloved by all (except one, whose ill report is his greatest praise) who had the pleasure of his acquaintance'. Heywood's later memories were of Fletcher Christian's boyish exuberance, competing physically always to be the best. Why, the memory went, Fletcher could make a standing jump out of one barrel into another.

Charles, in his autobiography of 1811, was in a better position to reflect on mutinies and their causes, and on the character of his younger brother. Interestingly, his first references to Fletcher concerned his exuberance and physicality. 'He was then [when they met at Spithead] full of professional Ambition and Hope. He bared his Arm, and I was amazed at its Brawniness. "This", says he, "has been acquired by hard labour. I delight to set men an example. I not only can do every part of a Common Sailor's Duty, but am upon a par with a principal part of the officers".'

Charles Christian added that in India he had met up with companions of Fletcher who had been with him on HMS *Eurydice* before he sailed with Bligh. His captain on the *Eurydice*, like Bligh, had appointed him acting lieutenant in charge of a watch. 'They said he was strict, yet as it were, played while he wrought with men – he made a toil a pleasure and ruled over them in a superior, pleasant manner to any young officer they had seen.'

Charles had no explanation for Fletcher's part in the mutiny, but he had this reflection: 'when men are cooped up for a long time in the interior of a ship, there oft prevails such a jarring discordancy of tempers and conduct that it is enough on many occasions by repeated acts of irritation and offence to change the disposition of a lamb into that of an animal fierce and resentful'.

After Rarotonga and Mangaia, Christian was still looking for his uninhabited island. He took a slightly more northerly course, passed through some of the Tongan islands, and came across Ono-i-lau in the Southern Lau Group of the Fijis. This took him south and west of Tofua, the island of his mutiny. He was strangely close to his past. Had Ono-i-lau been uninhabited, Jenny reported, he would have destroyed the *Bounty* and stayed there. The lottery of his search was against him. They turned back into the wind and beat eastward in a long southern loop to Pitcairn. They had now added two more tedious months of tacking to the two months of their searching. They were discouraged enough even to think of returning to Tahiti.

In the end, Fletcher Christian made better navigation to Pitcairn than Captain Cook, who looked for it twice but could not find it. (There was an error of some five degrees of latitude in Hawkesworth's transcription of Carteret and an actual error of some three degrees of longitude in Carteret's account. Anyone needed some luck to find Pitcairn.) The island fitted Christian's image of where the *Bounty* should and could be. There were no natives; it was out of the way; there was no easy landing to invite visitors. It was fertile and had water. He came back from his first reconnaissance exhilarated.

The *Bounty* anchored in what little shelter there was off the dangerous landing place. The men unloaded and stripped her of what they could. They seem to have raised some dispute over whether they would beach her, giving them the possibility of using every last plank and nail either for shelter or for some later escapes, or whether they would sink her and erase every sign of their presence. Matthew Quintal decided for them all by setting fire to her. She sank in waters shallow enough to allow the retrieval of bits and pieces over the years by divers and archaeologists. They are to be found in museums around the world. If confidence in their capacity to make their Island out of the island's environment is to be measured by the ease with which the mutineers let much of value in the *Bounty* go, then those days after January 15, 1790, were days of remarkable resolve. We do not know how many times they climbed the Hill of Difficulty, as they came to call it, from the landing place to the Edge, where the old *marae* stood and behind which they were to build their settlement. Nor do we know their mood, although they now had, at last, some sense of permanence and, by that, some sense of social contract.

Christian seemed to have lost his earlier illusions. There was now no sense of play in the discipline he enforced. There was now no talk of forts or castles. Instead, the men built temporary shelters and planted a screen of trees behind which they would build a more permanent village – around a village square, it is true. With breadfruit, yams, taro, bananas and coconuts already growing, with plentiful fish in the sea, with a myriad of seabirds nesting in the cliffs, there was no urgency to begin gardens. But William Brown, the assistant botanist on the breadfruit voyage, chosen by Joseph Banks himself and supplied by him, was eager to transplant the

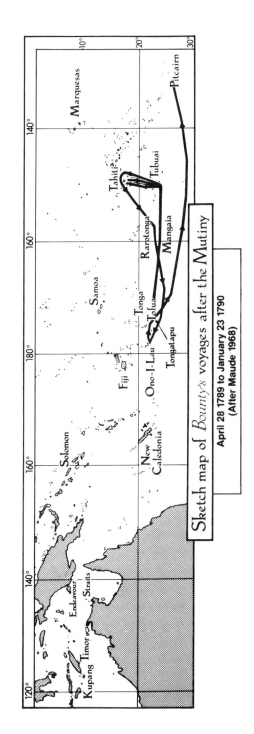

Figure 18.
The *Bounty*'s last voyage, April 28, 1789 to January 23, 1790 (After Maude 1968).

fruit trees and better varieties of food plants they had brought with them. He discovered a spring of water: water's distance was to be an inconvenience, its scarcity a problem. Brown surveyed the arable land. There was not much to survey. Only about 90 acres, of the island's 1,120 acres, were level enough to cultivate.

As a sign of what was urgent in their relations with one another, they divided the land of the island into nine equal portions, and each, using seamen's ways, took his part by lottery. Nine portions, nine mutineers; there was no land for the 'blacks' (as they called the natives). Neither the six men from Tubuai, Tahiti and Raiatea nor the twelve women and infant girl from Tahiti were allocated land. In that blatant injustice, the mutineers planted the seeds of their own destruction. They would soon have their own mutiny out of the discontent that arose, more violent and deadly than theirs against Bligh. They had snatched the 'blacks' of Tahiti on the night of September 22, 1789. Some of the women had been their companions on Tubuai. Two of the men, Tubuaians, had endangered their own lives by their loyalties to Christian while he built Fort George, and were still with the mutineers freely. Christian had quietly cut anchor on the rest and forced them to accompany him on his odyssey. He had forced overboard, however, six women who were too old for their needs or too ugly for their tastes. The women they divided, as they were to divide the land, into nine equal shares. The remaining three women were given to the six native men: Tararo, a Raiataian and a man of some superior social status, had one woman for his wife, while the five others shared two women. In that, too, the mutineers planted seeds of their own destruction.

It should be said that if it has been the mutiny itself that has attracted our twentieth-century interests, it was its denouement on Pitcairn Island that set nineteenth-century England aquiver. For us, the *Bounty* has been a parable of the tensions of institutional man, the malpractices of authority. The nineteenth century, however, had savoured something of the romance of the inner goodness of a gentleman, Fletcher Christian, who had been 'in hell'. The English public ached for Fletcher Christian's return, or at least eagerly bought the books that suggested it. Lord Byron's harsh barbs against Fletcher Christian's character did not stick. A boyhood friend of Christian's from Cockermouth days replied to Byron with a poem of his own. For him, there was something electric in Christian as an icon.

Young Christian – victim to a tyrant's guile
His heart was open, generous and humane,
His was a heart that felt for other's pain
Yet quick of spirit as the electric beam
When from the clouds its darting lightnings gleam.

To see this electric, even holy, spirit one needs to be exposed to a fairly horrendous narrative of events on Pitcairn. Let me relieve that narrative of the tedium of all its 'ifs' and 'buts' and 'possibles' and all the lateral pursuits that must be followed even to justify the spelling of a name, let alone a sequence or an inner motive. The narrative comes out of histories that were made when the transformations of 'what happened' had taken place. That is not greatly different from the ordinary encounter with 'the past' in any historical inquiry, of course. Historians never observe process. They observe only process interpreted by texts. Quite often these texts are survivals of moments instantly gone, yet they retain the feel of being primary, of being as near to process as texted experience can be. Out of Pitcairn, the texts all come after experiences there were transformed into tales of Goodness and Beauty. And the texts were collected by those who were dazzled by a miracle. Miracle viewers do no always give a good ethnography. They do make lasting myth.

Christian seemed to have a sense of organic solidarity at all stages of the mutiny. In their life after the mutiny, the mutineers would be dependent on one another. His Island, wherever it would be, would need to call upon many skills. First among these was metalworking. The metal that the mutineers had in their weapons, in their tools and in the nails that held the ship together, was all the metal they had – iron, copper, lead. It would always need to be preserved or reworked. Earlier in the mutiny, Christian was prepared to force cooperation in this area of need by holding the *Bounty*'s armourer, Joseph Coleman, as his blacksmith. Coleman was most unwilling to help the mutineers in any way. Those left on the beach at Tahiti when they returned believed Christian had planned to kidnap Coleman on that September night. But John Williams was the assistant armourer and he was one of the Pitcairn nine. Bligh had had Williams flogged for some negligence in heaving the lead. Williams was 'a native of Guernsey and spoke French', as Bligh recorded it in his list of the men's identifying traits. Williams had also, early in the voyage and much to Bligh's chagrin, revealed publicly that he had taken some cheeses to Bligh's house, when Bligh was blustering over the identity of the man

who had 'stolen' them. Williams had as much reason as any of the men
for mutiny.

At Pitcairn, Williams quickly established a forge – it was still there
150 years later, and is perhaps still to be seen, a nice relic of industrial
archaeology. He had got his land and his woman, along with all the
others. Within months, however, his female companion died of some
disease of the throat. Williams endured his celibacy for a little while but
then declared that he would have a wife or take the cutter and go. The
cutter was of no great importance, but Williams' metalworking skills
were. The mutineers decided to take the wife of Tararo, the Raiataian,
and give her to Williams. All the 'blacks' were disaffected. The plotting
of three of them, including Tararo, was betrayed by Williams' new wife.
Confronted by Christian with a gun, they fled. The other Tahitians then
conspired with the whites to kill the three 'blacks' and were able to murder Tararo and one Tubuaian. Tetahiti, the principal Tubuaian, was allowed to return and, after being put in irons, lived in virtual serfdom to
Isaac Martin.

The four natives now began to live under violent and reckless oppres-
sion. They were, however, allowed to use muskets, probably because they
had become skilled marksmen in hunting and culling the pigs that now
ran wild. In the three years to March 1793, the group had achieved much.
They built their houses around a small square, two- and single-storey
dwellings, in hybrid and invented architecture. They planted their gardens around the houses and worked the plantations of their individual
allotments assiduously. Land they owned individually, but its products
were owned in common. They furnished their houses and clothed their
bodies with the litter of the *Bounty* and relied on the knowledge and
labour of the native men and women to exploit a familiar environment for
cloth, for basketry, for utensils for cooking, and food. And they begot
children. Mauatua – or 'Isabella' or 'Mainmast' – must have been pregnant most of her life with Christian. She bore him three children in the
little time they had.

It is difficult to locate any rhythm or structure in this society through
the texts that we have. There seemed to be some sense of a symbolic centre
in their preparedness to accept that each would put into the common store
what circumstance of skill or productive land allowed and take out what
each needed. Christian was always 'Mr. Christian' to them all and set
apart. They watched his moods carefully and were wary of them. Edward

Young, nephew of a knight, Sir George Young, and accepted by Bligh as a midshipman because of Sir George's petition, was always close to Christian. Bligh said Young was of dark complexion – he was born at St Kitts in the West Indies – and had a 'rather bad look'. His rotten teeth and the gaps among his foreteeth did not make him seem a gentleman, but he considered himself something of one. John Adams, who was the son of a Thames waterman and was to live on as sole survivor with Young, always was suspicious of his alliance with Christian. Indeed he blamed most of their troubles on Young's jealousy of Christian's status. Four of the nine men – Matthew Quintal, William McCoy, Isaac Martin, John Mills – were always a little on the margins of things, set apart by their brutality. So the society's structures were always brittle. Later accounts – whether written out of a memory or out of a need to have such a memory, we do not know – said of Christian that he established weekly religious services and twice daily expected the whole community to recite the words of the Prodigal Son.

Pitcairn's fragile social structures were always at risk. Alcohol threatened to break them up altogether. How much liquor had remained aboard the *Bounty* after two years of heavy use, we do not know. One skill that Christian probably did not want on his Island was the knowledge of the Aberdeen man, McCoy, how to distil spirits. But the *ti* plant on Pitcairn gave William McCoy the means to make a savagely potent drink that, in the end, would drive him insane and, in the last months before October 1793, incite his three companions to even crueller treatment of the four Tahitian men. The Tahitians were flogged, hung up in irons, tortured with salt poured on their wounds (perhaps not for any sadistic pleasure but to ensure such valuable items did not become sick). There was nowhere to hide on this two- by one-mile island, but in the end two of the Tahitians fled the settlement and plotted at a distance with their companions. On October 3, a day when they had somehow obtained muskets, they came together and stalked the white men. It was planting season, and the men were in their separate fields. Williams died first, then Christian, then Mills, then Martin, then Brown. The job was done with muskets and axes. There was some tug of reluctance in the Tahitians as individual *taio* faced them, but what violence one man could not do, the others did. Williams and Christian probably did not see what was happening to them. The others did, and died somewhat unbelieving that it could. Christian's last recorded words were 'Oh, Dear!'

In all this, Young and Adams had been slightly wounded but were hidden and protected by the women. McCoy had been with Mills when he was killed but had run off and joined Quintal. They were now in hiding in the mountains, away from the camp, scavenging for food.

There now followed a week or so of inexplicable quiet. The Tahitian men held most of the weapons, all of the liquor and eleven women. The character of the quiet is hard to understand. In their mortal fear, the Tahitians needed to trust somebody but after the killings there could be no trust. The women were not inclined to be merely the tools. They had lost more than they could have hoped to gain in the murders, but, in the trauma, they achieved what the men never would, a secure alliance among themselves.

Within a few days, in a drunken jealousy over a woman, one Tahitian shot another as he sat beside the woman playing the flute. Then he fled in fear to – of all people – McCoy and Quintal, who murdered him for his musket. The two remaining Tahitians were dispatched at the same time, one being axed by the woman with whom he was sleeping, the other shot by Edward Young. McCoy and Quintal insisted on being shown the heads and hands of the slain Tahitians before returning to the settlement. Why they should insist on being shown the hands as well as the heads is not clear.

The community, if that is the word to describe this traumatised group, was now divided into four polygamous households. Adams had four women and their children in his house; Young had three women, McCoy and Quintal had two. Three years later, in 1797, McCoy, in delirium from drink, threw himself off the cliffs, with a rock tied around his neck. Five years on, one of Quintal's women was accidentally killed while gathering seabirds' eggs. Berserk with liquor, Quintal demanded that he should have Christian's former wife. She was living now with Edward Young. Adams and Young agreed it would be safer to exterminate Quintal. Young killed him with an axe as he lay in a drunken stupor. A year after this, in 1800, Young himself died, the first of the mutineers to die a natural death. He wheezed his way asthmatically into eternity. John Adams, at the age of thirty-three years, was now alone with nine Polynesian women, one eleven-year-old Polynesian girl, and twenty-three children born on the Island (eleven girls and twelve boys). It was then that he had a disturbing dream. At thirty-three years, he was ripe for resurrection. A figure appeared to him when, as he admitted, he was in a drunken sleep –

he had continued to distil spirits. The vision threatened to pierce him through with a dart. 'Ah, I know who you are', Adams said, 'Michael the Archangel'. It should be noted, however, in the interests of psychohistory, that Edward Young, whom Adams hated but on whom he was dependent to learn to read and write, was tattooed on the chest with a large heart pierced by a dart – and dated, observed Bligh, 1788 or 1789.

It is the way of history to foster selected preoccupations. The history of the mutiny on the *Bounty* has always been primarily concerned with its Eurocentric romance. There is another unromantic story that needs to be told, how the *Bounty* cut a swath of death through native lives. The six 'blacks' on Pitcairn were only the last to be killed. There were another hundred and twenty or more on Tubuai, a dozen or so at Tahiti, even one man shot dead in the Cook islands by McCoy as the native triumphantly displayed a jacket given him by Christian. Who will say that more than 139 lives were less important than the five *Bounty* lives taken by natives at Pitcairn and Thompson's at Tahiti, Norton's at Tofua?

That 86 percent of the founding male population of Pitcairn should be individually murdered is reason enough for focusing a narrative on the episodes of mayhem. That John Adams should be surrounded, in 1800, by twenty-three children is a reminder, however, that in death there was living and that most of that living turned around the native women. The Island was as much what was in *their* minds and bodies as in the men's. The women reared the children and made the rhythm of every day. They made the first and lasting interpretation of all things to do with food, clothing and the knowledge of the physical environment. Perhaps the men, with wives who spoke little English, gave their own lives a shipboard character – entertained themselves separately, spent time in yarning. The women, by that, were separate too and tightly knit. They bore their children individually, of course, but they reared them communally. It was a common observation later that neither households nor separate mothers seemed to matter. For the children the Island was one household and every woman their mother. Who precisely the women were or how they managed their lives is almost impossible to describe. Only one of them is known to us in any detail. She was 'Jenny' or Teehuteatuanoa. At Tahiti, she had been John Adams' *taio* and had been claimed by him and initialled with a tattoo on her left arm, 'AS/1789'. (Adams had mustered on the *Bounty* under the name 'Alexander Smith'.) Teehuteatuanoa was the only woman to survive the first ten years at Pitcairn and remain childless. She was Isaac Martin's woman on Pitcairn. Independent and strong, she urged the women, at one point, to return to Tahiti and even built a boat to that purpose. She finally persuaded a whaling captain to take her away from Pitcairn. A desperate voyage via Chile and the Marquesas saw her back in Tahiti.

Teehuteatuanoa's story is virtually the only source of our knowledge of the *Bounty*'s trip from Tahiti to Pitcairn. She told it to several missionaries, trading captains and explorers in Tahiti. Her English, they said, was reasonable, but accented. They, in turn, told her story in the *Bengal Hurkuru* and the *Sydney Gazette*. Teehuteatuanoa was a remarkable woman by any standards. Yet there is no reason for us to believe that she was exceptional among the women, other than that, through accident, we know her story and that, being childless, she did not feel the pull of Pitcairn as the other women did.

Having said that, it seems logical to see the women as the chief socialising force on Pitcairn, but to admit that we cannot say precisely how. I should say that the language of Pitcairn – surely a sign of socialising forces – was English, well, English enough to be recognised and understood by visitors from outside. Out of a polygot of dialects – Philadelphian American English, London cockney, Aberdeen and Ross-shire Scots, as well as dialects of the North Country, Guernsey Island, St Kitts in the West Indies, Cornwall and Manx – came an English that has delighted phonologists. But it was not Tahitian. And we have the puzzle that English was the language of power – shall we say of the Sea? – and Tahitian the language of everyday social life – shall we say of the Land?

The women lived long lives on Pitcairn, averaging thirty-two years. They all came from Tahiti, except perhaps one from Raiatea and one from Tubuai. Two women, Christian's and Young's wives, were of the ranked and titled class of Tahitian society. Another, Vahineatua, Mills' wife, had a name that, in most of Polynesia, called attention to some degree of sacredness and connection with localised deities. She was also known as 'Bal'hadi' (Baldhead). It would be no surprise, given what followed, that from early on the women's alliance centred around some prophetess figure like Vahineatua who could interpret signs. Women, in most circumstances of contact with European strangers in Polynesia, mediated cultural change. They satisfied the sexual needs of the strangers and entered into exchanges that challenged their own cultural definitions and freed them, in the circumstances of that exchange, from rules that bound them. We saw the inventiveness of the Tahitians in the reverse situation, when they required the *Bounty* mutineers to don Tahitian clothing in order to take it off in deferential rituals to Pomare. In the women's intercourse with sailors, they felt themselves relieved of some of their most binding *tapu*, such as not eating with men or not eating certain categories of food. They were freed of the signs of Tahitianness in the marginal space of their contact.

On Pitcairn, it was the other way around. In circumstances in which they had to be inventive of virtually every aspect of their social relations, they clung to signs of gender and culture. They ate separately from men. Through thirty years, no inducement on the island or from visitors could persuade them to make a marginal space to breach that *tapu*.

The years that followed the first murders of the white men and the Tahitians were very disturbing for the surviving *Bounty* men. They were years in which they discovered how different the women really were. The women dug up the bones of Christian, Williams, Martin, Mills and Brown. They kept the skulls in their houses or carried them when they went into the fields. The women's Island now included the *'oromatua,* the active souls of their murdered husbands. They knew that, as guardians of the family welfare, these ghosts would occupy their own skulls and give a protective presence. Edward Young was the man most offended at this sign that the women's Island was so different from his, and he repeatedly made the matter an issue of challenge and submission.

The four white men were not strong enough to enforce their Island on the women, however. We know the women had their own conspiracies to kill the men. They made hideaways in the mountains, they captured muskets. They pulled the *Bounty* planks from the houses and made a boat or raft on which to escape. At times, they made war on the men, who then had to conceal weapons in safe places to which they could retreat. In the end, the women were broken. Their raft overturned on being put in the water. The men foiled their attacks and promised to kill the first woman who disobeyed. There was a submission, and the skulls and bones were finally buried. Indeed, there was an anniversary feast to celebrate the killing of the 'blacks'. There must be a suspicion that in this submission and ceremonial burial, the Island was changed. Or at least there was an emptiness in its landscape that needed to be filled. John Adams began its filling with his dream of Michael the Archangel.

'INNOCENCE BETTER IMAGINED THAN DESCRIBED'

The Island had a shallow past, only as deep as the experience of those who founded it. Its only history was of the mutiny that created it. There was a cargo of a deeper past, however: the *Bounty*'s cargo of books. It was not an encyclopaedic collection. It did not distil the wisdom and science of ages for this new society. And if it had, by the time John Adams had his dream, there was no one who could read it save himself in a halting way. There was Bligh's collection of books of exploration and discovery, anno-tated with his vitriolic hatreds, and where he saw himself uncredited for the role he played in Cook's fatal voyage. There were some pious books – Doddrige's *Sermons on Regeneration* among them. Most importantly, there were sacred texts, the Bible and the Book of Common Prayer. Christian had discovered his own Bible at the bottom of his sea-chest. Bligh had left behind a copy of the Book of Common Prayer, from which he custom-arily read the service before proclaiming the Articles of War. These sacred texts were the seeds of a fundamentalism that would fill the Island's empty landscape and be a sign to Victorian England that God's Providence works on the British in mysterious ways. This would be the miracle of Pitcairn.

John Adams, a man of a northern Ireland seafaring family and orphan of a Thames waterman, was neither priest nor prophet. He did not feel the authority of the one or the confidence of the other. No metaphors worked his mind: he had the literal-mindedness of the barely literate. When he looked for God after dreaming of St Michael, he found him incarnate in words more than in the Word. Words gave him a liturgy and a regime out of the Book of Common Prayer and rules out of the Bible. He began to bind his family, now the whole Island, to five services on Sunday, making no choice between the optional prayers and readings, feeling more secure in doing all. He had the people fast until evening and abstain from meat Wednesdays, Fridays and the Sabbath. The rules of work and preparations for the Sabbath found in the Old Testament suited his purpose. Every counsel in the sacred text became a law. Every law became an absolute, unrelativised by experience or reflection: simple prac-tices, such as prayers at sunrise and sunset and twice in between, became tests of literalness and correctness. Assembled on a slope halfway up a cliff, or fishing in a canoe, how could his people kneel, hands raised aloft to pray? Would standing do instead? Every gesture became a matter of conscience.

It was not the first time, or the last, that the Book was cargo on a Pacific island. It functioned elsewhere as a thing, an icon, unread – even unreadable – its mysteries somehow held back by those who knew its secrets. It functioned as an instrument in the civilising process, allowing the unexperienced to be experienced through being read, allowing the abstractions of reading to seem as real as the abstractions of power and institutions. On this Island, there was a difference. Only John Adams – and he with great awkwardness – could read. Only John Adams could write, even more hesitantly than he could read. He did not seem to have the energy or the confidence to teach the others to read or write. And the Book, the Bible, was one of a kind. It was 'printed' only in the physical sense. There were no other copies. How could it be fingered by many hands and survive? How could it be reproduced if none could write? (The Book, the Bible, is still on the Island. It had been taken away for more than a hundred years and ended up in the Connecticut Historical Society Library, just one of many other icons, the loot of another people's past. But the Connecticut Historical Society, less possessive than most such institutions, gave it back.) This Book only had a mediated presence. John Adams was its prophet. It was, by that, more fundamentalist in its possibilities. The poetics of its reading was limited by the Island's relationship with one man, Adams. He was the words-made-flesh. It was to be said later that 'Reckless Jack' – his nickname on the *Bounty* – was affected deeply by this mirroring. Under locks 'as white as driven snow', there was a countenance that was 'a perfect mould of benevolence'.

The social order of the Island became quite remarkable. The prescribed times of rising, playing, working, eating and relaxing were signalled at their proper moments by a bell. There was another book that Adams kept – a sort of muster roll – that registered every ounce or measure of produce, who contributed it and to whom it was distributed. The quarrels of a given day were, on biblical injunction, required to be resolved by evening. Adams would later protest to any outsider that their Island was the happiest of places. None who lived there or visited there denied it, although John Buffet, who lived for twenty-one years on Pitcairn in the last days of Adams' life, added less idealistically, 'my residence has convinced me that human nature is the same throughout the world'. Religious revelation did not blind Adams to the special problems of the Island. To the laws of the Bible, he added some of his own, notably the relatively late age at which young women would be allowed to marry. He wanted their labour in the fields more than their labours at birth. He knew, as well, that there were problems he had not solved, such as the ownership of land and the stress put on the island's resources from their rapidly increasing numbers. He had the relics of its previous inhabitants to remind him that the island had been abandoned before. He sensed that it would have to be deserted again. He could not be blamed for keeping at bay the problem of ages and cultures, namely, that land once divided would be inherited, that lineage and property were centripetal forces. But he hid the problem away, as long as the population was scarcely adult, in his enforced communalism.

On an ocean, crossed by as many ships and canoes as the Pacific, it was only a matter of time before the Island would be 'discovered' again. The people of Pitcairn had seen sails two or three times, and men had landed once on the side of the island opposite their settlement. In 1808, Captain Mayhew Folger, out of Boston in the *Topaz,* had his famous meeting with Friday October Christian, the young olive-skinned man who came out in a canoe, surprisingly spoke English and asked Folger if he knew Captain Bligh and whether, when the captain told him where he was from, America was in Ireland. And there was the navigator's little joke that Friday October Christian was renamed 'Thursday October Christian' because the Island, for all its careful calculations of the calendar year, was one day out, because the *Bounty* had crossed unknowingly what was later established as the International Date Line. It is difficult to know what sort of joke Christian was playing when he named his son, a Christian with no christian name. We do not know for certain whether Friday October was named for the October day in 1790 on which he was born, or for October 25, 1788, the day of the *Bounty*'s sighting of Tahiti, the date tattooed on Tom Ellison's arm. It would be satisfying to discover that Friday October's birthday was October 25. That date, however, was a Sunday by ship's time, a Saturday by civil time. Was it a Friday in Christian's memory? Or was this firstborn of the Island, a child destined to marry back into the first generation of Tahitian women, a sign of all that was skewed in his father's life, born into no past, no future, only into the day and month of his birth? Folger, excited by his discovery and presuming that the British Admiralty would be too, wrote them not once but twice, in 1809 and 1813. The Admiralty did not reply or do anything. They had a war with France to handle, some say, and were too distracted by it to be interested in a colony of mutineers. But Bligh was not yet dead and had had all those other embarrassing mutinies. Pitcairn could have been something about which the navy did not need to know.

Six years later, quite by the accident of maps that showed Pitcairn to be somewhere else and quite unwarned by the Admiralty, two British warships, the *Briton* and the and the *Tagus,* discovered again what Folger had found. The islanders, this time, had a fear, and old Adams himself was tremulous at his first navy visit. They need not have been alarmed. The captains and the crews were enchanted by what they saw – *Englishmen:* 'Their teeth are beautiful, without a single exception; and all, both men and women, bear strong resemblance to English faces. From so promising a stock, it is natural to expect a progeny of beautiful people upon the island'. Thursday October Christian impressed them especially. 'He is of a brown cast, not however, with that mixture of red so disgusting in wild Indians. With a great share of good humour, and a disposition and willingness to oblige, we were very glad to trace in his benevolent countenance all the features of an honest English face.' It was not just that good English blood came through a native screen. There was the triumph of the Island's remarkable culture. 'Tenderness and compassion' welled up in naval breasts as they saw what, in the end, a British tar could do. Tears welled, also. 'The parting with the men was almost worse [than with the officers]. To see big stout fellows crying, and hardly able to look up, was too much. All the officers were deeply affected; and I saw some of the men nearest me, old sturdy seamen and big mariners, not only wipe away a tear, but regularly crying.' There was no question of the majesty of the law and justice. There was another parable to be told. The British navy had begun its love affair with Pitcairn.

Ships came more frequently in the years that followed. They all tasted the delicious innocence of the Island. 'It is astonishing the feeling produced by the conduct and manners as well as the happiness in which these innocent people live have on all of us. For many days we talked of nothing else and in our dreams visited the island. In fact we almost desired to live with them.' 'The whole of us did not fail to take a parting kiss of the young women. They are in general handsome, fine figured, beautiful tresses, fine hair and being in such a state of nature combined with innocence, they have that effect upon our minds which might be better imagined than described.'

Although the navy was entranced at how well the *Bounty*'s story ended and at the propitious timing of its relevation, the Church had questions about the island's state of religious innocence. Pitcairn was a parable of the triumph of Good over Evil, and there were pulpits and pamphlets aplenty to broadcast its message. But those who believed that change of heart was a deeper, more mysterious thing than obedience to Levitical laws were a little suspicious of Adams' formalism. Enigmatically, he had said to John Buffet, the first outsider to come and live on Pitcairn, that 'he thought that people would neglect to do good if [they] thought to believe in Jesus alone for salvation'. On the other hand, more established churchmen were suspicious of Adams' mediating role. It was safer to read a book than hear a prophet:

'Great credit is due to Smith [i.e., Adams] as the patriarch of so well-ordered a community: and after he has done so much it would be cruel to censure him harshly for not having attempted more. Yet it is now fully ascertained that he has taught none of these young men, women and children to read; so that, unless the Christian beneficence of distant strangers (who might never have heard of them) prevent so deplorable a catastrophe, they will be left at his decease destitute of the means to learn the revered will of God, or even to keep alive in their remembrance what they have been taught to believe. Can all that Smith has done for them make amends to such a deficiency? Will *he* think so at the hour of death? Can the plea that "He had not a Spelling-book," be *then* satisfactory to his mind?' Samuel Greatheed, the intellectual of the London Missionary Society, who had made such good ethnographic sense of Tahiti out of the vocabularies and descriptions Heywood and Morrison had given him, made this point in his 'Authentic History of the *Mutineers of the Bounty*' (1820–1).

Pleas to help these unreading poor were instantly heard. Bibles, prayerbooks and spelling books were sent through the Calcutta Society for the Promotion of Christian Knowledge. Names such as Ramdulal Day, Rustemser Cowaster and Meer Eckrem Ally – I am making a point here made long ago by the most learned of all Pacific historians, H. E. Maude – subscribed to help the Quintals, Christians and McCoys. Within five years, every family of the island had a box of books. Among them were titles such as Allien's *Alarm to the Unconverted.*

But it was the converted who were alarmed by too much innocence and the prospects of unestablished religion. Pitcairn's soul, like the *Bounty*'s mutiny, would be a parable of something else.

'POORE ORFING'

As his fears that he would be made to pay for his mutiny died, John Adams enjoyed his Rip Van Winkle role. Visitors to Pitcairn, too, enjoyed awakening him to a world of revolutions and wars, and were charmed to report that when he learned of Nelson's victory at Trafalgar, he 'rose from his seat, took off his hat, swung it three times round his head, threw it on the ground sailor-like and cried out "Old England Forever" '. He still had his rolling sailor's gait, would take off his hat and smooth the sparse hair on his forehead whenever he addressed an officer. He was a memory of other days standing before them. He made gestures and spoke phrases of a navy twenty years out of date. They were kind to him for the nostalgia he created and the sense of their own modernity they found in his history. The *Bounty* was like the gaucheries of adolescence. It could not happen now: it was not them.

John Adams was generous to his visitors in their search for souvenirs. He pandered to their desire to boast of having spoken to a mutineer of the *Bounty*. He told the story of the mutiny to anyone who asked, a little differently to each. His own story became dialogic with the stories he began to hear from others. He laid claim in the end to have been the one to shout 'Huzzah for Otaheite' that only Bligh had heard. No doubt from having told it so often to those on Pitcairn, he came to believe that he was sick in his hammock when the mutiny happened, whereas he would have been one of the first to hang had he been caught. He had been among the four who had dragged Bligh from his cabin.

Things, as well as words, were John Adams' gift of souvenirs. He gave the *Bounty*'s chronometer, made by Larcun Kendall in 1771 and used by Cook on his third voyage, to the honest Captain Folger. Folger got Bligh's azimuth compass as well. Someone cadged Adams' sailor's pigtail from him, although the sceptical might think the pigtail is like that old museum joke, the skull of John the Baptist as a young man. The *Bounty*'s

Figure 19.
The Poore Orfing, John Adams. (H. Adlard, engraver; R. Beechey, artist. In Thomas Boyles Murray, *Pitcairn: The Island, the People and the Pastor; with a short account of the Mutiny of the Bounty.* Ferguson F13007. National Library of Australia.)

Bible was another gift. The boys of the island would dive to scavenge the sunken *Bounty* for wood from which sailors carved their curios. Then to Captain Reynolds of the *Sultan,* an American trader that took Teehutea-tuanoa away as well, Adams gave the *Bounty's* spyglass and two 'blank books'. They were not in fact blank at all. Hidden shyly in four separate spots were Adams' efforts to start his own history. He would not have been the first autobiographical author, or the last, to have found a blank page overawing, or to have said the one thing that needed to be said about his life and then become stumped for something else to say. Adams' first effort went thus: *I was Born at Stanford Hill in the parish of St John Hackney Middellsex of poor But honast parrents My father was Drowned in the Theames thearfore he left Me and 3 More poore Orfing Bot one was Married ot of All harmes.*

He tried again:

The life of John Adams Born November the 4 Or 5 in the Year Sixty Six at Stanford Hill in the parish of St John Hackney My farther was sarvent to Daniel Bell Coke Marchant My farther was drowned in the River Theames.

In an age as genealogically intent as ours, no man need have a history so short. John Adams' entry on the *Bounty* muster roll: No. 29 [Entry] 7th Sept 1787 [Whence and whether prest or not] Volr London [Age at time of entry in this ship] 20 [Qualities] AB [D. D.D. or R] R [Time of Discharge] 28th April 1789 [Whither or for what reason] Mutineer [Slops] £2-2-0 [Venereals] 30/- Huggan [Dead Men's Clothes] – [Beds] 9/8 [Tobacco] £3-19-2 [Two months advanced wage] £2-5-0. Bligh wrote this description of him in the launch: 'Alexr Smith, Aged 22 years, 5ft 5in High, Complexion Brown, Hair Brown, Make Strong, Marks Very much pitted with the small [pox] and very much tatowed on his Body, Legs, Arms and feet – and a scar on his Right foot where he has been cut with a Wood Ax'.

We have to presume that John Adams took the name 'Alexander Smith' to disguise his desertion from some other ship. But he seemed to stick with this alias all through his twenty years at Pitcairn till Captain Folger told him of President John Adams of the United States of America. Perhaps this discovery of being joined unknowingly to the outside world gave John Adams confidence to take up his own name again. 'Poor but honast parrents' and even 'orfings' are not easily lost to the registering forces of his church and state. Let it be said that John Adams' brothers and sisters, his parents, his parents' siblings and the children and children's children of all these can be traced, and have been. It is no mystery why he took Alexander Smith as his name. Smith was the maiden name of his Ulster grandmother and Alexander the name of his granduncle of a seafaring family. Or Smith was the married name of his sister who lived in Derby. Dina, Rachel, Jemima, Hannah, Jonathan are all names of first-generation Pitcairn children. They are names that stud the register for the Adams family in the parish of St John's, Hackney. Pitcairn Island was a very alien place, in the culture of its women, in the violence of its men. John Adams made a private space on it in the names he gave to its children. His stuttering starts to his histories cannot tell us of what those names reminded him.

If John Adams' own histories were short, there were others who did not blush to make them longer. In 1835 Captain Frederick Chamier, R.N., wrote *Jack Adams The Mutineer* in three volumes, 886 pages long. Chamier had no way of knowing that John Adams was the 'poore orfing' son a Thames waterman. He gave him a quintessential naval birth instead. He made him a 'son of a gun', born between the gun carriages of the lower deck of the *Renown,* and had him christened in rum with a tar for a god-father. Young Jack Adams would not put a foot on land for the first eleven years of his life. Chamier was at pains to caricature the sailor of the 1760s, the better to show how different the navy was in the 1830s. In the modern navy, eccentric religiosity had given way to conforming behaviour, the way rum had given way to tea, the way scruffy bodies and motley clothing had given way to personal cleanliness and uniforms. One thing was constant in Chamier's eyes, however – the general caring relationship between officers and men. The true dangers to the men came from outsiders, notably the 'kindhearted Jew' willing to gamble on future prize money and 100 percent interest.

Jack Adams, the boy, was different in one respect from his contemporaries. He had learned to read and write. The captain's clerk had taught him. It was half expected that a 'son of a gun' would be better educated than a landsman. Ships had men's total interest at heart compared with an uncaring land. But not four men in several hundred of a crew could read and write, and Jack Adams was marked by that. Reading made him dangerous, a 'sea lawyer'. Reading gave him a vicarious experience in an institution in which precedence was a total organising principle. Young Jack Adams discovered that his namesake had signed the petition for United States independence in 1776 and read the American grievances and declaration of rights with eyes flashing fire. 'Hush', the man who had christened him in rum said, 'I never heard tell of a mutiny that did not end in death and destruction. Never, boy, mention the word. It's a kind of upstart that never did well in this world and as sure as those Yankees have spouted all those long words to the king, so surely he'll hang them well without benefit of clergy'.

Because he came to save the life of a drowning midshipman, Jack Adams earned a gentleman's gratitude and got a patron who generously pensioned his mother, and in the end got him aboard the *Bounty*. Adams had left the navy for a while for the merchant service on runs to the West Indies. But he did not like merchants. Chamier makes them another sort of outsider, like the Jews, to the familial relations of a naval vessel. So Adams gladly takes his patron's offer to return him to the navy and introduce him to Bligh.

Bligh is introduced as a 'precious boy, they say, all smirks and smiles when he talks to the great men who came down to see the ship, all growls and curses when he speaks to any of the crew'. But nothing gainsays Bligh's seaman's skills. For all the coarseness of his language, he was presented as a true disciplinarian, not a tyrant. But the old tar who was Adams' godfather said he would never sail on the *Bounty* on her breadfruit voyage. 'Never liked your hermaphrodite craft, neither man of war nor merchant.' Disturbing ambivalences again! – in language, in the very structure of the ship.

Four hundred pages on the mutiny did not distract Chamier from his prime interest in Jack Adams and the island he made at Pitcairn. Nor did it change his judgement that the mutiny had no rightful cause. Bligh was low, harsh and vulgar. But the navy was big enough to see that. Bligh could have been court-martialled on his return for any act serious enough to have effected a rebellion. For Chamier, the true miracle of the mutiny was Pitcairn. It was Genesis all over again. Adams, the last man on earth on his isolated island, was Adam, the first man. Pitcairn was the Garden of Eden because the Word in the form of the Bible was unmediated by anything other than Adams' innocence – there was no interposition of schoolmen or bigots. The Bible was the prime source of divinity itself. It offered unpolluted wisdom. There was no knowledge of good and evil, no code of laws. 'The very name of certain crimes might induce some to practice them', so on Pitcairn sin had no name. Obedience, repentance, loneliness created their own evolutionary force. By this, heredity, prejudices, idolatry, cruelty were bred out of existence. Discipline, not laws, made paradise.

What do we finally learn from their history? Why, that liberated slaves make invariably the hardest taskmasters; that those who are so eager to disturb discipline are themselves driven to greater acts of tyranny in order to support their own authority; that popular clamour or encroachments upon regular government lead generally, step by step, to a nation's decay or overthrow. This also we learn – and it is consolatory to all who bear about them the hell of bad conscience – that there is a power above who listens to the voice of the repentant sinner, and who can raise up even from him, who had violated the laws of both God and man, one man just in all his actions – a worthy labourer in the vineyard of christianity, and one whom the historians may point out as a proof that good may come out of the greatest evil – that there is no crime so heinous that it may not obtain forgiveness and that the stirrings of an evil conscience may, by God's mercies, be turned to repose of mind, which may cheer up the repentant sinner, and give him courage to yield up his soul without fear and menace.

Jack Adams, the Mutineer, had this last piece of advice to sailors whose subjection to discipline could be expected to touch their souls, not just their backs. 'Go to your ship with this advice from one well entitled to give it – for experience is the best preceptor. Do your duty cheerfull – to your God, your king, and your captain; and remember the words of Jack Adams, the mutineer: No man sleeps soundly whose conscience is scarred with crime – no man knows the value of sincere repentance, but he who reads attentively this holy book from which I have learnt that to the really penitent sinner the hand of salvation is offered, the pardon he prays for is granted.'

The measurers of the new naval discipline were sensing victory.

POLITICS IN PITCAIRN

'Politics in Pitcairn' is a borrowed phrase. The late Sir Keith Hancock published a book of essays under that title in 1947. Sir Keith was one of the master historians of Australia, Britain and South Africa. He had written the essay 'Politics in Pitcairn' as a brilliant young historian.

The League of Nations still had its facade unbroken when I found Pitcairn the parody of European lawlessness and terror [in 1929]', he wrote in preface to his essays. 'Since then we have subdued three dangerous anarchs, but not the anarchy itself. Our victorious band has named itself the United Nations, but its members still eye each other mistrustfully. John Adams – which of the Great Powers is he? – wields now a more terrible axe.

So the Pitcairn parody is still relevant. It is, however, only a parody, not a true description. I never was cynical enough to confuse the two things. I told my trivial tale grandiloquently. I played that game of the mock-heroics which Machiavelli played in the days of his disillusioned uselessness; but I could not give myself to the game with Machiavelli's zest. I spoilt my squib with too much sermonizing. I was not at the time *italianizzato* to the very limits of detachment and despair. Nor am I now. I cannot rid myself, I do not wish to rid myself of my very British preoccupation with right conduct. After all, I belong to a people which by Machiavelli's own test remains 'uncorrupted', a people which lives in liberty under the law, and for all its conflicts of material interest is capable of passionate response to the call of civic duty.

The British are incorrigible moralisers of their politics, and this harbors a part of their strength, but it also leads them from time to time into great danger. At the root of things there exists a vital connection between ethics and politics; but there exists also an important sphere which belongs to *virtu* – the technique and mechanics and impulsers of power. Within this sphere, the irrelevant and optimistic application of ethical interpretations helps nobody except the more brutal and unscrupulous masters of power.

John Adams in Hancock's 'politics of Pitcairn' was a master of power. He may not have been Machiavellian and manipulative. He may not have known what Aristotle knew, that 'if men think that a ruler is religious and has a reverence for the gods . . . they are less disposed to conspire against him'. Adams may not have been expediently holy. He could have been honestly holy and had more frightening power because of that. Holiness was a very political *virtu* in a society that had lapsed into a Hobbesian state of nature, tooth and claw. Empire out of anarchy was very predictable – and timely.

There was an awful history to Pitcairn after Adams. Sharks did walk on the land. Power did belong to strangers from outside who came in a succession of 'canoes'. John Adams could not find a successor to his power among his own people of the land. He entrusted it briefly to a pious young man, John Buffet, permitted to leave a whaler and stay at Pitcairn. Then Adams was more impressed with the credentials of the Reverend George Hunn Nobbs, who sailed in one day all the way from Callao with a single dying companion in an eighteen-ton cutter. Nobbs had already led a profligate and adventurous life in the navy, in the convict settlement at Botany Bay, in the patriotic wars and prisons of South America. He had returned home to England only to be implored by his mother to go somewhere else. 'Go to Pitcairn's Island, my son; dwell there, and may the blessing of Almighty God be upon you.' The long, painful voyage to Pitcairn was George Nobbs' Road to Damascus. Nobbs wanted to be a Peter rather than a Paul, however, and went about establishing law and order in the place of Adams' more erratic rule. Adams died March 5,

1829. Buffet and Nobbs were rivals for a while. Nobbs finally won out when Pitcairn took that giant step in the civilising process and freed him of the labours of the community for subsistence so that he could be schoolteacher full time.

Someone in England, however, had decided that Pitcairn was facing a Malthusian crisis. Its population was growing too large for its resources. The residents must be saved. Putting such innocents among the wastes of British society in England's convict settlement in New South Wales was too horrible to contemplate. They must be sent back to Tahiti. The Government at home was sensible enough to try to discover whether the Pitcairners needed or wanted to go, and learned that the answer to both questions was no. But the philanthropy of empire once raised is difficult to stop, and the courage of bureaucrats at the fingertips of empire to countermand a philanthropic suggestion is slight. Willy-nilly, the Pitcairners were carried off to Tahiti, March 7, 1831.

The trouble was that the Pitcairners did not consider themselves 'blacks'. Tahiti to them was a land of 'blacks'. The first anniversaries they had celebrated on their Island were not commemorative of the burning of the *Bounty,* nor were they thanksgivings for their first harvests. They had celebrated, as it were, their first national day as the anniversary of the final murder of the Tahitian 'blacks'. Their myths about Fletcher Christian were ambivalent, but their myths about 'blacks' were unequivocal: they were treacherous, inferior, dangerous. The islanders would not even agree to being served by black servants on the ships that visited them. Part of their innocence, visitors discovered, was the disarming frankness with which they discussed the evils of being 'black' even with the Negroes they came upon.

It was a humiliating discovery for the Pitcairners to find that being special in British eyes did not elevate them to being white. Other physical immunities were low, as well. One in five Pitcairners died in the six months of their Tahitian stay, among them the firstborn of their island, Thursday October Christian. They were morally devastated by Tahiti as well – by its drunkenness and its forms of sexuality. They had only one source of capital by which to escape Tahiti. For forty years they had hoarded the copper bolts of the *Bounty*'s hull. With the sale of these, and by selling off everything the British had given them, they bought a passage home to Pitcairn. The *Bounty* thus took them back to start a second time.

There were hard times in this second beginning. Pitcairn had lost its innocence. Liquor made a bit of hell out of paradise, and visitors found morals at a low ebb and 'vices of a very deep dye hinted at in their mutual recriminations'. Hobbesian theory, it would see, might be tested again. Sure enough it was. Out of the sea came a bizarre figure, Joshua Hill. He was nearly a lord, he said, related to the Duke of Bedford. Otherwise he had all the characteristics of a travelling medicine man in the outreaches of the American West. He was all for temperance and discipline. He was sent by the British Government, he said, to redeem the people of Pitcairn with laws and systems. His credentials were the stories he told.

I have visited the four quarters of the globe, and . . . it has been my desire to maintain, as far as lay in my power, the standing of an English gentleman. I have lived a considerable time in a palace, and had my dinner parties with a princess on my right and a general's lady on my left. I have had a French cook, and a box at the opera. I have drove my dress-carriage (thought the neatest in Paris, where I spent five or six years; as well, I have known Calcutta) with the handsomest lady (said) Madame Recamier, to grace my carriage. I have drove a curricle with two outriders, and two saddle-horses, beside a travelling-carriage, a valet, a coachman, footman, groom, and, upon extraordinary occasions, my maitre d'hotel. I have (at her request) visited Madame Bonaparte at the Tuileries, St.Cloud, and Malmaison. . . . I have had the honour of being in company, i.e. at the same parties, with both his late Majesty George IV, then Prince-Regent, and his present Majesty William IV, then H. R. H. Duke of Clarence; as well as with their royal brothers. I have ridden in a royal duke's carriage, with four horses and three footmen, more than once; and have dined at his table, and drunk the old hock of his late father George III. I have visited the falls of Niagara and Montmorency, the great Reciprocating Fountain in Tennessee, the great Temple of Elephants at Bombay. I have dined with a prince, as well as with a princess; and with a count, a baron, an ambassador, a minister (ordinary and extraordinary) and have travelled with one for some weeks. I have dined with a Charge d'Affaires, and lived with consuls, etc. I have visited and conversed with 'Red Jacket', the great Indian warrior. I have visited and been visited by a bishop.

Hill collected into an arsenal all the arms on the island, made a government of elders and privy councillors, built a prison, passed a Treason Act, and set about purging the island of 'lousy foreigners' other than himself. Having written the laws of Pitcairn and having legislated them, he turned to the matter of John Buffet and George Nobbs. He judged them both guilty of treason, sentenced them to three dozen lashes on 'bare back and breech', and took off his own coat and proceeded to lash John Buffet mercilessly. Nobbs, being ill in bed, escaped his dozens of lashes. It was no time for protest. Hill was Leviathan. Buffet and Nobbs left before he could do something worse.

Perhaps Pitcairn really was blessed by a providence, however, or perhaps the navy took care of its own. After news reached England of what was happening in Pitcairn, HMS *Actaeon* was sent out to make inquiry. As it happened, the *Actaeon* was commanded by Lord Edward Russell, the Duke of Bedford's son. He could be expected to know how close a relation Joshua Hill was. 'Lord' Hill was banished. The Reverend Nobbs was reinstated.

Sir Keith Hancock preferred to call his *Politics in Pitcairn* a parody rather than a parable. In parody the representation of an author is mimicked in order to make it appear ridiculous – especially by applying the mimicry to a ludicrously inappropriate subject. In parable, the narrative leads to larger meanings than the story. Hancock would not have intended to demean Pitcairn's history. He was not the sort of historian to demean anything ordinary or common. He meant rather that the discourse of power, in the ways Machiavelli and Hobbes wrote of it, had the grandeur of princes and states to make it look serious. That Pitcairn should have a politics at all seems slightly ludicrous, when politics is about the way the world is changed by imperial and national power. That Pitcairn's history should be touched by anything universal seems equally ludicrous. The space of our knowledge, the time of our minds are not large enough, many would say, to be filled by something so trivial. History needs to be about something larger. Politics in Pitcairn really is parody.

I beg to differ. The *Bounty,* and with it politics in Pitcairn, is parable rather than parody. Hard-pressed over many years by students and scholars on how such apparently trivial pursuits as the *Bounty* and native pasts could be worth the years of toil, I am prompted to make some final reflections on representation and cultural literacy. On representation, because the past, as we know it, is indistinguishable from the ways in which it is realised in the present. On cultural literacy, because some of the priorities being proclaimed for what we should be literate about disturb me, and because I believe that in our day and age there is no cultural literacy without understanding of the processes of being literate. There is much of parable about ourselves in our peculiarly twentieth-century representations of the past of the *Bounty.*

Scene ii. *Reflection*

REPRESENTATION AND THE CONTRIBUTION OF ERROL FLYNN, CLARK GABLE, MARLON BRANDO AND MEL GIBSON TO CULTURAL LITERACY.

The bicentenary of the mutiny on the *Bounty*, April 28, 1989, has come and gone in the writing of this book. On the day itself you could have joined a charter group and stood on the deck of a reconstructed *Bounty* in the shadow of the volcano on Tofua, and relived all its dramatic moments. You could have learned in a whisper from Tongan guides that John Norton was not, after all, killed in the dusk on Tofua. Why! His descendants are still living on that island over there – or is it that other one?

Or you could have gone on April 28 to the National Maritime Museum in London to enjoy its exhibition of the Mutiny on the *Bounty*. The exhibition was spectacular in ways that would have made de Loutherbourg proud. It was in part an eidophusikon. You could stand in a darkened room, with only the launch, its eighteen figures and the seas before you, and be enveloped with the sights and sounds of that dreadful voyage. Or you could sit at the back of the court martial room and watch and hear an electronic, roboted Lord Hood give the death sentence to an electronically roboted John Millward. Your children could have entertained themselves in a *Bounty* playroom, while you perused the Museum's brilliant treasures – its own priceless objects and others borrowed from a global network of collectors. In an entrepreneurial age, museums need to make small fortunes in order to survive. Their greatest capital is their never-to-be-seen-elsewhere originals. Only in their display cases can be seen the delicacy of colour, the stamp of time, the marks of totally particular moments that can never be reproduced even in the most careful facsimile. You must make a pilgrimage to see the past in a museum. Pilgrims share the 'one-off-manship' of their places of pilgrimage. A pilgrim's representations add the experience of going there to the impression of seeing the past.

There were enough erratic relics of the *Bounty*'s past on display at the National Maritime Museum to make you gasp at the miracles of preservation. There was John Adams' pigtail, John Fryer's telescope, the *Bounty*'s Kendall chronometer, Thomas Huggan's copy of William Buchan's *Domestic Medicine,* Bligh's reading glasses and sword, Elizabeth Bligh's pendant of Tahitian pearls, the watch of the *Pandora*'s surgeon with its hands stopped at the moment of the wreck – 11.12 and 20 seconds. All these relics and the experience of seeing them rouse a primal antiquarianism. These objects, certified for their authenticity by the institutions in which we trust, are facts in action. They offer 'realistic' perspectives. Objects of wonder, they masquerade as history. They represent not so much the past as the art of collecting. Collecting raises its own discourse.

On April 28, you also could have gone to St Petersburg, Florida, and watched a re-enactment of the mutiny on the decks of the *Bounty* reconstructed for Marlon Brando's film. The actors wore 'authentic' costumes – authentically copied from the costumes of the film. Their authenticity was squared, as it were. All took place in a History Park, where the representations of the film were more important than the representation of the event itself. There is a sense that Marlon Brando and Trevor Howard belong to our past in ways that the *Bounty* does not.

That takes me to the question of cultural literacy. Cultural literacy, for those who deplore its disappearance, is that knowledge of the past that sustains the values of the present, that knowledge that 'plucks the mythic chords of memory'. Cultural literacy, in the words of the chief proponent of it, E. D. Hirsch, is 'less a system of skills than a system of information', a sort of database out of which a cultured person or a citizen is made. Dates, events, persons, achievements make up this database, but more importantly, if less explicitly, so do interpretations of what these facts mean. Implicit in this notion of cultural literacy is a demonology of Good and Evil. The history that is meant to pull on the 'mythic chords of memory' emplots the past with unequivocal portraits of Good and Evil in extravagant difference. History, then, is expected to be not interpretive. In the proper sort of history moral judgements can be learned like dates.

'Captain Bligh' is almost a cliché of our times for misused power. If ever there was a demonology embedded in our myths, it is in our twentieth-century images of 'Captain Bligh'. He makes a comfortable sort of villain in a century in which it is the banality of evil with which we do not easily cope. We do not mythologise the banality of evil very well.

The evil of those who hide their personal responsibilities behind the rule and role imposed upon them comes too near our everyday bad faith to let us make myths about it. 'Captain Bligh', however, is easily condemned.

I was reflecting on these paradoxes of cultural literacy during the bicentenary of the Mutiny on the *Bounty* and wondering why an image of 'Captain Bligh' as extraordinarily violent belonged to our twentieth-century cultural literacy and how my image of him in his 'bad language' would fare, when two strange things happened. Well, not strange, but interesting to me who had come so far on this *Bounty* voyage.

The first was the appearance of a cartoon in the *New Yorker*. The drawing in the cartoon caught that most famous scene in the mutiny of the *Bounty*, painted by Robert Dodd, depicting Bligh and his companions in the launch trailing behind the *Bounty*. In the painting, the mutineers are on the quarterdeck throwing swords and clothes to the men in the launch. Christian is poised high on the rear railing behind the *Bounty*'s flag box, breadfruit trees and a jeering crew beside him. Bligh, in his shirt sleeves, is gesticulating at him. In the cartoon, the mutineers all have their fingers in their ears. They are protesting that Bligh must go because they can take no more of his bad language—he ruthlessly throws split infinitives at them! These were further ambivalences of 'bad language' that I had not explored. That, I wanted to say to the cartoonist, J. B. Handelsman, was closer to my notion of cultural literacy.

What is required to laugh at that cartoon? A sense of irony that 'bad language' can have such different meanings? A sense of inconsequentiality that so macho an event as a mutiny could have so fey a cause? – our mythic memory of 'Captain Bligh' acts as foil to the silliness of the interpretation. Mostly it is our enjoyment of the creativity of language, a sense that words do not mirror the world but make it. By that, cultural literacy is more inventive than repetitive. Words, the instruments of our knowing, are the metaphors of reality, not the models of it, not the facts of it. To be culturally literate about the past we must recognise that words themselves have histories across time, across space. There is not a word that does not hold some surprise. History, since its object of observation is words, is always working the surprises in them, the *doubles entendres,* the novelties created by the ever-changing context of their expression. And since words expressed take on a life of their own, have their meaning in the reading of them or the hearing of them, who knows where their life ends? Their expression is the beginning of the death of the author. So

The crew can no longer tolerate Captain Bligh's
ruthless splitting of infinitives.

Figure 20.
Mr Bligh's other bad language. (*The New Yorker,* January 30 1989. Drawing by Handelsman. © 1989. The New Yorker Magazine, Inc.)

much is added to words in the reading – the mood and memory of the
reader, the shape of the page, the size of the font, the linearity of written-
down thought – that the text slides out of the author's possession and
begins a life of its own. All the tricks in the world will not change that

– not monotone, not passionless voice, not facts only facts, not logic, not adversarial poses. 'In the beginning was the Word and the Word was God' is the way we have mythologised our hankering for eternal authorship. But the 'Word' that is 'God' is the only word that has never been spoken. A word spoken is speech, in time, in place. It always has two dimensions – its language (its system, its grammar, the commonality that joins two speakers) and its expression (its speech, all that adds occasion and circumstance). Cultural literacy based on only one of those dimensions is a fraud. Reader, if you have come thus far with me, you will be no clearer than I on where the 'Mutiny on the *Bounty*' begins and ends. But that is the ultimate realism of our shared cultural literacy.

There was another strange/interesting occurrence in my celebration of the metric moments of the *Bounty*'s mutiny. It was the resignation speech on American Public Radio of U.S. Secretary of Education William Bennett. He had played a controversial role in President Ronald Reagan's administration and was now, in September 1988, leaving office. Mr Bennett was a strong proponent of E. D. Hirsch's brand of cultural literacy, and had voiced a fear being voiced in hundreds of places around the world, not just the United States, that children of today are ignorant of their history. There should be more history in American schools, Mr Bennett had been saying, but 'real history', history that children could learn. Every American child, he was saying now on Public Radio, should know, for example, why there was a mutiny on the *Bounty*. 'Mr. Bennett', I wanted to shout in this my moment of relevance, 'alien though I am, I am here and ready to tell every American child why there was a mutiny on the *Bounty*. I am writing a book that every American child should have.' Ah, well! Even an academic historian can dream.

I cannot really say why Mr Bennett thought every American boy and girl should know why there was a mutiny on the *Bounty*. My prejudices suggested to me that Mr Bennett would not have been the first in President Reagan's administration to confuse history with some product of the film industry. Charles Laughton's 'Captain Bligh' and Clark Gable's 'Fletcher Christian' in the 1935 Metro-Goldwyn-Mayer film *Mutiny on the Bounty* were perfect examples of the sort of demonology that in Mr Bennett's eyes made for 'real history'. 'A cardinal principle of education', Mr Bennett used to say, 'is social efficiency'. 'Facts, conditions, theories, activities that do not contribute rather directly to the appreciation of human betterment have no claim.' 'Our young must be taught the golden ideals of

liberty, justice, equality, limited government, betterment of human conditions, and they should know that a large part of the world thinks and
acts according to other principles.' The rub, of course, is whether human
betterment is advanced by learning these judgements like dates or by
experiencing what is true in them or what is not. And what is the measure
of 'social efficiency'? How efficient is it to learn the representation without
the representing? With the prejudice that demonology is destructive of
the values it aims to protect, and in the hope that in describing the representing as well as the representation I would make a more creative contribution to cultural literacy, I began the last phase of my *Bounty* voyage.
The Center for the Study of the Performing Arts of the New York Public
Library holds part of the Metro-Goldwyn-Mayer archives. I started there.
The film censors of the State of New York have collected some 55,000
scripts of films in the Cultural Archives, Albany, New York. I made
inquiries there as well.

There have been five Bounty films. The first was a 1916 Australian silent
movie, *The Mutiny on the Bounty*. It is extant now only in stills. Raymond
Longford, a pioneer of the Australian film industry, produced the film
and shot it in Rotorua, New Zealand, and Norfolk Island. From the cast
of characters and the reviews, it can be surmised that the film made some
dramatic play on the paradox of Bligh's brutality as captain of the *Bounty*
and his tenderness as father and husband within his family. 'Mrs Bligh',
'Mrs Heywood' and 'Nessie Heywood' got to play their parts. The paradox
touched on the dark days of Bligh's losses in his family, on Elizabeth
Bligh's bewilderment and on the Heywood women's terror at the threat
of the loss of son and brother. This has not been the usual paradox played
in representation of the *Bounty*. The paradox that most often came to be
stressed was the apparent contradiction between the brilliance of Bligh as
a seaman and his abject failure as a commander. This latter paradox, in
the way of *realpolitik,* has provided more acceptable excuses for Bligh. In
any case, the critics of seventy-five years ago lauded the historical accuracy
of the 1916 film, but deplored its weak human interest and lack of public
appeal. Perhaps, even then, its ambiguities of human motivations were
less popular than demonology.

The second *Bounty* film was another Australian version, this one released in 1933. It was Charles Chauvel's *In the Wake of the Bounty*. Chauvel
constructed an early drama documentary in which he mixed the story of

the mutiny as narrated by Michael Byrne, the half-blind Irish fiddler, with a travelogue on Chauvel's visit to Pitcairn Island in 1932. In some desperation at a turning point in the film industry, Chauvel had been looking for an exotic location – anywhere – that had not been filmed. The North and South Poles had been 'done', darkest Africa and Timbuktu as well. Chauvel's partner in his company, called 'Expeditionary Films', had pulled out and stayed over in Hollywood to film the lion farms of the movie studios, saying that 'when everything else is exhausted, the roar of wild animals will bring them out – even on cold nights'. Sound in itself was then a novelty. Chauvel decided to make a series of films on remote islands – Tristan da Cunha, Juan Fernandez, Easter Island – and stumbled on Pitcairn. He remembered that, while visiting friends on a cattle station in Queensland, he had spent time rooting around in dusty station ledgers that logged such agricultural data as the planting of cereal crops and the inoculation of stock. He came across another sort of log. It was Bligh's own manuscript log of the *Providence,* his second breadfruit voyage. The owners of the station, the Nutting family, were descendants of Bligh – Mrs Lucy O'Connell Nutting subsequently donated the log of the *Providence* to the Mitchell Library, Sydney.

In the Wake of the Bounty was premiered at Prince Edward Theatre, Sydney, March 15, 1933, after some trouble with the censors about bare-breasted Tahitians and a graphic flogging scene. Tasmanian-born Errol Flynn made his debut as Fletcher Christian. There are several versions of the story of how Flynn came to make his debut – his photogenic potential was noted as he displayed his torso on Bondi Beach near Sydney, says one; he was modelling men's suits in a filmed commercial, says another. A third seems attractive for its ethnographic focus. Flynn had been captaining a New Guinea coastal trader working the tobacco crops at the time, the story goes. A German anthropologist, Dr H. F. Erbe, making an ethnographic film on head-hunting on the Sepik River, featured Flynn as captain of the vessel ferrying the expedition up the river. Chauvel saw the film, recognised Flynn's photogenic, if not thespian, qualities and offered him fifty pounds by telegram from Tahiti via Sydney and Port Moresby to play Fletcher Christian. 'I was without the least idea of what I was doing, except I was supposed to be an actor', Flynn said later. 'I had touched on something the world called an art form and it affected me deeply'. To his delight he found that movie actors, unlike stage actors, had to learn only those lines necessary for the day's shooting. 'It was a big discovery in a way', he said. Later – and through the alcoholic haze that began to envelop his life – he claimed that his family owned a sword of Fletcher Christian, which was probably not true, and that his mother was related to Edward Young, the mutineer from the West Indies whom Bligh described as having a 'dark and rather bad look', which we have no reason to doubt. Flynn happened to be in Sydney for the release of *In the Wake of the Bounty*. The theatre manager offered him two pounds to appear on the stage. Flynn said he would do anything for two pounds and appeared on the stage decked out in a bizarre naval uniform, wearing what he claimed to be one of only two wigs in Sydney, and looking, in his own words, like the elderly keeper of a whorehouse on King William St that he was prone to frequent. *In the Wake of the Bounty* never got much of a showing. MGM bought it up to clear the ground for their 1935 version. They parcelled it into two travelogue shorts on Pitcairn and included bits of it in their trailers for *Mutiny on the Bounty*.

There are three other *Bounty* films that belong more properly to modern cultural literacy. Seen as a trio, they have each proffered a different narrative to the same events. The 1935 Charles Laughton/Clark Gable version, with Laughton portraying a pathologically cruel Bligh and Gable a manly, honourable Christian, displayed the classic conflict between tyranny and a just cause. The struggle on the *Bounty* was a moral and an ideological one. The 1962 Trevor Howard/Marlon Brando version had Brando, clearly out of his director's control, lisping his way through the role of Christian as a gentleman fop finding true honour in standing up against Bligh's populist austerity. The struggle on the *Bounty* was political. In the 1984 Anthony Hopkins/Mel Gibson version, 'Mad Max' is tamed to a petulant, postering Christian with a Robinson Crusoe complex, while Bligh is a man bedevilled by nothing so much as his own vaguely homosexual jealousies. The struggle on the *Bounty* was psychological.

No use displaying all the inaccuracies of these versions, it was their purpose to be inaccurate. They could not say what they wanted to say without invention. The 1935 Laughton/Gable version needed the hyperbole reached by laying at Bligh's feet every violent and unjust happening in the early modern British navy, needed to meld Bligh and Captain Edwards into one character, construct a Bligh who recaptures his own mutineers and brings them back to England in his own 'Pandora's Box'. The 1962 Howard/Brando version needed to invent a trigger to the whole mutiny in Bligh's inhumane act of kicking a ladle of water out of Christian's hands as he comforted a dying seaman maddened by drinking sea water because of Bligh's austerities; just as it needed tons of white sand transported from the New Jersey coast and spilled over Tahitian black beaches to make a truly seductive Hollywood Pacific island. The 1984 Hopkins/Gibson version needed to transpose all the disciplinary issues on the *Bounty* to the master of the ship, John Fryer, and away from Bligh, so that Bligh and Christian could get on with their teasing one another.

Authenticity in each of these movie versions was a propman's concern, not a scriptwriter's goal. Exact re-creation of the visual environment made a living museum for the actors' actions. What actually happened was subordinated to what it would have looked like if it had happened. The *Campaign Books* that publicity agents put into the hands of the media – with suggested headlines about the film, potted reviews, catchy phrases and insider's information on the production – were full of the energy and cost that it took to be visually accurate. A reconstructed 'Bounty' was the proud accomplishment of each of them. The 1935 version had two reconstructed vessels. One was a full-sized replica. The other was scaled down to eighteen feet and sailed by two men below deck. The 1962 'Bounty' became the living museum at St Petersburg, where the public were invited to join 200,000 visitors a year to 'retrace history', 'experience the romance and excitement of the South Seas', 'relive stark human drama', 'hear the voices of Bligh and Christian', hear 'decks creak in soft tropic air', hear 'the sighs of mutineers in paradise'. Visitors could enter the Teloptikon enshrined in a grass hut and be engulfed in the sights and sounds of the voyage of this new 'Bounty' from the shipyards at Lunenburg, Nova Scotia, to Tahiti. 'Your children's children will not see the like again. Nor will you.' De Loutherbourg still lives! Eidophusikon, Teleptikon – realism is the wonder a viewer feels that sights and sounds can be so right. Historical accuracy is the antiquarian thrill that the buttons on an eighteenth-century coat are correct, that an eighteenth-century wooden leg – for someone who in real life never had one – is authentic.

To film critics, there really has been only one Mutiny on the *Bounty* film – the 1935 Laughton/Gable version. All the other adaptations have been measured against the brilliant clarity of Charles Laughton's portrayal of 'Captain Bligh' forcing impossible choices on honourable manly spirits. Each of the later versions has been declared unhistorical by the critics for omitting all that the 1935 version invented.

The 1935 *Mutiny on the Bounty* came out of Metro-Goldwyn-Mayer studios. Louis Mayer of MGM was, in the phrase of a Hollywood historian, Neal Gabler, one of those 'Jews who invented Hollywood'. Mayer had created MGM's extraordinary success out of his chauvinistic view of American culture. He made movie versions of Norman Rockwell stills. That is, his films were full of the fantasies of stylised beauty, idealised families and beatified mothers. Greta Garbo, Norma Shearer, Joan Crawford, Jean Harlow, Myrna Loy were some of his female stars. Mayer was not enthusiastic when Irving Thalberg, his vice-president, suggested a film about the *Bounty*. He did not want to produce a film in which mutineers were heroes. Nor did he like the notion of a film in which the women were uncivilised natives seducing good order. MGM had never made an outdoor adventure film, he protested. In any case, women chose the entertainment of their families and they would not choose violence.

Irving Thalberg had been Mayer's young genius. He had masterminded the success of MGM by providing out of its immense wealth the atmosphere in which talent could thrive. F. Scott Fitzgerald had registered his adulation for Thalberg's genius in *The Last Tycoon*. Thalberg's pale intensity –he had been a 'blue baby' – haunted Hollywood with its tragic sense of mortality. This made it difficult to play the usual cutthroat politics with him. But in 1931 he had begun to split with Mayer. Then, in 1932, at thirty-two years of age, he had a heart attack. Mayer could not let him go. Mayer could not let him stay. Thalberg went to Germany to convalesce and undergo surgery on his tonsils. In Germany he saw violent anti-Semitic demonstrations outside his hotel and discovered that his German doctor was reluctant to operate on him, fearing the consequences should an internationally famous Jew come to harm under his knife.

Then Thalberg was back in Hollywood. These were Depression days. Upton Sinclair and the 'leftist' scriptwriters were forming unions and writing scripts that disputed the unquestioning conservative politics of the film industry. There was a widespread questioning of the pristine American values that MGM had so consciously instilled. Thalberg, out of his German experience, feared fascism, but to him communism among the left scriptwriters was an even greater threat. In the internal politics of MGM, David Selznick had begun to take Thalberg's place. Left without easy access to the stars of MGM studios, Thalberg established a special unit of his own. He began a series of expensive, special and masterful films – *The Barretts of Wimpole St, Ruggles of Red Gap, Les Misérables*. His chief coup, in his own mind, was in bringing the sophistication and class of British acting to Hollywood, principally in the figure of Charles Laughton. Thalberg's Anglophilia was part studio politics, and part cultural cringe. But his sense of a world in tension between fascism and communism was to give a decisively strong political dimension to the sort of representation *Mutiny on the Bounty* came to be.

Against Mayer's fears about how women would receive the film, Thalberg had no scruples. 'It doesn't matter that there are no women in the cast. People are fascinated by cruelty and that's why the Mutiny will have appeal.' And in any case there were more than male sexual fantasies to titillate. The critics' first judgement on the *Mutiny on the Bounty* was that it was 'no woman's picture'. A second viewing, however, suggested to them that more footage in the film was devoted to Clark Gable's 'gams' and Franchot Tone's 'manly stems' than was ever given to Marlene Dietrich's legs. Women's sexual fantasies at this time may not yet have been marketed with anything more than a wink and a nudge, but the managers of Loew's theatres all over the United States remarked that the proportion of women among the hundreds of thousands who saw the film in its first week of release was high. They thought they knew why that was so.

Thalberg's explicit answer to Mayer's fears about the socially destabilising effect of a film idealising mutineers is not recorded. His real answer was to make a film in which the hero was not the mutineers at all, but the British Navy, and a British Navy that was a weapon of freedom in a threatened world. The Fade-In Forward and the Fade-Out Ending made that meaning of the film quite clear.

The Fade-In Forward scrolling before the audience read:

In December, 1787, HMS Bounty lay in Portsmouth Harbour on the eve of departure for Tahiti in the uncharted waters of the Great South Sea.
The Bounty's mission was to procure breadfruit trees for transplanting to the West Indies as cheap food for slaves.
Neither ship nor breadfruit reached the West Indies. Mutiny prevented it – mutiny against the abuse of harsh eighteenth century sea law. But this mutiny, famous in history and legend, helped bring about a new discipline, based upon mutual respect between officers and men, by which Britain's sea power is maintained as security for all who pass upon the seas.

What did it matter that the whole British fleet mutinied just ten years after the *Bounty* and thirty-six men were hanged? What did it matter that flogging went on in the navy for forty more years? Thalberg's message was that the act of mutiny, wrong in itself, had had good effects. The reason was that institutions of power are ultimately responsive to men of good will.

This didactic message of the *Mutiny on the Bounty* was played out in the final scenes. The writers, Charles Nordhoff and James Norman Hall, from whose trilogy on the *Bounty* the script of the film had been taken, had invented a character, 'Roger Byam'. Byam was their narrator. In all the things he did and that were done to him, Byam was Peter Heywood of the real *Bounty*. The film script dispensed with a narrator but kept 'Roger Byam' as a midshipman, played by Franchot Tone. The film ends with Byam making an impassioned speech to the officers of the court martial, just before being condemned to death. Bligh is made to be present at the court martial, as he had been also been made to be captain of the *Pandora*. Franchot Tone played the whole scene in one long filming. It was one of those famous Hollywood 'Cut it. Can it' feats. The whole film crew stood around and applauded:

Captain Bligh you've told your story of mutiny on the Bounty, how men plotted against you. Seized your ship, cast you adrift in an open boat. A great venture in science brought to nothing, two British ships lost.
But there's another story, Captain Bligh, of ten coconuts and two cheeses. The story of a man who robbed his seamen, cursed them, flogged them, not to punish them, but to break their spirit. A story of greed and tyranny and anger against it! Of what it cost! One man, My Lord, would not endure such tyranny. That's why you hounded him, that's why you hate him, hate his friends. And that's why you're beaten. Fletcher Christian is still free.
But Christian lost, too, My Lord. God knows he's judged himself more harshly than you could judge him. I say to his father, he was my friend. No finer man ever lived. I don't try to justify his crime, his mutiny. But I condemn the tyranny that drove him to it. I don't speak for myself alone, nor for the men you've condemned. I speak in their names, in Fletcher Christian's name, for all men at sea. These men don't ask for comfort, they don't ask for safety! If they could speak to you they'd say; let us choose to do our duty willingly, not the choice of a slave, but the choice of free Englishmen. They ask only the freedom that England expects for every man. Oh, if one man among you believed that. One man! He could command the fleets of England, he could sweep the seas for

England. If he called his men to their duty, not by flogging their backs, but by lifting up their hearts! Their hearts . . . that's all.

Lord Hood then condemns the mutineers to death. As the court disperses, Hood passes Bligh and refuses to shake his hand. Hood says: 'I must admire your seamanship and courage, but . . .'

The scene changes to St James' Palace where Sir Joseph Banks is pleading for the life of Byam before King George. 'We do not exaggerate when we say that a new understanding between officers and men has come to the Fleet. By returning Byam to duty, your Majesty will confirm that understanding, and not for today only, but for all time to come.'

Then the cameras move to a naval vessel. Roger Byam, now pardoned, is coming aboard as midshipman to one of the ships whose captain, Colpoys, had earlier condemned him to death.

[Read the filming instructions in the script in the following way: CS = Close Shot; o.s. = offscreen; b.g. = background; LAP = Overlap; ELS = Extreme Long Shot; MLS = Medium Long Shot]

No. Feet Frames

			Colpoys: Very glad to have you with us, lad.
42	709	2	**Byam:** Thank you, sir.
43			CS – Edwards and Byam – they shake hands and speak – Edwards exits left – Officer enters – shakes hands with Byam – then exits right – CAMERA MOVES up on Byam – he looks o.s. – smiles – turns to b.g.
			LAP Dissolve into
			Edwards: May I, Byam?
			Byam: Of course.
			Edwards: We're off for the Mediterranean, lad. We'll sweep the seas for England.
44	746	1	ELS – Ships of the British Fleet moving forward –
45			MLS – Shooting up to the sails of the ship – the British flag waving – superimposed title:
	765	0	THE END
			FADE OUT

The significance of these scenes did not escape the critics. Richard Watt, writing for the *New York Herald Tribune*, scoffed at 'Hollywood's romantic crush on Empire' and deplored its servile politeness and 'cringe in the presence of foreigners'. He looked forward to the sequel, 'Mutiny on the Pinafore'. No doubt Mayer escaped his dilemma and Thalberg plucked 'mythic chords of memory' in such dissolves and fade-outs. 'Captain Bligh' had become a metonymy of the right sort of institutional evil against which one can rebel.

Without labouring this point by introducing an elaborate aside, let me briefly consider another mutiny film, *The Caine Mutiny*, made in 1954. It also resolved a number of Mayer's dilemmas about idealising mutineers but in a significantly different way. *Caine Mutiny* was directed by Edward Dmytryk, one of the Hollywood Ten. As one of the 'Ten' he had been exposed to the vitriol of the McCarthy hearings and had been imprisoned for contempt of Congress after refusing to give information about writers with communist leanings in Hollywood. In 1954, Dmytryk had just been allowed to work again after his imprisonment, recantation and naming names. The 'Captain Bligh' of *The Caine Mutiny* was Captain Queeg (Humphrey Bogart), a weak, pathetic and paranoid character. And the 'Fletcher Christian' was Lieutenant Keefer (Fred MacMurray). Keefer was written into the script as an intellectual, by Hollywood standards, and it was he who persuaded the innocent Lt Steve Maryk (Van Johnson) to depose Queeg. It was Maryk, not Keefer, who was subsequently court-martialled, but was freed when Queeg was humiliated in court by a young Jewish lawyer, Greenwald (played by Jose Ferrer), who hated what he was forced to do in destroying Queeg. Keefer in the end has a cocktail thrown in his face for his cunning cowardice and is accused by Greenwald of being the true cause of the mutiny. There were no heroic mutineers in *The Caine Mutiny*. The message was that legitimate professional authority in a weak Queeg was calling for help. It was betrayed by self-interested liberals who had no loyalties to institutions. Keefer could have been a hero like 'Roger Byam' had he made his deferences to the institution's hegemony, had he scotched his own cynicism and been more trusting of power's good will.

In the Laughton/Gable *Mutiny on the Bounty*, Bligh's pathological cruelty made room for a hero. But the real hero finally was not an individual but an institution. Authoritarian and unbending as it was, the institution of the navy was portrayed as listening to committed men of good will, but only to committed men. Relativism, the agreement that things can be changed, comes in institutions only after an absolute submission. Then the mimesis of these responsive and commonsensical institutions makes you feel warm all over. Fade Out.

There were others reluctant to be involved in the filming of *Mutiny on the Bounty*. Clark Gable was even more reluctant than Louis Mayer. 'I'm a realistic kind of actor', he complained. 'I've never played a costume picture in my life. Now you want me to wear a pigtail and velvet kneepants and shoes with silver buckles. The audience will laugh me off the screen. And I'll be damned if I'll shave off my moustache because the British navy didn't allow them. This moustache has been damned lucky for me.' Gable had other problems too. He felt his accent would be flat against Laughton's. And he was uncertain how he would play the gentleman against Laughton's performance of violence. His macho father had always said that he would become a sissy if he became an actor. His problem was how he could be Good against violent Evil without being feminine – and to do it in kneepants that showed how bandied his legs really were.

Gable need not have worried. His 'gams' were seen as manly rather than bandy. His patent virility overrode his deficiencies in the techniques of acting. The tinge of rascal in his gentlemanly role made his Christian an American hero. Wallace Beery had been considered for the role of Bligh but had been rejected because he was 'too American'. It is significant that none of the American versions of the Mutiny of the *Bounty* could cope with an American actor as Bligh. The 'mythic chords of memory' were plucked by older, more colonial demonologies. Gable's Christian, full of sexuality, had a chauvinist dimension as well.

Laughton was not reluctant to play the role of Bligh, but once he had begun he was stricken with self-doubts. All the scenes of the film involving the cast were shot on Catalina Island off the California coast. The logistical feats accomplished during these eighty-eight days of filming became, like the price paid for a masterpiece in an art gallery, a sign of the film's greatness. Five old sailing ships were assembled there as well as the reproductions of the *Bounty*. Speedboats and seaplanes ferried visitors and supplies to the encampment. The filming took on a life of its own, as the crew and cast managed the peaks and troughs of intensive activity and vacuous boredom. The very first day of shooting exploded in a savage dispute between Gable and Laughton. Laughton had begun to play his Bligh with arrogant dismissiveness, looking off screen and not at Gable. Gable thought Laughton's acting was a kind of soliloquy, in which he,

Gable, was being reduced to an extra. Gable also punched a makeup man for some comment made while powdering his face. Meanwhile, Laughton was beginning to feel physically ill with the loathsomeness of the character he was creating. By telephone and seaplane visits, Thalberg managed to quieten Laughton's and Gable's rivalries and promote their self-confidence, only to find the actors turning their venom on the director, Frank Lloyd, who wanted to make the *Bounty* ship – or so they thought – the star of the movie.

Laughton's 'Bligh' dominated the sets of the movie. Soon, comics in nightclubs and on radio began to play the ironies of his chilling phrases. 'Mr Christian, come here!' became one of those catch phrases, raising a sort of nervous laughter at the sentiments and an appreciation of the realism of the caricature. The audiences could laugh off the seriousness of their engagement in the poetics of the Mutiny on the *Bounty* in a caricature of a caricature, in a mimicry of Laughton mimicking Bligh. Those that filmed the *Mutiny on the Bounty* were dominated by something other than the figure of Bligh. They were awed by Laughton's cultural literacy. They savoured his historical diligence but, more, the historical continuities that he was able to establish with Bligh. Laughton told of going to Gieves, the military tailors on Savile Row, London, with inquiries about eighteenth-century naval uniforms. He was told by the clerk assisting him that, if he would wait, they would check Mr Bligh's measurements from an account on the last uniform Bligh had ordered. Laughton himself lost fifty-five pounds in some historical awe at his discovery. Then when the propmen went looking for something as arcane and foreign to their experience as a Book of Common Prayer, they were staggered to find that Laughton not only knew of it but could recite passages from it because of his brief experience in the navy. Of an evening on Catalina he would read plays or declaim Shakespeare. Laughton had been educated by the Jesuits at Stonyhurst and been strongly affected by their long theatrical tradition. His theatrical ambitions had disturbed his parents and undermined their ambitions for him to be an hotel clerk and manager. He came to Catalina Island with an educated touch of class that mesmerised those around him.

Frank Lloyd, the director, had been shrewdly entrepreneurial about the *Mutiny on the Bounty*. He had seen the potential of Charles Nordhoff and James Norman Hall's fictional trilogy, *Mutiny on the Bounty, Men against the Sea* and *Pitcairn Island*. He had bought the film rights for $12,500 and had offered them to Irving Thalberg on condition that he direct the film.

The *Bounty* trilogy had been a publishing triumph. An estimated twenty-five million people read the books even before seeing the film. It was serialised in the *Saturday Evening Post.* There seems to have been hardly a second-hand bookshop anywhere in the world where one could not buy copies. (My copies, before me now as I write, come from the China Coast Club, Hongkong, the Australian Red Cross Society NSW Book Depot, the Argosy Lending Library, 1290 Hutt St., City, Sydney – 'Latest Books Arriving Weekly. Books are constantly fumigated'.) Nordhoff and Hall had made their names as writers by writing a history of the Lafayette Escadrille, the volunteer American squadron flying for France in the First World War. They had been flyers in that squadron. They had persuaded publishers to advance funds for them to do a tour of the Pacific, following Robert Louis Stevenson's example. Settled in Tahiti, they were distracted from their broader project by the *Bounty*. 'Rare primeval stuff of which romance is made', they wrote.

Thalberg gave one of the most prominent scriptwriters in Hollywood, Carey Wilson, responsibility for the script, but took it away from him when he discovered that Wilson was moonlighting for Sam Goldwyn and working on two scripts at the same time. Talbot Jennings finished it, with much input from Thalberg himself. Lloyd's preoccupation was always with the representation of the realism of the ship and the exotic background of Tahiti. Thalberg's preoccupation was managing the dramatic intensity of the passions of the mutiny.

To effect his realism, Lloyd took the reconstructed *Bounty* and *Pandora* to Tahiti with sixty technicians, nine camera outfits and a hundreds tons of equipment. At Tahiti he engaged 2,500 'semi-savage natives' as extras. He supplied them with every spear and club that Hollywood prop warehouses could provide. He came, like Bligh, prepared to barter for their labour. Bligh had had adzes, shirts and beads. Lloyd had birdcages, snakes-in-a-box, harmonicas, mirrors, pocket-knives, wristwatches, celluloid dolls, straw hats, bracelets, necklaces, earrings and Spanish combs. Unfortunately, nature's own realism played its part. The first 80,000 feet of scenic and sound film were destroyed by mildew and had to be done again. Lloyd's own efforts to transplant full-grown breadfruit trees back to Catalina Island failed against the social realism of California plant quarantine laws. He had to be content with papier-mâché copies made frenetically as the customs officers destroyed the trees. Lloyd's true love was the *Bounty* itself and the portrayal on it of the rhythms of naval life. Ten athletes from California college football teams and the recent Los Angeles Olympic games were trained in seamanship and clambered the *Bounty*'s rigging with speed and dexterity.

Historicity, however, needed something more. No director, after all, could be totally unaware of how realism is invented. Lloyd needed an authenticating experience. Representation through intimacy, one is tempted to call it – the cultural literacy that comes from knowing something happened in the past because one has touched a thing or a document that has survived. Lloyd's authenticating experience came in a strange place. He was sitting in the Blue Lagoon Cafe in Papeete, bemoaning with Norman Hall that he had looked the world over for Bligh's logs and had not found them. A 'little white-haired lady' at the next table overheard him and said 'I know where they are.' That lady is a figure of some reverence in Pacific History circles. She was Ida Leeson, Librarian of the Mitchell Library, Sydney, NSW. She was new in her position and was making the library one of the great repositories of material connected with William Bligh. Not that seeing the copies of Bligh's logs made any difference to Lloyd's representation. Seeing them, however, made him confident that what he was doing was true.

Thalberg's interventions concerned the dramatic realism of the representation of the mutiny. He was concerned with the poetics of the portrayal of the 'true' Bligh and how something made 'true' by extravagant caricature could be believable. He made Bligh's pathological and inhuman cruelty believable by inventing two clowns, Smith, the cook (Herbert Mundin), and 'Bacchus' or Thomas Huggan, the surgeon (Dudley Digges). The cook's continual dilemma in getting rid of the slops against the wind underscored the ambivalences of Bligh's language and the absurdity of his rages. Bacchus' ever-changing story of how he got his wooden leg offered his peccadilloes as the human foil to Bligh's righteous evil. The cook, Bacchus and Bligh all made one another believable.

Not many Hollywood films are reflective on their own poetics. But there seemed to be an almost missionary zeal in proving the film's historical authenticity. The *Campaign Books* were full of the film's accuracies and of efforts to make it factual. The producers went so far as to produce a Teacher's Manual for distribution through U.S. high schools. It is an interesting primer in the sort of cultural literacy Hollywood thought it was promoting. Dr William Lewis of Weegahie High School, Newark, New Jersey, helped produce it and was invited to observe some of the filming. The Manual begins with the protest that there is 'nothing in it of dogmatic theory, but merely helpful suggestions which may serve the dual purpose of aiding the teacher and of enlarging the literary knowledge of the student'. It suggests that students use as texts the Nordhoff and Hall trilogy, Sir John Barrow's *Mutiny on the* Bounty (available in World Classics in 1928), Owen Rutter's *Trial of the* Bounty *Mutineers* (1931), Lord Byron's *The Island*. The Manual suggests to the teacher that the questionnaires requiring answers from students are designed to help generate impressions of the film, to alert them to indicators of judgement, tastes and emotional development, and to act as an introduction to training in story and setting.

Students in one set of questions were asked to describe the themes of the film and its leading characters in a sentence. They were asked to describe the most dramatic scene, the scenes they liked best, the 'scene [that] best displays the art of the motion picture', who of the players acted the best, whether the mutiny was justified. Ah yes! and 'Did you like the ending? Give reasons.' The questions, not to put too great an emphasis on Hollywood's short-term educational ambitions, were small exercises in cultural literacy, small lessons in discovering the cultural operators in narrative forms. What were – to ask a question that can have only surmise for an answer – the cultural functions of the ending? Surmise: the warm optimism that came from 'Roger Byam's' reinstatement, the ultimate goodwill of institutions of power, the inspiration that came from true justice being done and righteous patriotism expressed find rooms in the 'memory palace' of the public mind. The hegemony of commonsense makes the narrative naturally believable, even mythic.

The second set of questions in the Teacher's Manual concerned critical skills in interpretation. Students were asked 'In what way does the film differ from Nordhoff and Hall? In what respect does Nordhoff and Hall differ from actual history?' Students were invited to make living museums of themselves – as press-ganged sailors or as Bligh himself or as a native of Tahiti or as a seaman of the *Pandora* – and to record their experiences. They were asked as well to put themselves at various points of moral dilemma in the narrative – would they have gone with Bligh in the launch or stayed on the *Bounty*? – would they have waited at Tahiti or gone with Christian? The thrust of these questions was to stress familiarity rather than difference. And where authenticity of the narrative was explicitly questioned – in the first question about the differing histories of the mutiny – it is interesting to follow the answers in the crib. Facticity and difference in the answer are subordinated entirely to effectiveness in expressing the meaning of the narrative.

So when the students had read the fiction of Nordhoff and Hall, the histories of Barrow and Rutter and seen the film, they inevitably would have discovered that much of what Nordhoff and Hall had described as the cruelty of other British naval captains and of what Captain Edwards had done on the *Pandora* had been made to be Bligh's responsibility in the film. There was an 'obvious reason' for this, the crib answer said: 'The actions of Captains Courtney and Edwards were typical of the class of ship commanders to which Bligh belonged. The transference of these actions to Bligh allowed a closeknit, strong and more comprehensive study of Bligh's character and thus the exclusion of characters, who, having little or no part in the actual story, might have possibly confused the issue.' Ambivalence, multivalency, alternate interpretation do tend to create a different sort of cultural literacy than demonology.

Audience response when the film was released in November 1935 was extraordinary. In an unprecedented move, all of Loew's theatres showed only this film. Record attendances were reported from every city where it was shown. Within six weeks 600,000 people had seen it. The Capitol Theatre in New York, with its 5,400 seats always filled, held the film for an unheard-of four weeks, and ended its showing only when Harpo Marx made unpleasant scenes about the delay of the premieres of *A Night at the Opera*. Five hundred stores around the Capitol reported sales up by 40 percent. The Depression was firmly upon them. The headlines about the film stressed the extravagance of its cost, the size of its returns, the consequences of its success – employment, sales, relief to the needy from MGM's American Christmas and Relief Fund. Hopefulness in bad times was as much the film's contribution to cultural literacy as its demonology.

'No woman's picture', 'hard-boiled', 'strong meat' were among the critics' responses. There was some complaint that all the 'flogging and torture stuff' made the film 131 minutes long and posed problems for theatre managers in serving peanuts and popcorn. Doyens among the critics – Joseph Alsop and Otis Ferguson – thought the film brilliant. Laughton was overpowering, the 'ship a living thing'. The only sour note came from Richard Watts of the *New York Herald Tribune*, who, on a second viewing, remarked that much of the film was 'slightly embarrassing nonsense'. *Variety* offered a reflection on the sort of cultural literacy with which the film would be seen: 'The Polynesians are considered members of the white race by many experts, but whether they are so held by the majority of laymen is questionable. And Gable's and Tone's girlfriends are very much Polynesian in appearance. But it is all done so neatly the kicks won't be numerous'. Gable had sailed into New York for the premiere after a much-publicised lubricious cruise of South America. There was much smirking condescension in the reviews as they remarked on how this 'no woman's picture' roused female sexuality. Gable's 'gams' and Tone's 'manly stems' were seen to be as much a triumph of theatricality as the use of 'unspoiled girls rather than Hollywood temptresses'.

We have no 'cultural literacy meter' to measure the various poetics of representation in the 1935 *Mutiny on the Bounty*. What 'mystic chords of memory', we might have asked, does lubricity play? What poetic did 'gams' and 'unspoiled' girls contribute to the narrative and its reading? The images of mind of the millions who saw the film in its immediate cultural context are gone. Our own images are cluttered with fifty-five years of experience in between. Let me be modest, then, in my certainties, and merely list what I think was there to be read: a sense that the extravagant violence of authority excused rebellion but did not legitimate it; a sense that institutions of power were ultimately goodwilled and responded to the ideals of men committed to them; a sense that the historical narrative is not divorced from the total ambience of its representation – that its meaning can be found as much in its cost of production as in its plots; a sense that historicity is more a matter of visual consistency than interpretation. Above all, in this period of technological revolution in representation through sound film, there was a growing confidence in the realism of illusions. Five old hulks in a bay of Catalina Island could be the British fleet at Portsmouth. Tahitians at Matavai on Tahiti could appear to converse with 'Fletcher Christian' at 'Matavai' on Catalina. A set on a bobbing barge in an open sea could be the deck of the *Bounty* so long as the light and the camera angles were right. Illusions make things true; truth does not dispel illusion.

There seems common agreement that the 1962 film of the *Mutiny on the Bounty* was the beginning of the end of Marlon Brando as an actor. The whole venture was grossly decadent – from its $27 million cost, the sensual wallowing of the whole crew for months at Tahiti, Brando's use of his $6 million to buy a Tahitian island (Tetiaroa, to which Millward,

Burkitt and Churchill had deserted), his marriage to the Tahitian 'un-spoiled girl' (actually Mexican) who had played Franchot Tone's girlfriend in the 1935 version, Brando's unprofessional behaviour in the filming, the near-obscene cultural arrogance in changing Tahitian landscape, di-verting rivers, making black sands white, the presumption of the film-makers that their own sexual fantasies of the Tahitians were the reality. The lowest of many low points in the film undoubtedly came when, to depict the irrational conflict between Bligh and Christian, Christian was ordered to copulate with the 'King's daughter' so that Bligh could get his breadfruit. A smirking Brando reports his obedience, peeling a banana, with 'Rule Britannia' playing in the background.

To do him justice, Brando never wanted to do the film. It was the producer's decadence and greed that made him accept Brando's near-im-possible terms. Certainly Brando did not want to do the adventure film constructed by Eric Ambler's script. Brando wanted to do a film with what his more sardonic critics called 'more philosophy' in it. Brando did not even want to be Fletcher Christian. He wanted to be John Adams, the final survivor of all the mutineers on Pitcairn Island. The 'philosophy' he wanted to present was not that of heroic mutiny against outrageous tyranny, but the mystery of violence in human nature. Even when the mutineers had had a chance to make an island paradise on Pitcairn, they were self-destructive. Brando wanted to show 'man's inhumanity to man'. 'I wanted to draw a parallel with what's happening in Africa today,' he said.

In the end, all was total disaster. Brando's liberalism did not fare well at all. The film, wrote the *New York Times* critic, was full of 'hoarse platitudes of witless optimism until at last it is swamped with sentimental bilge'. The script, taken again out of Nordhoff and Hall, was finally credited to Charles Lederer, but not before it had gone successively through the hands of Eric Ambler, William L. Driscoll, Border Chase, John Gay and Ben Hecht. On the script alone, $327,000 was spent. Brando, in response to criticism of his behaviour on the set in constantly mulling his lines, claimed that there were scenes for which he had seen eleven different scripts.

Brando made a study of the *Bounty*. It was part of his acting technique to read himself into the context of a part. One press release said he had read a million words on the mutiny. He grasped at what he saw out of his reading to be the essential conflict between Bligh and Christian. Bligh was not a gentleman, and Christian was. Bligh was uneducated. Christian had all the superior knowledge of his class. For Brando, a Restoration dandy was the 'ideal type' of gentleman. He proceeded to make Christian a wealthy, irresponsible fop, constantly making a fool of Bligh. Trevor Howard played Bligh much less psychopathologically than had Laughton. The conflict on the deck of the *Bounty* was class warfare.

Aaron Rosenberg, the producer, chose Carol Reed as director. Reed's strengths were other than in creating the spectacular. He crafted spare, intense films, such as *The Third Man*. Reed was also British. He did not cope easily with Brando's indiscipline. There is more than a hint in the constant conflict on the sets that Brando's caricature of an English gentleman put an edge on relationships with Reed, with Trevor Howard, and with Richard Harris, who played the part of John Mills, seen in the film as instigator of the mutiny. Brando's preposterous accent, among other things, picked at the scabs of old cultural wounds. In the 1962 *Mutiny on the Bounty* there was no accommodation given to the ultimate propriety of the British navy. Forces of cultural literacy that made it impossible to have an American actor play Captain Bligh were also at work on the film sets. The British actors had to wonder whether Christian's conflict with Bligh was not also Brando's conflict with their Britishness.

One whole season of filming on Tahiti in 1960 was botched. The final script came long after the crew had established themselves at Tahiti. The rainy season interrupted filming. Reed's health was ruined. He could not guarantee that the film, whose costs were now rising wildly, would be completed on schedule. MGM replaced him with the seventy-year-old Lewis Milestone. Milestone, in filming a second season at Tahiti, did no better than Reed. Three men were killed in accidents. The reconstructed 'Bounty', overloaded with filming equipment, was dangerous. The farce was being touched with tragedy. Milestone, demeaned by Brando's behaviour in countermanding his direction, also quit. Brando, still hankering to make the whole film turn on Pitcairn, was secretly given charge of the scripts and direction of the final scenes.

These last scenes have come to be seen as among the most bizarre of movie history. Brando as Christian is dying on the cliffs of Pitcairn, having heroically tried to stop the others from burning the *Bounty*. (The real Christian, it may be remembered, was murdered by Tahitian slaves some

four years after the landing at Pitcairn.) Brando is lying on 200 pounds
of ice so that he can 'method' the tremors of death. The cold, however,
makes him forget his Tahitian lines. The crew write them in crayon on
Maimiti's forehead as she leans over him as he dies.

[Read the filming instructions in the following way: MCS = Medium Close
Shot; o.s. = offscreen; f.g. = foreground; CS = Close Shot; CU = Closeup;
MCU = Medium Closeup]

MCS – Mills and Williams – Camera shooting past Young and Brown as they
rise into scene, Brown holding Young back – Minarii enters left, pushing Williams and Mills back – Brown pulls Young o.s. right – CAMERA TRUCKS in
as other natives enter f.g.,pushing Williams and Mills away – natives exit f.g.
– CONTINUES TRUCKING in – Williams tries to explain –

> Young: . . . scum!
> Brown: Ned. Ned, stop!
> Williams: No – I'll swear that I gave him bad for good. I never done
> out anybody in my whole life before.

CS – Christian, as Brown strokes his brow – Camera shooting past latter in left
f.g. and Young in right f.g. – Brown holds Christian down as he tries to sit up
–

> Christian: Brown – wh-what's happened. Brown?
> Brown: We're on the beach, Mr Christian. There was an accident.
> You've been burned and you must lie still.
> Christian: Was I hurt badly?
> Brown: Not too bad. You're going to be all right, but – but it's im-
> portant that you stay as – as still as possible.
> Christian: The *Bounty*?
> Brown: It's hopeless.
> Christian: It's gone. The sextant – did we – did we – Have we lost it?
> Brown: No, I have it here, ...

MCS – Mills, McCoy, and Birkett, as Mills comes forward – CAMERA
TRUCKS back

> Brown: o.s.: . . . Mr Christian
> Christian o.s.: Hide it, Brown. Hide it quickly.

MLS – Camera shooting past Christian, Brown and Young, to Mills as he
comes forward – CAMERA PANS down and TRUCKS in as he kneels before
Christian – crew in b.g.

Christian: So, it was your work. The burning, was it? You filth!

MCS – Mills – Camera shooting past Christian in f.g. and past Brown and
  Young at right –

  Mills: I have no want in me to harm you. For the love of God, believe,
  I regret what has happened to you. We all do. But each man has to
  follow his own belief, no matter what.

CU – Christian__

  Mills o.s.: You've said this many times, after the mutiny. What I did –
  what I thought I had to do – . . .

MCU – Mills –

  Mills: . . . I burned the *Bounty* for the good of all. It wasn't in bad
  faith. It was just bad luck.

Ext. Shore – Night – CU – Christian

  Christian: For the good of all, Mills? Mmm?

MCU – Mills

  Mills: Yes, Sir.

CU – Christian –

  Christian: But why did you have to burn the *Bounty*? You'd no reason
  to fear me.

MCU – Mills

  Mills: We were afraid, Mr Christian. We were afraid you were going to
  take us to London by force.

CU – Christian

  Christian: Oh, God –
  Mills o.s.: We're sick and sorry for what's happened to you. We'll never
  forget what you've done for us.
  Christian: It's all right, Mills. It wasn't your fault. Bligh left his mark
  on all of us.

MCU – Mills

  Mills: Goodbye, Mr Christian. May God have mercy on you.

CU – Christian reacts – lifts his head slightly –

  Christian: Uhh – am I – am-m I – am I dying, Brown?

MCU – Brown and Young –

  Brown: Yes, Mr Christian.

CU – Christian –

>   Christian: What a useless way to die.

CU – Young –

>   Young: It's not useless, Fletcher. I swear it. Maybe we'll get to London, or maybe not. But the Blighs will lose. We'll tell our story somehow, to someone.

CU – Christian –

>   Young o.s.: It only needs one of us to survive.

CS – Mills – looks to b.g., then rises – CAMERA PANS up – he exits right as Maimiti runs forward, looking down to o.s. Christian –

CU – Christian reacts –

CS – Maimiti – CAMERA PANS down as she kneels – pours some medicine –

CU – Christian –

>   Christian: Never mind that, Maimiti. We haven't much time.

CS – Maimiti –

CS – Christian – shivers –

>   Christian: Please – Please know that – that I – loved you, – more than I knew.

MCU – Maimiti

>   Christian o.s.: And – if I'd only had time to –

CU – Christian – dies – Maimiti sobs o.s. –

>   Christian: to –

CS – Maimiti, her hands covering her face as she sobs – Camera shooting past Christian in f.g., as she embraces him – CAMERA PANS down – PANS her up, as she looks at him – CAMERA TRUCKS right past them to *Bounty* as it sinks –

>   Maimiti: Oh, Fletcher – (in Tahitian)

                                                                    FADE OUT:

Historicity did not loom large in the claims for the 1962 version of the *Mutiny on the Bounty*. Instead the *Campaign Books* suggested the headlines such as: 'Bounty Blockbuster with Style', '$20 million Mutiny Film Topnotch Excitement', 'Brilliant – That's the Word for Brando'. A fishing sequence filmed with a thousand islanders as extras on Bora-Bora near Tahiti roused the strongest claims for primitive realism. Historical realism was left for the postfilm experience of the Living Museum of the

Bounty at St Petersburg. The 1935 *Campaign Book* had been full of suggestions as to how a wider audience could be made to be engaged in the
film's historicity – ship model contests (a 'million stores cooperate'), sea
scouts' knot-tying competitions, navigation displays in museums, log-
books for sale, Sailors' Chantey Centers, *Bounty* cut-outs, striped sweaters
in a seaman's mode, love songs of Tahiti. By 1962, the targets of the
publicity men had changed. In that year, the *Campaign Books* were featuring sarongs modelled by Tavita (the film's 'unspoiled girl'), table decorations of coconuts and melons (or grapes and plums as substitute), raw fish
recipes, hair and skin care from the Pacific islands, *poi* as a gourmet dish,
Tahitian drums and songs, and travel tours. Perhaps advertising agents
are not as expert ethnographers of our symbolic nature as their fees claim
them to be, but it is clear that they must have believed that the 1962
Mutiny film tapped a different form of cultural literacy. They must have
thought the body, social standing, the present would spring to mind in a
reading of the film, not institutions, not social change, not the past.

Seven successive scriptwriters were, in any case, likely to leave historicity in some sort of limbo. The final script ruthlessly subordinated time,
space, actions, event and agency on the *Bounty* to making mutiny by
decadent fop halfway credible. So out of the 'natural' logic that Bligh was
preoccupied with the breadfruit, that the breadfruit needed more water
than the *Bounty* carried, that men would go crazy with thirst as they were
brutally ordered to work the ship without water, that someone would
drink seawater in these circumstances, that a gentleman like Christian
would finally have to choose between breadfruit and a seaman's life –
comes the mutiny. Mutiny finally happens when Bligh kicks a ladle of
water from Christian's hands as he helps a dying, mad Williams. 'You
snob', Bligh calls Christian as he does this last unforgivable act. He had
been taunted into absolute inhumanity by Christian's aristocratic condescension.

Charles Lederer, who was responsible for the final script, said it was a
'most rewarding creative experience'. He had read a hundred books on the
Bounty to get it right. What he had right, no doubt, was his sense of
cultural literacy. His script was not of what happened on the *Bounty* but
of what would have happened if all the common expectancies of cultural
literacy were true. The 'natural' logic of the events is the reading to which
cultural literacy responds. The 'mythic chords of memory' in this case are
all the vague cultural memories that men will go mad drinking sea water,

that madness creates responsibilities in other higher-than-institutional loyalties. The cultural literacy that Lederer taps says that it does not matter that there was no ladle kicked out of anybody's hands, there would have been a mutiny if there had been.

These many years my contribution to cultural literacy has been to teach the history of the *Bounty* to undergraduates in their senior years. I have always put it to them that history is something we make rather than something we learn. I have always been confident that out of events and people apparently so trivial and unimportant as the *Bounty* they would discover questions large enough for them to answer as well as the creativity to find the mode of their answering them. Of course, as their teacher I am not innocent. I want to persuade them to certain things. I want to persuade them that any question worth asking about the past is ultimately about the present. I want to persuade them that any history they make will be fiction − not fantasy, fiction, something sculpted to its expressive purpose. I want them to be ethnographic − to describe with the carefulness and realism of a poem what they observe of the past in the signs that the past has left. It is my hope that they make themselves culturally literate in giving ear to the questions women and men around them are asking about themselves and that they find in their history-making the capacity to represent human agency in the way in which it happens, mysteriously combining the totally particular and the universal.

My students respond enthusiastically to this patently presentist, relativist notion of history. It seems 'soft', no hard facts to learn. It warms their prejudice that history is just opinion, one as good as another. There is some alarm among them in the beginning at how empty their minds are of questions and there grows an awful realisation that if they look at their navel too long all they will see is a bellybutton. There is also a growing chagrin at how hard one must work at being creative and how elusive the past is.

It is not until my students have begun to produce their various historical fictions on the *Bounty* that I show them the Laughton/Gable and the Brando/Howard films. The films inevitably make them angry and scornful. They see the films as irresponsible, negligent of the rights of an historical past to be properly represented. They laugh at how obviously the films fail to cope with either the differences between the present and the past or with the differences between cultures. They discover that their own presentism, relativism and fictions have responsibilities. I call that cultural literacy. I find it is acquired somewhere between theatre and living.

Figure 21.
'You remarkable pig. You can thank whatever pig-god you pray to, you haven't quite turned me into a murderer.'
The real gentleman triumphs. (A still from the 1962 *Mutiny on the Bounty* film; © 1962 Turner Entertainment Co. All Rights Reserved).

Epilogue

There is a last word that I have delayed using till this final moment, when the drama is done and the author or the actor or 'everyman' confronts the audience with what it has seen. That word is 'claptrap'. 'Claptrap' is a word that comes from the eighteenth-century theatre. I flirt dangerously with it. It has a vulgar feel. The 1811 *Dictionary of the Vulgar Tongue and Dictionary of Buckish Slang, University Wit and Pickpocket Eloquence* defined 'clap' as a 'venereal taint'. 'He went out by Had'em and came round by Clapham home; i.e. He went out wenching and got a clap!', the *Dictionary* explains. Trapped the clap, we might surmise. But 'claptrap' is more innocent than that. The 'clap' that is trapped is a handclap, applause. Actors trapped a clap when they evoked applause in the middle of a dramatic scene for the brilliance of their acting. By a gesture, a pose, a look, a pause, an actor drew the attention of the audience away from the part being acted to the acting of the part.

Claptrap was a delicate, dangerous moment, a disturbing transformation. Creating spontaneous response is full of artifice. It requires timing, a sense of audience, of occasional topicality, even of the time of day – is it matinee? is it opening night? Claptrap was often seen as self-indulgence on the part of the actor and showing the artificiality of theatricality. Sometimes actors ineptly drew attention to themselves or craved the applause they did not deserve. By the early nineteenth century, theatres had invented a 'claptrap' machine that made a first clap to trigger an audience's spontaneity. Claptrap was now a sign of emptiness, the sort of 'canned laughter' that we would recognise as the ultimate forgery of the theatre. So nowadays we would be comfortable with *Roget's Thesaurus'* equivalences of claptrap: 'blither, blather, blah-blah, flap-doodle, guff, pi-jaw, poppycock, humbug'. Indeed, in the incipiently post-postmodernist age we are experiencing, any form of representation that calls attention to its own representing is decried as an insidious evil. From conference room floors and platforms, from new journals and monographs comes the call to end the claptrap and return to the good old modernist days when a fact was a fact was a fact.

I have a more positive sense of claptrap. I see it as the moment of theatricality in any representation. It is the space created by the performance consciousness of the presenter in which the audience – or the reader or the viewer – participates in the creative process of representing. It need not distract or disturb. It can enhance the realisation of the representation. I have quoted the critics' praise for the performances of David Garrick, the eighteenth-century actor. Garrick opposed all forms of formalistic representation. On the contrary, he 'realised the fiction. His business was not to methodize words but to express passions'. 'Realise the fiction', 'not to methodize words', 'express passions' – those are phrases that any historian, I should think, would like on his or her epitaph, or even in a review.

The years of our concern with the *Bounty* were three decades towards the end of a period in which European *philosophes* were exhilaratingly and self-consciously aware of themselves as 'enlightened'. Identity with those who, as Emmanuel Kant described them, 'dared to know', belonged to the naming process of discourse. We know the comfort that brings. The 'Enlightenment' of one century is the 'structuralism', 'neo-Marxism' or 'postmodernism' of another. Recognition of keywords, a sensitivity for the metaphoric nature of styles of thought, a feeling that what one has just read is what one was about to say, knowing the truth in the caricatures made by one's associates of oppositional stands, knowing on the other hand how untrue are the stereotypifications of oneself – all the stuff by which paradigms are made and seen – had given for nearly a hundred years a tribal sense to the lovers of criticism, the 'enlightened'. They had been to the top of the mountain with Petrarch and opened Augustine's *Confessions* there: 'Men went forth to behold the high mountains and the mighty surge of the sea, and the broad stretches of the rivers and the inexhaustible ocean, and the paths of the stars and so doing lose themselves in wonderment'. 'A new thought seized me', Petrarch had written, 'transporting me from space into time'. To have discovered that everything in nature, everything in human beings, was in time, that the abstractions of law, science and the market, even God himself were in time was indeed enlightening. It made for a season of observing.

In that season for observing, the years between 1767 (when Samuel Wallis 'discovered' Tahiti) and 1797 (when the first sustained missionary efforts of the London Missionary Society began in Tahiti) were a short and intensive period in which the Pacific was *theatrum mundi*. It was a period when the nations of Europe and the Americas saw themselves acting out their scientific, humanistic selves. Government-sponsored expeditions from England, France and Spain followed one another, self-righteously conscious of their obligations to observe, describe and publish, to be humane and to contribute to the civilising process of natives out of their superior arts and greater material wealth. It was a time of intensive theatre of the civilised to the native, but of even more intensive theatre of the civilised to one another. The civilised jostled to see what the Pacific said to them of their relations of dominance. They vied in testing the extensions of their sovereignty and the effectiveness of their presence – through territorial possessions, protected lines of communication, exemplary empire. They shouted at natives, in that loud and slow way we use to communicate with those who do not share our language, the meanings of flags and cannons and property and trade, all the lessons of civilised behaviour. But they were always conscious that this theatre was a play within a play – about world systems of power, about reifying empire, about encompassing the globe and hegemony. Historians for decades have poured scorn on the metaphor of the 'expansion' of Europe. The theatre of the Pacific was about making that unreal metaphor real at home and abroad.

In that season for observing during which the Pacific became *theatrum mundi*, England itself was something of a theatre to the world. Anglophilia was strong among the 'enlightened', mostly because the English were deemed to have managed time so well, so expediently and so stylishly – in government, in law, in political economy, in religion, in moral philosophy. Joseph Addison had helped make it so as 'the spectator' in *The Spectator*. 'I live in the World rather as a Spectator of Mankind, than as one of the Species.' 'I have acted all the Parts of my life as a Looker-On.' Irony was the enlightened's trope, the spectator's worldliness. Irony requires a perspective, a line of vision that the onlooker has but not the participant. Of course, this can often be merely a matter of physical angles of vision in which one can be enlightened by seeing something from a different angle. But perspective is more composed than that. Perspective is the persuasion that vision is geometric and that our representations are the more real by that. Roland Barthes, as we have seen, has commented on the relationship between geometry and theatre: 'The theater is precisely that practice which calculates the place of things *as they are observed:*

if I set the spectacle here, the spectator will see this; if I put it elsewhere he will not, and I can avail myself of this masking effect and play on the illusions it provides. . . . Representation is not defined directly by imitation: even if one gets rid of the "real", of the *"vraisemblable"*, of the "copy", there will still be representation for so long as a subject (author, reader, spectator, or *voyeur*) casts his *gaze* toward a horizon on which he cuts out the base of a triangle, his eye (or his mind) forming the apex'. The tricks of seeing the parts of the world 'as if' from the point of the pyramid of one's mind's eye are many. They were largely elaborated in the Enlightenment. They belong to our modernity. They help us see the world 'as it really is'. The tricks are most untheatrical.

The exhilaration of seeing something different, from a new perspective, lends a sort of self-righteousness to perspectiving. The passion for the beauty of the experience gives a dispassionate claim to its science, authenticates its disinterestedness, lends a moral quality to discipline. The world becomes more factual the more passionately the disinterestedness of the observer is displayed. Claptrap about such disinterestedness suddenly seems distasteful, immoral even, certainly political.

I think that if there had been more claptrap in the *theatrum mundi* of the Pacific there would have been less blood. I think that if Bligh had had a better sense of claptrap, he would not have had a mutiny. I think that if the court martial had had a better sense of claptrap, Millward, Burkitt and Ellison would not have hanged. I think it was claptrap that made the 'Bountys' political. In so far as the mythologies caught up in 200 years of representation of the mutiny on the *Bounty* emplot our lives, claptrap liberates us.

Notes

PROLOGUE

The politics and poetics of prologues have a long (Knapp 1961; Hogan 1968: 1: lxxiv) and more recent history (Agnew 1986: 112; Stallybrass and White 1986: 84). Prologues, like soliloquies (as Agnew points out), are 'ontologically subversive'. That a history of so apparently an 'un-world-changing' event as the mutiny on the *Bounty* need be ontologically subversive could be questioned. However, this book is written with an 'anti-antitheatrical prejudice' and is meant to be subversive of polarities of all descriptions but especially of the polarities of unthinking positivism and overthinking postmodernism.

The book is written in the belief that Roland Barthes' and Michel Foucault's notion of the 'death of the author' is not so much an ominous portent as an invitation to enjoy the mysteriousness of discourse. I personally am more inclined to celebrate knowledge than to argue about it. In that sense *Mr Bligh's Bad Language* is a celebratory narrative of what I have learned of ethnography from James Boon (1973, 1982), James Clifford (1988), James Fernandez (1986), Clifford Geertz (1973), Kirsten Hastrup (1990), Georges Marcus (Clifford and Marcus 1984), Paul Rabinow (1986); what I have learned of ethnographic history from Inga Clendinnen (1987), Robert Darnton (1984), Rhys Isaac (1982), Richard Price (1983, 1990), Marshall Sahlins (1981, 1985), Hayden White (1975); what I have learned of theatre and film from Jean-Christophe Agnew (1986), Jonas Barish (1981), Marvin Carlson (1984), Neal Gabler (1988), David Marshall (1986), Michael Rogin (1987), Peter Stallybrass and Allon White (1986); what I have learned on mimesis and acting performance from Stephen Halliwell (1986), Richard Handler and William Saxton (1988), Martin Meisel (1983), Karl Morrison (1982), Richard Schechner (1985), Victor Turner (1982, 1989) and the editors John Gassner and Ralph Allen (1964) and Philip Rosen (1986). The plagiarism inherent in reliving the past for the historian and entering the other for the anthropologist has

long been a mystery for me. It did not surprise me that someone such as
Thomas Tomkis in 1615 had the same thought:

> This Poet is that Poet's plagiary,
> And he a third's, till they end all in *Homer.*
> And *Homer* filch't all from an Aegyptian Preestesse.
> The world's a Theater of theft.
> [Quoted Agnew 1986: 64]

The *Bounty* and what happened on her and around her is now transformed into texts — logs, journals, court transcriptions, newspaper pieces,
pamphlets, letters, oral interviews written down. Two hundred years of
historical industry have seen much of this 'primary' material published.
Owen Rutter and George Mackaness have been the most assiduous editors
of these texts contemporary with the events — William Bligh's log of the
Bounty and correspondence (Bligh 1937; Mackaness 1949, 1960); John
Fryer's journal and notes (Rutter 1934, 1939); James Morrison's journal
(Morrison 1935); Edward Christian's pamphlet in defence of his brother
and Stephen Barney's notes on the trial of the mutineers (Mackaness 1938);
the official transcripts of the mutineers' court martial (Rutter 1931). The
Australian National Library has reproduced a facsimile version of Bligh's
launch notebook with a transcribed and annotated version edited by John
Bach (1986). There have been other facsimile editions as well, of Bligh's
Providence log (Bligh 1976), of his first letters describing his mutiny (Bligh
1989), of Fryer's account of the launch voyage (Fryer 1979). Rolf E. Du
Rietz has been the great bibliographer of the *Bounty* (Du Rietz 1963,
1979*a*, 1979*b*, 1986) and in his privately printed *Studia Bountyana* and
Banksia series has kept academic scholars on their toes. Douglas Oliver's
contexting of all the *Bounty* material as it related to Tahiti is a vital contribution of secondary editing (Oliver 1974, 1988). George Mackaness'
(1931) biography of Bligh will never be fully supplanted, but Gavin Kennedy (1978, 1989) has come near to it. Captain Edward Edwards of the
Pandora confiscated whatever papers he found on the mutineers when he
captured them at Tahiti. These were lost when the *Pandora* was wrecked.
Peter Heywood lost nearly a hundred drawings and other memorabilia as
well. But Edwards made extracts of Heywood's and George Stewart's midshipman's logs and the extracts are preserved (Edwards 1789, 1790). Nessie Heywood's collection of letters from her brother and hers to him are
in her unpublished diary (Heywood n.d.), but a substantial number of

Peter Heywood's letters were made public in an early biography (Tagart 1832). The Muster Rolls of the *Bounty*, being so repetitive and extensive, have not been published but, together with all the other muster rolls and logs of British naval vessels coming into the Pacific, are available on microfilm in the Australian Joint Copying Project (Muster Rolls 1787–90). D. Bonner Smith (1936) has transcribed and printed biographical details from the rolls. A 'Guide to the papers of William Bligh and the Bligh Family in the Mitchell Library, State Library of NSW' (Egan 1989) is an indispensable tool for research on the *Bounty*. Glynn Christian (1982) uncovered much that was new about Fletcher Christian by pursuing him in the Christian family records. C. S. Wilkinson (1953), a firm believer in Fletcher Christian's return to England and in a Wordsworthian conspiracy to conceal it, is full of marvellous lateral and antiquarian pursuits that will shame any more conventional historian for his energy to uncover new sources, but where they are remains his secret. Gavin Kennedy's edition of Sir John Barrow's *Eventful History of the Mutiny and Piratical Seizure of HMS* Bounty: *Its Causes and Consequences* (Barrow 1980) is the most prolific source of illustrations of the *Bounty* voyage.

THE SHIP

The physical space of the *Bounty* has been very precisely described (Knight 1936; McKay 1989). The social space is much more a matter of interpretation. Michael Lewis' classic surveys of the social structures of the Georgian navy (1960, 1965), like E. P. Thompson in his *Making of the English Working Class* (1964), displayed the spaces of power and privilege in the navy as relational. Later historical studies, notably N.A.M. Rodger (1986) and John D. Byrn (1989), have set the different roles performed by men in the navy in a more precise and actual context. Marcus Rediker (1987), working mostly on American merchant shipping and inspired by the earlier passionate work of Jesse Lemisch (1968, 1969), offers a more complete picture of the symbolic environment of a ship and the politics it generated. By studying pirates as well as merchant and naval seamen, Rediker shows the different dimensions of public and private space of a ship. Jerome R. Garitee (1977) and Patrick Crowhurst (1989) offer similar advantages in their studies of American and French privateering. Students of ships as institutions (Aubert 1982; Weibust 1967) have found Goffman's (1961) model of 'total institutions' useful to display the tensions at the boundaries of public and private space. Elias (1950) long ago pointed to the structural tensions of a fighting ship created by the division of authority between those who were given it by sovereign power and those who earned it by experience. My reflection on discipline offers a description of the perceptions of contemporaries as to what those tensions were and how they might be overcome.

Fatal histories

That public trials and executions may be conceived of as theatre and ritual is no analytically new concept. Masur, *Rites of Execution* (1989), and before him Foucault, *Discipline and Punishment* (1979), Spierenburg, *The Spectacle of Suffering* (1984), Douglas Hay et al., *Albion's Fatal Tree* (1975) (and Langbein's 1983 critique of *Albion's Fatal Tree*) display all the advantages (and disadvantages) of the theatre/ritual concept. The problem for any historian is to discover what is being signified in this theatre and how any meaning in it is privileged over any other meaning. The producers of this theatre – in this case a range of admirals, captains, lieutenants, petty officers, seamen, lawyers and civil officials – bind themselves with a set of rubrics that often prescribe what the meanings should be (Delafons 1805; Hannay 1914; McArthur 1813: 2: 343, 409; Maltby 1813: 116). This rhetoric of ritual or official commonsense is easily discovered. How the theatre and ritual were actually seen has to be discovered more indirectly in the language, tone and metaphors of those who experienced them and who happened to write their experiences down. The transcripts of the courts martial (Rutter 1931; Mackaness 1938) are the richest sources of this more actual commonsense, but there were also newspaper accounts (Newspapers 1790–2: the London *Times* Sept. 10, 18, Oct. 30, 31, 1792; *London Chronicle* Oct. 30–Nov. 1, 1792; *Annual Register* 1792; Knapp and Baldwin's (1820) *Newgate Calendar* 1792). These are greatly enlarged by 'W.L.' (1792) in his letter to *Gentleman's Magazine* and also by Nessie Heywood (n.d.) with her description of the legal manoeuvres of her brother. History writing, however, is full of lateral pursuits, and Scott (1982) pursuing the family of John Adams, Greatheed (1820) recording the role of the London Missionary Society in the *Bounty* affair, Leeson (1939) and Montgomerie (1941) debating the authenticity of James Morrison's journal, Wilkinson (1953) pursuing the sociopolitical network that grew around the Christian family all throw light on how the rituals were actually ex-

perienced as distinct from the rhetoric of how they should have been experienced.

'Fatal Histories', in my conception of it, is more than a narrative of the
trial and execution of the mutineers. In other places, I have described the
varieties of histories in any culture, their poetics and their function in the
construction of any sociocultural present (Dening 1983, 1988*b*, 1988*c*,
1990*a*, 1990*b*). I would like here to make the political nature of these
histories quite explicit, because it is sometimes presumed that such ethnographic description of them is apolitical. I would hope that from my
narrative the reader will have a greater understanding of the hegemonic
processes in varied history-making, some insight into the dialogic nature
of power and the exchanges it entails, some knowledge of how class and
institutional hegemony are a matter of negotiation, of how commonsense
is a matter of invention as much as consensus.

Mr Bligh's bad language

'Patterns of discourse are regulated through the forms of corporate assembly in which they are produced. Alehouse, coffeehouse, church, law-court,
library, drawing-room of country mansion: each place of assembly is a
different site of intercourse requiring different manners and morals. Discourse space is never completely independent of social space and the formation of new kinds of speech can be traced through the emergence of
new public sites of discourse and the transformation of old ones' (Stallybrass and White 1986: 80). Add a ship to this list of places of discourse.
Add the space created by the collective sense of being 'navy'. Add tonal-
ity, silence, looks and glances, winks and nudges, and a sense of corporate
reaction to our understanding of the ways in which language and discourse
are expressed. The Wooden World of sailors was classified in a complex
system of signs whose mastery gave seamen their identity and set them
apart. (Aubert 1982: 263; Gilbert 1980: 118; Parry 1948; Rediker 1987:
5, 11; Rockwell 1842: 388–90; Rodger 1986: 118).

That the realisations and politics of this world should turn on such
apparently trivial matters as ducking, yarning and dancing should not
surprise us. Institutions in the end are talk, and, in the social dramas that
talk makes, institutional men become the most adept critics. Of such
criticism and theatricality politics are easily born. On a revolutionary scale,
these may be only 'sub-politics', as Thompson (1964: 167) has suggested.

That is not necessarily so, however, as I think Dugan (1965), Lemisch (1968, 1969) and Rediker (1987) have shown. My thesis in 'Mr Bligh's Bad Language' is that the 'Bountys' political sense was raised by their crosscultural experience at Tahiti, by the marginality of the *Bounty* as a semiprivate ship in a very public institution and by the inability of Bligh to understand the theatrical nature of institutional life. I do not think political ideology was the cause of the mutiny, but I think the extraordinary silences during the mutiny were a sign of its politics. Teitler's (1977) description of the professionalisation of European officer corps and Foucault's (1979) thesis on the changing epistemes of European institutions of coercion show how Bligh's language could have been 'bad' in a time of institutional transformation.

It has long been my ambition to write the anthropology of an eighteenth-century ship. Great though my admiration of the classic descriptions of seamen's sociocultural life is (Lewis 1939, 1957, 1960, 1965; Lloyd 1968; Marcus 1961, 1971, 1974; Masefield 1920), they do not satisfy my ethnographic hopes. I count my description of the ceremonies of Crossing the Line and of yarning as a small lien on something still to come. Henningsen (1954, 1961) has scoured the maritime sources of half a dozen nations for descriptions of sailors' baptisms. Lydenburg (1957) is another who has devoted many years to the subject. Williams (1989) has attached some of their perceptions to Bligh on the *Bounty* and the *Providence*. The English ceremonies of the late eighteenth century elaborated the reverse world element more extensively than other nations. The ducking, paralleling as it did a hanging, underlined the seriousness of the clowning and, in my eyes, showed the extent to which power on a ship was a matter of negotiation.

James Morrison's Journal (1935, 1966) is one of the great masterpieces of seamen's literature of the Pacific, although defenders of Bligh have always been disparaging of it. Rolf Du Rietz (1986) has described the evolution of its text and the role its suppression played in a final settlement of the mutiny that did the least damage to Bligh's public institutional character. Whether it is accurate or true in relation to Bligh is less interesting in my view than the fact that it represented the ways in which, in Stallybrass and White's words, 'the patterns of discourse are regulated through the forms of corporate assembly in which they are produced', and show the politics of yarning.

Mr Christian's lot

Sources on what happened after the mutiny are sparse (Heywood 1789; Morrison 1935; Stewart 1789; Teehuteatuaonoa 1819, 1829). Harry Maude (1964a, 1968) has reconstructed the *Bounty*'s voyages under Christian. Glynn Christian (1989) has made his own pilgrimage to Tubuai and has stepped out 'Fort George', whose relics had been described a hundred and fifty years and surveyed eighty-five years before (Moerenhout 1837: 1: 149; Maude 1968:11). Robert Aitken (1930) has described the ethnology of Tubuai. George Mortimer (1791) reported the puzzlement of those on board the *Mercury* about the stories of the comings and goings of the *Bounty* to Tahiti and their realisation on their return to England that they had almost discovered the mutineers within weeks of their mutiny.

Sad passion and damned oeconomy

Bligh's published account of his famous launch voyage (Bligh 1790), his reproduced notebook (Bach 1986), and his letters to his wife, Elizabeth, Duncan Campbell and Sir Joseph Banks, since published (Bligh 1989), together with John Fryer's notes and recollections (Fryer 1979; Rutter 1934, 1939) are the principal sources for my narrative. Vicky Leong, dear friend, used her nutritionist skills to count the calories for me. Kennedy (1989) covers the miserable events after Timor in considerable detail, as does George Mackaness (1931). Thomas Ledward's letters can be found in Ledward (1903). Cook's visit to Nomuka and his sightings of Tofua, as well as Anderson's criticism of Cook's dealings with the Tongans, can be found in Beaglehole (1967: 101–3, 869–70). Delano (1817: 111–52) related what he knew of the *Bounty*, Pitcairn and Mayhew Folger quite extensively.

Some cliometrics of violence

James E. Valle, *Rocks and Shoals. Order and Discipline in the Old Navy 1800–1861* (1980) and John D. Byrn, *Crime and Punishment in the Royal Navy* (1989), are the most extensive studies of discipline in the American and British navies. Clavel (1954), Gilbert (1976, 1980), Glenn (1984), Horan (1970), Langley (1967) and Rasor (1972) are indispensable aids as well. It is difficult to discover firsthand descriptions of either the giving or the receiving of physical punishment. Those with the ability to express themselves, such as Richard Dana (n.d. [1849]), Melville (1970), Nord-

Table 1. *British naval vessels in the Central Pacific, 1764–95*

Ship's name	Commander	Years of voyage
HMS *Tamar*	Patrick Mouat	1764–6
HMS *Dolphin*	John Byron	1764–6
HMS *Swallow*	Philip Carteret	1766–9
HMS *Dolphin*	Samuel Wallis	1766–8
HMS *Endeavour*	James Cook	1768–71
HMS *Adventure*	Tobias Furneaux	1772–4
HMS *Resolution*	James Cook	1772–5
HMS *Discovery*	James Burney	1776–80
HMS *Resolution*	James Cook	1776–80
HMS *Bounty*	William Bligh	1787–9
HMS *Pandora*	Edward Edwards	1790–1
HMS *Assistant*	Nathaniel Portlock	1791–3
HMS *Providence*	William Bligh	1791–3
HMS *Chatham*	William Broughton	1791–5
HMS *Discovery*	George Vancouver	1791–5

hoff (1883), are deemed too literary to be believed, while those who had a passion to change the system such as 'Jack Nastyface' (1973), 'Tiphys Aegyptus' (1843), Solomon Sanborn (1841), are seen as too politically committed to be trusted. The *realpolitik* of those such as Glascock (1831), who argued that sailors, being hard as granite, preferred physical pain to the mental pain of guilt and anguish, was really a blindman's bluff and presumed that institutions of coercion such as navies were immune to sociocultural change. To those comfortable in an unchanging navy, the notion that authority did not need privilege was a serious challenge to the privileges that power gave them.

My cliometrics come from the voyages of the following British naval vessels under the commanders and for the years listed in Table 1.

Of the 1,556 men of this group of ships, the ratings were as shown in Table 2. Men aged between 12 and 30 years made up 82.1 percent of the crews. Some 14.3 percent were aged between 30 and 40 years.

Table 3 offers general statistics concerning the number who died on a voyage from disease or accident or were killed by natives, the number who were drowned, who deserted, who were punished and repeatedly punished, who had the 'venereals'. The bracketed figures are percentages.

Table 2. *Ratings of British naval seamen in the Central Pacific, 1764–95*

Marines	151	9.7%
Seamen	874	56.2%
Petty officers	353	22.7%
Warrant officers	129	8.3%
Commissioned officers	48	3.1%

Table 4 reduces to twelve categories the offences for which naval seamen in the Central Pacific, 1764–95, were flogged. It indicates the number of men flogged for these offences and whether the flogging was the sailor's first, second, etc., flogging. Thus, 77 men were flogged for insolence for their first flogging on their voyage; 30 men were flogged for insolence on their second flogging; 11 men on their third, and so on.

Most men (135) received 12 lashes during a whole voyage; 17 received 18 lashes; 55, 24 lashes; 13, 36 lashes; 11, 48 lashes; 22 received between 50 and 100 lashes; 5 between 100 and 120. Three men broke the 200 level (204,210,252). See Table 5.

There are those who consider Sir John Barrow's comments about Bligh not being a gentleman because he was not educated in the midshipmen's cockpit a 'calumny' (Barrow 1980: 160; Gavin Kennedy's editorial comment, 14). Perhaps a social prejudice, perhaps a puzzle as to how it could be true, but not a calumny, I think. George Borrow in an appendix on gentility to *The Romany Rye* (1906: 342,365) remarked that he had known a companion of Bligh in the launch. This man had died in Borrow's provincial town in 1822. He had believed that Fletcher Christian and George Young had influence over the 'Bountys' because they were 'genteely connected'. Money or birth was the mark of 'gentlemen', Borrow thought. Bligh had neither and, for whatever reason, had not acquired the language of the 'as if' gentility of a professional officer.

Some non-cliometrics of violence

Francis Pinkney's story is gleaned from the official and unofficial, the published and unpublished accounts of Samuel Wallis's circumnavigation in the *Dolphin*, 1766–1768 (Furneaux 1900; Gore 1766–1767; Hawkesworth 1773; Robertson 1948; S. Wallis 1768, H. Wallis 1965). Richard

Table 3. *Deaths, health and discipline of British naval seamen in the Central Pacific, 1764–95 (numbers and percentages)*

Ship	Crew	Died	Drowned	Deserted	Punished	Repeat. punished	VD
Tamar	109	5 (4.58)	4 (3.66)	7 (6.42)	11 (10.09)	1 (0.91)	20 (18.34)
Dolphin	148	5 (3.37)	1 (0.67)	7 (4.72)	14 (9.45)	4 (2.70)	22 (14.86)
Swallow	112	29 (25.89)	1 (0.89)	6 (5.35)	22 (19.64)	11 (9.82)	8 (7.14)
Dolphin	155	7 (4.51)	1 (0.64)	—	10 (6.45)	5 (3.22)	28 (18.06)
Endeavour	116	31 (26.72)	3 (2.58)	4 (3.44)	15 (12.93)	8 (6.89)	39 (33.62)
Adventure	90	13 (14.44)	—	—	19 (21.11)	4 (4.44)	17 (18.88)
Resolution	122	2 (1.63)	2 (1.63)	2 (1.63)	16 (13.11)	16 (13.11)	31 (25.40)
Discovery	68	2 (2.94)	2 (2.94)	5 (7.35)	15 (22.05)	4 (5.88)	30 (44.11)
Resolution	125	11 (8.8)	—	3 (2.00)	32 (25.6)	14 (11.2)	71 (56.8)
Bounty	46	7 (15.21)	—	21 (45.65)	5 (10.86)	4 (8.69)	18 (39.13)
Pandora	136	19 (13.47)	36 (26.47)	—	—	—	27 (19.85)
Assistant	31	1 (3.22)	—	1 (3.22)	4 (12.90)	1 (3.22)	9 (29.03)
Providence	120	3 (2.50)	1 (0.83)	10 (8.33)	6 (5.00)	4 (3.33)	44 (36.66)
Chatham	54	—	—	5 (9.25)	9 (16.66)	11 (20.37)	32 (59.25)
Discovery	124	2 (1.61)	3 (2.41)	7 (5.64)	24 (19.35)	32 (52.80)	41 (33.06)
Total	1556	137 (8.80)	54 (3.47)	78 (5.01)	201 (12.92)	119 (7.65)	437 (28.08)

Table 4. *The number of British naval seamen flogged, their offence and the occasion of their flogging, 1764–95*

Offence	Flogging					
	1st	2nd	3rd	4th	5th	6th +
Insolence	77	30	11	7	2	2
Assaulting superior	4	2		2		
Desertion	7	2	1			
Stealing, general	38	15	3			1
Disorderly conduct	18	3	3			
Stealing from natives	2	3				
Other offences on natives	4	1				
Drunk and neglect of duty	29	11	7	4	1	
Drunk and other offences	21	9	2	2	1	
Neglect of duty	89	27	13	6	3	2
Offences concerning food, clothing, bedding	8	3				
Personal hygiene	2	1				

Richardson, the barber of the *Dolphin*, put his account into verse (Richardson 1768, 1965).

Iudicatio *(law)* and coercitio *(force)*

Brand, *Roman Military Law* (1968), offers a most insightful interpretation of military law. Thring (1877), Aycock and Wurfel (1955), Sherrill (1969) offer histories through two millennia of military law. See Valle (1980), Byrn (1989) for more particular reference to navies. Polybius (1923, Book VI), is forever the classic description of *coercitio* and Edward Gibbon (1896: 1: 11) is obviously dependent on him. My understanding of *iudicatio, coercitio* and *provocatio* come from Grant (1974), Lintott (1972), Strachan-Davidson (1969).

Dreams of perfect naval discipline

Contemporary (Pugh 1787) and later (Hutchins 1940) biographies of Jonas Hanway, and short studies of his maritime school at Chelsea and his County Naval Free Schools on Wastelands (Bosanquet 1921, 1922), do not do

Table 5. *The number of lashes given at each occasion of a flogging*

No. of lashes at a flogging	Floggings						Total fl'gs	Total lashes
	1st	2nd	3rd	4th	5th	6th+		
6	34	12	6	1			52	312
7	1						1	7
8		2					2	16
12	198	62	17	11	4	2	294	3528
15	1						1	15
18	13	4	1	1			19	342
19	1						1	19
24	38	14	9	4	2		67	1608
30	1						1	30
36	9	9	3	2	1		24	864
48	3	4	4	2		2	15	720
114						1	1	114
144		1					1	144
							479	7719

full justice to a remarkable man. His writings discussed here (Hanway 1757*a*, 1757*b*, 1761, 1783) display him as the essential utilitarian modernist. I am attracted to him in a reflection on discipline because he represents in person and ideas the transformation of epistemes of public discipline that Michel Foucault alerted us to in *Discipline and Punishment*.

Midshipmanship
Historians and social commentators have often reiterated 'Jack Nastyface's' (1973: 55) denunciation of the tyrannical disposition of midshipmen (Gilbert 1980: 117; Glenn 1984: 94; Neale 1985: 24; 'Tiphys Aegyptus' 1843: 11). Christopher Claxton, *The Naval Monitor* (1815), belonged to a long line of writers from the time of Erasmus and before who believed that the civilising process of the young could be given a grammar by typologising the actualities of behaviour so that the young could have a crib on sociocultural rules.

Captaining
Dandeker (1985) stresses the tensions created for institutions of coercion by bureaucratisation of state power and the growing polarities of class.

Buker (1970: 139), Glascock (1854), Lewis (1939: 55–8), Marcus (1961: 350–73), Richmond (1927: 11), Teitler (1977: 19), Vagts (1937: 11) describe the institutional and personal qualities required in the professionalisation of officers. James Dugan (1965: 63), who perhaps better than most naval historians describes the contradictions and tensions as they were worked through in the Great Nore Mutiny, quotes the classic history of naval administrations (Oppenheim 1896) to show how issues of naval discipline and class politics were not independent of one another: 'throughout the history of the navy any improvement of the man-o'-wars' men is found to bear a direct relationship to the momentary needs of the governing class'. Rear Admiral Richard Kempenfelt's reflections on discipline in a changing navy are to be found in his letters to Lord Barham, Admiral of the Red Squadron (Barham 1906).

Texts for discipline

The texts of the British Articles of War are most easily found in Rodger (1982) and collected in Admiralty (1810). The Regulations, being fuller, need to be read as they were published. See Admiralty (1772, 1790, 1808, 1826). For their legal history I am dependent on the older historians of military law, Aycock and Wurfel (1955: 3); Brand (1968: vii–xvi); Oppenheim (1896: 311–3); Paullin (1968: 5–6); Thring (1861: 5–6); Wiener (1967: 9); Winthrop (1920: 15), and on the more modern historians of discipline, such as Byrn (1989: 10–18, 274–5); Valle (1980: 38).

My reflections on the founding of the U.S. navy and on the invention of a gentlemanly language of command for it by such men as John Paul Jones are not so lateral to considerations of the *Bounty* as they may at first sight seem. My thesis is that fundamentalism of the sort that both John Adams and William Bligh exhibited inevitably led to 'bad language'. The ultimate cause of that, I think, comes from a further thesis of the reflection: there is no way in which an institution of coercion, such as a navy, can be isolated from either the politics or the cultural operators of the society of which it is a part. Contradictions between the *iudicatio* of that society and the *coercitio* of the institution inevitably make discipline a subject of politics and social reform (Glenn 1984; Langley 1967). Christopher McKee, *A Gentlemanly and Honorable Profession: The Creation of the U.S. Naval Officer Corps, 1794–1815* (1991), has arrived too late for me to do any more than acknowledge its seminal pertinence to my concerns.

My history of these contradictions is written out of the papers of John Adams (1850, 1961), the naval documents of the American revolution and the archives of the Continental Congress (Clark 1966; Continental Congress 1775). But various historians made it easier: Braugh 1965; Clark 1941, 1960; Coletta 1980; Cunliffe 1968; Fowler 1974, 1984; Smelser 1958; Symonds 1980, 1981. John Paul Jones proved fascinating as another who played out military modernism in his person (De Koven n.d.; Morison 1959). Had I given my anthropological ambitions their full play, I would have described duelling much more particularly, although I have made a start elsewhere (Dening 1983). See Paullin (1909); Castronono (1987).

The commentator with the poor opinion of American sailors is Charles Rockwell (1842:2: 389), but as I suggested earlier in the narrative there was a way in which sailors played the grotesque to a bourgeois hegemony. Examples can be seen in Rodger (1986: 15, 37, 118); Rediker (1987: 11, 17, 147). Robinson, *The British Tar in Fact and Fiction* (1909) – and Watson (1931) – can be read in this light, and the vast fictional literature about seamen and seagoing, listed in Parkinson, *Portsmouth Point* [1949], can be understood as *theatrum mundi*.

White jacket

I have described Herman Melville's beachcombing and vicarious ethnographic experience in the Pacific (Dening 1988*a*: 147–50). Rogin's splendid subversions in *Subversive Genealogy: The Politics and Art of Herman Melville* (1985) do not deter me from using Melville's actual seaman's experience ethnographically. *White Jacket* is fiction, not fantasy. Charles Robert Anderson (1937) edited the journal of the USS *United States* on which Melville sailed. My cliometrics for discipline aboard US naval vessels in the Pacific comes from the information in Table 6.

Sharks that walk on the land

Marshall Sahlins would describe himself as an 'old-fashioned historian' in the intensity with which he attaches himself to the empirical evidence of the past. But there is not much else that is old-fashioned in his *Historical Metaphors and Mythical Realities: Structure in the Early History of the Sandwich Islands Kingdom* (1981) and his later publications (1985, 1988). They are his narratives of the death of Captain Cook. It is *Historical Metaphors* that I transform to my present purposes. Sahlins is not the first to write on the death of Captain Cook (see Beaglehole 1974; Daws 1968), and the radical

Table 6. *U.S. naval vessels in the Central Pacific, 1812–45*

Ship	Commander	Voyage dates
USS *Essex*	David Porter	1812–4
USS *Dolphin*	John Percival	1825–6
USS *Peacock*	T. Ap Catesby Jones	1824–6
USS *Vincennes*	W. Bolton Finch	1829
USS *Potomac*	John Downes	1832–3
USS *Vincennes*	John H. Aulich	1835
USS *Peacock*	E. P. Kennedy	1836–7
USS *Enterprise*	Geo. N. Hollins	1836–7
USS *Constitution*	Daniel Turner	1839–41
USS *Columbia*	George C. Read	1839–40
USS *John Adams*	Thomas Wyman	1839–40
USS *Constellation*	Lawrence Kearney	1843
USS *Cyane*	C. E. Stribling	1843
USS *Eyrie*	Alex J. Dallas	1844
USS *United States*	T. Ap Catesby Jones	1843
USS *Brandywine*	Foxhall A. Parker	1844–5
USS *St Louis*	Isaac McKeever	1844–5
USS *Perry*	John S. Paine	1844–5

brilliance of his interpretation ensures that he will not be the last as his views are enlarged and debated.

I see no point in either entering or closing that debate. Instead, liberated by my own understanding of the nature of historical certainty and interpretation, and by my own researches that have followed Sahlins in a limited way, I simply touch up and colour his view with my perceptions and interests. In other places and other ways, I have made other contributions to the question (Dening 1982, 1984, 1988*b*).

The beach

Ancient Tahitian society is described in Oliver's volumes (1974). Urged on by his admiration of Bligh as an observer of Tahiti, Oliver has followed these classic and indispensable ethnographies with *Return to Tahiti: Bligh's Second Breadfruit Voyage* (1988). Bligh's and Tobin's paintings and drawings (see also Bligh [n.d.], and Tobin [n.d.] for the originals) are there splendidly reproduced. If the spirit of Bligh has been restless for nearly

200 years at the neglect of his scientific contributions, it must be quieted a little by Oliver's latest work. Driessen (1982), Gunson (1963), Newbury (1961, 1967a, 1967b, 1980), Langdon (1968) offer the most authoritative histories of Tahitian-European exchanges. The archaeology of Roger and Kaye Green (1968), the museum studies of Rose (1978), the library work of Lewthwaite (1964, 1966) and Charles Nordhoff's (1930) enjoyment of fishing give vicarious authenticity to my judgements and interpretations.

Between land and sea

Gore (1776), Hawkesworth (1773: 2: 213 ff.), Robertson (1948: 138 ff.), Wallis (1778) are the sources of my account of the *Dolphin*'s bloody arrival at Tahiti, and James Morrison's journal (1935) is at its most valuable in narrating the mutineers' stay at Tahiti and in describing Tahitian culture. Keller, *Creation of Rights of Sovereignty through Symbolic Acts 1400–1800* (1938) incited me to be anthropological about possession rituals and to pursue them through the Pacific in the French (Bougainville 1772: 232–3, 238) and Spanish possessions (Corney 1913: 1: 153–7, 257). Teuira Henry's (1928: 157–77, 120–7) somewhat romantic description of Tahitian rituals and practices can be modified by pursuing the following subjects in Oliver's (1974) index: 'Oro, *maro ura*, feathers, *arioi*, sacrifice. Rose (1978) offers a specific study of feather girdles of Tahiti and Hawaii, and Kaeppler (1970, 1979) adds special considerations for Hawaii.

An icon of the beach

James Morrison (1935) lovingly describes his boatbuilding. Maude (1964*b*) in 'The Voyage of the *Pandora*'s Tender' gives a full history of the *Resolution* become *Matavy*, and A. F. C. David (1977*b*) and Alan Reid (1978) follow her career through South-east Asia and the China Coast.

Flags and feather girdles

Oliver's chapter on the 'Wars of the Bounty Mutineers' (1974: 1256–71) is the masterly source of my sureness in my narrative.

Interlude on sacrifice

The Interlude really began when I read Peter Brown, *The Cult of the Saints* (1981). Brown works the irony that an apparent surrender by the early christian bishops to popular religion in the cult of martyrs' bones was really the first step in establishing universal church structures against the powerful kin focus of late Roman times. I saw something of this spatialising of institutions in the colonising processes of 'Oro's Taputapuatea temples. It is difficult not to think that the accomplishment of such extension of power and the experience of it in material symbols is not critical in the civilising process and the establishment of political and cultural hegemonies. I think it is the responsibility of ethographic history to portray the ambivalences and paradoxes of symbolic experiences as well as their certainties.

That part of Maximo Rodriguez's journal and the accounts of the Spanish friars that have survived can be found in Corney (1913). The execution of the rebels by Pomare is described in Newbury (1961: 252) and the letters and journals of the London Missionary Society of the times.

Another sort of altar stone

The Greens (1968) long ago provided the best description of the *marae* at Tarahoi and with that description a review of the various eyewitnesses to rituals there. Oliver (1988) transcribes the texts of Bligh's witnessing from Bligh (1976: July 12, 1792), George Tobin (1791–3: May 2, 1792) and Godolphin Bond (Mackaness 1960: 41–2). James Cook and his companions (Beaglehole 1967: 198–205; 1968: 533; 1969: 217, 978–85) add further dimensions.

For Pomare III's coronation, see Montgomery (1831: 91) and Malardé (1931).

Managing the sublime

The Muster Rolls of the *Pandora* survive but not much else. For archaeological relics and the most recent account of the *Pandora,* see Marden (1985) and Coleman (1989). The narrative of the surgeon, George Hamilton (1794), has been the prime source of most histories. Captain Edwards' own papers (1789, 1790) are scrappy. Morrison (1935) and Peter Heywood (Nessie Heywood n.d.) give the alternative story. Rawson (1963 [*pace* Rolf du Rietz 1963]) has been the prime authority on the *Pandora* for perhaps too long.

What interested me in Edmund Burke (1904*b,* 1904*c*) was that he experienced the contradictions of cultural hegemony with the rest of us. Symbolic action, when it is either Sublime or Beautiful, seems to be naturally effective of the meanings it signifies. At the same time, it is subject to manipulation and invention that betray both its politics and its self-interest. The rule of law, in the late eighteenth century, was a 'potent fiction', John Brewer has written (1980: 15–16). Its reality was that it was a 'crucible of conflict' in which its discretionary application was an instrument of domination (see Hay 1975: 58 as well). In the end, I do not think the perception of the mutineers as victims of sacrifice to be fantasy at all.

In the name of the Revolution . . . of the King . . . of the President.

My fuller narrative of these possession rituals in the Marquesas can be found in *Islands and Beaches* (Dening 1988a). There, too, are fuller reflections on the social and cultural scandal created by beachcombing.

Going native

There is enough of a sense of titillation in the correspondence from and to Nessie Heywood (Heywood n.d.) to wonder at what it meant. We will see below in 'Possessing others with a laugh' that the feminisation of the Other, of the Native, allowed cultural differences to be ignored and native 'wantonness' to be the excuse for the civilised to be savage. Stafford, *Voyage into Substance* (1984), shows that, at this time, the voice of science and discovery was deemed to be male in opposition to that of style, nuance, poetry, which was feminine. I think that the voice of the law as expressed by the Admiralty, court martial panels and officers of the navy was also gendered. They clothe brutality and *realpolitik* with Nessie's maidenhood and 'Peter's' demasculined boyhood and discover their better selves excused from responsibility. They can turn their backs on what they did to Millward, Burkitt and Ellison and see their 'true' selves mirrored in their punctilio with Nessie.

Possessing others with a laugh

Said (1989: 213) has remarked on the fetishism of otherness that has marked the European encompassing of the world. Indeed as the discovery of Tahiti has been represented, Europe seemed to bathe in the 'deepdown freshness' (G. M. Hopkins) of the Noble Savage. Who can deny either the delirious escapism of the late eighteenth century or the visionary nostalgia of the twentieth? But I think it is not otherness but normality that is the fetish, as this reflection borrowed from an earlier piece of mine (Dening 1986) is meant to show. Stallybrass and White's (1986: 14) phrase, 'grotesque realism', is a better one. Laughter degrades difference and appreciates normality at the same time. Laughter possesses self in possessing others. The fetish of otherness is more a fear of modernity.

The trouble with that as a historical thesis is that the delirium of philosophers and painters gets frozen on pages and canvas while the laughter of crowds is evanescent. Take my reflection then not so much as a thesis as a sample – with more to come – of what theatrical history may be.

Poor John Hawkesworth is easy to find. See Abbott (1982). So is the real Omai on his visit to England. See McCormick (1977), Clark (1940). The flood of verse mocking Joseph Banks' fetish of otherness and reducing natives to comic spectacle was great: Blosset [Pseud.] (1774), English Alphabet (1786), Oberea [Pseud.] (1771), Banks [Pseud.] (n.d.), Omiah [Pseud.] (1775), Oberea [Pseud.] (1779), Omai [Pseud.] (1780), Anon. (1779), Omiah [Pseud.] (1776), Oberea [Pseud.] (n.d.), Anon. (1777). See Roderick (1972) for a more literary critique.

That a pantomime should have both mythical and topical significance is no new insight (Allen 1965; Mayer 1969). *Omai or a Trip Round the World* has been the subject of considerable research: Allen (1962); Huse (1936); Irvin (1970); Joppien (1979); Thiersch (1972). The pantomime's programme (O'Keeffe 1785), the reviews in London newspapers and magazines, December 1785 (*European Magazine, New London Magazine, London Chronicle, Universal Daily Register, Rambler's Magazine,* London *Times*), John O'Keeffe's recollections (1826), various histories and annals of the London stage (Dibdin n.d.; Dobson 1917; Hogan 1968; Pyne 1823; Wyndham 1906) make up the primary sources for this parable of possession.

Henry Adams (1901, 1964), Teuira Henry (1928), read with the understanding offered by Oliver (1974) and the cautions of Gunson (1963), help me repossess Tahiti yet again.

Ralph Wewitzer: the first 'Captain Bligh'.
This Entr'acte, like the interlude on sacrifice, like the narrative on fatal histories, like the reflection on possessing, concerns the dynamics of representation. I confess to having been fascinated by Diderot's *Paradox of Acting* the moment I read it and pursued him and it wherever I could: Barthes (1986); Cole and Chinoy (1949); Diderot (1958, 1964); Elkner (1973); Fried (1980); Guilhamet (1974); Hagpood (1958); Seznec (1975);

Wilson (1961, 1972). He drove me to Aristotle and Plato (Halliwell 1986; Havelock 1963), to discovering the dimensions of the antitheatrical prejudice (Barish 1981), to exploring the social and epistemological significance of theatre theory (Carlson 1984; Morrison 1982) and to unravelling the interplay within theatre of material environment and dramatic meaning (Gassner and Allen 1964; Kuritz 1988; Nicholl 1927; Pedicord 1954; Roose-Evans 1977; Sherson 1925) as well as the interplay of the theatre and a wider society (Kelly 1936; McCabe 1983; Meisel 1983; Paulson 1983; Watson 1906). All this because I felt Diderot, in stressing the paradoxical nature of representation, was inviting us to describe symbolising 'as it actually is', not 'as if' it were controlled by some model. Of course one does not make that discovery alone (Schechner 1985; Turner 1969, 1982, 1989).

Outside of newspaper advertisements (Newspapers 1790–2), Ralph Wewitzer left few relics of his life (Baker: 1812: 1; Oxberry 1825: 1–209, 2–176; Russell n.d.: 214). William Bourke, by alphabetical precedence, now has a place in an incomplete dictionary (Highfill 1975). The Royalty Theatre and its turbulent history won more concern (Doran n.d.: 3: 8–9; Genest 1832: 6/458; Sherson 1925: 43; Watson 1906: 104).

De Loutherbourg's pivotal role in theatre and painting is well recorded (R. G. Allen 1964, 1966; Highfill 1975; Joppien 1979; Rosenfield 1972). He appears in many diaries and memoirs of the time (Dobson 1917: 94–110; Farington n.d., 1978 [n.d. has an index!]; Pyne 1823; Seznec 1975).

One needs to learn how to read eighteenth-century newspapers. Aspinall (1949), Boyce and Curran (1978), Read (1961), Werkmeister (1963, 1967) will help. Charles Beecher Hogan, *The London Stage 1600–1800: Part 5 1776–1800* (1968), is the first and last resort for anything concerning London theatre.

The island

Fosberg (Ed.), *Man's Place in the Island Ecosystem* (1965), describes the sifting and species-making processes in the isolated habitats of Pacific Islands. Cartaret's discovery of Pitcairn Island, Wallis (1965: 1–149).

A murderous settlement

Teehuteatuaonoa (1819, 1829) is virtually our only source of knowledge of the *Bounty*'s voyage to Pitcairn, but Maude's 'In Search of a Home' (1968: 1–34) is a wonderful enlargement of her account and is worth reading just to see a master historian/researcher at work. The history of Pitcairn is available in many places – Maude (1964a) himself; Ball (1973); Brodie (1851); Nicolson (1966). John Buffet (1846) wrote a narrative of twenty years' residence for *The Friend*. The Harvard anthropologist Harry L. Shapiro tried to unravel the physical and cultural heritage of this new society (1929, 1936). Scott (1989), Glynn Christian (1982), Kennedy (1989) have their modifications of earlier histories.

'Innocence better imagined than described'

Sir Joseph Banks maintained his interest in Bligh and the *Bounty* for many years. In his papers in the Mitchell Library can be found all the tidbits that those who knew his interests fed him. So much of what was later published came to him in manuscript form: Beechey (1831), Folger (1808), Pipon (1814), Shillibeer (1817). Sir John Barrow (1833) used his position in the Admiralty to distribute, out of captains' reports, the good news of the miracle of Pitcairn. Published (Bechervaise 1839) and unpublished accounts (Edwardson 1820; Ramsey 1821) glowed with the same sense of graceful beauty. *Poole's Index of Periodical Literature* of Victorian England (Poole 1963) lists dozens of sermons and pious narratives that edified the faithful on the subject.

'Poore orfing'

Brian Scott (1982) gives us an archaeology of John Adams, but Adams himself (Adams 1825) deposited several versions of his story on different ears. Chamier (1835) and Aleck (1855) are only two of the further stratifications of that archaeology.

Politics on Pitcairn

Keith Hancock's essay (1947) survives the years. The general histories of Pitcairn, cited above, tell the sad tale of the later years of tyranny and pilgrimage. Rosalind Amelia Young (1924), 'native daughter', great-granddaughter of John Adams, gives an insider's view gently, piously.

Representation of cultural literacy

Films as cultural artefacts have a disembodied feel. Their function is to be seen, but writing the history of seeing is a difficult thing. A film in its can is not like a book on its shelf or a manuscript in an archive file. In a text written down, one can see the author, the environment of its origins, the environment to which it is addressed. The possibilities of its meaning can be reduced to probabilities. Reading and living have become very close, and historians move easily between them. With a film it is different. Everything is subterfuge and camouflage. Living is out of camera view and off set. We see films in crowds and argue with one another over what we have seen. Maybe some time in the future somebody will write on *The Film*, as Henri Lefevre wrote on *The Book*, and Walter Ong on *The Word*.

Not now. Moving uncomfortably between hagiography and scatology of the 'stars', I embraced Michael Rogin (1987) and Neal Gabler (1988) with enthusiasm because they began to teach me how to 'read' a film. But mostly I blessed two sorts of people I thought I would never bless – film censors and studio publicity agents. They gave me texts that I could really read: 'Mutiny on the Bounty' (1935, 1962), Press Book (1935, 1962), Campaign Book (1935).

There are a series of general research tools that are indispensable for this sort of history: F. N. Magill (1980); Jay Robert Nash and Stanley Ralph Ross (1986); David Thomson (1975); James Vinson (1986).

Such information as I have about the 1916 and 1932 Australian films comes from Chauvel (1933), Cunningham (1991), Flynn (1959), Freedland (1978), Pike and Cooper (1980), Peter Valenti (1984).

There is a plethora of biographies and reminiscenses surrounding the production and the stars of both the 1935 and 1962 versions of the 'Mutiny on the Bounty'. My selection out of them was these:

1935: Paul L. Briand (1966); George Carpozi (1961); Bosley Crowther (1960); Kathleen Gable (1961); Jean Garceau (1961); James Norman Hall (1952); Warren G. Harris (1974); Charles Higham (1976); Rene Jordan (1973); Elsa Lanchester (1938); Samuel Marx (1975); Robert Roulston (1978); Kurt Singer (1954); Bob Thomas (1969); Lyn Tornabene (1976); Jane Ellen Wayne (1987). *1962:* Ann Kashfi Brando and E. P. Stein (1979); Gary Carey (1973); Francois Guerif (1977); Charles Higham (1987); Rene Jordan (1975); Metro-Goldwyn-Mayer (1962); Bob Thomas (1975).

Mr William Bennett is perhaps a walk-on 'extra' to my theatre of the *Bounty*. His ideas on history and his plans for it in American education can be found in William J. Bennett (1987*a*, 1987*b*, 1988*a*, 1988*b*).

No student of the *Bounty* should be without the guide and programme to the bicentenary exhibition at the National Maritime Museum, Greenwich – *Mutiny on the Bounty* (1989).

Reference Bibliography

Abbott, John Lawrence. 1982. *John Hawkesworth. Eighteenth-Century Man of Letters.* Madison: The University of Wisconsin Press.

Adams, Henry (Ed.). 1901. *Memoirs of Arii Taimai E Marama of Eimeo, Teriirere of Tooarai, Teriinui of Tahiti.* Paris: Privately printed.

Adams, Henry (Ed.). 1964. *Mémoires d'Arii Taimai.* (Suzanne and André Lebois, trans. Marie-Thérèse and Bengt Danielsson, Intro.) Paris: Société des Océanistes.

Adams, John. 1825. 'Autograph MS Narrative of the Mutiny of the Bounty, given to Captain Beechey in Dec. 1825.' Sydney: Mitchell Library, ML A 1804.

Adams, John. 1850. *The Works of John Adams.* Boston: Charles C. Little and James Brown.

Adams, John. 1961. *Diary and Autobiography of John Adams* (L. H. Butterfield, ed.). Cambridge, Mass.: Belknap Press.

Admiralty. 1772. *Regulations and Instructions Relating to His Majesty's Service at Sea,* 11th ed. London: Admiralty.

Admiralty. 1790. *Regulations and Instructions Relating to His Majesty's Service at Sea,* 13th ed. London: Admiralty.

Admiralty. 1808. *Regulations and Instructions Relating to His Majesty's Service at Sea Established by His Majesty's Council.* London: Admiralty.

Admiralty. 1810. *A Collection of the Statutes Relating to the Admiralty, Navy, Shipping and Navigators down to the Fifteenth of George III inclusive.* London: Admiralty.

Admiralty. 1826. *Regulations and Instructions Relating to His Majesty's Service at Sea.* London: Admiralty.

Agnew, Jean-Christophe. 1986. *Worlds Apart: The Market and the Theater in Anglo-American Thought, 1550–1750.* Cambridge: Cambridge University Press.

Aitken, Robert T. 1930. *Ethnology of Tubuai.* Honolulu: Bishop Museum Bulletin 4.

Aldridge, A. Owen. 1975. *Voltaire and the Century of Life.* Princeton: Princeton University Press.

Aleck. 1855. *Aleck and the Mutineers of the Bounty. A Remarkable Illustration of the Influence of the Bible,* new ed. Boston: Massachusetts Sabbath School Society.

Allen, Gardner W. 1962[1913]. *A Naval History of the American Revolution.* New York: Russell and Russell.

Allen, Ralph G. 1962. 'De Loutherbourg and Captain Cook.' *Theatre Research* 4: 195–211.

Allen, Ralph G. 1964. ' "The Wonder of Derbyshire": A Spectacular Eighteenth Century Travelogue.' In Gassner and Allen 1964: 1035–47.

Allen, Ralph G. 1965. 'Topical Scenes from Pantomime.' *Education Theatre Journal* 17: 289–300.

Allen, Ralph G. 1966. 'The Eidophusikon.' *Theatre Design and Technology* 7: 12–6.

American Theatrical Arts. 1971. *A Guide to Manuscripts and Special Collections in the United States and Canada.* New York: William C. Young.

Anderson, Charles Robert. 1937. *Journal of a Cruise to the Pacific Ocean 1842– 1844 in the Frigate* United States. Durham: Duke University Press.

Anon. 1777. *Seventeen Hundred and Seventy Seven or a Picture of the Manners and Character of the Age. In a Poetical Epistle from a Lady of Quality.* London: T. Evans.

Anon. 1779. *Mimosa or the Sensitive Plant: A Poem dedicated to Kitt Frederick, Dutchess of Queensberry Elect.* London: Printed for W. Sandwich near the Admiralty to be sold by all the Booksellers within the Bills of Mortality.

Anon. 1790. 'Narrative of the Loss of HM Frigate *Pandora.*' Sydney: Mitchell Library, Manuscript, Safe 1/30.

Anon. 1792*a*. *An Account of the Mutinous Seizure of the Bounty with the Succeeding Hardship of the Crew to which are Added Secret Anecdotes of the Otaheitean Females.*London: Robert Turner.

Anon. 1792*b*. *A New Theatrical Dictionary.* London: S. Beadon.

Anon. 1831*a*. 'A Sketch of the Career of the Late Capt. Peter Heywood R.N.' *United Services Journal* 1: 468–87.

Anon. 1831*b*. 'The *Bounty* Again.' *United Services Journal* 3: 305–15.

Anon. 1831*c*. 'Pitcairn Island Extracts 1831–81.' Sydney: Mitchell Library, MS F 999.7 P.

Anon. 1842. 'The Last of the "Pandoras".' *United Service Magazine* 3: 1–13.

Anon. 1843. 'The *Pandora* Again.' *United Services Journal* 1: 411–20.

Ansted, A. 1947. *A Dictionary of Sea Terms.* Glasgow: Brown, Sons and Ferguson.

Archer, William. 1888. *Masks of Races? A Study of the Psychology of Acting.* London: Longman Green.

Aspinall, A. 1949. *Politics and the Press c. 1780–1850.* London: Home and Van Thal.

Asquith, Ivan. 1978. 'The Structure, Ownership and Control of the Press 1780– 1855.' In Boyce and Curran 1978: 98–116.

Aubert, Vilhelm. 1982. *The Hidden Society.* New Brunswick: Transactions Books.

Auerbach, Erich. 1968. *Mimesis: The Representation of Reality in Western Literature.* Princeton: Princeton University Press.

Aycock, William B., and Seymour W. Wurfel. 1955. *Military Law under the Uniform Code of Military Justice.* Chapel Hill: University of North Carolina Press.

Bach, John. 1963. 'The Royal Navy in the Pacific Islands.' *Journal of Pacific History* 3: 3–20.

Bach, John. (Ed.). 1986. *The Bligh Notebook.* 2 vols. Canberra: National Library of Australia.

Baker, David Erskine. 1812. *Biographical Dramatica.* London: Longman Hurst.

Baker, Ian M. 1973. *Pitcairn: Children of the Bounty.* London: Victor Gollancz.

Ball, Ian M. 1973. *Pitcairn. Children of the* Bounty. London: Victor Gollancz.

Banks, Sir Joseph. 1787–94. 'Sir Joseph Banks Papers.' Sydney: Mitchell Library, Brabourne Collection, vol. 5.

Banks, Sir Joseph [Pseud.]. n.d. *An epistle from Mr Banks Voyager, Monster Hunter and Amoroso to Oberea, Queen of Otaheite Translated by ABC Esq. Second Professor of the Otaheite and every other unknown tongue.* London: Privately printed.

Barham, Lord Charles. 1906. *Letters and Papers of Charles, Lord Barham, Admiral of the Red Squadron 1758–1813.* London: Navy Records Society.

Barish, Jonas. 1981. *The Anti-Theatrical Prejudice.* Berkeley: University of California Press.

Barrow, Sir John. 1831. *The Eventful History of the Mutiny and Piratical Seizure of H.M.S.* Bounty*; its cause and consequences.* London: J. Murray.

Barrow, Sir John. 1980. *The Mutiny of the* Bounty (Gavin Kennedy, ed.) Boston: David R. Godine.

Barthes, Roland. 1986. 'Diderot, Brecht, Eisenstein.' In Rosen 1986: 172–8.

Bassett, Fletcher S. 1971. *Legends and Superstitions of the Sea and of Sailors.* Detroit: Singing Tree Press.

Baston, G. A. R. 1790. *Narration d'Omai.* 4 vols. Paris: Buisson.

Bauss, Rudy. 1981. 'Rio de Janeiro; Strategic Base for Global Designs of the British Royal Navy 1777–1815.' In Symonds 1981: 75–89.

Baynham, Henry. 1969. *From the Lower Deck. The Old Navy 1780–1840.* London: Hutchinson.

Baynham, Henry. 1971. *Before the Mast.* London: Hutchinson.

Beaglehole, J. C. (Ed.). 1967. *The Journals of Captain James Cook on His Voyages of Discovery. The Voyage of the* Resolution *and* Discovery, *1776–1780.* Cambridge: Hakluyt Society, extra series xxxvi.

Beaglehole, J. C. (Ed.). 1968. *The Journals of Captain James Cook on His Voyages of Discovery. The Voyage of the* Endeavour, *1768–1771.* Cambridge: Hakluyt Society, extra series xxxiv.

Beaglehole, J. C. (Ed.). 1969. *The Journals of Captain James Cook on His Voyages of Discovery. The Voyage of the* Resolution *and* Adventure, *1772–1775.* Cambridge: Hakluyt Society, extra series xxxv.

Beaglehole, J. C. 1974. *The Life of Captain James Cook*. Stanford: Stanford University Press.

Beatson, Robert. 1804. *Naval and Military Memoirs of Great Britain from 1729 to 1783*. 6 vols. London: Longman Hurst.

Bechervaise, John. 1839. *Thirty-Six Years of Sea-Faring Life*. Portsea: Longman.

Beechey, F. W. 1831. *Narrative of a Voyage to the Pacific and Beerings Strait*. London: H. Colburn and R. Bentley.

Belased, David. 1964. "Some of My Stage Effects." In Gassner and Allen 1964: 972–8.

Belcher, Lady Diana. 1870. *The Mutineers of the* Bounty *and Their Descendants in Pitcairn and Norfolk Islands*. London: J. Murray.

Bennett, F. D. 1840. *Narrative of a Whaling Voyage Round the Globe for the Years 1833–1836*. 2 vols. London: R. Bentley.

Bennett, Stanley. 1968. *The Price of Admiralty*. London: Robert Hale.

Bennett, William J. 1987a. *James Madison High School*. Washington: U.S. Department of Education.

Bennett, William J. 1987b. *What Works. Research about Teaching and Learning*. Washington: U.S. Department of Education.

Bennett, William J. 1988a. *Our Children and Our Country*. New York: Simon and Schuster.

Bennett, William J. 1988b. *American Education. Making It Work. Report to the President*. Washington: U.S. Department of Education.

Blane, Gilbert, 1785. *Observations on Diseases Incident to Seamen*. London: Joseph Cooper.

Blane, Gilbert. 1822. *Selected Dissertations on Several Subjects of Medical Science*. London: Thomas and George Underwood.

Bligh, William. n. d. 'Drawings.' Sydney: Mitchell Library, MS Px A 565 f18, 19, 52.

Bligh, William. 1790. *A Narrative of the Mutiny on Board His Majesty's Ship the* Bounty *and subsequent voyage of part of the crew in the ship's boat from Tofoa, one of the Friendly Islands, to Timor, a Dutch settlement in the East Indies, illustrated with charts*. London: G. Nicol.

Bligh, William 1792. *A Voyage to the South Seas, undertaken by command of His Majesty, for the purpose of conveying the breadfruit tree to the West Indies in His Majesty's Ship the* Bounty. London: G. Nicol.

Bligh, William. 1794. *Answer to Certain Assertions contained in the Appendix to a pamphlet entitled 'Minutes of the Proceedings of the Court-martial . . . on ten persons charged with mutiny on board His Majesty's Ship* Bounty'. London: G. Nicol.

Bligh, William. 1937 [1787–9]. *The Log of the* Bounty (Owen Rutter, ed.). 2 vols. London: Golden Cockerell Press.

Bligh, William. 1976 [1791–3]. *The Log of the* Providence. London: Genesis Publications.

Bligh, William. 1981. *The Mutiny on Board H.M.S.* Bounty. *The Log in Facsimile* (Stephen Walters, ed.). Guilford, Surrey: Pageminster Press.

Bligh, William. 1989. *Awake, Bold Bligh! William Bligh's letters describing the mutiny on HMS* Bounty. (Paul Brunton, ed.) Sydney: Allen and Unwin.

Blosset, Harriet [Pseud.]. 1774. *The Court of Apollo. An Heroic Epistle from the injured Harriet, Mistress to Mr Banks, to Oberea Queen of Otaheite.* London: Westminster Magazine.

Boon, James. 1973. 'Further Operations of Culture in Anthropology.' In Schneider and Bonjean 1973: 1–32.

Boon, James. 1982. *Other Tribes, Other Scribes: Symbolic Anthropology in the Comparative Study of Cultures, Histories, Religions, and Texts.* New York: Cambridge University Press.

Borrow, George. 1906 [1857]. *The Romany Rye.* London: Dent, Everyman's Library.

Bosanquet, Henry T. A. 1921. 'The Maritime School at Chelsea.' *Mariner's Mirror* 7: 322–9.

Bosanquet, Henry T. A. 1922. 'County Naval Free Schools on Waste Lands.' *Mariner's Mirror* 8: 101–8.

Bougainville, Louis de. 1772. *A Voyage Round the World. Performed by order of His Most Christian Majesty, in the years 1766, 1767, 1768 and 1769* (John Reinhold Forster, trans.). London: J. Nourse.

Bowman, Hildebrand [Pseud.]. 1778. *The Travels of Hildebrand Bowman Esq.* London: W. Strahan and Cadell.

Boyce, George, and Pauline Wingate Curran. 1978. *Newspaper History.* London: Constable.

Bradley, W. 1789. 'A Voyage to New South Wales.' Sydney: Mitchell Library, MS A 3631.

Brand, C. E. 1968. *Roman Military Law.* Austin: University of Texas Press.

Brando, Anna Kashfi, and E. P. Stein. 1979. *Brando for Breakfast.* New York: Crown.

Braugh, Daniel A. 1965. *British Naval Administration in the Age of Walpole.* Princeton: Princeton University Press.

Braunholtz, H. J. 1970. *Sir Hans Sloane and Ethnography* (W. Fagg, ed.). London: British Museum.

Brewer, John, and J. Styles (Eds.). 1980. *An Ungovernable People.* London: Hutchinson.

Briand, Paul L. 1966. *In Search of Paradise. The Nordhoff-Hall Story.* New York: Duell, Sloan and Pearce.

Brissenden, R. F. (Ed.). 1973. *Studies in the Eighteenth Century II.* Canberra: ANU Press.

Brodie, Walter. 1851. *Pitcairn's Island and the Islanders in 1850.* London: Whittaker.

Brown, Andrew. 1793. *A Sermon on the Dangers and Duties of the Seafaring Life.* Boston: Belknap and Hall.

Brown, P. R. L. 1981. *The Cult of the Saints.* Chicago: University of Chicago Press.

Buffet, John. 1846. 'A Narrative of 20 Years Residence on Pitcairn Island.' *The Friend* 4: 2–3, 20–1, 27–8, 34–5, 50–1, 66–7.

Buker, George C. 1970. 'Captain's Mast: Conservatism vs Liberalism.' *American Neptune* 30: 139–46.

Burke, Edmund. 1904*a*. *The Works of the Right Honourable Edmund Burke.* 8 vols. Boston: Little, Brown.

Burke, Edmund. 1904*b*. 'A Philosophical Inquiry into the Origin of our Ideas of the Sublime and Beautiful; with an Introductory Discourse concerning Taste.' In Burke 1904*a*: 1: 67–262.

Burke, Edmund. 1904*c*. 'Some Thoughts on the Approaching Executions, Humbly Offered to Consideration.' In Burke 1904*a*: 6: 245–53.

Burke, Peter. 1876. *Celebrated Naval and Military Trials.* London: W. H. Allen.

Burnim, Kalman A. 1964. 'David Garrick: Plot and Practice.' In Gassner and Allen 1964: 1011–34.

Burr, Henry L. 1939. 'Education in the Early Navy.' Ph.D. diss., Temple University, Philadelphia.

Byrn, John D. 1989. *Crime and Punishment in the Royal Navy. Discipline on the Leeward Islands Station 1784–1812.* Brookfield, Vermont: Scolar Press.

Byron, George Gordon. 1823. *The Island or Christian and His Comrades.* London: J. Hunt.

Callender, Geoffrey. 1936. 'Portraiture of Bligh.' *Mariner's Mirror* 22: 172–8.

Campaign Book. 1935. *Mutiny on the Bounty Campaign Book.* New York: Public Library, Center for the Study of Performing Arts. ZAN-T8, reel 35, NC 199–202.

Caramello, Charles. 1983. *Silverless Mirrors. Book, Self, and Postmodern American Fiction.* Gainesville: University Presses of Florida/Talahassee.

Carey, Gary. 1973. *Brando.* New York: Simon and Schuster.

Carlson, Marvin. 1984. *Theories of the Theatre: A Historical and Critical Survey from the Greeks to the Present.* Ithaca: Cornell University Press.

Carpozi, George, Jr. 1961. *Clark Gable.* New York: Pyramid.

Castronono, David. 1987. *The English Gentleman: Images and Ideals in Literature and Society*. New York: Unger.

Catalogue. 1818. *A Catalogue of the Genuine Collection of Ancient and Modern Prints of the Late Admiral Bligh (of Farningham Kent) Comprising the Production of the Principal Artists of the various Schools, British and Foreign Portraits, A Large Collection of Theatrical Prints, Drawings of Natural History by Van Huysun etc. Valuable Books of Prints Among which will be found Le Brun, Dusselroff, Poullain, Lambert, Farnese, Pamfili, D'Aiguillea and other Celebrated Galleries. English and Foreign Topography. The Works of Hogarth, Morland, Capt. Baillie. The Houghton Collection etc. Useful Volumes of Maps and Charts and Portfolios which will be sold by auction On Monday, July 27, 1818 and three following days, at Twelve O'Clock*. London: Sothebys.

Chamier, Captain Frederick. 1835. *Jack Adams: The Mutineer*. 3 vols. London: Henry Colburn.

Chapelle, Howard J. 1949. *The History of the American Sailing Navy*. New York: W. W. Norton.

Chapelle, Howard J. 1967. *The Search for Speed under Sail*. New York: W. W. Norton.

Chauvel, Charles. 1933. *In the Wake of 'The Bounty': To Tahiti and Pitcairn Island*. Sydney: Endeavour Press.

Christian, Edward. 1819. *Charges Delivered to Grand Juries in the Isle of Ely Upon Libels, Criminal Law, Vagrants, Religion, Rebellious Assemblies, etc. for the Use of Magistrates and Students of the Law*, 2d ed. London: T. Clarke and Sons.

Christian, Fletcher [Pseud.]. 1809. 'Statements of the Loss of Her Majesty's New Ship The *Bounty*.' *Mariner's Marvellous Magazine* 2.

Christian, Fletcher [Pseud.]. 1984 [1796]. *Letters from Mr. Fletcher Christian* (Stephen Walters, ed.) Guilford: Genesis Publications.

Christian, Glynn. 1982. *Fragile Paradise: The Discovery of Fletcher Christian* Bounty Mutineer. Boston: Little, Brown.

Clark, Thomas Blake. 1940. *Omai. First Polynesian Ambassador to England*. Honolulu: Colt Press.

Clark, William Bell. 1941. 'American Naval Policy 1775–1776.' *American Neptune* 1: 26–41.

Clark, William Bell. 1960. *George Washington's Navy*. Baton Rouge: Louisiana State University Press.

Clark, William Bell (Ed.). 1966. *Naval Documents of the American Revolution*. Washington: Office of Naval Operations.

Clavel, Scott. 1954. *Under the Lash*. London: Torchstream.

Claxton, Christopher. 1815. *The Naval Monitor: Containing many useful hints both for the public and private conduct of young gentlemen in, or entering, the profession, in all branches, in the course of which and under the remarks on gunnery, are some observations on the naval actions with America also A Plan for improving the naval system, as far as it regards that most useful set of petty officers, the midshipmen.* London: Law and Whittaker.

Clendinnen, Inga. 1987. *Ambivalent Conquests. Maya and Spaniards in Yucatan, 1517–1570.* Cambridge: Cambridge University Press.

Clifford, James. 1988. *The Predicament of Culture: Twentieth Century Ethnography, Literature and Art.* Cambridge, Mass.: Harvard University Press.

Clifford, James, and George E. Marcus (Eds.). 1984. *Writing Culture.* Berkeley: University of California Press.

Clippings. 1935. 'Mutiny on the *Bounty* 1935.' New York: Public Library, Center for Study of Performing Arts.

Cole, Toby, and Helen Krich Chinoy. 1949. *Actors on Acting.* New York: Crown.

Coleman, George. 1830. *Random Records.* London: Henry Colburn.

Coleman, Ronald A. 1989. 'Tragedy of the *Pandora.*' In 'Mutiny on the *Bounty*' 1989: 116–23.

Coletta, Paolo E. 1980. *American Secretaries of the Navy 1775–1913.* Annapolis: Naval Institute Press.

Collection. 1810. *A Collection of the Statutes Relating to the Admiralty, Navy, Shipping and Navigation down to the fifteenth of George III inclusive.* London: Admiralty.

Connolly, L. W. 1971. 'A Case of Political Censorship at the Little Theatre in the Haymarket in 1794 . . .' *Restoration and Eighteenth Century Theatre Research* 10: 34–40.

Continental Congress. 1775 [1905]. *Journals of the Continental Congress 1774–1789.* Washington: Library of Congress, vol. III, September 21–December 30.

Cook, Captain James. 1979. *Captain Cook and the South Pacific* (T. C. Mitchell, ed.). London: British Museum, yearbook 3.

Corney, Bolton Glanvill (Ed.). 1913. *The Quest and Occupation of Tahiti.* Cambridge: Hakluyt Society, series 2: 32, 36, 43.

Course, A. G. 1962. *A Dictionary of Nautical Terms.* London: ARCO Publications.

Creswell, John. 1972. *British Admirals of the Eighteenth Century.* Hamden, Conn.: Shoe String Press.

Crosby, Alfred. 1986. *Ecological Imperialism. The Biological Expansion of Europe 900–1900.* Cambridge: Cambridge University Press.

Crossland, Cyril. 1928. 'The Island of Tahiti.' *Geographical Journal* 71: 561–85.

Crowhurst, Patrick. 1989. *The French War on Trade. Privateering 1793–1815.* Aldershot: Scolar Press.

Crowther, Bosley. 1960. *Hollywood Raja: The Life and Times of Louis B. Mayer.* New York: Henry Holt and Co.

Cunliffe, Marcus. 1968. *Soldiers and Civilians: The Martial Spirit in America.* Boston: Little, Brown.

Cunningham, Stuart. 1991. *Featuring Australia: The Cinema of Charles Chauvel.* Sydney: Allen and Unwin.

Cuzent, G. 1860. *Iles de la Société.* Rochefort: C. Thèze.

Dana, Richard Henry. n.d. [1840]. *Two Years Before the Mast. A Personal Narrative of Life at Sea.* London: Blackie and Son.

Dana, Richard Henry. 1854. *The Seaman's Friend,* 7th ed. Boston: Thomas Groom.

Dandeker, Christopher. 1985. 'The Old Navy and Social Change: Discipline, Punishment and Authority in the Royal Navy 1780–1860.' In Department of History, U.S. Naval Institute, 1985: 93–107.

Danielsson, Bengt. 1962. *What Happened on the* Bounty? London: George Allen and Unwin.

Darby, Madge. 1965. *What Caused the Mutiny on the* Bounty? Sydney: Angus and Robertson.

Darby, Madge. 1966. *The Causes of the* Bounty *Mutiny. A Short Reply to Dr Rolf du Rietz's Comments.* Uppsala: Studia Bountyana, no. 2.

Darnton, Robert. 1984. *The Great Cat Massacre, and Other Episodes in French Cultural History.* New York: Vintage Books.

David, A. F. C. 1977a. 'Surveys of William Bligh.' *Mariner's Mirror* 63: 69–70.

David, A. F. C. 1977b. 'Broughton's Schooner and the *Bounty* Mutineers.' *Mariner's Mirror* 63: 207–13.

David, A. F. C. 1981. 'Bligh's Notes on Cook's Last Voyage.' *Mariner's Mirror* 67: 102.

Davis, George B. 1915. *A Treatise on the Military Law of the United States,* 3d ed. New York: John Wiley.

Davis, John. 1813. *The Post-Captain: or, The Wooden Walls Well Manned comprehending a view of Naval Society and Manners.* Brooklyn: Spooner and Sleight.

Davis, Ralph. 1962. *The Rise of the English Shipping Industry.* London: Macmillan.

Daws, Gavin. 1968. 'Kealakekua Bay Revisited: A Note on the Death of Captain Cook.' *Journal of Pacific History* 3: 21–3.

De Koven, Anna. n.d. *Life and Letters of John Paul Jones.* 2 vols. London: T. Werner Laurie.

Delafons, John. 1805. *A Treatise on Naval Courts Martial.* London: P. Steel.

Delano, Amasa. 1970 [1817]. *A Narrative of Voyages and Travels in the Northern and Southern Hemispheres.* New York: Praeger.

Dening, Greg. 1982. 'Sharks That Walk on the Land.' *Meanjin* 41: 417–37.

Dening, Greg. 1983. 'The Face of Battle: Valparaiso, 1814.' *War and Society* 1: 25–42.

Dening, Greg. 1984. *The Death of Captain Cook.* Sydney: Library Society, State Library of NSW.

Dening, Greg. 1986. 'Possessing Tahiti.' *Archaeology in Oceania* 21: 103–18.

Dening, Greg. 1988*a. Islands and Beaches. Discourse on a Silent Land: Marquesas 1774–1880.* Chicago: Dorsey Press.

Dening, Greg. 1988*b. History's Anthropology. The Death of William Gooch.* Washington: University Press of America, ASAO Special Publications no. 2.

Dening, Greg. 1988*c. The* Bounty: *An Ethnographic History.* Melbourne: Melbourne University History Monograph no. 1.

Dening, Greg. 1988*d.* 'Southern Cross/Northern Crosses: The Poetics of Hemisphere.' In Hardy and Frost 1988: 233–43.

Dening, Greg. 1990*a.* 'Ethnography on My Mind.' In *Boundaries of the Past* (Bain Attwood, ed.). Melbourne: Historical Institute, Victoria.

Dening, Greg. 1990*b.* 'A Poetic for Histories: Transformations that Present the Past.' In *Clio in Oceania* (Aletta Biersack, ed.). Washington: Smithsonian Institution.

Department of History, US Naval Institute. 1985. *New Aspects of Naval History.* Baltimore: Nautical and Aviation Publishing Co.

Dibble, Sheldon. 1938. *History and General Views of the Sandwich Islands Mission.* New York: Taylor and Dodd.

Dibdin, Charles. n.d. *A Complete History of the Stage.* 5 vols. London: Privately printed.

Diderot, Denis. 1935. *Supplément au Voyage de Bougainville.* Paris: E. Druz.

Diderot, Denis. 1958. *Paradox sur le Comédien.* Paris: Libraire Théâtrale.

Diderot, Denis. 1964. 'On Dramatic Poetry.' In Gassner and Allen 1964: 464–79.

Dobson, Austin. 1917. *At Prior Park and Other Papers.* London: Chatto and Windus.

Doran, John. n.d. *Their Majesty's Servants or Annals of the English Stage.* Boston: F. A. Nicolls.

Driessen, H. A. H. 1982. 'Outriggerless Canoes and Glorious Beings.' *Journal of Pacific History* 17: 3–28.

Duffy, Christopher. 1988. *The Military Experience in the Age of Reason.* New York: Atheneum.

Dugan, James. 1965. *The Great Mutiny.* New York: G. P. Putnam.

Dunmore, John. 1972. 'The Explorer and the Philosopher.' In Viet 1972: 54–66.

Du Rietz, Rolf E. 1963. 'The Voyage of HMS *Pandora* 1790–2.' *Ethnos* 28: 210–8.

Du Rietz, Rolf E. 1979*a*. *Thoughts of the Present State of Bligh Scholarship.* Uppsala: Dahlia Books, Banksia 1.

Du Rietz, Rolf E. 1979*b*. *Fresh Light on John Fryer of the* Bounty. Uppsala: Dahlia Books, Banksia 2.

Du Rietz, Rolf E. 1986. *Peter Heywood's Tahitian Vocabulary and the Narrative by James Morrison. Some Notes on Their Origin and History.* Uppsala: Dahlia Books, Banksia 3.

Edwards, Edward. 1789. 'Admiral Edwards Commanding HMS *Pandora,* Concerning the Mutiny of the *Bounty* and the Voyage of the *Pandora* 1789–91.' London: Admiralty Library; Sydney: Mitchell Library, microfilm FM4 2098.

Edwards, Edward. 1790. 'Letters to the Admiralty.' Sydney: Mitchell Library, Australian Joint Copying Project, 'Captains' Letters' 3270, no. 1763.

Edwards, Edward, and George Hamilton. 1915. *Voyage of the HMS* Pandora *Despatched to Arrest the Mutineers of the* Bounty *in the South Seas, 1789–1791.* London: F. Edward.

Edwardson, W. E. 1820. 'Journal of a Voyage from London to New South Wales and Van Diemen's Land.' Sydney: Mitchell Library, MS A 131.

Egan, Elizabeth (Compiler). 1989. *Guide to the Papers of William Bligh and the Bligh Family in the Mitchell Library, State Library of NSW.* Sydney: Library Council of NSW.

Elias, Norbert. 1950. 'Studies on the Genesis of the Naval Profession.' *British Journal of Sociology* 1: 291–301.

Elkner, Brian A. 1973. 'Diderot and the Sublime. The Artist as Hero.' In Brissenden 1973: 143–62.

Ellis, William. 1782. *An Authentic Narrative of a Voyage Performed by Captain Cook and Captain Clerke in His Majesty's Ships* Resolution *and* Discovery *During the Years 1776–1780.* 2 vols. London: G. Robinson.

Ellis, William. 1831. *Polynesian Researches.* London: Fisher and Jackson.

Emory, Kenneth P. 1931. 'The Cook's Marae.' *Bulletin de Société des Etudes Océaniennes* 4: 195–203.

Emory, Kenneth P. 1933. *Stone Remains in the Society Islands.* Honolulu: B. P. Bishop Museum Bulletin 116.

Emory, Kenneth P. 1969. 'A Re-Examination of East Polynesian Marae: Many Marae Later.' *Pacific Anthropological Records* 11: 73–92.

English Alphabet. 1786. *An English Alphabet for the Use of Foreigners; wherein the Pronunciation of the Vowels or Voice Letters is explained in twelve Short General Rules, with the several exceptions as abridged {for the Instruction of Omiah} from a larger work.* London: J. W. Galabin.

Evans-Pritchard, E. E. 1937. *Witchcraft Oracles and Magic among the Azande.* Oxford: Clarendon Press.

Evans-Pritchard E. E. 1956. *Nuer Religion*. Oxford: Clarendon Press.

Fabian, Johannes. 1983. *Time and the Other*. New York: Columbia University Press.

Falconer, William. 1930. *Falconer's Celebrated Marine Dictionary. The Wooden Walls* (Claude S. Gill, ed.). London: W. and G. Foyle.

Farington, Joseph. n.d. *The Farington Diary*, 2d ed. 8 vols. (James Greg, ed.). London:Hutchinson.

Farington, Joseph. 1978. *The Diary of Joseph Farington* (Kenneth Garlick and Angus Macintyre, eds.). 25 vols. New Haven: Yale University Press.

Fernandez, James W. 1986. *Persuasions and Performances: The Play of Tropes in Culture*. Bloomington: Indiana University Press.

Fisher, Robin, and Hugh Johnston. 1979. *Captain James Cook and His Times*. Canberra: ANU Press.

Flynn, Errol. 1959. *My Wicked, Wicked Ways*. New York: G. P. Putnam.

Folger, Mayhew. 1808. 'Extract from the Log Book of Capt. Folger of the American Ship *Topaz* of Boston.' Sydney: Mitchell Library, Brabourne Collection, Banks Papers, vol. 1.

Folger, Mayhew. 1809. 'Extract from log of *Topaz*. Capt. Folger.' *Naval Chronicle* 21: 454–5.

Fosberg, F. R. (Ed.). 1965. *Man's Place in the Island Ecosystem*. Honolulu: British Museum Press.

Foucault, Michel. 1979. *Discipline and Punish: The Birth of the Prison*. New York: Vintage.

Fowler, William M. 1974. 'The Non Volunteer Navy.' *US Naval Institute Proceedings* 100: 74–8.

Fowler, William M. 1976. *Rebels under Sail*. New York: Scribner's.

Fowler, William M. 1984. *Jack Tars and Commodores 1783–1815*. Boston: Houghton Mifflin.

Freedland, Michael. 1978. *Errol Flynn*. London: Arthur Baker.

Fried, Michael. 1980. *Absorption and Theatricality: Painting and Beholder in the Age of Diderot*. Berkeley: University of California Press.

Fryer, John. 1979. *The Voyage of the* Bounty's *Launch. John Fryer's Narrative* (Stephen Walter, ed.). Guilford, Surrey: Genesis Publications.

Furneaux, Rupert. 1900. *Tobias Furneaux*. London: Cassell.

Gable, Kathleen. 1961. *Clark Gable: A Personal Portrait*. Englewood Cliffs, N.J.: Prentice-Hall.

Gabler, Neal. 1988. *An Empire of Their Own: How the Jews Invented Hollywood*. New York: Crown.

Gallagher, Robert E. (Ed.). 1964. *Byron's Journal of His Circumnavigation 1764–1765*. Cambridge: Hakluyt Society, 2d series, cxxii.

Garceau, Jean. 1961. *"Dear Mr G – ": The Biography of Clark Gable*. Boston: Little, Brown.

Garitee, Jerome R. 1977. *The Republic's Private Navy*. Middletown: Wesleyan University Press.

Gassner, John, and Ralph G. Allen (Eds.). 1964. *Theatre and Drama in the Making*. 2 vols. Boston: Houghton Mifflin.

Gebser, Jean. 1984. *The Ever Present Origin*. Athens: Ohio University Press.

Geertz, Clifford. 1973. *The Interpretation of Cultures*. New York: Basic Books.

Genest, John. 1832. *Some Account of the English Stage from the Restoration in 1660 to 1830*. 10 vols. Bath: H. E. Carrington.

Gibbon, Edward. 1896. *The History of the Decline and Fall of the Roman Empire* (J. B. Bury, ed.). 7 vols. London: Methuen.

Gilbert, A. N. 1976. 'Buggery and the British Navy 1700–1861.' *Journal of Social History* 10: 72–98.

Gilbert, A. N. 1980. 'Crime as Disorder: Criminality and the Symbolic Universe of the Eighteenth Century British Naval Officer.' In Love 1980: 110–22.

Glascock, W. N. 1831. *Naval Sketchbook*. 2 vols. London: H. Colburn.

Glascock, W. N. 1854. *The Naval Officer's Manual*, 3d ed. London: Parker, Furnwall.

Glenn, Myra C. 1984. *Campaigns against Corporal Punishment*. Albany: State University of New York Press.

Goffman, Erving. 1961. *Asylums*. Garden City, N.Y.: Doubleday.

Goldman. Irving. 1970. *Ancient Polynesian Society*. Chicago: University of Chicago Press.

Goodwin, H. B. 1890. 'The Navy of the Georges.' *United Service Magazine* 4: 178–90.

Gore, John. 1766–77. 'Logbook of HMS *Dolphin*, August 21, 1766–October, 1767.' Sydney: Mitchell Library, MS B 1533–B 1534.

Gould, Rupert T. 1928. 'Bligh's Notes on Cook's Last Voyage.' *Mariner's Mirror* 14: 371–385.

Gouriet, J. B. 1811. *Personnages Célèbres dans les Rues de Paris*. 2 vols. Paris: Lerouge.

Grant, Michael. 1974. *The Army of the Caesars*. London: Weidenfeld and Nicolson.

Greatheed, Samuel ('Nausistratus'). 1820–1. 'Authentic History of the Mutineers of the *Bounty*.' *Sailor's Magazine and Naval Miscellany* 1: 402–6, 449–56; 2: 1–8.

Green, Roger, and Kaye Green. 1968. 'Religious Structures of the Society Islands.' *New Zealand Journal of History* 2: 66–89.

Grego, Joseph. 1980. *Rowlandson the Caricaturist*. 2 vols. New York: J. W. Bouton.

Guerif, François. 1977. *Marlon Brando*. Paris: Collection Têtes d'Affiches.

Guilhamet, Leon. 1974. *The Sincere Ideal. Studies on Sincerity in Eighteenth Century English Literature*. Montreal: McGill–Queens University Press.

Gunson, W. Niel. 1963. 'A Note on the Difficulties of Ethnohistorical Writing with Special Reference to Tahiti.' *Journal of the Polynesian Society* 72: 414–19.

Gunson, W. Niel. 1980. 'Cover's Notes on the Tahitians 1802.' *Journal of Pacific History* 15: 217–24.

Hall, James Norman. 1916 [1952]. *My Island Home*. Boston: Little, Brown.

Halliwell, Stephen. 1986. *Aristotle's Poetics*. Chapel Hill: University of North Carolina Press.

Hamilton, George. 1794. *A Voyage Round the World in Her Majesty's Frigate Pandora Performed under the Direction of Captain Edwards in the Years 1790, 1791, and 1792*. Berwick: W. Phorson.

Hancock, W. K. 1947. *Politics in Pitcairn and Other Essays*. London: Macmillan.

Handler, Richard, and William Saxton. 1988. 'Dyssimulation: Reflexivity, Narrative and the Quest for the Authenticity in "Living History".' *Cultural Anthropology* 3: 242–60.

Handy, E. S. C., and E. G. Handy. 1972. *Native Planters in Old Hawaii*. Honolulu: Bishop Museum.

Hannay, David. 1914. *Naval Courts Martial*. Cambridge: Cambridge University Press.

Hanway, Jonas. 1757a. *A Letter from a Member of the Marine Society, Shewing the Piety, Generosity and Utility of their Design with respect to the Sea-Service, at this Important Crisis. Addressed to all true friends of their country*, 4th ed. London: J. Waugh.

Hanway, Jonas. 1757b. *A Journal of Eight Days Journey from Portsmouth to Kingston upon Thames*. 2 vols. London: H. Woodfall.

Hanway, Jonas. 1761. *Reflections, Essays and Meditations on Life and Religion*. 2 vols. London: John Rivington.

Hanway, Jonas. 1783. *Proposal for County Naval Free-Schools to be built on Waste Lands giving such effectual Instructions to Poor Boys as may nurse them for the Sea Service, teaching them also to cultivate the Earth that in due time they may furnish their own food, and to spin, knit, weave, make shoes, etc., with a view to provide their own raiment while good Regulation and Discipline diffuse a moral and religious Oeconomy through the Land*. London: Privately printed.

Hapgood, Elizabeth Reynolds (Ed.). 1958. *Stanislavski's Legacy. Comments on Some Aspects of an Actor's Art and Life*. London: Max Reinhardt.

Harding, Robert. 1989. 'The Inauguration Ceremony in Ancient Tahiti.' *Pacific Island Focus* 1: 45–60.

Hardy, John, and Alan Frost (Eds.). 1988. *Studies from Terra Australis to Australia*. Canberra: Australian Academy of the Humanities.

Harland, John. 1984. *Seamanship in the Age of Sail: An Account of the Shiphandling of the Sailing Man-of-War, 1600–1860, Based on Contemporary Sources.* Annapolis: Naval Institute Press.

Harris, John. 1837. *Zebulon; or, The Moral Claims of Seamen Stated and Enforced,* 3d ed. (1st U.S.). Boston: Gould, Kendall and Lincoln.

Harris, Warren G. 1974. *Gable and Lombard.* New York: Simon and Schuster.

Hastrup, Kirsten. 1990. 'The Ethnographic Present: A Reinvention.' *Cultural Anthropology* 5: 45–61.

Havelock, Eric A. 1963. *Preface to Plato.* Cambridge, Mass.: Belknap Press.

Haweis Papers. n.d. 'Haweis Papers Supplement.' Sydney: Mitchell Library, A1963.

Hawkesworth, John. 1773. *An Account of the Voyages Undertaken by the Order of His Present Majesty for Making Discoveries in the Southern Hemisphere.* 3 vols. London: W. Strahan and T. Cadell.

Hay, Douglas, et al. (Eds.). 1975. *Albion's Fatal Tree: Crime and Society in Eighteenth Century England.* New York: Random House.

Hayes, Frederic H. 1965. 'John Adams and American Sea Power.' *American Neptune* 25: 35–45.

Hearsay, John E. N. 1976. *Voltaire.* London: Constable.

Henningsen, Henning. 1954. 'Sailor's Baptism in Scandinavian Waters.' *Mariner's Mirror* 40: 196–205.

Henningsen, Henning. 1961. *Crossing the Equator: Sailor's Baptisms and Other Initiation Rites.* Munksgaarde.

Henry, T. 1928. *Ancient Tahiti.* Honolulu: Bishop Museum Bulletin 48.

Hernardi, Paul. 1985. *Interpreting Events: Tragicomedies of History on the Modern Stage.* Ithaca: Cornell University Press.

Hervé, Georges. 1914. 'Autourou ou le Taïtien à Paris'. *Revue Anthropologique* 24: 209–19.

Heywood, Nessie. n.d. 'Correspondence.' Chicago: Newberry Library, MS E 5. H 5078.

Heywood, Peter. 1789. 'Extracts from Journal.' In Edwards 1789.

Hickman, William. 1851. *A Treatise on the Law and Practice of Naval Courts Martial.* London: John Murray.

Higham, Charles. 1976. *Charles Laughton: An Intimate Biography.* Garden City, N.Y.: Doubleday.

Higham, Charles. 1987. *Brando. The Unauthorized Biography.* New York: New America Library.

Highfill, Philip H., et al. (Eds.). 1975. *A Biographical Dictionary.* Carbondale: Southern Illinois University Press.

Hill, Jonathan D. (Ed.). 1988. *Rethinking History and Myth. Indigenous Southern American Perspectives on the Past.* Urbana: University of Illinois Press.

Hogan, Charles Beecher. 1968. *The London Stage 1660–1800: Part 5 1776–1800*. 3 vols. Carbondale: Southern Illinois University Press.

Hood, Ronald Chalmers. 1985. *Royal Republicans*. Baton Rouge: Louisiana State University Press.

Horan, Leo F. S. 1970. 'Flogging in the United States Navy.' *US Naval Institute Proceedings* 76: 969–75.

Hough, Richard. 1973. *Captain Bligh and Mr Christian*. New York: E. P. Dutton.

Hough, Richard. 1975. *A History of Fighting Ships*. London: Octopus.

Hough, William. 1855. *Precedents in Military Law*. London: W. H. Allen.

Houlding, J. A. 1981. *'Fit for Service'. The Training of The British Army 1715–1795*. Oxford: Clarendon.

Hubert, Henri, and Marcel Mauss. 1964 [1898]. *Sacrifice: Its Nature and Function* (W. D. Halls, trans.). Chicago: University of Chicago Press.

Hugill, Stan. 1967. *Sailortown*. London: Routledge and Kegan Paul.

Hunter, Rosemary. 1989. 'Surviving the Pacific: Captain Bligh's Record of Health and Disease.' *Pacific Island Focus* 1(2): 23–44.

Huse, William. 1936. 'A Noble Savage on the Stage.' *Modern Philology* 33: 303–16.

Hutchins, John H. 1940. *Jonas Hanway 1712–1786*. London: Society for Promoting Christian Knowledge.

Irvin, Ric. 1970. 'Cashing in on Cook.' *Masque* 14: 14–17.

Isaac, Rhys. 1982. *The Transformation of Virginia 1740–1790*. Chapel Hill: University of North Carolina Press.

J.R. 1792. 'J.R. to Mr Urban. Sept 24.' *Gentleman's Magazine* 62: 879.

Jackson, John W. 1974. *The Pennsylvania Navy 1775–1781*. New Brunswick: Rutgers University Press.

Jacob, Giles. 1719. *The Law Military*. Ann Arbor: University Microfilms International.

Jarvie, I. C. 1970. *Towards a Sociology of the Cinema*. London: Routledge and Kegan Paul.

Jefferson, Thomas. 1961. *The Papers of Thomas Jefferson*. Vol. 16. (Julian P. Boyd, ed.), Princeton: Princeton University Press.

Jones, George C. 1829. *'A Civilian'. Sketches of Naval Life with notices of Men, Manners and Scenery on the Shores of the Mediterranean in a series of letters from the Brandywine and Constitution, Frigates*. 2 vols. New Haven: Hezekiah Howe.

Joppien, Rudiger. 1979. 'Philippe Jacques de Loutherbourg's Pantomime "Omai, or a Trip Round the World" and the Artists of Captain Cook's Voyages.' In Cook 1979: 81–136.

Jordan, Gerald. 1981. 'Admiral Nelson as Popular Hero. The Nation and the Navy, 1795–1805.' In Symonds 1981: 109–19.

Jordan, Rene. 1973. *Clark Gable: A Pyramid Illustrated History of the Movies.* New York: Pyramid.

Jordan, Rene. 1975. *Marlon Brando.* London: W. H. Allen.

Kaeppler, Adrienne L. 1970. *Feather Cloaks, Ships, Captains and Lords.* Honolulu: Bishop Museum, Occasional Papers xxiv, no. 6.

Kaeppler, Adrienne L. 1979. 'Tracing the History of Hawaiian Cook Voyage Artefacts in the Museum of Mankind.' In Cook 1979: 167–98.

Karsten, Peter. 1972. *The Naval Aristocracy.* New York: Free Press.

Keller, A. S., O. J. Lissitzyn, and F. J. Mann. 1938. *Creation of Rights of Sovereignty through Symbolic Acts, 1400–1800.* New York: Columbia University Press.

Kelly, John Alexander. 1936. *German Visitors to English Theaters in the Eighteenth Century.* Princeton: Princeton University Press.

Kemp, Peter K. 1946. *Prize Money.* Aldershot: Wellington Press.

Kemp, Peter K. 1970. *The British Sailor: A Social History of the Lower Deck.* London: J. M. Dent and Sons.

Kennedy, Gavin. 1978. *Bligh.* London: Duckworth.

Kennedy, Gavin. 1979. 'Bligh and the *Defiance* Mutiny.' *Mariner's Mirror* 65: 65–8.

Kennedy, Gavin. 1989. *Captain Bligh. The Man and His Mutinies.* Trowbridge: Duckworth.

Kling, Georges. 1965. *Tahiti, Moorea, BoraBora.* Paris: Libraire Hachette.

Knapp, A., and W. Baldwin. 1820. *The Newgate Calendar.* London: J. Robins.

Knapp, Bettina. 1980. *Theatre and Alchemy.* Detroit: Wayne State University Press.

Knapp, Mary E. 1961. *Prologues and Epilogues of the Eighteenth Century.* New Haven: Yale University Press.

Knight, C. 1936. 'H.M. Armed Vessel *Bounty.*' *Mariner's Mirror* 22: 183–99.

Knight, Roger. 1988. 'The First Fleet. Its State and Preparation 1786–1787.' In Hardy and Frost 1988: 121–36.

Kuritz, Paul. 1988. *The Making of Theatre History.* Englewood Cliffs, N.J.: Prentice-Hall.

Ladurie, E. Le Roy. 1979. *The Territory of the Historian.* Chicago: University of Chicago Press.

Lanchester, Elsa. 1938. *Charles Laughton and I.* New York: Harcourt, Brace.

Langbein, John H. 1983. 'Albion's Fatal Flaws.' *Past and Present* 96: 96–120.

Langdon, Robert. 1968. *Tahiti. Island of Love.* Sydney: Pacific Publications.

Langley, Harold. 1967. *Social Reform in the United States Navy, 1798–1862.* Urbana: University of Illinois Press.

Layton, C. N. T. 1955. *Dictionary of Nautical Words and Terms.* Glasgow: Brown Sons and Ferguson.

Ledward, Thomas Denman. 1903. 'Captain Bligh and The Mutiny on the *Bounty*' (A. Denman, Ed.). *Notes and Queries* (Series 9) 12: 501–2.

Lee, Ida. 1920. *Captain Bligh's Second Voyage to the South Seas.* London: Longman Green.

Leeson, Ida. 1939. 'The Morrison Myth.' *Mariner's Mirror* 25: 433–8.

Lemisch, Jesse. 1968. 'Jack Tar in the Streets: Merchant Seamen in the Politics of Revolutionary America.' *William and Mary Quarterly* 25: 371–407.

Lemisch, Jesse. 1969. 'Listening to the "Inarticulate": William Widger's Dream and the Loyalties of American Revolutionary Seamen in British Prisons.' *Journal of Social History* 3: 1–29.

Lévi-Strauss, Claude. 1972. *Triste Tropiques.* New York: Atheneum.

Lewis, Michael. 1939. *England's Sea Officers.* London: George Allen and Unwin.

Lewis, Michael. 1957. *The History of the British Navy.* Harmondsworth: Penguin.

Lewis, Michael. 1960. *A Social History of the Navy 1793–1815.* London: George Allen and Unwin.

Lewis, Michael. 1965. *The Navy in Transition 1816–1864.* London: Hodder and Stoughton.

Lewthwaite, G. R. 1964. 'Man and Land in Early Tahiti: Polynesian Agriculture through European Eyes.' *Pacific Viewpoint* 5: 11–34.

Lewthwaite, G. R. 1966. 'Man and the Sea in Early Tahiti. Maritime Economy through European Eyes.' *Pacific Viewpoint* 4: 28–53.

Linebaugh, Peter. 1975. 'The Tyburn Riot against the Surgeons.' In Hay et al. 1975: 65–117.

Lintott, A. W. 1972. 'Provocatio. From the Struggle of the Orders to the Principate.' In *Aufstieg und Niedergan der Romisch Welt* 1: 2, 226–67.

Lloyd, Christopher. 1968. *The British Seaman 1200–1860.* London: Collins.

Lloyd, Christopher. 1979. 'Cook and Scurvy.' *Mariner's Mirror* 65: 23–8.

Lloyd, Christopher, and J. L. S. Coulter. 1961. *Medicine and the Navy.* Vol. 3, *1714–1815.* Edinburgh: Livingstone.

Longridge, C. Nepean. 1977. *The Anatomy of Nelson's Ships.* Watford, Hertfordshire: Argus Books.

Love, Robert William (Ed.). 1980. *Changing Interpretations and New Sources in Naval History.* New York: Garland.

Lovette, Leland P. 1939. *Naval Customs.* Annapolis: Naval Institute Press.

Lucas, Sir Charles. 1929. *The Pitcairn Island Register Book.* London: Society for Promoting Christian Knowledge.

Lydenberg, Harry Miller. 1957. *Crossing the Line*. New York: New York Public Library.

Lysaght, A. M. 1979. 'Banks' Artists and His *Endeavour* Collections.' In Cook 1979: 9–80.

McArthur, John. 1813. *Principles and Practice of Naval and Military Courts Martial*, 4th ed. 2 vols. London: A. Strahan.

McCabe, William H. 1983. *An Introduction to the Jesuit Theatre*. St Louis: Institute for Jesuit Sources.

McCormick, E. H. 1977. *Omai. Pacific Envoy*. Auckland: Auckland University Press.

McGann, Jerome J. 1968. *Fiery Dust. Byron's Poetic Development*. Chicago: University of Chicago Press.

Mack, William P., and Royal E. Connell. 1980. *Naval Ceremonies, Customs, and Traditions*, 5th ed. Annapolis: Naval Institute Press.

Mackaness, George. 1931. *The Life of Vice-Admiral William Bligh*. Sydney: Angus and Robertson.

Mackaness, George (Ed.). 1938. *A Book of the* Bounty. London: J. M. Dent.

Mackaness, George. 1949. *Fresh Light on Bligh. Some Correspondence of Captain William Bligh RN with John and Francis Godolphin Bond, 1776–1811*. Sydney: Ford Printers.

Mackaness, George. 1960. 'Extracts from a Log-Book of HMS *Providence* Kept by Lt. Francis Godolphin Bond RN.' *Royal Australian Historical Society Journal* 46: 24–66.

McKay, John. 1989. *Anatomy of the Ship. The Armed Transport* Bounty. London: Conway Maritime Press.

McKee, Christopher. 1978. 'Fantasies of Mutiny and Murder.' *Armed Forces and Society* 4: 293–304.

McKee, Christopher. 1991. *A Gentlemanly and Honorable Profession: The Creation of the U.S. Naval Officer Corps, 1794–1815*. Annapolis: Naval Institute Press.

Magill, F. N. (Ed.). 1980. *Magill's Survey of Cinema*. Englewood Cliffs, N.J.: Salem Press.

Mahan, Alfred Thayer. 1879; 1888; 1893. *Naval Education, the Necessity and Object of a Naval War College, The Practical Character of the Naval War College*. Annapolis: Proceedings of United States Naval Institute.

Mahan, Alfred Thayer. 1901. *Types of Naval Officers*. Freeport, N.Y.: Books for Libraries Press.

Malardé, Yves. 1931. 'Attributes Royaux.' *Bulletin de Société des Etudes Océaniennes* 4: 204–9.

Maloney, Linda. 1980. 'The US Navy's Pacific Squadron 1824–1827.' In Love 1980: 180–91.

Maltby, Isaac. 1813. *A Treatise on Courts Martial and Military Law.* Boston: Thomas B. Wait.

Marcus, G. J. 1961. *A Naval History of England: The Formative Centuries.* Boston: Little, Brown.

Marcus, G. J. 1971. *The Age of Nelson.* New York: Viking Press.

Marcus, G. J. 1974. *Heart of Oak. A Survey of British Sea Power in the Georgian Era.* London: Oxford University Press.

Marden, Luis. 1985. 'Tragic Sequel to *Bounty* Mutiny. Wreck of H.M.S. *Pandora.' National Geographic* 168: 423–51.

Marshall, David. 1986. *The Figure of Theater.* New York: Columbia University Press.

Marshall, James Stuart, and Carrie Marshall. 1960. *Pacific Voyages.* Portland, Ore.: Binford and Mort.

Marshall, John. 1825. 'Peter Heywood. Esq.' *Royal Naval Biography* II: 2: 747–97. London: Longman, Hurst.

Marx, Samuel, 1975. *Mayer and Thalberg: The Make Believe Saints.* New York: Random House.

Masefield, John. 1920. *Sea Life in Nelson's Time,* 2d ed. London: Sphere Books.

Mason, Hadyn. 1981. *Voltaire:: A Biography.* London: Granada.

Masur, Louis P. 1989. *Rites of Execution: Capital Punishment and the Transformation of American Culture, 1776–1865.* New York: Oxford University Press.

Maude, H. E. 1964*a*. 'History of Pitcairn Island.' In Ross 1964: 45–101.

Maude, H. E. 1964*b*. 'The Voyage of the *Pandora*'s Tender.' *Mariner's Mirror* 50: 217–35.

Maude, H. E. 1968. *Of Islands and Men.* Melbourne: Oxford University Press.

Mayer, David, III. 1969. *Harlequin in His Element: The English Pantomime 1806–1836.* Cambridge, Mass.: Harvard University Press.

Meisel, Martin. 1983. *Realization. Narrative, Pictorial and Theatrical Arts in Nineteenth Century England.* Princeton: Princeton University Press.

Melville, Herman. 1970 [1850]. *White Jacket or the World of a Man of War.* Chicago: Northwestern University Press and The Newberry Library.

Metro-Goldwyn-Mayer. 1962. *M.G.M. Presents Mutiny on the* Bounty. London: Arcola Picture.

Milgram, Stanley. 1963. 'Behavioural Study of Obedience.' *Journal of Abnormal and Social Psychology* 67: 371–8.

Milton-Thompson, G. J. 1974. 'The Changing Character of the Sailor's Diet and Its Influence on Disease.' In *Problems of Medicine at Sea.* Greenwich: National Maritime Museum, Maritime Monographs no. 12.

Mintz, Sydney W. 1985. *Sweetness and Power: The Place of Sugar in Modern History.* New York: Viking Penguin.

Moerenhout, J. A. 1837. *Voyages aux îles du Grand Océan*. Paris: Adrien Maison-neuve.

Moffat, Hugh. 1965. 'George Tobin RN.' *Sea Breezes* 39: 562–6.

Montaine, William. 1783. *The Seaman's Vade Mecum and Defensive War at Sea*. London: Mont and Page.

Montgomerie, H. S. 1941. 'The Morrison Myth.' *Mariner's Mirror* 27: 69–76.

Montgomery, James. 1831. *Journal of Voyages and Travels by the Rev. Daniel Tyer-man and George Bennett*. London: F. Westley and A. H. Davis.

Moore, J. J. 1801. *The British Mariner's Vocabulary or Universal Dictionary*. London: T. Hurst.

Morison, Samuel Eliot. 1959. *John Paul Jones*. Boston: Little, Brown.

Morrisby, Edwin. 1987. 'Unpackaged Tours.' *Quadrant* 31: 46–50.

Morrison, James. 1935. *The Journal of James Morrison* (Owen Rutter, Ed.). London: Golden Cockerell Press.

Morrison, James. 1966. *Journal de James Morrison* (Bertrand Jaunez, trans.). Paris: Société des Océanistes.

Morrison, Karl R. 1982. *The Mimetic Tradition of Reform in the West*. Princeton, Princeton University Press.

Mortimer, George. 1791. *Observations and Remarks Made During a Voyage to the Islands of Teneriffe, Amsterdam, Sandwich Islands, Owhyee, The Fox Islands on the North West Coast of America, Tinian, and from there to Canton in the Brig* Mercury *commanded by John Henry Cox*. London: T. Cadell.

Morton, Harry. 1975. *The Wind Commands. Sailors and Sailing Ships in the Pacific*. Dunedin: John Indore.

Musher, Daniel M. 1967. 'The Medical Views of Dr Tobias Smollett (1721–1771).' *Bulletin of the History of Medicine* 45: 455–62.

Muster Rolls. 1787–90. 'Bounty (Ship) 16th August 1787–19th November 1790. Commander: William Bligh.' London: Public Record Office, England (Admiralty) Muster Books 1768–98. Mic E 58.

'Mutiny on the Bounty'. 1935. 'Mutiny on the *Bounty*.' Dialogue Continuity. Hollywood: Metro-Goldwyn-Mayer. Copy: Albany, New York State Archives.

'Mutiny on the Bounty'. 1962. 'Mutiny on the *Bounty*.' Dialogue Continuity. Hollywood: Metro-Goldwyn-Mayer. Copy: Albany, New York State Archives.

Mutiny on the *Bounty*. 1989. *Mutiny on the* Bounty. *Bi-centenary Exhibition, National Maritime Museum, Greenwich*. London: Manorial Research PLC.

Nash, Jay Robert, and Stanley Ralph Ross. 1986. *The Motion Picture Guide 1927–1983*. Chicago: Cinebooks.

Nastyface, Jack (William Robinson). 1973 [1836]. *Memoirs of an English Seaman* (Oliver Warner, ed.). Annapolis: Naval Institute Press.

Neale, Jonathan. 1985. *The Cutlass and the Lash*. London: Photo Press.

Newbury, Colin W. (Ed.). 1961. *John Davies. The History of the Tahitian Mission*. Cambridge: Cambridge University Press. Hakluyt Society, 2nd Series, cxvi.

Newbury, Colin W. 1967*a*. 'Aspects of Cultural Change in French Polynesia: The Decline of the Arii.' *Journal of the Polynesian Society* 76: 7–26.

Newbury, Colin W. 1967*b*. 'Te Hau Pahu Rahi. Pomare III and the Concept of Interisland Government in Eastern Polynesia.' *Journal of the Polynesian Society* 76: 477–514.

Newbury, Colin W. 1980. *Tahiti Nui. Change and Survival in French Polynesia*. Honolulu: University Press of Hawaii.

Newspapers 1790–2

Annual Register 1790.

Diary or Woodfall's Register 1790, May–June, July 1, 3; 1792, Oct. 28, 30.

English Chronicle and Universal Evening Post 1790, March 16–18.

European Magazine 1789. Dec. pp. 468–9. 'Omai: or a Trip Around the World: A Pantomime Performed the first time, Covent Garden.'

European Magazine and London Review 1790, April, June.

Evening Mail 1792, Oct. 29–31.

Gazetteer and New Daily Advertiser 1790, March 16; May–June; July 1, 6, 23.

General Evening Post 1790, March 16–18; July 1.

Gentleman's Magazine 1790, May, p. 463.

London Chronicle 1790, March 13–16, 18; June 19; Sept. 1, 7: 1792 Oct. 30–Nov. 1.

New London Magazine 1785, Dec. Supplement 1: 380.

Oracle 1792, Oct. 28–31.

Public Advertiser 1790, May 3; June 28.

Rambler's Magazine. December, 1785.

The Star 1792, Oct. 28–30.

St James Chronicle or British Evening Post 1790, May 15–18.

The Times (London) 1790, March 17, 26, 31; May 1, 3; 1792, Oct. 28–30; 1816, April 16; 1823, July 28.

Universal Diary Register 1785, Dec. 22.

World. 1790, March 16, May–June.

Nicholl, Allardyce. 1927. *A History of Late Eighteenth Century Drama, 1750–1800*. Cambridge: Cambridge University Press.

Nicholson, Watson. 1906. *The Struggle for a Free Stage in London*. Boston: Houghton Mifflin.

Nicolson, Robert B. 1966. *The Pitcairners*. Melbourne: Angus and Robertson.

Nordhoff, Charles. 1883.[1855]. *Man-of-War Life*. New York: Dodd, Mead.

Nordhoff, Charles. 1930. 'Note on the Off-Shore Fishing of the Society Islands.' *Journal of the Polynesian Society* 39: 137–73, 221–62.

Nordhoff, Charles, and James Norman Hall. 1933. *The Mutiny on the* Bounty. London: Chapman and Hall.

Nordhoff, Charles, and James Norman Hall. 1934. *Men Against the Sea.* London: Chapman and Hall.

Nordhoff, Charles, and James Norman Hall. 1935. *Pitcairn's Island.* London: Chapman and Hall.

Oberea [Pseud.]. 1771. *Epistle from Oberea, Queen of Otaheite, to Joseph Banks Esq. Translated by TQZ Esq. Professor of the Otaheite Language in Dublin, and of all the languages of the undiscovered islands in the South Seas,* 3d ed. London: J. Almon.

Oberea [Pseud.]. n.d. *A Second Letter from Oberea Queen of Otaheite to Joseph Banks.* London: T. J. Carnegay.

Oberea [Pseud.]. 1779. *The Injured Islanders or the Influence of Art upon the Happiness of Nature. A Poetical epistle from Oberea of Otaheite to Captain Wallis. By the Author of the Academical Sportsmen.* Dublin: T. T. Faulkner. 1985.

O'Keeffe, John. 1785. *Omai, or a Trip Round the World.* Pantomime Programme. Canberra: Australian National Library, R Bq Misc 1991.

O'Keeffe, John. 1826. *Recollections of the Life of John O'Keeffe, Written by Himself.* 2 vols. London: Henry Colburn.

Oliver, Douglas. 1974. *Ancient Tahiti Society.* 3 vols. Honolulu: University Press of Hawaii.

Oliver, Douglas. 1988. *Return to Tahiti. Bligh's Second Breadfruit Voyage.* Melbourne: Melbourne University Press.

Omai [Pseud.]. 1780. *A Letter from Omai to the Right Honourable the Earl of ******** Late – Lord of the – . Translated from the Ulaeitea Tongue in which, amongst other things, is fairly and irrefragably stated the Nature of Original Sin, together with a proposal for planting Christianity in the islands of the Pacific Ocean.* London: J. Bell.

Omiah. [Pseud.]. 1775. *An Historic Epistle from Omiah to the Queen of Otaheite.* London: T. Evans.

Omiah. [Pseud.] 1776. *Omiah's Farewell Inscribed to the Ladies of London.* London: G. Kearsley.

Oppenheim, M. 1896 [1961]. *A History of the Administration of the Royal Navy and of Merchant Shipping in Relation to the Navy from 1509–1660.* London: Shoe String Press.

O'Reilly, Patrick, and Edouard Reitman. 1967. *Bibliographie de Tahiti et de la Polynésie Française.* Paris: Société des Océanistes.

O'Reilly, Patrick, and Raoul Teissier. 1975. *Tahitiens. Répertoire biographique de la Polynésie Française,* 2d ed. Paris: Société des Océanistes.

Oxberry, William. 1825. *Oxberry's Dramatic Biography and Histrionic Anecdote.* London: G. Virtue.

Parkinson, C. Northcote. 1949. *Portsmouth Point. The British Navy in Fiction 1793–1815.* Cambridge, Mass.: Harvard University Press.

Parry, Albert. 1933. *Tattoo. Secrets of a Strange Art as Practised among the Natives of the United States.* New York: Simon and Schuster.

Parry, J. H. 1948. 'Sailors' English.' *Cambridge Journal* 2: 660–70.

Parry, J. H. 1974. *The Discovery of the Sea.* London: Weidenfeld and Nicolson.

Parson, William, and William White. 1829. *History, Directory and Gazetteer of the Countries of Cumberland and Westmoreland.* Leeds: W. White.

Paullin, Charles Oscar. 1909. 'Duelling in the Old Navy.' *US Naval Institute Proceedings* 35: 1155–97.

Paullin, Charles Oscar. 1968 [1906–14]. *Paullin's History of Naval Administration 1775–1911.* Annapolis: Naval Institute Press.

Paulson, Ronald. 1983. *Representation of Revolution 1789–1820.* New Haven: Yale University Press.

Pedicord, Henry William. 1954. *The Theatrical Public in the Time of Garrick.* New York: King's Crown Press.

Pelham, Camden. 1887. *The Chronicles of Crime or the New Newgate Calendar.* 2 vols. London: T. Miles.

Pemberton, Charles Reece. 1929. *The Autobiography of Pel. Verjuice.* London: Scholars Press.

Phillips, Henry. 1980. *The Theatre and Its Critics in Seventeenth Century France.* London: Oxford University Press.

Pickering, Jerry. 1978. *Theatre. A History of the Art.* St Paul: West Publishing Co.

Pike, Andrew, and Ross Cooper. 1980. *Australian Film 1900–1937.* Melbourne: Oxford University Press.

Pipon, Capt. P. 1814. 'Narrative of the State Mutineers of H.M. *Bounty* . . .' Sydney: Mitchell Library, Brabourne Collection, Banks Papers 1: 17–51.

Pocknee, Cyril E. 1963. *The Christian Altar.* Westminster: Canterbury Press.

Polybius. 1923. *The Histories.* 6 vols. London: Heinemann.

Poole, William Frederick. 1963. *Poole's Index to Periodical Literature,* rev. ed. Gloucester, Mass.: Peter Smith.

Powell, Dulcie A. 1966. 'The Voyage of the Plant Nursery, HMS *Providence* 1791–1793.' Sydney: Mitchell Library, MS 1314.

Press Book. 1935. 'Mutiny on the *Bounty* 1935 Pressbook.' New York: New York Public Library, Center for the Study of Performing Arts. MFL x NC 1561.

Press Book. 1962. 'Mutiny on the *Bounty* 1962 Press Book.' New York: New York Public Library, Center for the Study of Performing Arts. ZAN-T8 Reel 35. NC 199–202.

Price, Richard. 1983. *First Time: The Historical Vision of an Afro-American People*. Baltimore: Johns Hopkins University Press.

Price, Richard. 1990. *Alabi's World*. Baltimore: Johns Hopkins University Press.

Price, Hon. R. M. 1852. *Speech on the Bill for the Enforcement of Discipline in the Navy*. Washington: Congressional Globe Office.

Pugh, John. 1787. *Remarkable Occurrences in the Life of Jonas Hanway*. London: J. Davis.

Pyne, William Henry. 1823. *Wine and Walnuts or After Dinner Chit-Chat by Ephraim Hardcastle, Citizen and Dry-Salter*. 2 vols. London: Longman Hurst.

Rabinow, Paul. 1986. 'Discourse on Power: On the Limits of Ethnographic Texts.' *Dialectical Anthropology* 10: 1–14.

Raidier, Jean. 1968. *Men and Ships Around Cape Horn 1616–1939*. London: A. Barker.

Ramsay, David. 1821. 'Scrapbook of Log of Ship Surrey, written by the Ship's Doctor.' Sydney: Mitchell Library, MS AS 125/1.

Rasor, Eugene Latimer. 1972. 'The Problem of Discipline in the Mid-19th Century Royal Navy.' Ph.D. diss., University of Virginia, Charlottesville.

Rawson, Geoffrey. 1963. Pandora's *Last Voyage*. New York: Harcourt, Brace and World.

Read, Donald. 1961. *Press and People 1790–1850*. Westport, Conn.: Greenwood Press.

Rediker, Marcus. 1987. *Between the Devil and the Deep Blue Sea. Merchant Seamen, Pirates, and the Anglo American Maritime World, 1700–1750*. Cambridge: Cambridge University Press.

Reid, Alan. 1978. 'Broughton's Schooner.' *Mariner's Mirror* 64: 241–2.

Rey-Lescure, Philippe. 1953. 'Les Premier Européens à Tahiti.' *Bulletin de la Société des Etudes Océaniennes* 9: 162–75.

Richards, Kenneth, and Peter Thomson (Eds.). 1972. *Essays on the Eighteenth Century English Stage*. London: Methuen.

Richardson, R. 1768. *The* Dolphin's *Journal Epitomized in a Poetical Essay*. London: Privately printed.

Richardson, R. 1965. *A Poetical Essay on the* Dolphin *Sailing Round the World in the Years 1764, 1767, 1768 by R. Richardson, Barber of the Said Ship* (Phyllis Mander-Jones, Introd.). Paris: Société des Océanistes.

Richmond, Sir Herbert W. 1927. *Command and Discipline*. London: Ed: Stanford.

Robertson, George. 1948. *The Discovery of Tahiti. A Journal of the Second Voyage of HMS* Dolphin *Round the World 1766–1768* (H. Carrington, ed.). London: Hakluyt Society, Series 2, 98.

Robinson, Charles Napier. 1909. *The British Tar in Fact and Fiction*. London: Harper Brothers.

Rockwell, Charles. 1842. *Sketches of Foreign Travel and Life at Sea.* Boston: Tappan and Dennet.

Roderick, Colin. 1972. 'Sir Joseph Banks, Queen Oberea and the Satirists.' In Viet 1972: 67–89.

Rodger, N. A. M. 1982. *Articles of War.* Homewell: Kenneth Mason.

Rodger, N. A. M. 1986. *The Wooden World: An Anatomy of the Georgian Navy.* Annapolis: Naval Institute Press.

Rogin, Michael Paul. 1985. *Subversive Genealogy: The Politics and Art of Herman Melville.* Berkeley: University of California Press.

Rogin, Michael Paul. 1987. *Ronald Reagan the Movie and Other Episodes in Political Demonology.* Berkeley: University of California Press.

Roose-Evans, James. 1970. *Experimental Theatre from Stanislavsky to Today.* New York: Universe Books.

Roose-Evans, James. 1977. *London Theatre.* Oxford: Phaidon.

Rose, Roger, G. 1978. *Symbols of Sovereignty: Feather Girdles of Tahiti and Hawaii.* Honolulu: Pacific Anthropology Records 28.

Rosen, Philip (Ed.). 1986. *Narrative, Apparatus, Ideology.* New York: Columbia University Press.

Rosenfield, Sybil. 1972. 'Landscape in English Scenery in the 18th Century.' In Richards and Thomson 1972: 171–8.

Ross, A. S. C. 1964. *The Pitcairnese Language.* London: André Deutsch.

Roulston, Robert. 1978. *James Norman Hall.* Boston: Twayne.

Russell, W. Clark. n.d. *Representative Actors.* London: Frederick Warne.

Rutter, Owen (Ed.). 1931. *The Courtmartial of the* 'Bounty' *Mutineers.* Edinburgh: William Hodge.

Rutter, Owen. 1934. *The Voyage of the* Bounty's *Launch as related in William Bligh's Despatch to the Admiralty and the Journal of John Fryer.* London: Golden Cockerell Press.

Rutter, Owen. 1936. 'Bligh's Log.' *Mariner's Mirror* 22: 179–182.

Rutter, Owen (Ed.). 1939. *John Fryer of the Bounty. Notes on His Career Written by his Daughter Mary Ann (Gamble).* London: Golden Cockerell Press.

Rydell, R. A. 1952. *Cape Horn to the Pacific.* Berkeley: University of California Press.

Sadler's Wells. 1823. 'The Island or Christian and His Comrades.' Sadler's Wells Handbill. New York: New York Center for Study of Performing Arts, Stead Collection, MWEZ and nc 766–7.

Sahlins, Marshall. 1958. *Social Stratification in Polynesia.* Seattle: University of Washington Press.

Sahlins, Marshall. 1981. *Historical Metaphors and Mythical Realities: Structure in the Early History of the Sandwich Islands Kingdom.* Ann Arbor: University of Michigan Press.

Sahlins, Marshall. 1985. *Islands of History*. Chicago: University of Chicago Press.

Sahlins, Marshall. 1989. 'Captain Cook in Hawaii.' *Journal of the Polynesian Society* 98: 371–423.

Said, Edward. 1989. 'Representing the Colonized: Anthropology's Interlocutors.' *Critical Inquiry* 15: 205–25.

Sailing Directions. 1940. *Sailing Directions for the Pacific Islands*. 5th ed. Vol. 2 Washington: Government Printing Office.

Sales, Roger. 1983. *English Literature in History 1780–1830. Pastoral and Politics*. New York: St Martin's Press.

Sanborn, Solomon H. 1841. *An Exposition of Official Tyranny in the United States Navy*. New York: n.p.

Schechner, Richard. 1985. *Between Theater and Anthropology*. Philadelphia: University of Pennsylvania Press.

Schneider, L. and C. Bonjean (Eds.). 1973. *The Idea of Culture in the Social Sciences*. Cambridge: Cambridge University Press.

Scott, Brian W. 1982. 'The True Identity of John Adams.' *Mariner's Mirror* 68: 31–9.

Scott, Brian W. 1989. 'Pitcairn: What Happened.' In 1989: 124–36.

Seznec, Jean, and Jean Adhemar. 1975. *Diderot Salons*. 2d ed. 4 vols. Oxford: Clarendon Press.

Shackleton, Jasper. 1989. 'Elizabeth Bligh – Her Beginning'. In Mutiny on the Bounty 1989: 153–9.

Shapiro, Harry L. 1929. *Descendants of the Mutineers of the* Bounty. Honolulu: Bishop Museum Memoirs XI.

Shapiro, H. L. 1936. *The Heritage of the* Bounty. London: Victor Gollancz.

Sharp, Andrew. 1960. *The Discovery of the Pacific Islands*. Oxford: Clarendon.

Sherrill, Robert. 1969. *Military Justice Is to Justice as Military Music Is to Music*. New York: Harper and Row.

Sherson, Errol. 1925. *London's Lost Theatres of the Nineteenth Century*. London: John Lane.

Shillibeer, J. 1814. 'Extracts from Voyage to Pitcairn's Island of HMS *Briton* 1814.' Sydney: Mitchell Library, Doc.566.

Shillibeer, J. 1817. *A Narrative of the* Briton's *Voyage to Pitcairn Island*. Taunton: Law and Whittaker.

Shirley, Graham, and Brian Adams. 1983. *Australian Cinema. The First Eighty Years*. Sydney: Angus and Robertson.

Singer, Kurt. 1954. *The Charles Laughton Story*. London: Robert Hale.

Smelser, Marshal. 1958. 'The Passage of the Naval Act of 1794.' *Military Affairs* 22: 1–12.

Smith, D. Bonner. 1936. 'Some Remarks about the Mutiny on the *Bounty*.' *Mariner's Mirror* 200–41.

Smith, D. Bonner. 1937. 'More Light on Bligh and the *Bounty.' Mariner's Mirror* 23: 210–28.

Smith, Howard M. 1975. 'The Introduction of Venereal Disease into Tahiti: A Re-Examination.' *Journal of the Polynesian Society* 10: 38–45.

Smith, William Robertson. 1892. 'Sacrifice.' *Encyclopaedia Britannica,* 9th ed. 21: 132–8.

Smyth, W. H. ['X.Y.Z.']. 1829. 'Letter to the Editor.' *United Service Journal* 2: 366–7.

Smyth, W. H. 1831*a*. 'Sketch of the Career of the Late Capt. Peter Heywood, R.N.' *United Service Journal* 1: 468–81.

Smyth, W. H. 1831*b*. 'The *Bounty* Again.' *United Service Journal* 3: 305–15.

Smyth, W. H. 1867. *The Sailor's Word Book.* London: Whitmore and Fenn.

Soule, C. C. 1923. *Naval Terms and Definitions.* 3d ed. New York: Van Nostrand.

Spence, Sydney Alfred. 1970. *Captain William Bligh (1754–1817) and Where to Find Him.* London: Privately printed.

Spierenburg, Pieter. 1984. *The Spectacle of Suffering.* Cambridge: Cambridge University Press.

Stafford, Barbara. 1984. *Voyage into Substance: Art, Science and the Illustrated Travel Account 1760–1840.* Cambridge, Mass.: MIT Press.

Staine[s], Sir Thomas, and Capt. P. Pipon. n.d. 'Interesting Report of the Only Remaining Mutineers.' Sydney: Mitchell Library, MS 999.7s.

Staines, Sir Thomas. 1815. 'Account of the Descendants of Christian and Other Mutineers of the *Bounty.' Naval Chronicle* 33: 217–18.

Stallybrass, Peter, and Allon White. 1986. *The Politics and Poetics of Transgression.* Ithaca: Cornell University Press.

Starr, Chester G. 1960. *The Roman Imperial Navy 31 BC – AD 324,* 2d ed. New York: Barnes and Noble.

Stennis, E. H. 1965. *Portrait of the Isle of Man.* London: Robert Hale.

Stevenson, Karen. 1990. ' "Heiva": Continuity and Change of a Tahitian Celebration.' *The Contemporary Pacific* 2: 255–78.

Stewart, George. 1789. 'Extract from Journal.' In Edwards 1789.

Stone, George Winchester, and George M. Kahrl. 1979. *David Garrick. A Critical Biography.* Carbondale: Southern Illinois University Press.

Strachan-Davidson, James Leigh. 1969. *Problems of the Roman Criminal Law.* Amsterdam: Rodopi.

Swainson, William. 1822. *A Catalogue of the Rare and Valuable Shells which formed the Celebrated Collection of the late Mrs Bligh.* London: W. Smith (Sotheby Sale, May 20, 1822).

Symonds, Craig L. 1980. *Navalists and Antinavalists.* Newark: University of Delaware Press.

Symonds, Craig L. (Ed.). 1981. *New Aspects of Naval History.* Annapolis: Naval Institute Press.

Tagart, Edward. 1832. *A Memoir of the Late Captain Peter Heywood R.N.* London: E. Wilson.

Taillemite, E. 1968. 'Le Séjour de Bougainville à Tahiti.' *Journal de la Société des Océanistes* 24: 3–10.

Tanner, J. R. 1974 [1920]. *Samuel Pepys and the Royal Navy.* Cambridge: Foxcraft Library.

Taussig, Michael. 1987. *Shamanism, Colonialism and the Wild Man: A Study in Terror and Healing.* Chicago: University of Chicago Press.

Teehuteatuaonoa ['Jenny']. 1819. 'Account of the mutineers of the Ship *Bounty* and their Descendants at Pitcairn's Island.' *Sydney Gazette* July 17: 817.

Teehuteatuaonoa ['Jenny']. 1829. 'Account of Jenny, an Otaheitian Woman . . .' *United Service Journal* 2: 589–93.

Teitler, G. 1977. *The Genesis of the Professional Officer Corps.* Beverly Hills: Sage Publications.

Thiersch, Marlies. 1972. 'Cook Plays Now and Then.' In Viet 1972: 43–53.

Thomas, Bob. 1969. *Thalberg: Life and Legend.* Garden City, N.Y.: Doubleday.

Thomas, Bob. 1975. *Brando. Portrait of a Rebel and an Artist.* London: W. H. Allen.

Thompson, E. P. 1964. *The Making of the English Working Class.* New York: Pantheon.

Thomson, Basil (Ed.). 1915. *The Voyage of the* Pandora. London: Francis Edwards.

Thomson, David. 1975. *A Biographical Dictionary of the Cinema.* London: Secker and Warburg.

Thomson, Robert. n.d. 'History of Tahiti.' Sydney: Mitchell Library, Australian Joint Copying Project, Microfilm of London Missionary Society, Miscellany, FM4/3032.

Thring, Theodore. 1861. *A Treatise on the Criminal Law of the Navy.* London: V. and R. Stevens.

Thring, Theodore. 1877. *Thring's Criminal Law in the Navy.* 2d ed. London: Stevens and Sons.

Tilley, John A. 1987. *The British Navy and the American Revolution.* Columbia: University of South Carolina Press.

'Tiphys Aegyptus.' 1843. *The Navy's Friend or Reminiscences of the Navy Containing Memoirs of a Cruise in the US Schooner* Enterprise. Baltimore: Privately printed.

Tobin, George. n.d. 'Sketches.' Sydney: Mitchell Library, PX A 563 fi.

Tobin, George. 1791–3. 'Journal on HMS *Providence* 1791–1793.' Sydney: Mitchell Library, CY A 562.

Tobin, George. 1817. 'Letter to Captain Bond, December 15, 1817.' Sydney: Mitchell Library Ab 60/8.

Tornabene, Lyn. 1976. *Long Live the King: A Biography of Clark Gable.* New York: G. P. Putnam.

Trotter, Thomas. 1797. *Medicina Nautica.* London: T. Cadell and W. Dames.

Turner, Terence. 1988. 'Ethno-Ethnohistory: Myth and History in Native America. Representations of Contact with Western Society.' In Hill 1988: 235–81.

Turner, Victor. 1969. *The Ritual Process. Structure and Anti-Structure.* Chicago: Aldine.

Turner, Victor. 1982. *From Ritual to Theater.* New York: Performing Arts Journal Publications.

Turner, Victor. 1989. *The Anthropology of Performance.* New York: Performing Arts Journal Publications.

Vagts, Alfred. 1937. *A History of Militarism.* New York: W. W. Norton.

Valenti, Peter. 1984. *Errol Flynn.* Westport, Conn.: Greenwood Press.

Valeri, Valerio. 1982. 'The Transformations of a Transformation: A Structural Essay on an Aspect of Hawaiian History (1809–1819).' *Social Analysis* 10: 3–41.

Valeri, Valerio. 1985. *Kingship and Sacrifice: Ritual and Society in Ancient Hawaii.* Chicago: University of Chicago Press.

Valle, James E. 1980. *Rocks and Shoals.* Annapolis: Naval Institute Press.

Vernon, Admiral Edward. 1958. *Vernon Papers.* London: Naval Record Society.

Viet, Walter (Ed.). 1972. *Captain James Cook. Image and Impact.* Melbourne: Hawthorn Press.

Vinson, James. 1986. *International Dictionary of Films and Filmmakers.* 3 vols. Chicago: St James Press.

'W.L.' 1792. 'Letter from W.L.' *Gentleman's Magazine* 62: 1097–8.

Wallis, Helen (Ed.). 1965. *Carteret's Voyage Round the World 1766–1769.* Cambridge: Hakluyt Society, Series 2, 124.

Wallis, Samuel. 1768. 'Logbook and Sketchbook of Captain Samuel Wallis.' Sydney: Mitchell Library, MS Safe 1/98.

Ward, Edward. 1707 [1929]. *The Wooden World* (Geoffrey Callender, ed.). London: Society for Nautical Research, Occasional Papers II.

Watkin, R. C. 1970. 'Mutiny on the *Bounty*.' *Isle of Man Natural History and Antiquarian Society.* 7: 374–400.

Watson, Harold Francis. 1931. *The Sailor in English Fiction and Drama, 1550–1800.* New York: Columbia University Press.

Watson, Nicholson. 1906. *The Struggle for the Free Stage in London.* Boston: Houghton Mifflin and Co.

Watt, Sir James. 1979. 'Medical Aspects and Consequences of Cook's Voyages.' In Fisher and Johnston 1979: 129–57.

Watt, Sir James. 1988. 'The Colony's Health.' In Hardy and Frost 1988: 137–53.

Wayne, Jane Ellen. 1987. *Gable's Women*. Englewood Cliffs, N.J.: Prentice-Hall.

Weate, Philip, and Caroline Graham. 1972. *Captain William Bligh*. Dee Why West, NSW: Paul Hamlyn.

Weibust, Knut. 1967. *Deep Sea Sailors*. Stockholm: Nordiska Museets Hanlingar 71.

Werkmeister, Lucyle. 1963. *The London Daily Press, 1772–1792*. Lincoln: University of Nebraska Press.

Werkmeister, Lucyle. 1967. *A Newspaper History of England, 1792–1793*. Lincoln: University of Nebraska Press.

Wesseling, H. L. (Ed.). 1978. *Expansion and Reaction*. Leiden: Leiden University Press.

White, Elipha. 1827. *The Claims of Seamen. A Sermon*. Charleston, S.C.: Port Society.

White, Hayden. 1975. *Metahistory: The Historical Imagination in Nineteenth Century Europe*. Baltimore: Johns Hopkins University Press.

Wiener, Frederick Bernays. 1967. *Civilians under Military Justice*. Chicago: University of Chicago Press.

Wilkinson, C. S. 1953. *The Wake of the* Bounty. London: Cassell.

Williams, Anne. 1989. 'Sowse Over Head: Crossing the Line on the *Providence*.' *Pacific Island Focus* 1: 3–22.

Wilson, Arthur M. 1961. 'The Biographical Implications of Diderot's *Paradox sur le Comédien*.' *Diderot Studies* 3: 369–83.

Wilson, Arthur M. 1972. *Diderot*. New York: Oxford University Press.

Winthrop, William. 1920. *Military Law and Precedents*, 2d ed. Washington: Government Printing Office.

Wolf, Eric R. 1982. *Europe and the People without History*. Berkeley: University of California Press.

Wyndham, Henry Saxe. 1906. *The Annals of Covent Garden Theatre from 1732 to 1898*. 2 vols. London: Chatto and Windus.

Young, Rosalind Amelia. 1924. *Mutiny of the* Bounty *and Story of Pitcairn Island*. Auckland: Dawson.

Index

Numbers in italic type indicate illustrations.

violence (*cont.*)
  some non-cliometrics 124–30
  officers as beneficiaries 156
  rights of officers 65
  in United States navy 153–6
  of Wallis 125–7
  see also discipline; floggings; punish-
    ment

Wake of the Bounty, In the, (Chauvel 1933
    film) 344–6
  Fletcher Christian represented by Errol
    Flynn 345–6
'W. L.' 46–7
Wallis, Captain Samuel
  at Tahiti 181, 184, 191–203
  takes possession of Tahiti 198–200
    depicted 264–5, 265
  voyage to Pacific 125–7
Webber, John
  adviser on *Omai* 270, 271–2
  portraits 48, 49, 54
Wedgeborough, William 121
Williams, John (assistant armourer)
  flogged 84, 127, 317
  murdered 319
  on Pitcairn 317–18
  yarn on cheeses 74, 317–18
women
  brutality of mutineers towards 217,
    230

  as chiefs 279
  discarded by mutineers 94, 316
  grief after capture of mutineers 239
  at Hawaii 170
  on Pitcairn 316, 320
    dig up bones of mutineers 323
    dispute over 320
    murder Tahitian 320
    rank 322
    rebellion 323
    solidarity 320, 321–2
    tapu 323
  Polynesian 322–3
  at Tahiti 125, 193, 195
    not sacrificial victims 190
  taken to Pitcairn 94, 316
  at Tubuai 90, 91, 92
  see also 'Oberea'
Wordsworth, Dorothy 11
Wordsworth, William 11, 311

yarning *see* language, of sea
Young, Edward (midshipman) 21, 25,
    28, 321
  described by Bligh 319, 346
  genteel connections 383
  on Pitcairn 318–19, 320, 321
    challenges women 323
    death 320
    murders Quintal 320
    murders Tahitian 320